Praise for *The Ghost*

"The best book ever written about the strangest CIA chief who ever lived. No screenwriter or novelist could conjure a character like Angleton, but Morley's stellar reporting and superb writing animate every page of this work. It's essential history and highly entertaining biography."

—Tim Weiner, National Book Award–winning author of *Legacy of Ashes*

"*The Ghost* is the compulsively readable, often bizarre true-life story of American spymaster James Jesus Angleton. Capturing the extent of Angleton's eccentricity, duplicity, and alcohol-fueled paranoia would have challenged the writing skills of a le Carré or Ludlum, and Jeff Morley has done it with flair."

—Philip Shenon, author of *A Cruel and Shocking Act*

"James Angleton's real life is the most intriguing, moving, and at times shocking spy story in American history. In *The Ghost,* Jeff Morley has captured the man in all his brilliant and sometimes delusional eccentricity. Angleton is woven through many of the strangest episodes of the 1950s and 60s—including the Kennedy assassination—in what was invisible thread, until Morley's book. A 'must-read' for anyone who wants to understand just how strange and secretive the CIA was at the height of the Cold War."

—David Ignatius, columnist for *The Washington Post* and author of *The Director*

"Americans are finally coming to know the Cold War spymasters and other hidden figures who lived their lives in secrecy while shaping our national destiny. *The Ghost* reveals a fascinating chapter of this hidden history. It is a chilling look at the global power that is wielded in Washington by people who are never known—until a book comes out to spill their secrets."

—Stephen Kinzer, author of *The Brothers*

"Anyone interested in the CIA should not fail t
tered James Angleton time and again, not on

T0003289

but also, one memorable evening, literally. I say 'memorable,' but only because—amongst hundreds of interviews I have conducted—he indeed came over as a phantom, seemingly cooperative yet always inscrutable. Nobody has focused on him, mined what can be mined, as Jefferson Morley has now done. Essential reading for anyone intrigued by the vital mysteries of U.S. intelligence at a pivotal time in our history."

—Anthony Summers, Pulitzer Prize finalist for *The Eleventh Day*

"[Morley] does a fine job of filleting out [Angleton's] talents and charisma from the dark deeds he committed. . . . Morley adeptly builds a picture of a spymaster weaving a web in which his concept of duty gradually eroded his moral sense."
—Ben Macintyre, *The Times* (London)

"A page-turning biography of an eccentric spy hunter . . . In Angleton, [Morley] has a character beyond the imagination of John le Carré, perhaps even of Patricia Highsmith."
—*Star Tribune* (Minneapolis)

"Scintillating . . . [the book] delves into an important and rarely visited terrain."
—*Mondoweiss*

"Essential reading for anyone interested in how our intelligence network operated during the Cold War."
—LewRockwell.com

"Easy to read and understand; for those interested in U.S. intelligence history and the Kennedy assassination."
—*Library Journal*, starred review

"Serving up a suitably intriguing profile of this quintessential spy, journalist Morley's mosaic-like biography painstakingly pieces together the complex webs of subterfuge and deception Angleton created during his storied career."
—*Booklist*

THE GHOST

ALSO BY JEFFERSON MORLEY

Our Man in Mexico: Winston Scott and the Hidden History of the CIA

Snow-Storm in August: Washington City, Francis Scott Key, and the Forgotten Race Riot of 1835

THE GHOST

THE SECRET LIFE OF
CIA SPYMASTER
JAMES JESUS ANGLETON

Jefferson Morley

ST. MARTIN'S GRIFFIN 🐦 NEW YORK

THE GHOST. Copyright © 2017 by Jefferson Morley. All rights reserved. Printed in the United States of America. For information, address St. Martin's Press, 175 Fifth Avenue, New York, NY 10010.

www.stmartins.com

"One Thousand Fearful Words for Fidel Castro" by Lawrence Ferlinghetti, from *Starting from San Francisco,* copyright © 1961 by Lawrence Ferlinghetti. Reprinted by permission of New Directions Publishing Corp.

"Excerpts from unpublished letters by Ezra Pound" from New Directions Pub. acting as agent, copyright © 2017 by Mary de Rachewiltz and the Estate of Omar S. Pound. Reprinted by permission of New Directions Publishing Corp.

Excerpts from "Gerontion" and "East Coker" from *Collected Poems* 1909–1962, Copyright 1936 by Houghton Mifflin Harcourt Publishing Company. Copyright © renewed 1964 by Thomas Stearns Eliot. Reprinted by permission of Houghton Mifflin Harcourt Publishing Company. All rights reserved.

The Library of Congress has cataloged the hardcover edition as follows:

Names: Morley, Jefferson, author.
Title: The ghost : the secret life of CIA spymaster James Jesus Angleton / Jefferson Morley.
Description: New York, NY : St. Martin's Press, 2017. | Includes bibliographical references and index.
Identifiers: LCCN 2017023616 | ISBN 9781250080615 (hardcover) | ISBN 9781250139108 (ebook)
Subjects: LCSH: Angleton, James, 1917–1987. | United States. Central Intelligence Agency—History—20th century. | United States. Central Intelligence Agency—Officials and employees—Biography. | Intelligence service—United States—History—20th century. | Intelligence officers—United States—Biography.
Classification: LCC JK468.I6 M67 2017 | DDC 327.12730092 [B]— dc23
LC record available at https://lccn.loc.gov/2017023616

ISBN 978-1-250-16730-9 (trade paperback)

Our books may be purchased in bulk for promotional, educational, or business use. Please contact your local bookseller or the Macmillan Corporate and Premium Sales Department at 1-800-221-7945, extension 5442, or by email at MacmillanSpecialMarkets@macmillan.com.

First St. Martin's Griffin Edition: October 2018

D 11

CONTENTS

Introduction xi

PART I

POETRY 1

Pound 3

Salesman 8

Wife 13

Secretary 17

Black Prince 21

Nazi 27

Monsignor 33

Reunion 39

"Homo Circles" 44

Philby 48

Mossad 54

LSD 57

PART II

POWER 65

Counterintelligence 67

Zionist 73

Fisherman 78

COINTELPRO 82

Mole 84

Oswald 86

JFK 91

Cuba 93

"Hit Him" 98

Empire 104

Golitsyn 106

Blackmail 110

Hamlet 113

PART III
IMPUNITY   121

   Kim   123
   Provocation   127
   "Go Easy"   131
   Mole Hunts   133
   Oswald Again   136
   Dallas   141
   Noah's Cloak   149
   Loathing   154
   Defector   158
   Mary   163
   Cicely   169
   Bomb   171
   War   178
   CHAOS   184
   Two Boxers   188
   Heist   192
   Kim Again   194

PART IV
LEGEND   199

   Nixon   201
   Golem   209
   Ghoul   210
   Widow   213
   Helms   216
   Colby   220
   Smoking Gun   228
   Desolate   233
   Cheney   240
   Warning   245
   Inconceivable   252
   Legacy   256
   Legend   266
   Jerusalem   270

   Acknowledgments   275
   Bibliographic Note   279
   Notes   281
   Index   315

INTRODUCTION

When I started writing the biography of James Angleton in January 2015, the notion that a "deep state" shaped American politics was largely unknown. When I finished *The Ghost* two years later, the term commanded belief from the president of the United States and a near majority of the citizenry.

In April 2017 ABC News pollsters asked Americans about the possible existence of a deep state—defined as "military, intelligence, and government officials who try to secretly manipulate government policy." A plurality of respondents—48 percent—agreed while 35 percent described the idea as a conspiracy theory. The belief in a deep state ran equally strong among Republicans and Democrats.

I did not rely on the concept of a deep state in researching Angleton's career. But I wanted to tell his story precisely because I had encountered spectral glimpses of his handiwork in my reporting for *The Washington Post* and for my first book, *Our Man in Mexico*. When I finished *The Ghost,* I realized Angleton and his conspiratorial mode of thinking illuminated the new discourse of the deep state.

But how? Among the various theories of the deep state, the only common denominator is the role of the secret agencies created by the National Security Act—what Professor Michael J. Glennon calls "double government." Since 1947, Glennon notes, the three branches of the republican government founded in 1789 have been joined by a fourth branch of military and intelligence organizations, which wield power largely beyond the view of the Madisonian government and the voting public.

Whatever the label applied to the national security sector of the U.S.

government, Angleton embodied its ascendancy after World War II. Thus *The Ghost* is a biography that interrogates today's headlines: Was James Angleton a defender of the republic? An exemplar of double government? Or an avatar of the emerging deep state?

This is his story, insofar as it is known.

PART I

POETRY

POUND

THE YOUNG AMERICAN PEERED through the viewfinder at the naked poet. James Angleton squeezed the shutter once and then again. Ezra Pound went right on talking, as if he didn't care.[1] Jim, as Pound called him, had just come down from Milan. Upon arrival, the Yale man with black hair and high brown cheekbones had spotted the abode of the expatriate poet from the waterfront below. It took some ingenuity to locate the entrance to number 12 via Marsala in the narrow cobblestone street around back. He hiked up the darkened stairs to the fifth floor and emerged into the bright light of the terraced apartment, where Pound and his wife, Dorothy, welcomed him like an old friend.

In fact, that summer day in 1938 was the first time Jim Angleton and Ezra Pound had met. Pound was fifty-two years old, Angleton a rising college sophomore and expatriate resident of Italy. He knew of Pound through the crystalline poetry of his books *Personae* and the *Cantos* ("Songs" in English). He felt something of a personal connection, too. During his freshman year, he had come across a sketch of Pound in a campus magazine, above the caption "From Idaho to Rapallo."[2] Jim had made that same intercontinental journey. Born in Boise, he had lived there and in Dayton, Ohio, until he was sixteen years old, when his family moved to Milan. In the poet's odyssey from Idaho to Italy, Angleton might have seen the arc of possibility in his own life.

Angleton was taller than his host. He had a Latin complexion and the lithe build of a soccer player. His English accent announced old-world courtesy and quiet good manners. His piercing dark eyes and the perpetual hint of a smile suggested an ironic approach to life.

The couple welcomed Angleton into their neat apartment. Pound, ever alert for potential patrons, knew of Jim's father, a parvenu who ran the Italian-American Chamber of Commerce in Milan. Hugh Angleton was one of the best-known Americans in northern Italy.[3] He mixed easily among the businessmen and officials associated with the government of Benito Mussolini. For Pound, who admired Mussolini, this was recommendation enough. He also supposed that the young Angleton could derive from his teaching a necessary education in the complexities of debt, trade, and paper money. And eventually (the poet may well have calculated), Jim's father might be of some service.

For five days in August 1938, Angleton made himself at home with the Pounds. He had come in search of greatness and found it. He had read the dense poetry of *The Fifth Decade of Cantos*, published in 1937. He especially admired an early poem of Pound's, *Hugh Selwyn Mauberley*, about the universal beauty of poetry. Angleton knew, too, of Pound's interest in economics, articulated in a series of publications with pedantic titles such as *ABC of Economics*, *Social Credit*, and *Jefferson and/or Mussolini*—the latter a frankly laudatory portrait of the Italian fascist leader. Poetry could not be insulated from revolution and money, Pound insisted. So Jim gave close attention to his political writings as well as to his poetry.[4]

JAMES JESUS ANGLETON WAS born on December 9, 1917, the first of four children of James Hugh Angleton and his wife, Carmen Moreno Angleton. Hugh, as he was known, had grown up in central Illinois, working as a schoolteacher until he moved to Idaho, where he started out as a candy salesman. He was serving in the Idaho National Guard at a U.S. military post in Nogales, Arizona, when he met Carmen Moreno, born in Mexico but naturalized as a U.S. citizen. It was, according to one account, "a case of love at first sight." The bride was "one of the Spanish beauties of Nogales and exceedingly popular."[5] They were married in December 1916 and returned to Boise, where their first child was born, a son. They named him James, and Carmen gave him a Spanish middle name, "Jesus," which later he would shun. The Angletons lived in a two-story, two-bedroom bungalow on Washington Avenue in Boise.[6] Hugh took a job as a sales agent for the National Cash Register Company.[7] Sociable and engaging, he was soon promoted.

In 1927, Hugh and Carmen Angleton moved their family to Dayton, Ohio, where Hugh became a vice president of National Cash Register. Jim attended Oakwood Junior High, a public school.[8] In 1933, Hugh bought out NCR's Italian subsidiary and moved the family to Milan, where he opened his own company, selling cash registers and business machines. Suddenly, the candy salesman was a wealthy man.

In raising their children, Hugh and Carmen emphasized the importance of education and travel. They sent Jim to Malvern College, an exclusive red-brick boarding school in Worcestershire, England.[9] It was there, he said years later, that he learned the importance of duty.[10] His younger brother, Hugh, was sent to Harrow, an even more exclusive English prep school. Carmen, the elder daughter, went to a convent school in Milan and then a girls' school in Switzerland. Delores, the youngest, would also go to school in England. In the summers, the family reunited in Milan.

Angleton's upwardly mobile childhood was formative. By the time he arrived at Yale in September 1937, he had resided in three countries, at-tended public and private schools, spoke three languages, and had lived in circumstances both modest and luxurious. He was an outdoorsman with advanced tastes in poetry, an athlete with an original mind. He displayed a distinctive social style, and—perceptible under the surface—an ambition fueled by the rapid success of his father.

After his freshman year at Yale, he returned to Milan for the summer. He called up the American embassy, asking for the address of the expatri-ate writer Ezra Pound, and he didn't relent until he was given it. Then he wrote straightaway. Jim explained he was the photography editor of *The Yale Literary Magazine,* not mentioning that said journal did not actually publish photographs.[11] Receiving no answer, Jim wrote another letter in longhand ten days later.

"I want only to get a few spirited ideas from you together with a photo. . . ."[12]

This plea extracted the desired invitation from the Pounds. And so Angleton drove down from Milan to Genoa and then traced the coastal road to Rapallo. In their summer idyll, the esoteric master and the vora-cious schoolboy talked and smoked.[13]

Pound doted on the company of disciples, and Angleton was looking for wisdom. Angleton wanted to find coherence in the world, and Pound's mythic poetry offered a place where he could speak a higher language of art. Angleton felt free to wield his camera around the apartment. When they went out onto the apartment's rooftop terrace overlooking the Gulf of Tigullio one overcast day, Pound stood up and stared into the distance. Jim snapped another photo and later gave it to the poet. Pound thought it the best picture of himself that he had ever seen.[14]

BY THE TIME ANGLETON got back to New Haven in September, his five days with the world-famous Ezra Pound had become, in the retelling, close to five weeks. In one gulp, Angleton had taken in the surface effects of a worldly education. Pound's reckless ambition, his will to cultural power, his elitism, his conspiratorial convictions, his self-taught craftsmanship, and his omnivorous powers of observation—all these would have influence on the maturing mind of James Angleton.

Angleton took a room at 312 Temple Street with his best friend from freshman year, another aspiring poet, Reed Whittemore. Reed had led a more prosaic childhood as a doctor's son in New Haven. Whittemore recommended T. S. Eliot's poem "Gerontion" to his roommate, and Angleton loved it. With its apparent insight into history and its obscure intimations of danger, Eliot's poem foreshadowed the life of adventure to which Angleton would aspire.

> After such knowledge, what forgiveness? Think now
> History has many cunning passages, contrived corridors
> And issues, deceives with whispering ambitions,
> Guides us by vanities. Think now
> She gives when our attention is distracted
> And what she gives, gives with such supple confusions
> That the giving famishes the craving . . .

"He was quite British in his ways," Whittemore said of his friend. "He was a mixture of pixiness and earnestness, very much at home in Italian literature, especially Dante, as well as the fine points of handicapping horses."[15]

Angleton's solitary style was already evident. A student of fly-fishing, he liked to borrow Whittemore's car and drive off to streams in northwestern Connecticut, where he would spend long hours casting for trout. Yet Whittemore said he never saw a single catch. Angleton spoke of visiting a female friend whom he knew from some other life, but Whittemore never saw her, either. With his English accent, Italian suits, and lofty manner, he was, in Whittemore's words, "a mystery man."[16]

YALE COLLEGE OCCUPIED a high position in American intellectual life. Not as patrician as Harvard, nor as provincial as Princeton, Yale served students from a wider range of backgrounds, and it served them differently.[17] The classrooms scattered around the campus in New Haven contained intense islands of scholars, students, and aspiring poets who spoke of a new way of thinking about literature. Angleton, it turned out, had entered one of the more powerful intellectual milieus of midcentury America. Yale was the place where the enduring influence of New Criticism began to be felt.

The New Critics were a cohort of literature professors who converged on Yale in the 1930s. They favored a canon of English poetry centered on Shakespeare; the metaphysical poets of the seventeenth century, led by John Donne; and select moderns, such as William Butler Yeats and T. S. Eliot. Angleton took English 10, an introductory course on poetry, fiction, and drama, with Maynard Mack, a young professor who admired Pound's poetry. Mack encouraged Angleton's interest.[18] Mack's undergraduate seminars were presented as laboratories for young literary scientists, the model for research being drawn from two original-minded English critics, I. A. Richards and William Empson. Richards had been an influential lecturer in English and moral sciences at Cambridge University. In 1939, he became a professor at Harvard. Bill Empson was his most gifted student, a mathematician and poet whose undergraduate thesis became a famous work of literary criticism, *Seven Types of Ambiguity*.

In the book, Empson offers an argument, supported by interpretations of poems, for the relationship between verbal ambiguity and imaginative value. From its first publication in 1930, *Seven Types of Ambiguity* has never gone out of print. Yet at the time, it had not been published in the United States—a neglect that surprised Angleton. When Empson visited Yale, Angleton introduced himself and took the critic out for a long evening of wine and literary talk. He said he would find Empson an American publisher.[19]

The New Criticism that Angleton treasured was a powerful method, not merely for its insights into poetry but for its implicitly conservative worldview. It was not value-free. On the contrary, its proponents would argue vigorously that it was a method deeply rooted in a particular set of values, a method, in the final analysis, for promulgating those values. The elevated strictures of the New Criticism that exalted his favorite poets would prove formative for Angleton. He would come to value coded language, textual analysis, ambiguity, and close control as the means to illuminate the amoral arts of spying that became his job. Literary criticism led him to the profession of secret intelligence. Poetry gave birth to a spy.

SALESMAN

ANGLETON EXTRACTED A FISTFUL of letters from his mailbox in the cramped confines of Yale Station. One of the letters was postmarked "Rapallo." When he sliced open the envelope, he had to decipher Ezra Pound's inimitable orthography.

> Dear Jim,
> All this is vurry fine and active. How the hell am I to do my own work and take two months off to collect my own bibliography I don't see. Does the Yale lib/[rary] expect to BUY . . . ?[20]

The poet was steamed that Angleton had not fulfilled his promise of compiling a complete bibliography of Pound's work. Ezra wanted to sell some manuscripts and pay some debts. He was always short of money.

By return mail, Angleton responded with flattering familiarity: "Dear Ezra."

He reported he was rereading Confucius's *Ta Hio* and Pound's opera *Cavalcanti*. He saved his biggest news for the last page: He and Reed Whittemore were launching a new magazine called *Furioso*. "Would you be the Godfather of this?"[21]

Angleton was pleased to get Pound's response ten days later.

"Yes, I'll back up any and all the proposals in yrs. 19th instant," Pound wrote. "But we had better think out WHAT will do the job best. The 'text book' ought to be ready soon/you can quote from advance copy of that."[22]

The idea that the great Ezra Pound was sending them a "text book"—whatever that was—sounded more than promising. Angleton described himself as "a very excited piece of protoplasm."[23]

Nonetheless, he was disappointed—no, dismayed—when Pound sent him the long-awaited "text book." It was not a canto. It was not even poetry. It was a list of Pound's favorite quotes about coinage, paper money, and debt from John Adams, Thomas Jefferson, and other Founding Fathers. Angleton wasn't pleased.

He wrote to Pound, deflecting the gift and asking for something more literary.

"Right at this moment Ezra, we are awaiting a canto or something," Angleton said. "We have to have some verse from you."[24]

Pound did not answer. With Whittemore's help, Angleton improvised a solution. They dressed up the "text book" quotes with some Roman numerals and stashed it at the back of the issue before they went to press. The red-trimmed first issue of *Furioso,* adorned by an impish devil wielding a switch, was mailed out in May 1939. Costing just thirty cents, the publication was a literary bargain. In its twenty-eight pages, there was Pound's odd contribution, and a letter from the poet Archibald MacLeish arguing that the new communications medium of broadcast radio would be the salvation of poetry. Angleton's friend E. E. Cummings, also a known poet, contributed a poem. The soon to be renowned Dr. William Carlos Williams added three more.[25]

One canny Yale graduate student named Norman Holmes Pearson was especially impressed with this collection of fresh, arresting literary work.

Pearson was a gimpy young man, almost a hunchback. He smoked a pipe and read Sherlock Holmes detective stories for pleasure, which proved to be good cover for the unlikeliest of spies. Pearson made a point of introducing himself to Angleton.[26]

WHEN YALE CLASSES ENDED in May 1939 Angleton returned to Milan by boat. The ten-day voyage took him from New York to Genoa. A train took him to Milan and a reunion with his parents and siblings. Angleton wrote a letter to Pound, asking if he might visit him in Rapallo again. He wanted Pound to meet his father.

Hugh Angleton, then fifty years old, was not a poet or a writer. He was a man of business. Like Ezra Pound, he admired the ambitions and spirit of Italian fascism. "Hugh Angleton was a very tough character," recalled William Gowen, a young army captain, who would meet both father and son in Rome a few years later. "Jim worshipped his father. Hugh was very aggressive and masculine. Jim was not."[27]

Hugh was an outgoing man, solidly built at five foot eleven, with serious gray eyes.[28] He had installed his family in the Palazzo Castiglioni, an art nouveau palace in the center of Milan. An extrovert and a fine horseman, he betrayed few traces of the raw western frontier from which he came. In the Italian-American Chamber of Commerce, he cultivated friends, dinner companions, and business partners.

In his office on via Dante, Hugh Angleton received visitors from all over Europe. From friends in manufacturing, he learned about the German arms industry. At the Rotary Club, he talked to financiers and industrialists.[29] As a member of the Knights of Malta, he knew influential Catholics.[30] As a Mason, he drew on his friends in the secretive order to keep himself informed about Italian politics. As a man with connections, Hugh wanted to get to know his son's friend, the great poet, who dared to say fascism and Americanism were two sides of the same coin. Angleton gravitated toward Pound's view that Italy and America were not enemies.[31] Hugh didn't disagree.

The newspapers brought more foreboding news every day. Armies were mobilizing across Europe. In August 1914, a global war had erupted, seemingly out of nowhere. In the summer of 1939, the older generation could sense another cataclysm coming.

A few weeks later, on September 1, 1939, Germany invaded Poland, and the war in Europe had begun. Two days later, England and France mobilized to fight Germany. Mussolini rallied to Hitler's defense, passing a series of anti-Semitic decrees in November 1939. The United States then sanctioned Italy. Angleton's adopted country was now an enemy of the United States of America.

IN THE FALL OF 1939, Angleton and Whittemore moved into room 1456 of Pierson College, a pleasant enclosed quadrangle in the heart of the Yale campus.[32] They went to work on the second issue of *Furioso*, which proved even better than the first, flush with poems from the famous and the promising. Pound's contribution, alas, was again disappointing. Generously titled "Five Poems," it consisted of five fragments, alternately whimsical, vulgar, and slight.[33]

In his own writing, Angleton had adopted Pound's resentment of Jews and verbal abuse of President Roosevelt. In February 1940, he wrote to Pound: "There is hell of a lot of Rooseveltian shillyshally here in America." He complained the American press favored London over Berlin. "Everything is definitely British and the jews [*sic*] cause a devil of a lot of stink. Here in New York will be the next great pogrom, and they do need about a thousand ghettos in America. Jew, Jew and Jew, even the Irish are losing out.[34]

But Angleton did not write to debate politics. He knew Pound was squeezed by wartime financial measures. He wanted to offer money.

"I talked to Dad on the telephone the day before the war and mentioned the little shekel you might need, say a couple of thousand, and he said o.k.," Angleton wrote. "So I hope you will oblige by writing him and accept it as a favor."[35]

Pound responded by return mail, acknowledging Angleton's offer, if not his own acceptance of money.

"Dear JIM, Thanks fr/ yr/ air mail. I am not yet starved to the wall yet but thanks for the practical intentions in yr/ epistle. Neither, of course do

I have any intention of relapsing into reminiscence of the Celtic Twilight during a period when twilight sleep is NOT, by hell, being used, for the birth of a new Euroope [*sic*]."

Pound had something more important in mind than money: a cause.

"A NEW god damn it NEW EUROPE," he wrote. "All midwives to hand and ready."[36]

As the poet championed the "new Europe" of Benito Mussolini and Adolf Hitler, he sought out Hugh Angleton and his generosity. Pound wrote him in June 1940:

> Dear Mr. Angleton,
> Jim is all het up for fear that I with poetic imprudence might have failed to putt [*sic*] by a few biglietti di mille [meaning he had failed to save a few thousand dollars]. I shall still eat/ even if Morgenthau, Hull, and that ass F.D. Roosevelt have succeeded in having the mails blocked and payment on U.S cheques suspended.

In the same letter, he signaled that he was short of funds, at the same time saying that he wished to talk about something "more important than my personal affairs." He wanted Hugh Angleton's help in spreading his political views.

"Time has come when I might be a business asset (wild as the idea wd/ appear)," he wrote. "I don't mean in an office but sitting at the seat of news."[37] Pound wanted to be a practical asset to a businessman like Angleton. Within six months, he began to broadcast his commentaries for Radio Rome, the Italian news outlet heard from Sicily to the Pyrenees.

"What will remain from this struggle is an idea," Pound declared in early 1941. "What spreads and will spread from the determination to have a New Europe is an idea: the idea of a home for every family in the country. The idea that every family in the country shall have a sane house, and that means a house well built, with no breeding space for tuberculosis bugs. . . ."

Pound likened twentieth-century European fascism to nineteenth-century American democracy in its rejection of collectivism. The new

Europe, he said, was merely following in the path of the United States.[38] Over the next four years, Pound would deliver more than 120 speeches over Radio Rome, most of them rife with folksy language, images of infestation, historical references, and anti-Semitism, all wrapped in a belligerent spirit of racial chauvinism.

Angleton had not been uncomfortable with fascism or fascists at Yale, sometimes to the consternation of his more liberal classmates. Anti-Semitism didn't seem to bother him. But Pound's overwrought vehemence did. As his bright college years came to a close in the spring of 1941, Angleton was ready to graduate from Yale College and the school of Ezra Pound. Apparently, they never corresponded again.[39]

WIFE

ONE RAINY DAY IN September 1941, Cicely d'Autremont, Vassar class of 1944, walked down Brattle Street in Cambridge. An impish sophomore from Arizona, she was out on a date with a Yale boy who wanted her to meet a friend who had just started at Harvard Law School. Cicely and the boy climbed up three flights of narrow stairs in an old apartment building. They walked into a bare living room that was unfurnished save for a reproduction of El Greco's painting *View of Toledo*. A tall man stood next to the picture of an unearthly green landscape.

"How do?" he said.

This first encounter so impressed Cicely d'Autremont Angleton that decades later she recalled the moment.

"If anything went together it was him and the picture," she told a reporter. "I fell madly in love at first sight. I'd never meet anyone like him in my life. He was so charismatic. It was as if the lightning in the picture had suddenly struck me. He had an El Greco face. It was extraordinary."[40]

Another decade after that disclosure, when Cicely Angleton was a grandmother, she again relived that chance encounter, writing a poem tinged with rueful hindsight.

> *Beware, she warned, of hollow cheeks,*
> *and auras sketched in lightning.*[41]

Cicely d'Autremont didn't know to beware of hollow cheeks. She was barely more than a schoolgirl, born into comfort and privilege. The marriage of her mother and father in 1919 joined two of the wealthiest families in Duluth, Minnesota. Her father, Hubert, was a scion of the d'Autremonts, who had vast holdings in mining and lumber.[42] Her mother, Helen, was a Congdon, who had more of the same, in addition to a fabulous mansion. Helen and Hubert moved to Tucson, Arizona, where he became a banker, while she was active in charitable work. During the Depression years, the d'Autremonts were known as the largest contributors to Tucson charities.[43] Cicely was born in 1922, their second child and first daughter.[44]

Cicely was drawn to Angleton's exotic intensity. "Jim was a Chicano and I loved him for it," she said. "I never saw anyone as Mexican as he was. He was Latino, an Apache, he was a gut fighter."[45]

ANGLETON DID NOT RETURN Cicely's passion, at least not immediately. In his last year at Yale, Angleton's charmed life had suffered unsettling setbacks. At a time when the U.S. Army was welcoming hundreds of thousands of young men, he was rejected by the Selective Service, probably because of his recurring tuberculosis.[46] Optimistically, he applied to Harvard Law School, despite the fact that his poor grades pulled him down to the bottom quarter of the Yale class of 1941.[47] He was rejected.

Angleton's friend Norman Holmes Pearson wrote a letter to Harvard, asking them to reconsider.[48] Pearson, then thirty-two years old, surely qualifies as the most improbable spymaster in American history.[49] An assistant literature professor from a prosperous New England family, Pearson had few obvious qualifications for a life of deception and intrigue. He was a genteel man of unobtrusive appearance who walked with a limp, left over from a spinal injury in childhood. He was also a founding spirit of the global enterprise of espionage, propaganda, and violence known as the Central Intelligence Agency.

Pearson's letter to Harvard proved convincing, and Angleton was admitted.[50] Reprieved from unemployment, Angleton intended to make good by studying international law and contracts and then going into the family business.[51] He was headed for a career of selling cash registers or perhaps publishing poets, but Norman Pearson wasn't done with him.

Pearson, like many other young Ivy League professors, went to war by joining the newly created Office of Strategic Services. The OSS, as it was known, resembled an elite university in its mission to collect and disseminate information. The OSS was the brainchild of William Donovan, a Wall Street lawyer known as "Wild Bill" for his aerial heroics in World War I. For years, Donovan had been telling his friend Franklin Roosevelt that the rise of Adolf Hitler's Nazi Germany meant there would be another war in Europe, one that the United States would have to join. America needed a foreign intelligence service, and probably sooner rather than later, he told FDR. After Pearl Harbor, Donovan had won the argument.

The British already had a foreign intelligence agency, the Secret Intelligence Service (SIS), established in 1909, sometimes known as MI6. So the officers of the new American OSS were sent to school at the British intelligence facility in Bletchley Park, north of London. There, Pearson joined the SIS men in teaching the novice Americans the arts of espionage and special operations as perfected by the world's greatest colonial power.

IN LAW SCHOOL, ANGLETON learned the consequences of his friendship with Ezra Pound. The poet's speeches on Radio Rome did not attract a big audience in Italy, nor were they broadcast in the United States. But the Federal Communications Commission in Washington was recording them,[52] and J. Edgar Hoover was listening. In his midfifties, the FBI director was a heavyset man who favored shiny suits. He had built the Bureau of Investigation, a small office within the Justice Department, into a national police force. In April 1942, Hoover ordered his men to investigate Pound on suspicion of aiding America's enemies.[53]

An FBI agent visited Angleton at his Brattle Street flat. Angleton explained he admired Pound's poetry and found his political theories convincing, though distorted by his prejudices against Jews and bankers. Angleton agreed that Pound's radio speeches were incoherent and indefensible. He said he would testify to that effect and provide the names of others who knew Pound.[54]

In spring 1943, Angleton was drafted into the army and passed his physical exam. He identified himself as James Hugh Angleton, Jr., proof that he did not care for his given middle name, Jesus.[55] Though he could have used his father's contacts and become an officer, he chose to begin army life as an enlisted man.[56]

He also proposed to Cicely, although Hugh and Carmen disapproved.[57] They didn't know Cicely d'Autremont or her family. Jim didn't have a job or professional degree. The couple endured a painful meeting with his parents, but the young lovers did not relent. They set a date for a wedding in July near the army base where Angleton was training. On one of Jim's few days off, he and Cicely got married at a church outside Fort Custer, Michigan, an unromantic beginning to a troubled lifelong commitment.[58]

CICELY WENT BACK TO Arizona and Jim left on a train eastbound to Washington. Norman Pearson had arranged for him to join the OSS. Before long, he was immersed in another form of basic training, this one in the hills of Maryland. Sixty OSS recruits marched up hills, danced through obstacle courses, and took night compass runs through the woods. The men who passed through the OSS training course became Angleton's colleagues and friends for life.

Some came from similarly privileged backgrounds. Frank Wisner, the scion of a wealthy Mississippi family, had attended the University of Virginia. Others were older men of humbler origins, experienced in ways unknown to Angleton's Yale classmates. Winston Scott, a former FBI agent, had grown up in a railroad boxcar in rural Alabama. He had a photographic memory and a Ph.D. in mathematics. Tom Karamessines was a taciturn lawyer who had worked as a prosecutor in New York City. Bill Colby was a Princeton man and army paratrooper who would lead sabotage raids in occupied Norway. Dick Helms was a white-shoed navy lieutenant who had worked as a wire-service reporter and once interviewed Adolf Hitler.

Angleton would know these men for as long as they lived.

Before shipping out to England, the OSS Officers' Training Corps passed through what was known as the New York staging area for some final polishing, including a course in the art of picking locks. The instructor, a muscular and profane whirlwind named George Hunter White, was a career agent with the Federal Bureau of Narcotics.[59] White had met Hugh Angleton and took a liking to his son.[60]

George White was as tough a character as Angleton had ever met. The FBN regulated the transshipment of narcotics in both legal and illegal transactions. Working undercover, White relished breaking the law in order to enforce it, a trait Angleton would come to share.[61] He was a new sort of associate for Angleton, a man who expressed himself not with words but with fists or a gun. There was nothing poetic about him.

Angleton and his OSS brothers then sailed to England on a stormy North Atlantic sea, a stomach-turning ten-day voyage.[62] When he disembarked with the duffel-toting throng at Southampton, Angleton had arrived where he wanted to be: the war front.

SECRETARY

THE HIDEOUS CRACK OF the missile blast jolted the floorboards, shattered the windows, buffeted the typewriters, and drove glass into every cranny of the cramped room at 14 Ryder Street in central London. Not long after, Angleton arrived for work at the OSS headquarters. It was raining hard and a brisk gale blew through the jagged panes as he went up to the second-floor office. Many nights, he slept on a cot by the desk. Luckily, Angleton had spent the previous night elsewhere, a twist of fate that might have saved his life.

It was March 1944. Angleton had gone through OSS training school in Bletchley Park, where he was reunited with Norman Pearson, who was responsible for the X-2 indoctrination training of the American arrivals. "X-2" served as shorthand for counterintelligence. Pearson also called on a British colleague, Harold Philby, an SIS section chief known to all as Kim, to explain the workings of a wartime intelligence station.[63]

After completing his training, Angleton was assigned to the Ryder Street office. The city was under siege from long-range German rockets fired from Flanders across the English Channel. Every day and night, V-2 missiles slammed into apartment blocks, office buildings, pubs, churches, and schools around the city, killing randomly and terrorizing generally.

Angleton's secretary, Perdita Macpherson, found him stamping around the drafty, shattered office in his overcoat. Angleton swept the glass off his chair and sat down to work.[64]

JIM ANGLETON LEARNED THE craft of counterintelligence from two masters: Norman Pearson and Kim Philby.

Pearson was the more intellectual of two. Now living in England, he liked nothing more than to spend his Sundays sipping tea in the flat of his friend Hilda Doolittle, the poet known as H.D.[65] The rest of the week, he taught the subtle arts of counterintelligence, defined as "information gathered and activities conducted to protect against espionage, sabotage or assassinations conducted for or on behalf of foreign powers, organizations, or persons."[66] Angleton would prove to be his most brilliant student.

Kim Philby was more of a rising civil servant. He had grown up in a well-to-do and well-traveled family. His father, Harry St. John Philby, had parlayed his livelihood as an Anglo-Indian tea planter into a career as a confidant to the royal family of Saudi Arabia.[67] His son, Kim, was educated at Cambridge and dabbled in journalism before joining the Secret Service in 1940. From the start Philby distinguished himself from his more conventional colleagues with a casual wardrobe, incisive memoranda, and a mastery of Soviet intelligence operations in Spain and Portugal. He taught Angleton how to run double-agent operations, to intercept wireless and mail messages, and to feed false information to the enemy. Angleton would prove to be his most trusting friend.

Angleton had found a calling and a mentor.

Once he met Philby the world of intelligence that had once interested him consumed him. "He had taken on the Nazis and the Fascists head-on and penetrated their operations in Spain and Germany," he said. "His sophistication and experience appealed to us. . . . Kim taught me a great deal."[68]

SO DID NORMAN PEARSON. He imparted to Angleton his knowledge about one of the most significant activities housed at Bletchley Park: ULTRA, the code-breaking operation that enabled the British to decipher all of Germany's military communications and read them in real time. By May 1944, the British believed they had, for perhaps for the first time in modern military history, a complete understanding of the enemy's intelligence resources.[69]

Pearson also sat on the committee that decided how to use the ULTRA information. He was let in on another, even more closely held British secret: the practice of "doubling" certain German agents to feed disinformation back to Berlin so as to shape the thinking and the actions of Hitler's generals.

It was a subtle, dirty game that Pearson shared with Angleton. The Germans had infiltrated dozens of spies into England with the mission of stealing information, identifying targets, and reporting back to listening posts on the Continent. When the British captured one of the German spies, they would "double" him—that is, compel him to send back a judicious mixture of false and accurate data, which would give the Germans a mistaken view of battlefield reality. In the run-up to the Normandy invasion of June 1944, the British had manipulated the Germans into massing their troops away from the selected landing point. The deception enabled the Allied armies to land at Normandy and start their drive toward Paris with the German resistance in disarray.

Angleton was learning how deception operations could shape the battlefield of powerful nations at war.

PERDITA MACPHERSON HAD ALREADY started working at the OSS offices on Ryder Street when Angleton turned up late one winter afternoon. He looked lean and taut, with a long-distance runner's build, she thought. He had cavernous cheekbones and black hair. After a cursory hello, he flung open files and drawers and started pulling out, leafing, and thumbing through papers. He had marvelous hands, she noticed: long, nervous, and expressive.

Perdita found him to be sensitive and knowledgeable and demanding.

"He proceeded to dictate a report of immense length, depth, and complexity," she remembered. "Leaning back in his chair, leaping up suddenly to pace like a panther. He quoted poetry . . . to strengthen an argument, to dramatize a point."

Macpherson liked Angleton, and she loved her job. The Yanks and Brits, the servicemen and civilians, SIS and OSS, all brisk banter and good cheer, working together in cramped quarters, going about their business of defeating the bloody Nazis. One of them was Angleton's friend, the affable Kim Philby, clad casually in a leather bomber jacket and exuding bonhomie with an endearing stammer.

"A real charmer," she recalled decades later. "So calm. So reliable."[70]

AS THE HEAD OF the X-2 Italy desk, Angleton was cleared for ULTRA material. He sent coded messages to the OSS station in Rome. With Macpherson's help, he prepared targeting material to be used as Allied forces entered the city of Florence in September 1944. The result, one memo noted, was "the speedy liquidation of a pre-arranged set of CE [counterespionage] targets," sixteen in all.[71] Angleton had become a lethal man.

In the face of danger, he was unmoved. After the Allied invasion at Normandy, the Germans stepped up their blitz of London with buzz bombs, also known as "doodlebugs," which announced their imminent arrival with a sizzling sound that suddenly ceased as the bomb fell toward its target.

"Whatever the name, the worst thing yet," Perdita Macpherson recalled. "Whenever one of them sputtered to a halt, my heart stopped. My typewriter stopped too."[72]

After the ensuing explosion, Angleton would look up at her quizzically and ask, "Is anything the matter?"

Angleton took a dim view of the females of the species, she noticed. "He censured my feminine traits, as he saw them," she recalled. "Lack of dedication, subjective thinking, faulty logic. And my problems, my endless problems; why did I have so many problems?"

One day, Angleton opined that Perdita wasn't working hard enough. Exasperated by the endless hours at the office, followed by standing on line to get a stale loaf of bread, she exploded.

"I told him I'd been fighting this war longer than he had," she recalled. "That I was tired of counter-espionage, and just plain tired."

Perdita took a holiday with friends in Cornwall, wondering what kind of reception might be awaiting her when she returned to Ryder Street. She was surprised.

"Jim was a person transformed," she said. "Luminous, effulgent. He hugged me and spun me all around. Cicely had borne him a son. . . . The rest of our days hummed along in sunny warmth. His commission came through. I had a spruce new lieutenant on my hands, as well as a new father. He was posted to Rome."

BLACK PRINCE

ANGLETON HURRIED UP TO the villa in Milan. Accompanying him toward the safe house was an Italian friend, Capt. Carlo Resio, a trusted naval officer, and a new acquaintance, Prince Junio Valerio Borghese. A commanding man, not yet forty years old, with a bold nose and a knowing squint in his eye, Borghese was perhaps the most famous fascist military commander in Italy. All three men knew that Borghese's life was in danger.

It was May 11, 1945, and the world was changing fast. Franklin Roosevelt had been dead for a month, Benito Mussolini for two weeks, Adolf Hitler for less than two. Germany had just surrendered three days before to the Allied forces of the United States and Great Britain. In northern Italy, the leftist partisans of the Committee for the Liberation of Italy were calling on the people to vanquish the fascists. Retribution was coming swiftly. Bodies were appearing on the streets of Milan.

Angleton, at twenty-seven years of age, was canny and well trained, already a student of power. He would later insist that he did not care for Borghese's fascist ideas, only for the tangible assistance he gave the U.S. government, a distinction that would prove not to make much of a difference.

The three men entered the villa and closed the door behind them.

JUNIO VALERIO BORGHESE, ANGLETON'S companion that day, was one of the few standouts in Italy's feckless military performance in

World War II. He came from a family with a storied name and a dissipated fortune. As a young man, Borghese was inspired by Mussolini's March on Rome in 1922, which brought the Fascist Party to power. He joined the navy, married a countess, and became a submarine commander. He fought with Generalissimo Francisco Franco in the Spanish Civil War, where his prowess in clandestine naval warfare won him the command of the prestigious Tenth Light Flotilla, also known as the Decima Mas. When Italy entered World War II, Borghese pioneered the use of speedboats, midget submarines, and frogmen. He had even planned an attack on U.S. ships in New York Harbor.[73]

When Rome capitulated to the incoming Allied forces in September 1943, Mussolini retreated north under the protection of the German army. Borghese joined him. He converted the maritime Decima Mas into a land-based fighting force. Thousands rallied under his banner, responding to his creed of God, home, and family. By the end of 1944, the Decima Mas had more than ten thousand men under arms.[74]

The motto of the Decima Mas was MAS: *Memento Audere Semper,* "Remember Always to Dare."[75] Borghese dared to defend the Nazis. When Gen. Karl Wolff, the German commandant for the region, directed Borghese to launch a war of reprisals against the partisans, Borghese obliged without hesitation or pity.

In the village of Borgo Ticino on August 18, 1944, a lieutenant under Borghese's command announced the Decima Mas response to a partisan attack on a convoy that killed three German soldiers. He wanted four Italians killed for every dead German, and he selected his victims at random from the town's residents. To underscore his point, the lieutenant decided to add a thirteenth man on a whim. All were executed on the spot.[76]

For the Decima Mas's promiscuous reliance on torture, rape, looting, summary executions, and collective punishment, Borghese gained a title he did nothing to discourage: the Black Prince.

IT WAS IN WARTIME Rome that the legend of James Angleton was born. Assuming command responsibilities for OSS counterintelligence, he made an immediate impression. His mission was daunting. Occupied Italy had to be cleansed of German informants left behind by the Sicherheitsdienst, the intelligence agency of the Nazi Party and sister organization of the more notorious Gestapo. It was Angleton's job to identify, catch, and interrogate so-called line crossers, German spies who sought to collect order-of-battle information on the advancing Allied forces.[77] From London, the reliable Kim Philby kept him supplied with the all-important Bletchley Park decrypts of what the German high command was planning.[78]

His father's contacts helped. Hugh Angleton had taken his family back to the United States in December 1941 to escape the coming war. He enlisted in the U.S. Army's School of Military Government in Virginia, which was planning for the occupation of Italy and Germany. Hugh Angleton was assigned to the staff of Gen. Mark Clark, the commander of the U.S. invasion of Italy. He returned to Italy with the U.S. invasion forces in August 1943. After the royalist government surrendered in September 1943 and Mussolini fled north, the Americans took control of the southern part of the country.

Hugh Angleton, calling on friends in business and government, served as an OSS representative in discussions with leaders of the Italian military, intelligence services, and police. The American collaboration with elements connected to the Fascist Party and regime—court prefects, police chiefs, and local leaders—was part of a deliberate choice made by the Allies to create conservative coalitions to oppose Italy's left-wing political factions, especially the Communists and the labor movement.[79]

In his new job, Angleton followed his father's political path.

IN ROME, ANGLETON WORKED out of a three-story office building on the via Sicilia that also housed the offices of the British SIS and U.S. Army Counterintelligence. In OSS communications his code name was ARTIFICE.

From the ULTRA intercepts, he knew the Germans were planning to retreat north and leave their Italian allies behind in strategic centers. Other information suggested that Valerio Borghese would be responsible for the organization that the Nazis were leaving behind. Angleton crafted a scheme he called Plan IVY to dismantle the German intelligence and sabotage networks north of Florence. The plan relied on Captain Resio, a frigate commander and top official in the Italian naval intelligence agency.[80] Angleton gave him the seaworthy code name SALTY.

Resio provided Angleton with an understanding of what Borghese and his Decima Mas shock troops wanted. His SALTY reports dealt primarily with two themes: One was the threat of Communist insurgency in northern Italy and the Soviet Union's support for the same; the other, the existence of a fascist residue that had to be excised from the otherwise-worthy leadership of the Italian security services.

When Angleton sent these reports to X-2 headquarters in London, the response was dubious. The Soviet Union was an ally against the German-Italian axis. The Italian navy's intelligence service, his colleagues cautioned, had long been considered royalist and anti-Soviet: "Therefore, it seems possible that this information may well be in the nature of a propaganda plant."[81]

Angleton disagreed.

PLAN IVY WAS JUST one aspect of the OSS effort to disable and dismantle the German and Italian intelligence networks on behalf of the Allied armies. From the OSS station in Bern, Switzerland, Allen Dulles, a former State Department official turned Wall Street attorney, had opened private lines of communication in early 1945 with General Wolff about the possibility of surrender.

Dulles, an amoral pipe-smoking schemer, had long experience with—and high regard for—a number of German businessmen and financiers. Dulles regarded the rise of the Nazis as an unfortunate aberration that should not taint the reputation of the good Germans who did not support them. While President Franklin Roosevelt and Prime Minister Winston Churchill were insisting on unconditional Nazi surrender, Dulles had a different idea: a separate peace with responsible Germans to end the war more quickly. If Wolff and others broke with Hitler and ceased fighting, Dulles intimated they would be treated well by the victorious Allies.

Dulles called it Operation Sunrise. It was designed to blunt the advance of Communist forces in Europe. The Soviet army was advancing from the east toward Austria. Communist-led partisans were vanquishing the fascist regimes in the Balkans and they were surging in Italy. Dulles predicted that Hitler and his most loyal followers would retreat to Bavaria, where they would fight to the end. Angleton followed Dulles's lead.

"Around February 1945," Angleton later recalled, "the OSS learned from very reliable sources that the Nazi regime was setting up a plan for the creation of a last zone of resistance in Austria, after the complete destruction of northern Italy by its retreating troops. This 'scorched earth' policy, which would have cost Italy all her ports, her factories and her lines of communication, was intended to create a 'revolutionary situation' which could have resulted in an encounter between the Soviets and the Western allies from which Hitler hoped to profit."[82]

The goal of Angleton's Plan IVY was to convince Borghese not to join in any plans for a "scorched earth" retreat. If the Decima Mas commander and his men were spared the ignominy of surrender, northern Italy would not be razed. To make contact with Borghese, Angleton chose Commander Antonio Marceglia, a former member of the Decima Mas.[83] Marceglia relayed Angleton's offer to Borghese.

"If he agreed to cooperate with the allies and line up his units to prevent the Germans from blowing up the port, he would be saved from the partisans who planned to gun him down in the streets of Milan."[84]

Borghese warily agreed. He provided the Americans with detailed maps of explosive mines laid in the port of Livorno. Then he surrendered, or, as he preferred to put it, demobilized. The men of the Decima Mas laid down their arms and flag at five o'clock on the afternoon of April 26, 1945, in a ceremony in their barracks at Fiume Square in Milan.[85]

Suddenly, the fascist collapse came faster and was uglier than anyone had expected. Angleton had received the sickening news at his office in Rome. Benito Mussolini, his mistress, Clara Petacci, and three of his top men were dead, captured by the partisans at Lake Como and executed. To prove the fascists were truly dead, the partisans had brought their bodies back to Milan and strung them up by their feet from the latticed roof of the Esso gas station in Piazzale Loreto, a bustling traffic circle not far from the heart of the city. Soon jeering crowds gathered to desecrate the upside-down bodies of the dead dictator, his mistress, and their friends.

The location was personal for Angleton. The Piazzale Loreto was located less than ten minutes from the Angleton home in Milan. Angleton might have filled up the family car at the gasoline pumps of that Esso station.

Angleton summoned Resio and drove north with a contingent of U.S. soldiers as bodyguards. On May 9, he met with Borghese and delivered a friendly message: Admiral de Courten, commander of Allied forces in Italy, wanted him to come to Rome. Angleton felt that Borghese had fulfilled his end of the Operation Sunrise bargain. Besides, the partisans had discovered where he was staying and would soon come to get him. Borghese was wary of a trick but had little choice: trust this earnest American or wind up as a public carcass like his friends Benito and Clara.

ANGLETON WAS A MAN in demand. On the night of May 11, 1945, he had a dinner date that he could not break. He had previously invited a British colleague to have supper at the villa. Angleton did not want to cancel, so he installed Borghese and Resio elsewhere in the villa and returned to prepare the table for his visitor. His guest had just returned from the surrender negotiations between the Allies and the Germans.

"Among other things," Angleton recounted later, "my guest told me that he had asked the Germans to bring him the fascist ringleaders: Valerio Borghese and Col. DeLeo." The British planned to question the men, his guest said, and then hand them over to the partisans for immediate execution.[86]

Angleton had to swallow his alarm as he ate. He said nothing of Borghese's whereabouts to his guest, even though the man the British wanted was sitting nearby. The two men finished their meal, and Angleton bade his friend farewell. The next morning, Angleton dressed the fascist Borghese in an American serviceman's uniform and they drove south.

In Rome, Angleton installed Borghese in an OSS safe house on via Archimedes.[87] On May 19, 1945, Borghese was formally arrested and taken to the Allied military base in Caserta, south of Rome, where prosecutors for the war-crimes tribunals were gathering evidence. Someone in the OSS, perhaps Angleton himself, arranged for Borghese's arrest record to be falsified so that the Italian government would not learn that he was in custody.[88] As Angleton later explained, he had saved Borghese's life because he thought the U.S. government had a "long term interest" in retaining his services.[89]

Borghese, never charged with the war crimes of the Decima Mas, would be convicted of lesser offenses and released in 1949. He and his wife were the only fascists of the period who were formally rescued by the authority of the U.S. government.[90] Thanks to Angleton, Borghese survived to become titular and spiritual leader of postwar Italian fascism.

"ANGLETON'S APPROACH CAN BE best understood as the implementation of what might be called 'Total Counterespionage,'" wrote historian Timothy Naftali. ". . . He believed that a counterespionage service had to have an insatiable appetite for information about foreign activities so as to be in a position to restrict, eliminate, or control the ways by which other states collected their intelligence."[91]

Imbued with fascist sympathies and anti-Communist passion, Angleton channeled his convictions into Anglo-American hegemonic ambition. With the analytic skills forged in Yale literary criticism and secret intelligence training imparted by the British SIS, he had unique aspirations. Angleton was intent on nurturing an intelligence network in service of the new American millennium. Recruiting the Black Prince was just the beginning.

NAZI

EUGEN DOLLMANN SAT IN a darkened, empty cinema as the matinee romance *Kisses You Dream Of* flickered on the screen.[92] It was another leisurely, lonely day in the life of a dapper man who had preened for the popping flashbulbs at fashionable events in Rome society throughout the 1930s. With his impeccable Italian and native German and ingratiating personality, Dollmann had flourished as a translator in the decade when Mussolini's Social Republic and Adolf Hilter's Third Reich made common cause.[93]

These days, Herr Dollmann could not be quite so outgoing. His membership in the SS, the Schutzstaffel ("Protection Squadron") of the Nazi Party, was sufficient cause for his immediate arrest.[94] Just five years before, he had sat between Mussolini and Hitler as they traveled in German-occupied Russia.[95] Now he sat in the darkness of the cinema between two empty seats.

There was a firm hand on his shoulder and a quiet voice in his ear.

"Kindly leave the cinema with me."

Outside, the man, a plainclothes detective, showed a badge. Dollmann said there must be some mistake. Two armed carabinieri boxed him in and pushed him toward a waiting car. Dollmann said that he was Alfredo Cassani, an employee of the American government.[96] What was the problem?

The three men took Dollmann to a holding room in a nearby police station. A pudgy American in a military uniform entered, trailed by a young soldier. The officer introduced himself as Maj. Leo Pagnotta, deputy chief of the 428th U.S. Army Counterintelligence Corps. The soldier was a twenty-year-old CIC special agent, William Gowen. He had grown up in Italy, and his father was an aide to Myron Taylor, President Roosevelt's personal emissary to the Vatican.

Decades later, Gowen still remembered the conversation.

"I am Cassani," said Dollmann, proffering his papers again.

"I think you're Dollmann." Pagnotta shrugged. He returned the document with barely a glance. He didn't care for forgeries, no matter how faithful. As their exchanges wore on without much emotion or resolution, Dollmann reconsidered his dwindling options. Finally, he extracted a piece of paper from his pocket and handed it to Pagnotta.

"Please call this number," he said in an altered tone. "Ask for Major Angleton. *He* knows who I am."[97]

BY THE END OF 1946, Jim Angleton had risen to the top of U.S. intelligence activities in Italy. He had survived President Harry Truman's abrupt abolition of the OSS without much disruption of his duties. His authority was growing.

In September 1945, the world war was over and America had to build a new peace. The new president agreed with the critics who warned that the OSS, as a secret intelligence agency, could turn into an American version of the Gestapo, the German police force that had repressed the opposition to Hitler. The overseas stations and personnel of the OSS were transferred overnight to the War Department; Angleton's work did not change much, but his cryptonym did.[98] ARTIFICE was now addressed in the cable traffic as "Major O'Brien."[99]

Angleton and his staff at the via Sicilia office were expected to monitor local political activities, especially those of the Communist Party, and to gather evidence for the war-crime trials of the Nazis.[100] Angleton preferred the former to the latter.

LIFE WAS RETURNING TO normal for the Angleton family. For the first time since 1941, they were all living in Italy. Hugh and Carmen chose to resettle in Rome, where Hugh returned to selling business machines. Jim's younger sister Carmen, who had helped continue publication of Furioso during the war, came to Rome and soon acquired a fiancé, Ernest Hauser, a journalist from Germany. They would be married in January 1947.[101] Brother Hugh had graduated from Yale and would marry a Polish woman. The youngest of the Angleton siblings, Delores, was headed for preparatory school in England.

Hugh Angleton wanted his son to resign his government job and take over the family business. Hugh told Jim the business would enable him to take care of Cicely and their son, Jamie, who were living with Cicely's parents in Tucson. Angleton had other plans. He would not leave secret intelligence work.

EZRA POUND WAS NOW confined to St. Elizabeths Hospital in southeast Washington. His radio speeches had resulted in an indictment for treason. In the last days of the war, he was arrested by U.S. military police in Rapallo and taken back to the United States for trial. His literary friends persuaded him to plead insanity, and he was committed to the hospital instead of prison. Angleton still appreciated Pound as an artist but thought he was mad.

"Pound probably had the finest ear as far as the English language is concerned," Angleton told a journalist many years later, "but he never stayed with one style and developed it. He was an innovator, but he had a philosophy which didn't really hang together. The fact he called one book *Personae*, or 'masks,' is reflective of his poetry and the different façades that he had. I don't think anyone ever took Pound's politics seriously."[102]

Of course, Angleton *had* taken Pound's politics seriously, at least as an undergraduate, and he still thought fondly of the man. In drawing up a will in 1948, he would bequeath a "bottle of spirits" to his friend, the incarcerated poet.[103]

IN OCTOBER 1945, ANGLETON met Allen Dulles and his wife, Clover, for the first time. After the abolition of the OSS, Dulles left Switzerland for a holiday in Rome. He wanted to vet the precocious young man who had so ably assisted in Operation Sunrise. They met at the Hotel Hassler, and it didn't take long for Dulles to appreciate the reflexes he saw at work in this gaunt young man. He had a passionate meticulousness, exemplified by what one chronicler called his "instinct to chew something twice and taste it three times."[104] Allen and Clover Dulles found Angleton immensely attractive.[105]

Angleton was not happy in marriage. Back in Arizona, Cicely was lonely and frustrated. She was living at her parents' shady estate in the heart of Tucson, raising Jamie. When Angleton returned to the United States for a two-week consultancy about the future of U.S. intelligence, his reunion with Cicely was dismal.

"It was exactly what his father had warned us about in 1943," Cicely said later. "Jim no longer cared about our relationship. He just wanted to get back to Italy, to the life he knew and loved. He didn't want a family."[106]

Cicely began to compile reasons for a divorce. She blamed herself for making him miserable. But in their misery, the young couple did not know how to separate. They stayed in the family guesthouse and fought.[107]

He returned to Rome. She remained in Tucson. She'd had an awful war, losing both of her brothers during the course of 1944. Her elder brother, Charles d'Autremont, a sailor on a U.S. warship, was killed in a German bombing raid in February 1944.[108] Her other brother, Hugh, not yet twenty years old, died ten months later.[109] With baby Jamie underfoot and her husband missing in action, Cicely filed for divorce in June 1946.[110] Then she discovered she was pregnant again.

She dropped divorce proceedings and settled for the company of her own thoughts. In time, she would become the poet of the family, not Jim. Late in life, she composed two books of poems about old age, nature, and youth, suffused with intimate details of a troubled marriage. Not yet thirty years old, Cicely was a wife and mother but lonely as a little girl.

ANGLETON'S OFFICE WAS THE seat of his incipient empire. He had taken on a deputy, an OSS officer named Ray Rocca, who was competent, loyal, and handy with a pistol. Rocca would work with Angleton for the next thirty years. Angleton told Norman Pearson he had already amassed more than fifty informants in seven intelligence services.[111]

Angleton even penetrated his office neighbors in the Army Counterintelligence Corps. Capt. Mario Brod, the commanding officer of the CIC unit in Palermo, became an OSS informant.[112] Thanks to Brod, Angleton gained a connection to the American Mafia, which he would find useful in the years to come. With regard to Angleton's liaison with the Italian security forces, one superior said it was "spectacularly productive."[113]

Angleton remained in touch with Kim Philby, who paid an unannounced visit to Rome not long after the liquidation of the OSS. They stayed up late talking about matters both professional and personal.[114] Angleton admitted he was worried about his marriage. Philby, a father of four and now married for the second time, was the voice of experience. "He helped me think it through," Angleton recalled.[115]

ANGLETON WAS NOT SURPRISED when Major Pagnotta called about Dollmann. Some months earlier, Angleton had learned from one of his Vatican contacts that two known Nazis, Eugen Dollmann and Eugen Wenner, had escaped from a minimum-security British detention camp. They had taken refuge in a hospital outside Milan.[116]

Angleton knew of Dollmann. He had represented General Wolff in the secret surrender talks with Dulles in early 1945, thus preparing the way for the culmination of Operation Sunrise.[117] Angleton feared Dollmann's arrest might be a propaganda coup for the Communists. Dulles had always claimed that he had not violated FDR's policy of unconditional surrender and denied promising leniency to Nazis like Wolff and Dollmann. In fact, Dollmann had received American help after the war and might testify to that effect if brought to trial.

Angleton sent a car to Milan to fetch Dollmann and Wenner and bring them back to Rome in order to "keep them quiet"[118]

When Angleton met Dollmann in person, he asked for his help.

"You see, for us of the American Secret Service, the struggle against Communism is only just beginning," he said, according to Dollmann. He proposed Dollmann take a six-week course and then "build up a really good espionage organization against the Russians."

Dollmann objected that his reputation as a Nazi might inhibit his usefulness in Germany. Angleton waved him off. "We're the masters of the world," he said. "No one can touch you."

Dollmann disdained Angleton. "He was talking like a young university lecturer who dabbled a bit in espionage in his spare time," he said later. But he didn't disdain Angleton's offer of money, identification papers, and a place to stay in Rome.[119]

LEO PAGNOTTA, THE ARMY CIC investigator, and Bill Gowen, the special agent, paid a visit to Dollmann's residence on via Archimedes.[120]

The man who answered the door was Eugen Wenner, who had also played a role in the Operation Sunrise negotiations.[121] Pagnotta asked about the third man living in the apartment. Wenner replied that he was traveling. He was Walter Rauff, another former SS commander who had worked as adjutant to General Wolff in northern Italy. Rauff had also helped design the Black Raven gas wagons that predated the gas chambers as the method for the mass killing of Jews.[122] An estimated 250,000 people died in Rauff's mobile killing machines. U.S. war-crimes prosecutors were determined to bring Rauff to trial. Thanks to Angleton, Rauff lived as a free man for the rest of his life.

"We couldn't believe Angleton put these men up in a safe house," Bill Gowen said. "It was inexplicable."[123]

When Pagnotta informed Angleton that Dollmann was wanted for questioning about war crimes, Angleton had to acquiesce in his detention. Italian prosecutors probed Dollmann's possible role in the 1943 Ardeatine Caves massacre in which the Nazis executed 335 Italian prisoners of war. After the authorities absolved Dollmann of involvement, Angleton resumed his effort to secure his release.

When Pagnotta returned to civilian life in the United States in the spring of 1947, Angleton was free to act. As "Major O'Brien," he visited Dollmann in his squalid jail cell and gave him five hundred Swiss francs.[124] He then supervised a team of agents who spirited Dollmann from the premises on a stretcher. Dollmann was whisked off to the U.S military base in Frankfurt, Germany.[125] In October 1947, he was given another small cash payment and a new set of valid identification papers and was released on the condition that he report weekly to U.S. officials.

Dollmann continued to serve as a CIA source for at least five more years while writing a memoir of life in Nazi Rome that sold well. In 1951, he was arrested for a homosexual tryst with a Swiss man. Unnamed CIA officials arranged for him to escape back to Italy. When Dollmann attempted in 1951 to pass off a batch of forged Nazi documents as authentic, the CIA cut him off.

Angleton's rescue of Eugen Dollmann was far from the most important intelligence operation he ran in Rome after the war, but it was one of the most revealing. As with the Black Prince, Angleton said sparing the Nazi translator from justice was a matter of honor.

MONSIGNOR

BY 1947, WELL-PLACED AMERICANS in Italy were saying, sotte voce, that young Jim Angleton had great sources in the Vatican. Some went so far as to say he was meeting on a weekly basis with Monsignor Giovanni Battista Montini, the Vatican's undersecretary of state for Italian affairs.[126]

Angleton did not boast of such connections. It was his job to know what was going on in Italian politics, and he made sure he did.

The relationship between the monsignor and the American spy was more transactional than spiritual. Baptized as a Catholic and raised as an Episcopalian, Angleton acknowledged Jesus Christ as his Savior.[127] His meetings with Montini concerned more earthly matters.

Montini was a dark, slim, self-effacing man, the son of a lawyer. One U.S. intelligence report described him as "the most authoritative person in the Vatican," not the least because of his daily personal contact with Pope Pius XII.[128] The lessons Angleton learned when he met with Monsignor Montini taught him certain timeless truths about the management of power. Yesterday's war criminal was today's asset. If the world was indifferent to the fate of the Jews, the Jews would return the favor. On the grounds of the Vatican, Angleton learned the religion of realism. He refused to rank ideologies of America's adversaries in terms of morality.[129]

Angleton put his principles into practice. When Montini learned that U.S. Army CIC investigators were asking questions about certain Croatian fascists sought by the Allied war-crimes tribunals, the monsignor complained to Angleton. The Croatians were steadfast in their support for the Church and in their rejection of communistic atheism. They were also notorious for massacring Jews and looting the banks of Zagreb. When the Nazis withdrew from southeast Europe, their local allies fled to the relative safety of Rome.[130]

The CIC men thought Montini might be sheltering the Croatians at the San Girolamo seminary, located a mile from the Vatican. And they suspected that the Croatians' loot, in the form of gold coins stolen from state banks and dead Jews, might be stashed nearby. Through an inside agent, William Gowen was able to copy the registration books listing visitors to various Vatican properties. A check of CIC files found that twenty of the men hosted by the Vatican were suspected war criminals. Gowen reported the information to his superiors, with a copy to Angleton.

In return, he received an order from Joe Greene, Angleton's friend at the U.S. embassy. The CIC was to stand down. The Croatians were an Italian, not American, responsibility. Gowen concluded that Angleton, as a favor to Montini, had thwarted the CIC's plans to arrest the Croatians and seize their ill-gotten gains.

"Angleton was way too smart to put it in writing," Gowen said. "He had other people do it."[131]

THE POWERFUL SOVIET-AMERICAN ALLIANCE that had crushed Hitler's Reich in a colossal pincer movement in 1945 evaporated in just two years. The two victorious powers were now bristling rivals confronting each other across Europe from the Baltic Sea to the Balkan Mountains. In every country where the war had been fought, local Communist parties were bidding for power. Even the most remote conflicts became part of a new global struggle between West and East.

The U.S. government mobilized for a cold war. In March 1947, President Truman announced the United States would support the royalist government in Greece, which had collaborated with the Nazis, against the Communists who had fought them. Truman pledged the United States would "support free peoples who are resisting attempted subjugation by armed minorities or by outside pressures."[132] The United States would also help rebuild the economy of its European allies under a plan announced by Secretary of State George Marshall in a speech given at Harvard in June 1947.

In July, Congress approved the National Security Act, which created the new Central Intelligence Agency. The CIA was charged with coordinating intelligence-collection activities, advising the newly created National Security Council in the White House, and distributing finished intelligence to other agencies.[133]

President Truman reversed his opposition to a peacetime intelligence agency and signed the act. But Truman insisted on language banning CIA operations on U.S. soil, reiterating that he did not want an "American Gestapo."[134] To insulate the new agency from political pressures, a military man, Adm. Roscoe Hillenkoetter, was brought on to serve as director.

The National Security Act empowered the CIA to take on "such other functions and duties related to intelligence affecting the national security," an ambiguous phrase whose meaning was well understood in Washington.

"The 'other functions' the CIA was to perform were purposely not specified," admitted Clark Clifford, an aide to Truman, "but we understood that they would include covert activities."[135]

In November 1947, Angleton was summoned back to Washington to join the Agency. He was soon installed in a ten-by-twelve-foot room in offices housed in a series of ramshackle huts lining the Reflecting Pool in front of the Lincoln Memorial, in the heart of Washington. These shabby white buildings, which had sprouted during the war, were known as "tempos," as in temporary. They were drafty in winter and torpid in summer, and devoid of charm year-round.[136]

Angleton arrived just in time for the very first presidentially authorized CIA mission. On December 14, 1947, Truman issued directive NSC 4/A, placing responsibility for "psychological warfare" with the CIA.[137] The priority was Italy, where the Communists were strong. Truman ordered deployment of all practicable means to shore up the pro-American Christian Democrats, including overt measures, such as "an effective U.S. information program," and covert measures, such as the use of "unvouchered funds," the preferred euphemism for untraceable cash bribes. Within the CIA, the Office of Special Operations, OSO, responsible for espionage and counterespionage, was assigned to carry out the president's orders.

Angleton's job title was chief of operations for Staff A, which handled OSO's foreign intelligence gathering. He inherited the files of the OSS X-2 and assigned the task of sorting and filing them to a former Army Intelligence officer named Bill Hood.[138] Hood was impressed by Angleton's mastery of mundane detail.[139] Angleton, he noted, established and codified practices for clearing agents and for reporting on operations that would soon become standard procedure and would remain so for decades.[140]

ANGLETON'S CEREBRAL APPROACH ANNOYED one of his new colleagues, Bill Harvey, the chief of Staff C, which was responsible for counterintelligence. William King Harvey was a pudgy, goggle-eyed cop who had graduated at the top of his class from the University of Indiana Law School. He had made himself into the FBI's expert on the Soviet Union's extensive intelligence activities in America. After the war ended, Harvey had identified a network of supposedly loyal Americans—including a handful from the OSS—who were actually reporting to Moscow. Harvey's drinking got him in trouble with J. Edgar Hoover in 1947, so he joined the newly created CIA. Harvey came to the job with a fund of knowledge about Soviet espionage unmatched anywhere in the U.S. government. He did not think much of Angleton, at least not at first.

Their styles contrasted. Harvey had grown up in the same small midwestern town as his father and grandfather. Angleton had grown up all over America and Europe. Harvey collected firearms. Angleton constructed fishing lures. Angleton shambled along like a professor late to a lecture. Harvey walked with the stiff gait of a military man on patrol. They were prototypes of two strains of spies—OSS veterans and FBI exiles—who came together to share the higher calling of the CIA. One journalist who knew them both wrote that Harvey was a man of action, heeding a call to glory. Angleton, he said, was a man of ideas, following a path to power.[141]

NO SOONER HAD ANGLETON started to settle in Washington than his bosses sent him back to Italy. He was simply too knowledgeable and capable to be kept in Washington. The Italian Communist Party was already running strong in the campaign leading up to the April elections, which would determine the structure of the country's first postwar government.

The sense that Italy was on the brink of civil war was pervasive in the American press. "Italy Faces Her Worst Crisis," proclaimed *Look* magazine. "The Communist Party is extending its gains every day as poverty and hunger grip the nation. The opposition to communism is also stiffening, with the promise of American aid. But the resistance may not be strong enough."[142]

In his quest to make sure the Partito Comunista Italiano, or PCI, did not come to power, Angleton knit together friends, allies, and agents into a formidable action network. He could call on the Italian security forces, the Vatican, his father's associates in the business world, fraternal allies in the Knights of Malta, as well as contacts in the British and French secret services.

To stem the Communist tide, Angleton proposed raising $300,000 in private funds for radio and newspaper advertising and for the "personal expenses" of anti-Communist candidates. It wasn't enough. His bosses in Washington authorized tapping of the captured assets of the defeated Axis powers to pay for political action in Italy.[143] Ten million dollars was put into an account for CIA use.[144] A meeting was arranged at the Hotel Hassler. A satchel stuffed with millions of lira was passed from the Americans to their local allies.[145] With U.S. money pouring into Italy for the purposes of defeating communism, Monsignor Montini had his reward. He was given control of a campaign slush fund through the Vatican Bank.[146]

ANGLETON'S IMAGINATION HAD AN artistic dimension. As the story later circulated, he interrupted one embassy meeting in Rome in early 1948 to ask Ambassador James Dunn if he might offer an idea.

"I thought," he began mischievously, "we might take advantage of one of America's great natural resources: Greta Garbo."

The name of the Swedish actress invoked images of her sultry style. "I realize she once belonged to another country," Angleton said, "but I believe by now we're justified in claiming her as our own. So I suggest we import one of her best pictures." He paused. "I'd like to expose the Italians to *Ninotchka*."

Ninotchka, released in 1939, was a comedy in which Garbo spoofed Stalinist Russia. The ambassador ratified Angleton's proposal on the spot. Actually, Angleton wasn't the only wise guy with this idea. The Hollywood studios had printed extra copies of *Ninotchka* and made special arrangements to show the film in Italy as a way of contrasting golden America with ravaged Russia. At the end of the meeting, Angleton supposedly quipped, "Miss Garbo will prove a most lethal secret weapon."[147]

And so she did. The Christian Democrats emerged from the election of April 1948 with 48 percent of the vote and an absolute majority in parliament. In this rather open and extensive intervention by the United States,

Angleton had played a decisive role. His enemies, the Communists, would never gain control of the government in Rome, and his allies would mostly prosper. Within twenty years, Monsignor Montini would become Pope Paul VI.

REUNION

IN SEPTEMBER 1949, ANGLETON traveled across the Atlantic Ocean by boat, arriving at Southampton, England, the same port that had welcomed him five years earlier.[148] Then a novice, he was now an experienced spy. Upon landfall, he went straightaway to London, where he had lunch with his friend Win Scott, now chief of the CIA's London station. They then plunged into a week of meetings with senior British and American colleagues at SIS headquarters.[149]

The good news for Angleton was that Kim Philby would soon take command of the SIS station in Washington. He thought Philby was the best of the British service. The bad news for Angleton was the creation of a new enterprise within the CIA, the Office of Policy Coordination. The OPC was especially galling to Angleton because it was born of his personal success in Italy.

On May 4, 1948, barely three weeks after the Italian election, George Kennan, then a member of the State Department's Policy Planning Staff, had drafted a memo stating, "It would seem that the time is now fully ripe for the creation of a political warfare operations directorate within the Government."[150]

"We were alarmed at the inroads of the Russian influence in Western Europe beyond the point where the Russian troops had reached," Kennan later explained, "and we were alarmed particularly over the situation in France and Italy. . . . That is . . . why we thought we ought to have some facility for covert operations."[151]

Angleton's mission at OSO was narrow: "the conduct . . . of all organized Federal espionage and counterespionage operations outside of the United States."[152] Espionage was the theft of secrets, and counterespionage the prevention of the theft of secrets. OPC was entrusted with the more aggressive assignment: to wage political warfare, to manipulate the enemy's reality without disclosing the CIA's hand.

Angleton felt sidelined. He favored ambitious covert operations against the Soviet Union and its allies, but he insisted they required careful preparation and tight security, neither of which the OPC practiced. As OPC began to expand rapidly, Angleton believed the Agency was being taken over by amateurs. To fortify his position against office rivals, he went to London determined to consolidate his working relationship with Kim Philby, the rising star of SIS.

THE LEADERS OF CIA and SIS felt an urgent need to forge a more effective working relationship. More than a few people in Washington and London feared World War III might start in the near future. The dream of a cooperative postwar world was dead.[153] The strains between the Americans and the British services were dissipating under the growing Russian threat.[154]

The British wanted to preserve their "sphere of influence," the politest way of describing their shrinking empire. The country's self-appointed imperial mission had been battered during the war and besieged after it. In the course of a few months in 1947–1948, the British had had to accept the independence of India, once the crown jewel of their colonies, and then abandon Palestine to the Zionists, who established the state of Israel.

The Americans had a grander agenda. The newly created North Atlantic Treaty Organization would mobilize the armed forces necessary to deter any Soviet invasion of Western Europe. The Marshall Plan, funded by Congress, would provide an infusion of capital to rebuild Germany, France, and Italy as democratic countries allied with the United States. And the CIA would escalate secret operations against the Soviet Union and its allies to "roll back" the Communists from the countries where they had taken power.

The meeting of the minds in London in September 1949 settled on the requisite Anglo-American division of labor. The CIA needed expertise in running covert operations, an improved central file registry, and a more robust communications system—all of which the British had in place. SIS needed money and manpower—of which the Americans had a surplus. Kim Philby, all agreed, was just the man to make the new arrangements work in Washington.

After the meetings were over, Philby sailed to the United States, while Angleton flew on to Paris, then Rome and Athens, visiting CIA stations in each city. He visited his parents and wrote occasionally to Cicely, who remained in Tucson with five-year-old Jamie, one-year-old Helen, and the newborn Lucy. His wife was bored and envious of his travels.

Angleton was cavorting around Europe and Greece, and Cicely was complaining to a friend. "Really! The hush hush men deserve little pity and this isn't even considered a vacation."

By contrast, Cicely said, she was spending her time talking about babies. "They are wonderful," she wrote, "but as a topic of conversation can make a woman duller than canned orange juice."[155]

ANGLETON AND PHILBY RESUMED their friendship in December 1949, when they were reunited in Washington. Their bond, born in the classroom at Bletchley Park, nurtured in wartime London, and enhanced by professional collaboration, still had room to grow. Philby was working out of an office in the British embassy on Massachusetts Avenue. Angleton became his chief point of contact at the CIA.[156] They were the closest of friends, soul mates in espionage.

Angleton introduced Philby to the power rituals of Harvey's Seafood Grill on Connecticut Avenue. Located three blocks north of the White House, Harvey's was one of *the* places to be seen in the capital city. Harvey's claimed to have served every president since Ulysses S. Grant, a modest culinary distinction perhaps, but one that was irresistible to men with an appetite for power. Angleton didn't need to point out to his British friend the presence of J. Edgar Hoover, the sturdy and ominous director of the FBI, who often lunched with his cronies across the room.[157]

Philby embraced Angleton's tastes. He was a mentor to his American friend and a newcomer to his country. He sought Angleton's confidence.

"We formed the habit of lunching once a week at Harvey's where he demonstrated regularly that overwork was not his only vice," Philby would recall in a memoir. "He was one of the thinnest men I have ever met, and one of the biggest eaters. Lucky Jim! After years of keeping up with Angleton, I took the advice of an elderly lady, went on a diet and dropped from thirteen stone to about eleven in three months."[158]

For all their mutual affection, the two men vied for advantage as they talked espionage over lobsters.

"No matter how closely two intelligence services may cooperate, there are always things which are withheld," observed Jim McCargar, an OPC desk officer who worked with Angleton and Philby. "And there is, in the simple nature of things, a constant jockeying for advantage . . . it arouses no ill will, but it is, to the contrary, an accepted terrain for judging a man's professional abilities."[159]

Philby, the older man, was adept at these spy games. "The greater the trust between us overtly, the less he [Angleton] would suspect covert action," he explained. "Who gained the most from this complex game I cannot say. I knew what he was doing for CIA and he knew what I was doing for SIS. But the real nature of my interest was something he did not know."[160]

THE FRIENDSHIP BETWEEN ANGLETON and Philby was enhanced by mutual appreciation of the previously distant pleasures of marriage and family. Now settling in Washington, Philby and Angleton joined in conventional domesticity with their wives, the path of least resistance, and pleasing in its own ways.

Cicely had come from Tucson with the children. The Angletons bought a four-bedroom house on 33rd Road in north Arlington, on the Virginia side of the Potomac.[161] The Philbys settled into a modest rambler on Nebraska Avenue in Northwest Washington. Both wives began entertaining their husbands' friends and colleagues.

At the same time, both men maintained a life apart, working long hours and pursuing private interests. Angleton built a heated greenhouse to grow orchids. He installed a rock tumbler for polishing stones in his basement, where he made jewelry at night.[162] In his basement, Philby stored camera equipment, which he used for his own nocturnal pastimes.[163]

For all their chummy bonhomie, Angleton and Philby shared a certain ruthlessness, no doubt implanted by the example of their headstrong, successful fathers. The profession of secret intelligence demanded calculation, autonomy, cleverness, and mastery, qualities that they could not have failed to appreciate in each other. Angleton had seen his father trade dull success in Dayton for daring opportunity in Milan. Philby's father, St. John, had broken with British establishment to become a Muslim and political adviser to King Ibn Saud. He even helped broker the U.S. acquisition of the Saudi oil concession, infuriating his countrymen.

Philby's affable demeanor masked a hard streak that his more discerning associates glimpsed.

"He wore suede shoes, cravats and crumpled suits when the rest of the senior staff subscribed to a strict dress code," said McCargar. ". . . His smile, suggestive of complicity in a private joke, conveyed an unspoken understanding of the underlying ironies of our work. . . . Behind the modest, slightly crumpled exterior there was no mistaking a quick mind and a tenacious will."[164]

Philby was a formidable man. Robert McKenzie, the chief of security at the British embassy, had worked with St. John Philby and saw the influence on his son. "Philby had inherited from his father that same sense of dedicated idealism in which the means did not matter as long as the end was worthwhile," he said. ". . . This sense of dedication and purpose to whatever he was doing gleamed through and inspired men to follow. He was the sort of man who won worshippers. You didn't just like him, admire him, agree with him; you worshipped him."[165]

Angleton did not worship Philby—self-abasing emotion was not his style—but he did display a veneration bordering on the romantic for the older man. He, too, thought himself bold and ruthless. As he had told Eugen Dollmann, "We are masters of the world."

The friendship of these two masters extended into evenings and weekends when Jim and Cicely attended parties at Philby's sparsely furnished home on Nebraska Avenue. The entertainment usually consisted of a pitcher of martinis, a bottle or two of whiskey, some ice, and some glasses.[166] The ever-considerate Philby poured the first round and then the guests were on their own.

The thirsty attendees included many people who passed through Philby's office during the day. There were CIA men like McCargar and his wife. There were embassy colleagues, including Wilfred Mann, a nuclear scientist, and his wife, Miriam, who were close to the Angletons. There were experienced cops like Robert McKenzie, and sometimes savvy FBI men like Mickey Ladd and Bob Lamphere and their wives. Later that summer, Philby's new houseguest, an openly homosexual man named Guy Burgess, joined the party.[167] The consumption of liquor, observed McCargar, was "gargantuan."[168]

"HOMO CIRCLES"

THE SPRING OF 1950 was a sour season in Washington. Fears of war overseas bred fears of infiltration at home. In February, the previously obscure junior senator from Wisconsin, Joseph McCarthy, charged in a speech in Wheeling, West Virginia, that that there were two hundred Communists on the State Department payroll, an astonishing number if true. The charge made headlines, so McCarthy took his case to the floor of the U.S. Senate. In the course of a six-hour speech, he presented a case-by-case analysis of eighty-one people whom he described as "loyalty risks," without naming any of them. Over shouted objections, McCarthy led his Senate colleagues through each case. In most, he accused the unnamed officials of "palling around with Communists," joining Communist-front organizations, reading Soviet propaganda, or acting as Soviet agents. A few were homosexuals, McCarthy said. One "flagrantly homosexual" translator had been dismissed as a "bad security risk," he noted, but the man was later reinstated by a "high State Department official."[169]

As McCarthy and others on Capitol Hill began to weave together the threats of communism and homosexuality in 1950, Washington was engulfed with two popular passions: a wave of anti-Communist fervor that liberal historians would call "the Red Scare" and a widespread revulsion against homosexuals that gay historians would dub the "Lavender Scare." Both Communists and gays, it was said, should be purged from the federal government's workforce.[170]

The Lavender Scare was felt as an extraordinary political development. Homosexuality was all but unspeakable in American culture. Some newspapers would not even mention the word. Others, like the *Washington Times-Herald,* one of the capital's leading dailies, relied on abusive language. Gays and lesbians were "queers," "pansies," and "cookie-pushers." In any case, to even speak of such people was unheard of and scandalous.

And then there were the facts of the matter. While the florid-faced McCarthy was often reckless, his charges were not entirely imagined.[171] There *were* a lot of gays and lesbians in Washington. The federal government had quadrupled in size between 1930 and 1950.[172] More than a few of these governmental jobs were filled by gay people migrating into Washington, looking to escape the strictures of conventional families and small-town life.[173]

When Senator Millard Tydings, a liberal from Maryland, attacked McCarthy for the lack of specificity in his charges, the Wisconsin Republican responded with a true story, which Tydings could not refute. One known homosexual had been dismissed from the State Department, McCarthy said, only to be immediately rehired by the CIA.

"This man who was a homosexual . . . spent his time hanging around the men's room in Lafayette Park," he declared.[174]

Angleton knew the man McCarthy was talking about. His name was Carmel Offie. He worked for the CIA, and Angleton could not stand him.

CARMEL OFFIE WAS, by all accounts, an unusual and unscrupulous character. Born into a humble Italian family in Pennsylvania, he exhibited driving ambition at an early age. He studied dictation at a business school until he could take down conversations verbatim. He moved to Washington in the early 1930s, took a civil service exam, and was hired as a stenographer at the State Department. When William Bullitt, U.S. ambassador to the Soviet Union, asked for a first-class male stenographer, Offie was hired. In Moscow, he became Bullitt's assistant and lover. When Bullitt returned to the United States, he arranged for Offie to take the Foreign Service exam, which gained him a permanent job in the State Department.[175] Offie had a knack for shady financial schemes, which he used to keep powerful patrons in his debt.

Unusually for a gay man in those days, Offie did not hide his sexual preferences. He liked to refer to his bed as "the playing fields of Eton," the all-male English boarding school attended by the British elite. In 1943, he was arrested for propositioning an undercover police officer in Lafayette Park. After hours, the leafy park across the street from the White House was a popular place for gay men to congregate. The Washington police arrest report was the factual basis for McCarthy's charge.

At the time, Offie's bosses at the State Department defended him because he was simply too valuable to lose. They told the Washington police chief that Offie had gone to the park on departmental business. The charge was dropped and Offie kept his job.

When Frank Wisner, former chief of the OSS station in Romania, was selected to head the CIA's Office of Policy Coordination in 1948, one of the first people he hired was Carmel Offie. Amid the office power struggles, Angleton got to know Offie well.

He was a Machiavellian operator, Angleton told a friend, a "master intriguer. . . . [He] knew everybody. Superb bureaucratic infighter and guide." Angleton did not trust him. "He was capable of floating ruinous, scandalous rumors, wrecking careers," he said.[176]

Angleton was well acquainted with Offie's problems in the spring of 1950. In October 1949, Offie had propositioned a U.S. Army officer after an OPC meeting with an innuendo-laden digression about the foolishness of men who wasted money chasing women when there was a better alternative at hand.[177] The officer filed a complaint with his superiors, who ordered an investigation. Angleton heard about the incident; he soon acquired the police report on Offie's arrest in 1943.[178]

McCarthy's charges alarmed CIA director Roscoe Hillenkoetter. Hilly, as he was known, was a traditional man with traditional mores. He knew all about Offie's gay tendencies, having served on the staff of Ambassador Bullitt in the late 1930s. Hillenkoetter ordered Wisner to fire Offie.

Wisner did not carry out the order, at least not right away. He was simply too dependent on Offie's skills. He put Offie "on leave" while allowing him to remain at the CIA. But McCarthy's charges showed the ruse was wearing thin. Offie was looking for another job to relieve the pressure on his boss.

Angleton, no slouch at bureaucratic maneuvering, sensed opportunity. He asked Offie if he wanted to come to work for him at OSO. While he thought Offie had a "criminal mentality," he also thought his range of contacts could be put to good use. Angleton told a friend he wanted to use Offie "in homo circles in Europe."

Surprised, Offie asked Angleton why he would offer him a job, given that he hated him so much.

"That's just the reason," Angleton replied. "No one would ever suspect."[179]

Offie refused the odd offer and continued to use his many contacts to look for a position elsewhere in the government.

In May, Marquis Childs, a syndicated columnist for *The Washington Post,* heard that Offie was still working for the CIA, despite his scandalous reputation. He called Hillenkoetter's office, seeking comment.

"The individual in question," Hillenkoetter replied stiffly, "had been employed but was no longer in CIA employ."[180]

Unfortunately for the admiral, that was not quite true.

When Hillenkoetter called Frank Wisner, the latter said that his investigation of Offie's alleged offense "had failed to reveal any grounds to substantiate the charge."[181] Offie was still on the CIA payroll. On June 2, Childs called Hillenkoetter again, seeking "to verify that Mr. Carmel Offie was no longer employed by CIA."[182] Hillenkoetter assured Childs that Offie "has no connection with the organization." Just to be sure, the irate director then ordered Wisner "to put a memo in his personnel file to the effect that Carmel Offie was *never* to be rehired by CIA."[183]

And still Offie was protected. Wisner arranged for him to go to work for Jay Lovestone at the Free Trade Union Committee of the American Federation of Labor, which was subsidized by the CIA.[184] Even Angleton conceded that Offie did a good job. "He had many useful contacts in Europe," he said.[185]

Angleton's response to the Lavender Scare was telling. He was not repelled by Offie's homosexuality. He was not deterred by politics from coming to Offie's aid. He could—and would—keep secrets on behalf of a gay man if it served his purposes and the Agency's. One writer would later insist, without evidence, that Angleton himself was homosexual.[186] Angleton certainly didn't think of himself as gay in the way Carmel Offie did. Nor was he uncomfortable with such a man, even though he might dislike him otherwise. As always with Angleton, the imperatives of secret intelligence trumped the strictures of conventional morality.

PHILBY

KIM PHILBY'S FRIEND GUY Burgess was slightly taller than average in height with a combination of blue eyes, inquisitive nose, and curly hair that gave him the expression of an alert fox terrier. Said one British reporter, "He swam like an otter and drank, not like a feckless undergraduate, but like some Rabelaisian bottleswiper with a thirst unquenchable."[187] After a cocktail or two, his eyes lit up with a glint of a sexual appetite that was insatiable. Said one lover, "If anyone invented homosexuality, it was Guy Burgess."[188]

In mid-twentieth-century Washington, Burgess stood out even more than Carmel Offie. In a city where gay impulses were all but unmentionable, Burgess did not conceal his witty contempt for American conventions. Before Burgess took up his post in Washington, his boss in London, who knew full well of his sexual recklessness, warned him there were three taboos he must respect in America: homosexuality, communism, and the color line. Burgess pondered the advice.

"What you're trying to say in your nice, long-winded way," he deadpanned, "is—Guy, for God's sake don't make a pass at Paul Robeson," the statuesque African American actor known for his Communist sympathies.[189]

Philby welcomed Burgess to Washington in the summer of 1950. Philby's masculine style encompassed toleration, even affection, for Burgess. They might even have been lovers. Philby's colleague Basil Mann dropped by the house unannounced one morning and found Kim and Guy lounging together in Philby's bed, dressed in bathrobes, drinking champagne.[190]

In 1934, while students at Cambridge University, Philby and Burgess first met when Burgess collected money for the campus Socialist Society, of which Philby was treasurer.[191] They had stayed in touch ever since. During the war, Burgess worked at the British Broadcasting Company, where he produced a popular radio program.[192] He helped Philby get his first job in the Secret Service. Burgess became an aide to Hector McNeil, the minister of state for the Foreign Office, who sent him to Washington, in the fatuous hope that his scandalous private life would not stand out in a large embassy.

When Burgess arrived in August 1950, he stayed as a temporary guest in Philby's house at 5100 Nebraska Avenue.[193] Philby introduced Burgess to Angleton. Like many people, Angleton was half appalled and half charmed by Burgess's exuberance. He invited both men to his house, and Angleton's daughter remembered the drunken games they played.

"They'd start chasing each other through the house in this little choo-choo train," according to Siri Hari (Lucy) Angleton, "these men in their Eton ties, screaming and laughing!" At another raucous party, she recalled, "Philby's wife passed out, and was just lying on the floor. Mummy said, 'Oh, Kim, don't you want to see how Mrs. Philby is doing?' And he said, 'Ahhh . . .' and just stepped right over her to get another drink."[194]

Guy Burgess was an ornament in Angleton's social world. But he had a mean streak, too, as Angleton knew full well. Jim and Cicely attended a dinner party at the Philbys' in January 1951 in honor of Bill Harvey, who would soon head off to command the CIA's base in Berlin. Harvey's enduring resentment of the Ivy Leaguers who dominated the Agency had only been slightly mollified by his prestigious assignment. And his suspicions of the effete British had only been slightly eased by Philby's liquid hospitality. Harvey's wife, Libby, an unsophisticated midwesterner, had just begun to get comfortable with such cosmopolitan company.

Guy Burgess wandered into the house, vivacious and drunk, as usual. He exchanged pleasantries with the Harveys and let slip that he was a caricaturist and would be delighted to do a portrait in honor of Mrs. Harvey. He dashed off a drawing and presented it to the lady. The drawing depicted Libby Harvey (depending on which version of the story you believe) as either a homely hag or a wanton woman with her dress hiked up and legs obscenely spread. Enraged, Harvey threatened Burgess, and the two men had to be separated. The Harveys stalked out, and the party broke up.

Cicely and Miriam Mann consoled Aileen Philby, who was in tears, while Angleton commiserated with Basil Mann. All the while, Kim sat, head in hands, anguished by Burgess's outrageous ways for more reasons than his wife and friends could possibly imagine. Suddenly, he was weeping.

"How could you?" Philby sobbed. "How could you?"[195]

"I ALWAYS THOUGHT THERE was something wrong with Philby," Angleton would later tell fellow CIA officer John Hart.[196] He told journalist Andrew Boyle that he suspected as early as 1951 that Philby might be a spy. Such claims are not supported by any evidence.[197]

In fact, one of Angleton's friends raised doubts about Philby's loyalties at the time and Angleton did not act. The friend was Teddy Kollek, a British Zionist who had served as an SIS agent during the war before emigrating to Israel. Angleton had met Kollek in Rome after the war as the Jewish Agency organized the exodus of European Jews to Palestine. They were reunited when Kollek was assigned to work at the Israeli embassy in Washington. In the fall of 1950, Kollek paid a visit to CIA headquarters to see Angleton.

"I was walking towards Angleton's office," Kollek recounted, ". . . when suddenly I spotted a familiar face at the other end of the hallway. . . . I burst into Angleton's office and said 'Jim, you'll never guess who I saw in the hallway. It was Kim Philby!'"

Kollek knew Philby. He had lived in Austria in 1934 when a fascist government crushed a socialist insurgency that had drawn supporters from across Europe, including the young Philby. Kollek told Angleton that Philby may have been recruited as an agent of the Soviet Union. "Once a Communist, always a Communist," he said. Angleton stared back.

"Jim never reacted to anything," Kollek said. "The subject was dropped and never raised again."[198]

ON JUNE 25, 1950, the men and women of the Central Intelligence Agency were caught by surprise.[199] The army of Communist North Korea invaded South Korea. President Harry Truman was surprised, too. It wasn't until eight hours after the fighting began that the commander in chief received the news. Where was the CIA? the president wanted to know. Summoned to Capitol Hill to explain, director Hillenkoetter said of wars, "You can't predict the timing." When Truman heard that, he wanted a new CIA director.

Truman chose Gen. Walter Bedell Smith to replace Hillenkoetter. Smith, known as "Beetle," was serving as U.S. ambassador to Moscow. He was best known for starting out as a buck private in the Indiana National Guard and rising to become Gen. Dwight Eisenhower's chief of staff during World War II.[200] Smith was the product of military education, training, and tradition. He did not come to his new job with a high opinion of the fledgling CIA.

"I expect the worst and know I won't be disappointed," he wrote to one friend.[201]

Smith thought he was taking over an intelligence organization, only to discover the CIA was a sprawling entity that had acquired its own radio stations, newspapers, airlines, and even private armies.[202] A stickler for order, Smith set out to get control of the organization, particularly its covert operations.[203] He asked OSS veteran Allen Dulles, now a partner at the Sullivan & Cromwell law firm, to serve as a short-term consultant. Dulles moved to CIA headquarters in Washington for six weeks. He wound up staying for a decade.[204]

Angleton was delighted to be working with Dulles again. He was more critical of Smith, whom he thought had no appreciation for the difficulty of running covert operations. The acerbic general, in turn, had no special regard for Angleton, especially not after Guy Burgess, the obnoxious houseguest of Angleton's friend Kim Philby, turned out to be a Soviet spy.

ANGLETON LEARNED THE STORY after the Memorial Day holiday in May 1951. He might have heard it from Philby himself: Donald Maclean, a top official in the British embassy, had vanished while on home leave in England—and apparently Guy Burgess had vanished with him.

U.S. and British officials had come to suspect that Maclean was a spy. The U.S. Army's code-breaking office had deciphered a series of messages sent to the Soviets in 1944 and 1945 from a source identified only as "Homer," who spoke of a pregnant wife in New York whom he visited regularly. At the time, Maclean's wife was pregnant and lived in New York. British officials had just decided to summon Maclean for questioning when he disappeared.

The British traced his movements in England. They discovered that Burgess, also on home leave, had picked up Maclean in a rented car. The two men had boarded a ferry to France, where the trail went cold. The only possible explanation for Maclean's flight, just as he was about to face interrogation, was that he had been spying for the Soviet Union. The simultaneous disappearance of Burgess was a surprise, because he had not been suspected of spying. Had someone tipped them off that Maclean was in danger? Was there a third spy in Washington, a third man?

Suspicions focused on Kim Philby. Beetle Smith asked everyone on his staff who knew Burgess, Maclean, and Philby to assess their loyalties.

Bill Harvey responded first. He consulted with Win Scott, who knew Philby from his stints in London.[205] They agreed Philby was a Soviet spy and that he had tipped off Burgess and Maclean. In a memo dated June 13, Harvey noted Philby had been joint commander of a CIA-SIS operation in Albania, which was plagued with security problems. Philby had known about the code breakers' efforts to identify the Soviet agent known as "Homer." And, of course, Philby had shared his house with Burgess. Harvey argued forcefully that these constituted too many coincidences to allow an innocent conclusion.

A few days later, Angleton said Philby was guilty only of being too fond of Burgess.

"Philby had consistently 'sold' subject as a most gifted individual," Angleton wrote in his memo to Smith. "In this respect, he has served as subject's apologist on several occasions when subject's behavior has been a source of extreme embarrassment in the Philby household. Philby has explained away these idiosyncrasies on ground that subject suffered a severe brain concussion in an accident which had continued to affect him periodically." The tenor of Angleton's memo was that the trusting Philby could not be blamed for Burgess's treachery.[206]

Harvey scoffed. When he read Angleton's memo, he scrawled across the bottom, "Where's the rest of the story?"[207] Harvey speculated that there was a homosexual relationship between Philby and Angleton, or that the two were such good friends that Angleton just could not bring himself to face the possibility that Philby was a spy.[208]

Beetle Smith told the British that the CIA would have no contact with SIS until Philby was removed from his position in Washington. Philby prepared to return to London. When Angleton heard the news, he called Philby and suggested they meet for a drink. In his memoir, Philby said he thought his American friend seemed oddly clueless about his predicament. The CIA thought he was a spy, and SIS was calling him home. In fact, Philby had been spying for the Soviet Union for sixteen years and had been deceiving his friend Angleton for seven. He had tipped off Maclean about his imminent arrest, though he never expected Burgess to bolt with him. Angleton, confronted with the possibility that his deep and warm friendship was a sham, did not allow himself to believe it. At their last meeting, Angleton told Philby he expected they would meet again.

The poignant truth, as Jim McCargar discovered, was that Angleton believed Philby was innocent. One day in 1952, he ran into Angleton at the Hotel Crillon in Paris. They talked about the Philby affair.

"Knowing nothing of the facts," McCargar wrote later, "my feeling at the time was that Philby had been railroaded out of the British service by American pressure. I therefore told Jim unless he thought it undesirable for any reason, my intention was to invite Philby for drinks the next time I was in London. Jim said he thought it was a very good idea."

"I still feel Philby someday will head the British service," Angleton said.[209]

He didn't care what Bill Harvey and J. Edgar Hoover said. He still believed his great, good friend, Philby, was an honest man.

MOSSAD

AFTER PHILBY'S FORCED DEPARTURE, the upward trajectory of Angleton's career flattened for the first time. He was no longer the miracle worker of the Italian elections. The disaster of Burgess and Maclean did nothing to endear him to the dyspeptic Beetle Smith.

The arrival of Allen Dulles in the so-called tempo buildings on the Mall was a positive development for Angleton. The merger of OPC and OSO was not.[210] In 1952, Dulles merged the CIA's two competing divisions into a single clandestine service, known as the Directorate of Plans.[211] Smith anointed Frank Wisner to run it. To Angleton's way of thinking, Beetle Smith had had been hoodwinked by Wisner and his "psychological warfare" specialists.[212] Angleton argued that the Agency had to tighten security, focus on intelligence collection, and understand the history of Soviet intelligence operators before it could mount secret actions of its own. With his usual creativity, he looked for opportunities to prove his point.

ONE OPPORTUNITY WAS ISRAEL. The Zionists had gained their state in May 1948. Using moral appeals, bombs, assassination, and weapons provided by Eastern European Communists, they drove out the British, commandeered the strategic heights of historic Palestine, and declared a Jewish homeland. They expelled most of the Arab residents and defeated the combined armies of Arab nations, which could not imagine that Jews from distant Europe could establish their own country in their midst. They could and did.

Angleton was initially wary of Israel. Many Jews espoused communism, and the Soviet Union was the first nation to extend diplomatic recognition to the Jewish state. He thought the Soviet intelligence service would use Israel as a way station for inserting spies into the West. But Stalin's anti-Semitic purges in 1948 guaranteed that the Israelis would not fall under Soviet sway.

In 1950, Reuven Shiloah, the founder of Israel's first intelligence organization, visited Washington and came away impressed by the CIA. In April 1951, he reorganized the fractious Israeli security forces to create a new foreign intelligence agency, called the Institute for Intelligence and Special Tasks, inevitably known as the Mossad, the Hebrew word for "institute."[213]

In 1951, Prime Minister David Ben-Gurion came to the United States and brought Shiloah with him. Ben-Gurion met privately with President Truman and Walter Bedell Smith. Angleton arranged for Ben-Gurion to lunch with Allen Dulles.[214]

"The purpose of the meeting," said Efraim Halevy, retired director of the Mossad and a longtime friend of Angleton, "was to clarify in no uncertain terms that, notwithstanding what had happened between Israel and the United States in 1948, and notwithstanding that Russia had been a key factor in Israel's survival, Israel considered itself part of the Western world, and it would maintain the relationship with the United States in this spirit."[215]

Shiloah stayed on in Washington to work out the arrangements with Angleton. The resulting agreement laid the foundation for the exchange of secret information between the two services and committed them to report to each other on subjects of mutual interest.[216] Shiloah, according to his biographer, soon developed "a special relationship" with Angleton,[217] who became the CIA's exclusive liaison with the Mossad.[218]

Angleton returned the favor by visiting Israel.[219] Shiloah introduced him to Amos Manor, chief of counterespionage for Israel's domestic intelligence agency, known as Shabak or Shin Bet.[220] Manor was an attractive man—tall, athletic, and outgoing. Born in present-day Romania as Arthur Mendelovich, he had grown up in a wealthy Jewish family, most of whose members had died in the Holocaust. Put on a train bound for Auschwitz, he had jumped off and escaped to join the Jewish underground. He emigrated to Israel, using a forged passport. Manor joined the general security service and changed his name. He spoke Hebrew, English, French, Romanian, and

Hungarian, and he had uncanny understanding of how other people thought, perhaps the most important skill a counterintelligence officer can possess.[221]

Manor headed up what the Israelis called Operation Balsam, their conduit to the Americans.

"They told me I had to collect information about the Soviet bloc and transmit it to them," Manor later recalled. "I didn't know exactly what to do but then I had the idea of giving them the material we had gathered a year earlier about the efforts of the Eastern bloc to use Israel to bypass an American trade embargo. We edited the material and informed them that they should never ask us to identify sources."[222]

ANOTHER ARENA FOR ANGLETON'S ambition was organized labor. Early on, he grasped the truth that unions were a key to political power in the democratic West, and central to Communist strategy. He needed sources in the labor movement.

That's why he turned to Jay Lovestone, the chief of the American Federation of Labor's Free Trade Union Committee. Growing up as a Jewish immigrant in New York City, Lovestone became a Communist. As the leader of the American Communist Party in the 1920s, his independent ways were rebuked by Joseph Stalin himself. In a decade of intra-Communist struggle, Lovestone learned—and loved—to operate through front organizations to achieve his political goals. During World War II, he rejected communism and joined the staff of the AFL, one of the two largest confederations of American labor unions, rivaled only by the more left-wing Congress of Industrial Organizations, or CIO.[223]

In a mutually agreeable arrangement Angleton hired him. Lovestone handled the AFL's relations with labor unions around the world. The CIA funded him. He not only reported to Angleton but also helped him build his own intelligence network. Lovestone introduced Angleton to his friend Louise Page Morris, an attractive forty-five-year-old divorcée from New York City. She had worked at OSS and taken its former chief Bill Donovan as a lover for a while, so she knew the world of intelligence.[224] As an heiress to the Morris tobacco fortune, she didn't lack for money. She craved adventure and found it in one of the few roles available to independent-minded women of the era: assistant to a man of power.

When Morris met Angleton in the summer of 1949, she took care to look good. She wore a purple skirt, a tight white linen blouse with a high neck, tucked in at the waist, and white Italian sandals. She thought Angleton was handsome, with his high forehead, large brown eyes, and jutting jaw. She noticed he wore a double-breasted charcoal gray suit and a homburg-type hat in the Washington heat, as though trying to make himself look older. He was all of thirty-one years old at the time.

"Would you like to work with me?" Angleton asked. "Not for the CIA. Just for me. I want you to be my eyes and ears, go on special assignments, stay clear of the embassies . . . let things come your way naturally."[225]

Morris was hired on the spot. She was paid five hundred dollars a month with a generous expense account. Her cover was that she worked for Lovestone and ran the AFL's library in New York City. Her code name was MARTHA. She passed her reports to Mario Brod, Angleton's hustler pal from OSS days, who was now a lawyer in New York. In her reports to Lovestone, they referred to Angleton as SCARECROW.

Lovestone's biographer would describe Morris as Angleton's "Mata Hari," the Dutch-born singer and exotic dancer who spied on behalf of the German military command during World War I. Caught by the French police, Mata Hari was executed by a firing squad.

Morris would serve as Angleton's spy for a decade, traveling to Cairo, Baghdad, Berlin, Jakarta, and Japan. She never met a firing squad, but she did risk her life for Angleton on more than one occasion, a measure of his persuasive powers.

LSD

IN THE DARKNESS OF room 1018 of the Statler Hotel in New York City, someone or something lifted Frank Olson off his bare feet, off the carpet, and propelled him headfirst toward the window overlooking Seventh Avenue. Whether it was a man or mental demons, the source of the force was so powerful that Olson's body exploded through the glass window and sailed out into the cool night air of midtown Manhattan. In the first second, Frank Olson fell sixteen feet; in the second, sixty-four.

"It was like the guy was diving, his hands out in front of him, but then his body twisted and he was coming down feet first, his arms grabbing at the air above him," said the hotel doorman, who looked up at the sound of breaking glass.

The falling man struck a temporary wooden partition that shielded the construction under way on the hotel's facade, then tumbled to the sidewalk, landing on his back.[226]

It was 2:25 A.M. on Saturday, November 28, 1953.

Up on the tenth floor, inside the room from which Olson had been ejected, there was a wide-awake man named Robert Lashbrook. He was a chemist for the CIA's Technical Services Division. He looked out the shattered window. Olson's body lay on the sidewalk below. He had better things to do than go down to see if poor Olson was dead. Lashbrook could (and would) console himself with the thought that he himself hadn't killed Olson, and that he was forbidden by the Agency and the law from saying anything more about what had happened in room 1018.

The story Lashbrook couldn't tell was that he was under CIA orders to control Olson, a U.S. Army scientist. Olson had been given a dosage of LSD to see if it would compel him to tell the truth about what he knew of certain operational matters involving bioweapons research. The CIA had ordered Olson be taken to New York over the Thanksgiving holiday to talk to an Agency-cleared doctor. After a few days, Olson became upset. He wanted to go home, which was not allowed. Olson's will conflicted with the CIA's ways in room 1018 and Olson went out the window.

Now Lashbrook had a problem his bosses needed to know about. He uncradled the phone and called the hotel operator. She connected him to Dr. Harold Abramson, the Agency-cleared doctor whom Olson had been seeing. Abramson called himself a psychiatrist but was trained only as an allergist.

"Well, he's gone," Lashbrook said, according to the hotel operator, who listened in on the call.[227]

When two New York City police officers arrived forty minutes later, they took Lashbrook to the precinct house, where he gave a statement. He explained Olson's distressed mental state and the concerns of his army colleagues, without mentioning his work for the CIA or the use of LSD. Lashbrook returned to the Statler and checked into a new room.

Not long after the sun had risen, Lashbrook received a visitor, James McCord, from the CIA's Office of Security. McCord was a diligent and taciturn man, a former FBI agent tasked with reporting on what had happened. Lashbrook finally felt free to speak. He explained that his assignment involved Olson and security concerns about some sensitive chemical-weapons operations. McCord took it all down.[228]

And so began the cover-up of Frank Olson's wrongful death and the notorious CIA operation known as MKULTRA, which encompassed a wide range of experiments to control the workings of the human mind in the service of U.S. national security. It wasn't until many years later that Angleton's supporting role in the MKULTRA story emerged.

Angleton worked with narcotics agent George White, his friend from OSS days, to establish two CIA safe houses in New York and San Francisco, where LSD experiments were conducted on unsuspecting subjects for two decades. In the fall of 1952, Angleton had had several work meetings in Washington with Harold Abramson and Robert Lashbrook, the men who would accompany Olson during his fatal trip to New York a year later. Angleton wasn't involved in the events leading to Olson's death, but he did help give birth to the CIA's mind-control program.

THE TERM *MIND CONTROL* and the cryptonym MKULTRA have become notorious in the American imagination, and for good reason. The CIA's efforts in the 1950s and 1960s to manipulate human behavior through chemistry, hypnosis, and coercion constituted a far-flung conspiracy to experiment on unwitting people in the name of "national security." MKULTRA is shorthand for a government-sanctioned crime wave born in the peculiar circumstances of the world in the mid-twentieth century.

America in the 1950s was peaceful, prosperous, and fearful of subversion. In Washington, the Red Scare and the Lavender Scare (and the flight of Burgess and Maclean) lent credence to the charges of ambitious politicians like Senator McCarthy and Congressman Richard Nixon of California that the government was riddled with security threats. In the newsreels, Americans saw the Communists' 1949 show trial of Hungarian cardinal József Mindszenty, in which the zombielike defendant confessed to crimes he probably had not committed.[229] The word *brainwashing,* coined in 1950 to describe North Korea's treatment of U.S. prisoners of war, instantly entered the American lexicon, adding fear of mental manipulation to concerns about Communist infiltration.

The CIA's Office of Scientific Intelligence responded by creating Operation Bluebird.[230] The program had several objectives. The first was to discover ways to condition U.S. personnel to prevent "unauthorized extraction of information . . . by known means." Another goal was to outdo the Communists at brainwashing: to control people through use of "special interrogation techniques," including hypnosis and drugs. A third goal was "memory enhancement" to improve human intelligence collection; and the fourth was figuring how to prevent "hostile control" of Agency personnel.[231]

When the Korean War erupted, the Bluebird program grew rapidly. A year later, in July 1951, Beetle Smith received a list containing the names of eighty-two employees cleared for working on Bluebird. One of them was Angleton.[232]

In August 1952, the operation was renamed Artichoke, and responsibility for research was given to the Technical Services Division, or TSD, which provided operational support for CIA clandestine activities.[233] The TSD scientists were especially intrigued by the potential of a chemical known as LSD-25. It was an organic compound of lysergic acid discovered by a Swiss scientist in 1943. Even the tiniest of dosages seemed to induce anxiety, hysteria, imbalance, even insanity, but also clarity, calmness, insight, and wisdom.

For help in utilizing LSD, the Agency turned to Angleton's old friend George Hunter White.

GEORGE WHITE WAS A natural choice for CIA consultant on drug-related issues. At forty-four years of age, White was perhaps the best-known narcotics agent in the country. He had made headlines nationwide in

January 1949 for arresting jazz singer Billie Holiday in a San Francisco hotel room for possession of heroin. (Holiday was acquitted).[234] In October 1949, White received the U.S. Treasury Department's Exceptional Civilian Service Award for his work on "breaking up numerous illicit narcotics rings" while operating "at grave personal risk."[235]

The CIA men were intrigued by his expertise. When White went to Rome for an undercover narcotics operation in 1948, he called on Angleton for support, and deputy Ray Rocca loaned him a gun.[236] In 1950, White was introduced to Allen Dulles, and they stayed up until one in the morning, talking about his "truth drug" experiments in the OSS.[237] Their mutual attraction wasn't hard to figure. White was a streetwise cop who could carry out Angleton's secret missions; Angleton was a savvy insider who could give White entrée into the suites of the glamorous CIA.

WHITE RECORDED CERTAIN EPISODES of their collaboration in his pocket calendars, which wound up in the library at Stanford University. These diaries trace how Angleton pursued the use of psychoactive drugs for intelligence work.

White's role with the CIA was formalized in the spring of 1952, when he met Sidney Gottlieb, the chief of the Chemical Branch of the Technical Services Division."[238] To Gottlieb's surprise, White said that he had already had several discussions about LSD with Angleton.[239] Later that summer, Angleton and White met in a Washington restaurant to discuss a "special teaching assignment" for White.[240]

In September 1952, Angleton met with White and Gottlieb in New York before going out to dinner with TSD colleagues, including Bob Lashbrook and Harold Abramson, the men who later concocted the story that Frank Olson had thrown himself through a window as a way to kill himself. On October 30, 1952, Angleton met again with White, who went on to a meeting with Lashbrook about "TD," White's code for "truth drugs."[241]

Angleton's interest in LSD was not purely professional. He tried the drug a few weeks later, according to White. In a letter to his lawyer, White said that Angleton came to have Thanksgiving dinner with him and his wife, Albertine, at their New York City apartment. The next evening, after

Albertine went to work, White and Angleton drank gin and tonics laced with LSD. White recounted that he had a "delayed reaction" to the drug, while Angleton had a "pleasurable experience." He said that Angleton, "after really coming under the effects of the drug," talked him into taking a taxi to Chinatown to have dinner. With plates of food before them, they began "laughing about something I can't remember now" and they "never got around to eating a bite."[242]

It may be coincidence, but after Angleton and White took LSD in November 1952, Angleton's name never again appeared in George White's diary. Over the course of the previous eight years, White had recorded a dozen meetings with Angleton, but not one after November 1952. Perhaps Angleton's psychedelic trip to Chinatown with White—its hallucinatory wonders, its negation of hunger, its comic immensity—ended their friendship or his interest in LSD or both.

ANGLETON HAD MORE IMPORTANT issues on his mind. Gen. Dwight D. Eisenhower, elected president of the United States of America on November 4, 1952, was the first Republican to occupy the White House in twenty years. He brought a new foreign policy agenda to Washington and new management to the CIA, which was all to the good as far as Angleton was concerned.

Eisenhower appointed John Foster Dulles, a career diplomat and older brother of Allen, as secretary of state. To ensure his control of the diplomatic corps on a day-to-day basis, Eisenhower also wanted Beetle Smith, his former executive officer, to serve as undersecretary of state. When Smith moved to that job, Allen Dulles became the director of Central Intelligence, the position he had been scheming to create and claim since 1945.

Angleton was feeling inspired by one of the most popular movies of 1952, *High Noon*. It was a tale of the Old West starring Gary Cooper, which made a lasting impression on Angleton as an allegory of America in the Cold War.

"The prosperous citizens in the frontier town of Hadleyville are suddenly confronted with the return of a menace which they thought had been banished forever," Angleton later explained in an essay on the movie. "The situation is classic because of its brilliant delineation of the opposed forces of good and evil."

In the movie, word flashes through Hadleyville that the gunslinger Frank Miller, who had terrorized residents until Marshal Kane (played by Cooper) brought him to justice, has been released from the penitentiary. To take revenge, Miller and his old gang are coming back to the town.

As in postwar America, prosperity had bred complacency in Hadleyville.

"But when Marshal Kane broke in upon the services at the church to ask for help, his plea fell on deaf ears," Angleton wrote. "The banker, the merchant, the lawyer, the town clerk, all drew back. Frank Miller, they argued, was the Marshal's responsibility—he was paid to handle it. So Kane, mindful of his duty, put aside everything he held dear—his bride, the honeymoon in which they were about to leave. He went out into the street alone and did the job."[243]

Angleton thought it was high noon in the Cold War. Like Marshal Kane, he believed the men of the CIA confronted an implacable evil foe. Like the marshal, he had to act alone because ordinary people would shy from the task. He was ready to sacrifice the comforts of family and safety so that others could enjoy their American freedoms.

He had a proposal for Mr. Dulles.

PART II

POWER

COUNTERINTELLIGENCE

HOW DID JAMES ANGLETON elevate himself from staff functionary at a new government agency to untouchable mandarin who would have an all but transcendent influence on U.S. intelligence operations for the next two decades?

With voracious intellect and compelling charm, said one Washingtonian who knew him late in life. He embodied the will to defeat communism. "Who presumed to rebut, watching [his] knitted, knotted, weaving, bobbing, stalking lexicon of body language of the Cold War," wrote journalist Burton Hersh. ". . . Who undertook to challenge that?"[1] Not many.

No one was more captivated by Angleton than his friend and mentor Allen Dulles, now director of Central Intelligence. Like Angleton, Dulles preferred collaborating with fascists to enabling Communists. Like Angleton he had little patience for liberals who embraced slogans like "land reform," "nonalignment," and "peaceful coexistence," which he regarded as so much camouflage for the confiscation of wealth. Like Angleton, Dulles was a man of action.

He wasted no time in redirecting the CIA. Whereas Beetle Smith had vetoed the idea of launching a covert operation against the government of Iran, Dulles approved. Iran's offense was pressing the British-controlled Anglo-Iranian Oil Company for more equitable royalty arrangements. Without much evidence, Dulles concluded this was a Soviet power play. In August 1953, the nationalist prime minister, Mohammad Mosaddegh, was overthrown by a joint CIA-SIS psychological warfare operation that relied on propaganda, diplomatic isolation, and paramilitary action. Iran's parliamentary democracy was crushed by a dictatorial monarchy that lasted until 1979.

In Guatemala, Beetle Smith had sided with the State Department in rejecting proposals for covert action against the country's reformist president,

Jacobo Arbenz, who was seeking to nationalize the unused property of the United Fruit Company. Dulles, who had done legal work for United Fruit, saw Arbenz as the first Communist interloper in the western hemisphere. In June 1954, a CIA psychological warfare operation drove Arbenz from power and replaced him with a more compliant military junta, which dismantled the country's democratic system and exiled Arbenz.

These operations impressed President Eisenhower, who marveled at their low-cost benefits to U.S. foreign policy. They also boosted morale in the Directorate of Plans in the CIA offices on the Mall. But they did not much affect the Agency's main enemy, the Soviet intelligence service, the Komitet Gosudarstvennoy Bezopasnosti (Committee for State Security), or KGB, which seemed to be operating as freely as ever in the United States. According to the National Security Agency's VENONA program, which deciphered Soviet communications, the KGB had cultivated an extensive network of informants in American institutions.

That was Angleton's opening. He was not an activist administrator like operations chief Frank Wisner or an efficient taskmaster like Dick Helms, Wisner's number two. Angleton was not a covert operator in the mode of Bill Harvey, who was digging a tunnel into Soviet-occupied Berlin, or Win Scott, who would take over the Mexico City station.

Angleton's specialty was more refined: intelligence collection, the running of agents, and the development of a counterintelligence archive to understand the techniques of the enemy. He spent much of 1954 talking to Dulles about how to ensure the confidentiality and security of CIA operations. Angleton thought there was much room for improvement. He admired Wisner as much as anyone for his tireless idealism and his willingness to try anything, but his approach was not working.

Angleton's oft-voiced skepticism had been vindicated in late 1952 when Wisner's biggest operation in Eastern Europe fell apart.[2] The CIA had pumped five million dollars' worth of guns, gold, and communications gear into Poland in support of an anti-Communist army called the Freedom and Independence Movement, known by its Polish acronym, WiN. The Agency had been helping the group's exiled leaders for years. Now with a force of five hundred soldiers and twenty thousand supporters inside the country, the CIA men felt they were ready to challenge Soviet domination of Poland.

In fact, they were fools. The Soviet and Polish intelligence services had been baiting the trap for years. When WiN dropped its agents into the country, the Communists detained them and forced them to send back false progress reports, along with requests for more money and men. Wisner's men had obliged all too willingly. In December 1952, the Poles went public with their ruse, revealing there was no anti-Communist opposition. To needle the United States, the Poles announced they were sending the CIA's funds to support the Communist Party in Italy.

In July 1954, President Eisenhower appointed a committee, headed by U.S. Army general James Doolittle, to conduct an independent review of CIA operations.[3] As chief of Foreign Intelligence, Angleton was asked to brief the committee. Behind closed doors, Angleton said the Agency's current setup had led to confusion, duplication, and waste of manpower and money. The Agency, he argued, needed a staff dedicated to counterintelligence, a staff that was knowledgeable about the KGB and its methods. Such a staff could oversee covert operations at a management level to make sure the Soviets had not penetrated the U.S. government or the CIA. Counterintelligence, he said, was both a body of knowledge and a way of seeing the world.[4] The Agency needed both.

Dulles was persuaded, and Angleton had found his mission.

"[Angleton] brooded longest, and perhaps with the greatest penetration, over the specialized methodology of counterintelligence," said his friend Robin Winks, a Yale historian. ". . . [He] was ends-oriented and could remember his own lies, surely a necessary brace of qualities for a successful spy."[5]

COUNTERINTELLIGENCE WAS A CHALLENGE very much like the literary criticism Angleton had learned at Yale. To interpret the enemy's communications and its documents required teasing meaning from texts that were filled with the kind of ambiguities his friend the critic William Empson delineated in poetry. Angleton's counterintelligence was radical in the sense that it went to the root of the CIA's functions. As one Agency chronicler put it, "Counterintelligence is to intelligence as epistemology is to philosophy. Both go back to the fundamental question of how we know things. Both challenge what we are inclined to take most for granted."[6]

Recalling a line from his favorite poem, "Gerontion," Angleton described KGB deception operations as a "wilderness of mirrors" designed to disorient the West. Taken to its extreme—and Angleton would take it there—counterintelligence suggested that the more reliable a source appeared to be, the more likely he was to be a Soviet agent. It was poetry of sorts. The improbable but undeniable impact of Ivy League literary criticism on geopolitics was embodied in Angleton.[7]

Angleton persuaded Dulles of a foundational principle: that counterintelligence, properly pursued, had to be proactive. He would have to see everything in the Agency's archives, including the Office of Security's personnel files. It was an unprecedented power that no one else in the Agency possessed. Angleton insisted, and Dulles approved.

In December 1954, the orders were issued and Angleton became chief of the new Counterintelligence Staff. He was now, in the words of one CIA watcher, "a ghost in the system, wired into the center of a Panopticon rendered in paperwork. He operated ahead of the conventional intel process, monitored all internal communications, and used a vast network extending far outside the official CIA to keep tabs on the entire intelligence establishment. From raw SIGINT [Signals Intelligence] to Special Operations, Angleton was an invisible supervisor."[8]

From this position, he built an empire, his own clandestine service housed within the CIA.

ANGLETON'S VISION WAS EXPANSIVE. No one was more important to his ambitions than FBI director J. Edgar Hoover. With the CIA barred by law from operating on U.S. soil, Angleton needed the FBI's counterintelligence capabilities to keep track of Soviet spies in the United States.

Hoover was not much interested. He ran his national police force and its thousands of field agents as an instrument of his personal and political will. He had no use for rival agencies. Hoover had welcomed the dissolution of the OSS in 1945 and resented its revival in the form of the CIA in

1947. Like Senator McCarthy, he regarded the Agency as a nest of liberals, atheists, homosexuals, professors, and otherwise feminized men who specialized in wasting the taxpayer dollar.

Hoover responded to Angleton's overture with disdain. He sent a junior agent to serve as a liaison with Angleton's office. Angleton responded by loading the young man with drinks and reams of high-quality reporting.[9] Hoover, who loved having dirt on his enemies, responded grudgingly. Angleton had only one requirement for his secrets: He did not want to be identified in FBI documents as the source of the information. Typically, the Bureau described information from the CIA as "Confidential Informant T-2, an agency of the U.S. government that conducts personnel and intelligence investigations."

Angleton refused the designation. The recipients of the documents, he noted, would inevitably surmise that the information came from the CIA. Angleton asked the Bureau to identify him only as "Bureau Source 100." Hoover approved.[10]

ANGLETON MOVED INTO A suite of offices in the L Building on the Mall. He now had several secretaries working for him,[11] along with a deputy, Herman Horton, who handled the daily issues of the office.[12] The staff's charter, written by Angleton and published in March 1955, established four offices in his new domain.

Angleton needed a liaison officer to handle daily contacts with the FBI and the other federal agencies. He brought on Jane Atherton Roman, who had worked with him in OSO. She was as reliable as they came. A graduate of Smith College, she married, divorced, and joined the OSS in 1944, where her research assignments in the X-2 branch took her to London and Berlin and then back to Washington.[13] In 1954, she had married a colleague, Howard Roman, an assistant to Dulles.[14] She was, in the words of Bill Hood, "a superadministrative, high-level secretary and desk operative. She was very experienced. Her job was to monitor the FBI. And the information that we passed to the FBI would go through her."[15]

Angleton established an office for research. He wanted to compile a body of knowledge about Soviet intelligence operations, with files on history, techniques, and personnel. For this job, he recalled Ray Rocca from the Rome station and named him chief of Research and Analysis.

He created an office, the Special Investigations Group, SIG, dedicated to looking for security breaches inside the Agency. The task of the SIG was to "perform the CI investigation and analysis of any known or potential security leak in the Clandestine Services organization, whether in head-quarters or in the field."[16] Concerned that no office in the U.S. government kept track of Americans who defected to the Soviet Union, Angleton assigned the SIG to monitor defectors, as well. Angleton called on Birch O'Neal, a former FBI man who had most recently served as station chief in Guatemala, to serve as chief of the SIG.

Finally, Angleton set up a Special Projects office to handle sensitive missions such as opening U.S. mail or doing deals with the Israelis.[17] For these tasks, he relied on Stephen Millett, a fair-haired and tight-lipped CIA man from Bristol, Rhode Island, who was working with Jay Lovestone and Carmel Offie at the Free Trade Union Confederation.[18]

Roman, O'Neal, Rocca, and Millett would work for Angleton for the rest of their careers. They carried out his orders and kept his secrets. They were loyal and discreet. They trusted his genius.

AS J. EDGAR HOOVER SENSED the advantages of working with Angleton, he sent a senior agent, Sam Papich, to serve as liaison with the Counterintelligence Staff. For the grouchy FBI director, this was an expression of respect, if not warmth. Papich, of course, was under strict orders to disclose as little as possible to the CIA while defending the Bureau's prerogatives at every turn.

In his first day on the new assignment, Papich was ushered into Angleton's office, a large corner room where a row of windows looked out on the Lincoln Memorial—or would have if the venetian blinds had not been shut against the light.[19]

Angleton lit a cigarette. He asked Papich about a recent case that he said the Bureau had mishandled. Papich took exception to Angleton's tone. Angleton barked at him; Papich shouted right back, then got up and walked out. An unpretentious man from Montana, Papich wasn't going to back down from this Ivy League bully.

Papich returned the next day. The men managed to be cordial in their meetings. Papich disclosed his fondness for fly-fishing, and Angleton was glad to discourse on a favorite hobby. Angleton invited Papich to go fishing for brown trout in West Virginia one weekend. Papich marveled at how carefully Angleton surveyed the stream, stalked the riverbank for insects, and then crafted lures to imitate the species he found. Papich realized Angleton was a master fisherman. The two men became friends.[20]

FROM THIS MODEST BEGINNING, Angleton's empire began to grow. He won authorization from Dulles to hire the necessary complement of secretaries, translators, typists, clerks, accountants, and the like. Within five years, the Counterintelligence Staff employed 171 people—96 professionals and 75 clerical workers.[21]

With this apparatus, Angleton would move the world. He had evolved from precocious youth to Cold War mandarin, a functionary who impressed presidents and prime ministers. Once raw and ingenuous, he was now sleek and refined. His small sculpted head—with each hair combed back—exposed his Edwardian integrity. As Burton Hersh observed, "When Angleton spoke, his mocha eyes shone, and as his lips parted, without warning, a grin would irradiate his hollow face." He was winning in every sense of the word.[22]

ZIONIST

THE LAND AND PEOPLE of Israel had captured Angleton's imagination. The revelations of the Nazis' extermination of the Jews during the war and his now regular visits to the newly created Jewish state had dissolved his inherited anti-Semitism. By the mid-1950s, Angleton liked nothing better than to leave the cramped office politics of Washington for the austere frontier of the Holy Land.

On his visits, Angleton stayed in Ramat Gan, on the suburban coastal plain north of Tel Aviv, the home to many Israeli intelligence officers and diplomats. When he traveled up to the hills of Jerusalem, he favored the plush elegance of the King David Hotel. The King David had been Britain's headquarters during its control of Palestine, which is why Zionist commandos planted a bomb there in 1947, killing scores of people and hastening the British departure.

The hotel's terrace offered Angleton a lovely view of the walls of the Old City, the ancient seat of both Christianity and Islam that the Zionists claimed as their modern capital. He saw the sandstone parapets adorned with barbed wire. He saw history in the making.

The Mossad had a new chief. Israeli prime minister David Ben-Gurion had replaced the furtive Reuven Shiloah with Isser Harel, an outgoing man and intuitive spy who believed secret intelligence was key to the survival of a small nation surrounded by enemies. Born to wealthy parents in tsarist Russia, his original name was Isser Halperin. His family fled to Lithuania after their vinegar business was confiscated by Russian revolutionaries, prompting Harel's lifelong aversion to Marxism.[23]

"Jim had enormous admiration for Isser, as he always called him," said Efraim Halevy, the Mossad veteran. "He often talked about Isser to me and to others as the epitome of Israel's success in collection and foreign intelligence operations."[24]

Angleton also bonded with Amos Manor, who served under Harel as the chief of Shin Bet, Israel's equivalent of the FBI.

"In Jim's eyes Isser was the 'ultimate' intelligence officer, just as Amos was the ultimate security chief foiling Soviet espionage and catching traitors and spies," Halevy said.

Angleton took to grilling Manor about his work.

"It wasn't easy to persuade the anti-communist Angleton that we could be friends," Manor recalled. "Even I was suspected by him—that I was a Soviet spy."[25]

In Manor's apartment in Tel Aviv, Angleton talked late into the night while sipping whiskey. "I didn't understand how a person could drink so much without getting drunk," Manor said.[26] Angleton later admitted to

Manor that he was examining him all the while to see if he might be a spy himself.[27]

"Jim's initial attitude toward us was very wary, but later he became a devoted admirer of Israel from an American standpoint," said Memi de Shalit, an Israeli diplomat. Angleton "changed his attitude toward us when he began to get to know people here and gradually grew stronger in his conviction that there was no great danger of Israel turning communist."[28]

Manor persuaded Angleton that Israel, with its population of immigrants from the Soviet Union and its East European satellites, was not a breeding ground for spies. Rather, it was an indispensable source for everything that interested the U.S. government about the Communist world, from the cost of potatoes to plans for new aircraft and ships.[29]

Angleton returned to Washington edified by these adepts and changed in his thinking about the Jewish people. It was true he had no qualms associating with, even helping, anti-Semites like Ezra Pound, Valerio Borghese, and Eugen Dollmann. It was true he did not care for Jewish businessmen—he found them grasping. He abhorred Jewish Communists for their amoral atheism.

The Zionist Jews were a different story. Angleton did not think they were greedy or amoral—far from it, in fact. The best of them were abstemious and principled, and they were nobody's victim. With enemies on every border, they were not tempted by compromise. The Israelis, he came to believe, were a model for the United States and the West. The anti-Semitic schoolboy had grown up to be an intuitive Zionist.

ANOTHER SOURCE OF ANGLETON'S power was his friend Jay Lovestone, the former Communist leader turned anti-Communist operative. As executive director of the Free Trade Union Confederation, Lovestone had a secret budget from the CIA and a global network of contacts. Before long, Angleton and Lovestone effectively controlled what American labor unions had to say about U.S. foreign policy.

"With their respective influence in the labor movement and the intelligence community," wrote Lovestone's biographer, "they formed a hidden power center bent on advancing a hard anti-Soviet line. [They were] particularly effective from 1953 to 1959, when John Foster Dulles was secretary of state."[30]

Angleton and Lovestone meshed personally given their unsentimental appreciation of power and dedication to the task at hand. Lovestone, an unmarried man, was romantically involved with fellow agent Louise Page Morris, but he had no family to speak of in New York City, where he lived. Three days a week, he traveled to Washington, and soon he was practically living at the Angletons' house in Arlington. He became close to Cicely, who understood her husband's devotion to him.

"He thought that Jay had struggled all his life to make his ideas prevail," Cicely said. "Many were the times when Jay came to dinner and he and Jim sat up talking into the night."[31]

Angleton's realm was growing when his Israeli friend Amos Manor delivered a timely package in April 1956. Then his power became unparalleled.

IT STARTED ONE FINE spring morning in Warsaw, Poland. Wiktor Grajewski, a journalist, went to see his girlfriend for their usual morning coffee. Grajewski, an editor at the Polish news agency, stopped at the offices of the Central Committee of the Polish Communist Party to see Lucia Baranowska. She, Jewish like Grajewski, was separated from her husband, a top party official, and knew what was happening around the office.[32]

He noticed (or she called his attention to) a red-covered booklet on her desk. It was emblazoned, in Russian, with the words "Top Secret" and "Comrade Khrushchev's Report to the 20th Congress of the CPSU." Grajewski knew the Soviet premier had recently given a speech hinting at criticism of Joseph Stalin, who had died in 1953.

"We heard that the United States had offered a prize of $1 million to anyone who could obtain the speech," he later recalled.[33]

Baranowska agreed to lend Grajewski the booklet. Grajewski put it in his pocket and went back to his apartment.

"On the Cult of the Individual and Its Consequences" was the title, and

Grajewski read it with mounting amazement. After the wartime propaganda about "Uncle Joe," both in Russia and the West, its candor was shocking.

Stalin had betrayed the legacy of Vladimir Lenin, Khrushchev declared:

> Terror was actually directed not at the remnants of the defeated exploiting classes but against the honest workers of the party; against them were made lying, slanderous and absurd accusations. Mass repressions contributed to the spreading of unhealthy suspicion, and sowed distrust among communists.[34]

It was incredible. The most reactionary sheets of the capitalist press might say such things about Stalin, but not the first secretary of the Communist Party.

Grajewski took the text to the Israeli embassy in Warsaw and gave it to the first secretary, Yaakov Barmor, who sent photographs of the document to Amos Manor in Tel Aviv. With permission from Prime Minister Ben-Gurion,[35] Manor passed the speech to the Israeli embassy in Washington with a note that it be delivered personally to Angleton.[36]

"Jim was in seventh heaven," Manor said. "He asked my permission to publish the material."

Manor consulted with Ben-Gurion, who agreed.[37]

On April 17, Angleton gave the speech to Dulles.[38] Two versions of the speech were released: one by John Foster Dulles at the State Department, who gave the text to *The New York Times;* the other version, edited by Angleton, consisted of the *Times* text with the addition of thirty-four paragraphs. Angleton inserted compromising remarks about the Chinese and the Indians that Khrushchev was known to have uttered at different times under different circumstances.[39] Angleton thus embellished propaganda with truths that would reach tens of millions of readers in India and China.

President Eisenhower was pleased; Dulles, delighted. Obtaining Khrushchev's secret speech was "one of the major intelligence coups of my tour of duty in intelligence," Dulles wrote in his memoirs.[40] Ray Cline, chief of the

Directorate of Intelligence, went further. He called it "one of the CIA's greatest coups of all time."[41]

OTHERS MISTRUSTED ANGLETON'S LIAISON with the Israelis. A few months later, in October 1956, the State Department learned that Israel was calling up its armed forces, including reserves, for unknown purposes. Robert Amory, an analyst in the Directorate of Intelligence, went to Dulles and called for an emergency meeting of the joint committee of all U.S. intelligence agencies. If war was going to break out in the Middle East, Amory wanted to make sure the president was informed.

In the meeting, Angleton and Amory both spoke. Amory predicted the Israelis would strike Egypt. Angleton countered by assuring those in the room that his Israeli friends were simply bolstering their border defenses with Jordan. Amory scoffed at the idea and called Angleton a "co-opted" Israeli agent to his face.[42]

Amory was right, at least about Israeli intentions. Within days, the Israeli Defense Forces had invaded Egypt's Sinai Desert, where they joined French and British forces who claimed to be protecting the Suez Canal from nationalization. They planned to decapitate the Egyptian government of Gamel Abdel Nasser and install a more cooperative regime.

Eisenhower was furious. He had not been consulted and he had no intention of compromising U.S. prestige to back up such a colonialist adventure. In the face of Washington's opposition, the Anglo-French-Israeli gambit was unsupportable. The Israelis had to surrender at the bargaining table what they had won on the ground. Angleton's confidence in his Israeli sources was unshaken.

FISHERMAN

THE ANGLETON HOME ON 33rd Road in north Arlington was unpretentious and comfortable. Jim and Cicely and the kids lived amid the clutter of his hobbies and her eclectic interior decorating, informed by her childhood in the deserts of Arizona. When Angleton was not at the office, he was clattering around in his workshop in the basement, where he perfected silver tiepins and cuff links as gifts for friends. On weekends, he spent long hours in the greenhouse working on his orchids.

Angleton's family was far away. His parents still lived in Rome, where his father still ran his business. His sister Carmen pursued the intellectual and literary interests Jim might have pursued if he had not joined the CIA. She became close friends with the novelist Mary McCarthy. His younger sister, Delores, married Luciano Guarnieri, a painter. Brother Hugh, a diminutive, elegant man, had divorced his wife and returned to Boise, where he opened a gift emporium called Angleton's. Impeccably dressed in suit and tie, Hugh Junior served as a kind of showroom director for an establishment overflowing with rare china, jewelry, and art objects.[43]

Among Angleton's closest friends was his new colleague Cord Meyer, who lived in McLean, Virginia. On the weekends the Angleton children, Jamie, Helen, and Lucy, played with the Meyers' boys, Michael, Mark, and Quentin, while the adults smoked and drank.

Cord Meyer had also gone to Yale, graduating after Angleton. After World War II, Meyer made his name as an eloquent student advocate of world government along the lines of the United Nations. When the Cold War extinguished that dream, he moved to the CIA to pursue a different vision of world government. In 1954, Allen Dulles persuaded him to take over the Agency's International Organizations division. In consultation with Angleton, Meyer orchestrated the Agency's covert funding of labor unions, newspapers, magazines, TV stations, and Hollywood movies. With the help of poets, painters, and editors, these two intellectuals disseminated the CIA's preferred narratives around the world.

Both Cord and his wife, Mary, came from families with money. The Meyers lived comfortably in a farmhouse deep in the woods. The next driveway down the road led to Hickory Hill, the estate where Robert and Ethel Kennedy and their growing brood lived. Bob was a staff attorney on Capitol Hill, and his brother John was the junior senator from Massachusetts. The neighborhood was full of paths and tree houses, gardens and hideaways.

"The Meyers' house in McLean, it was beautiful," said Peter Janney, another CIA kid who played with the Angleton and Meyer children. "It was literally next door to Hickory Hill and just a lot of woods back there, and space. A great place to be a kid growing up."[44]

Janney remembered the fathers in this crowd, all of them highly accomplished men. His father, Wistar Janney, had gone to Princeton and won a Navy Cross as a fighter pilot before joining the CIA. Cord Meyer, who had lost an eye in combat, was not shy about his certainties. Angleton was perhaps the most intimidating of all of them. In Janney's young eyes, he resembled no one so much as Ichabod Crane in "The Legend of Sleepy Hollow."

"He was always obsessed with whatever he and Cord were talking about or laughing about," Janney recalled in an interview. "You would never see Jim and Cord without both of them smoking and both of them having a drink in their hand. . . . Those two things were extensions of their bodies."

Janney was friends with the Meyer boys.

"As I got older," he said, "Michael and I would sometimes browbeat Cord to take us fishing down along the Potomac. A couple of times Jim came along. Jim, of course, was a master angler. . . . We would be casting these snag hooks out into the river to see if we could snag herring. . . . When Michael and I were doing it, we were constantly being criticized by Cord and Jim. We could never do it right, no matter what we did."

In this forest of towering masculine personalities, Peter found respite in the attentions of Mary Meyer, Michael's mother. Unlike Cord and Jim, Mary Meyer actually paid attention to Peter. She didn't live in another world like the dads, or even his own mom.

"You really felt she was there," Janney said. "She was listening to what you were saying. She responded to what you were saying. . . . You knew you were dealing with someone substantial who wasn't just blowing you off because you were a child."

Mary Meyer was a different kind of presence, a female one, and the boy sensed it. She had been born Mary Pinchot, the daughter of Amos and Ruth Pinchot, an established and progressive couple in Pennsylvania. Amos Pinchot spent his family fortune on conservation of nature. He and his wife raised their two daughters, Mary and Tony, without regard for conventional expectations of women.

Mary was an aspiring painter, and she made everyone around her feel good. Peter sensed she was especially close to Cicely Angleton, whom she took care of.

"I always had the impression that Cicely Angleton was somehow under-water," Janney said. "By that, I mean she was not terribly happy with her family and her family life."

Cicely was not socially ambitious. She avoided the Washington social circuit in favor of the company of a few good friends, such as Mary; Mary's sister, Tony Meyer Bradlee; and their friend Anne Truitt, all classmates from Vassar. Tony, the younger of the two Meyer sisters, had divorced and was now married to Ben Bradlee, a well-bred wise guy from Boston who had just joined *Newsweek*'s Washington bureau. Anne was married to James Truitt, a hard-drinking *Newsweek* correspondent who collected Asian art.

The Angletons, Meyers, Truitts, and Bradlees grew close, bound by interests in work, culture, and art.[45] Angleton was an entertaining friend, a man with "a very fascinating, romantic, Bohemian side," said one friend of Mary Meyer's. He sometimes played the piano after dinner.[46]

Cicely didn't always feel as smart as these accomplished people. In fact, she often felt exhausted, "worn to the bone," as she put it.[47] During the school year, she ran the car pool. In the summer, she arranged vacations in Arizona and northern Wisconsin, where the family had a home on the Brule River. In the summer, they visited with families she had known since childhood and Jim taught the kids how to cast a line and tie a fly. Those were the times Cicely liked the best.

CAROLINE MARSHALL SAW A different Jim Angleton than Peter Janney.[48] Her family had a house on the Brule River, where, as a little girl, she met Angleton for the first time. On lazy summer days, he taught her about the ways of the great brown trout, and she was fascinated. She felt welcomed by his attention and stimulated by his generous in-telligence.

"Browns are vicious, atavistic creatures," Angleton said, gently letting the girl know about the gross realities of nature. "They eat mice and frogs, baby chipmunks, their own kind."

"They're shy," he said of the great browns. "One feeding during the day, and the mere suggestion of a shadow passes—gone."

Angleton spoke with awe of these creatures. The sensitive little girl also heard his cunning.

"The patient game of waiting, silent, for the trusting quarry to expose itself, that is the game of fishing Jim Angleton played in the summer," Marshall later recalled. "How it might be said to resemble his other life with the CIA."

For Marshall, one memory of Angleton endured.

"I saw him one night when I was a child—coming suddenly wet, slippery, and silent as a huge brown, [coming] in from the dark, trailing rain, his fedora pinched and dripping, pulled low over his eyes, a fisherman wholly unlike others."

COINTELPRO

AT THE OFFICE, ANGLETON was voracious for information. As he built the Counterintelligence Staff, he ordered Steve Millet's Special Projects office to take over a sensitive program known by the code name LINGUAL. It would prove to be one of Angleton's greatest sources of power and perhaps his most flagrant violation of the law.

Surveillance of the U.S. mail was first proposed by officials in the CIA's Soviet Russia Division and the Office of Security in February 1952. They wanted to scan the exteriors of a handful of selected U.S. letters mailed to the Soviet Union and to record the names and addresses of the correspondents. The goal was to provide "live ammunition for psychological warfare," to identify possible agents with contacts in the Soviet Union, and to produce documentary material and intelligence. The letters themselves were not opened. The program was approved in 1953.[49]

In 1955, Angleton asked to take over this limited mail-surveillance program. In a memo to Dick Helms, he requested that the Counterintelligence Staff "gain access to all mail traffic to and from the U.S.S.R." He recommended the "raw information acquired be recorded, indexed, analyzed and various components of the Agency furnished items of information which would appear to be helpful to their missions." Most important, he proposed that the letters be opened and copied, something that had never been done before.[50] The expanded version of the mail-surveillance operation was approved in December 1955.

Angleton rented a room at New York's LaGuardia Airport to house the necessary staff and equipment. They proceeded to process two to six bags of mail every day. Selected letters were opened with the old-fashioned "kettle and stick" method. The glue on the envelope was softened by the steam from a teakettle and the letter was pried open with a stick.[51] The most skillful of the "flaps and seals" artists, as they were known, could open a letter in five to fifteen seconds.[52]

Under Angleton's direction LINGUAL burgeoned. In 1956, 832 letters were opened. In 1958, more than 8,000 letters were opened.[53] Angleton surely read many of them.

J. EDGAR HOOVER HAD MUCH the same idea about postal surveillance. In 1958, he sought authority from the postmaster general to open the mail of Communists and other people he regarded as a threat to the American way of life. When Angleton heard of the plan, he took Sam Papich aside and informed him, "on a personal basis," that the CIA was already conducting an extensive mail-opening operation.[54] Papich worried that "all hell was going to break loose" because the CIA was operating on U.S. soil, a violation of its charter and, worse, intruding on Hoover's domestic turf.

Angleton's response was deft. On February 6, 1958, he wrote to Hoover and offered to respond to FBI requests for mail opening. They would call it "Project HUNTER."[55] Hoover welcomed the gifts of "Bureau Source 100."

"Ours was shotgun treatment," Angleton later explained. "Theirs was rifle treatment. . . . We were covering a vast amount of mail. The Bureau's treatment was more or less pinpointed on matters that came as a result of a breakthrough or identification of some active case."[56]

Angleton was well aware that opening U.S. mail violated federal law.

"Existing federal statutes preclude the concoction of any legal excuse for the violation," wrote his deputy Jim Hunt in 1961 when the Office of Security expressed concern about the "flap potential" of the LINGUAL operation.

"No cover story is available to any government agency," Hunt warned.[57]

Hoover knew what he wanted to do with the HUNTER intelligence take. In 1956, he had revived the Bureau's Counterintelligence Program, known as COINTELPRO, originally created to counter pro-German subversives during World War II.[58] Hoover's first target was the American Communist Party, a shrinking organization discredited by Khrushchev's secret speech and American prosperity. With the bounty of personal information from LINGUAL/HUNTER, Hoover was able to expand the list of COINTELPRO targets in the years to come to include such enemies of the people as civil rights leader Martin Luther King, Jr., the Southern Christian Leadership Conference, the Nation of Islam, the Black Panthers, the Student Nonviolent Coordinating Committee, as well as the Socialist Workers Party and Women's Strike for Peace.

Historians and journalists usually describe COINTELPRO as a Hoover creation, which is not quite the case. It was created by Hoover with the critical help of Angleton, and it functioned as a joint FBI-CIA venture, with a bureaucratic division of labor. The Bureau took the lead in targeting dissident Americans inside the United States. The Agency took the lead outside the country. In the COINTELPRO attack on the Fair Play for Cuba Committee and its most famous member, Lee Harvey Oswald, the FBI and the CIA would work together.

Angleton used CIA mail surveillance to feed the COINTELPRO beast.[59]

MOLE

EZRA POUND WAS RELEASED from St. Elizabeths Hospital in April 1958. He was now seventy-two years old—still a favorite of conservatives but no longer enchanted with fascism. He had finished another book of cantos while incarcerated. Pound's psychiatrist found him a fascinating thinker and no danger to society.

Although Angleton gave former CIA officer Peter Sichel the impression that he had been in touch with Pound while the poet was at St. Elizabeths, there's no evidence Angleton ever visited or wrote.[60] After his release, Pound returned to Italy and connected with many old friends, but not with Angleton.[61]

Angleton was consumed by his work and its agonies. He felt intimations of bad news on October 18, 1959. A front-page story in *The New York Times* reported that Russell Langelle, chief security officer at the U.S. embassy in Moscow, had been arrested. The Soviet Foreign Ministry released a statement saying that Langelle had been seen giving a package to an unidentified passenger on a city bus, arousing suspicion. Langelle, who denied that he engaged in espionage, was expelled from the country.[62]

The counterintelligence implications were disturbing. Langelle was the Agency's contact with Pyotr Popov, a military officer and the best agent that the CIA had inside the Soviet Union. For seven years, Popov had been passing reports on the inner workings of the Red Army at incredible risk to himself and at virtually no cost to the Agency. At a time when Western intelligence services had little reliable information from inside the Soviet armed forces, Popov's reporting was priceless.

"He brought us so much," said George Kisevalter, one of the Agency's top Russian-speaking officers. "For instance when he was on duty at night, he could gain access to the monthly payroll. He copied the whole thing, and it contained all kinds of exotic information."[63]

Kisevalter was a bear of a man who wore rumpled clothes and spoke perfect Russian and German.[64] The only son of an émigré Russian engineer, he had served in the U.S. Army before joining the CIA in 1951. As a branch chief in the Soviet Russia Division,[65] his specialty was the handling of Russian agents. Over the course of six years, Kisevalter met more than a hundred times with Popov.[66]

The CIA soon learned that Popov was the unidentified bus passenger with whom Langelle had made contact. On December 20, 1959, the *Red Star* newspaper in Moscow reported what the CIA men already suspected: that the KGB had unmasked Popov as an American intelligence agent.[67]

———

THE CIA MEN DEBATED what had gone wrong.

Bill Harvey, chief of the Berlin base, thought Popov had been exposed by the sloppy tradecraft of one of his contacts in Moscow. Bill Hood, Angleton's friend, who also handled Popov, cited "several obvious clues" that supported this analysis.[68]

Angleton countered that the obvious clues did not necessarily provide the best answers to counterintelligence problems. Angleton suspected Popov had been betrayed by what he called "a mole," a spy within the ranks of the CIA.

In time, Angleton's suspicion would harden into a fixed idea, which fueled an ideological crusade that more than a few of his colleagues denounced as a witch hunt. It all began in October 1959, according to the CIA's in-house historian David Robarge. The seminal event was Pyotr Popov's arrest. "Angleton's fixation on the mole started around 1960, after Popov's then-unexplained compromise," he wrote.[69]

OSWALD

TWO WEEKS AFTER LANGELLE'S arrest, on Monday, November 2, 1959, Jane Roman received her daily call from Sam Papich. He asked her about a story that appeared on page A7 of Saturday's *Washington Post:* EX-MARINE ASKS SOVIET CITIZENSHIP.

The wire-service story reported that a twenty-year-old former marine from Texas named Lee Harvey Oswald had shown up at the U.S. embassy in Moscow and announced his intention to renounce his U.S. passport and become a citizen of the Soviet Union.

Papich wanted to know more. When Roman received a cable from the State Department about Oswald, she scrawled on the top, "Mr. Papich would like to know about this ex-marine who recently defected into the U.S.S.R." She routed the cable to a colleague who might have answers.

Two days later, Roman received another cable on Oswald, this one from the Office of Naval Intelligence. ONI had responsibility for Oswald because he had recently been discharged from the Marine Corps.

"Something of special interest," the sender wrote to Roman.

Another State Department cable came in, and soon Oswald's name was circled with an underlined note emphasizing "SAYS HAS OFFERED SOVIETS ANY INFORMATION HE HAD ACQUIRED AS ENLISTED RADAR OPERATOR."

Oswald was an obvious target for the Counterintelligence Staff. It wasn't unheard of for Americans to move to Moscow in 1959, but it was unusual. Few, if any, of the American defectors had ever announced their intention to give the Russians classified military information. Roman routed the cable about Oswald to Birch O'Neal and the Special Investigations Group, which was responsible for keeping files on defectors. Young Oswald was a person of interest.

THE CIA'S HANDLING OF information about Lee Harvey Oswald, the accused assassin of President John F. Kennedy, is a story shrouded in deception and perjury, theories and disinformation, lies and legends. But at least one aspect of the story cannot be disputed: Angleton controlled the CIA's file on Oswald for four years—from his defection in October 1959 until his death in November 1963.

Angleton would conceal this fact for the rest of his life. He hid it from the Warren Commission and he obfuscated about it with congressional investigators in the 1970s. The story only began to emerge when Congress ordered the declassification of long-secret JFK assassination records in the 1990s. While the full story has yet to be disclosed, much of it can now be told.

LEE OSWALD WAS THE object of intense CIA interest from the moment he arrived in Moscow. Angleton relied on the Special Investigations Group to monitor his movements. Birch O'Neal, the chief of the SIG, supervised a staff of eight people, including Elizabeth Ann Egerter, master of the office filing system. She controlled Oswald's file on behalf of Angleton.

Betty, as she was known, was a single woman from Croton, New York, who had worked as an interior designer and traveled around Europe with her husband, a professional musician.[70] They divorced, and she went to work for the CIA. She had no children. Her life focused on her work, which she took seriously and never spoke about except when compelled by sub-poena. Egerter liked to describe the SIG as "the office that spied on spies."[71]

The SIG was dedicated to exploiting the actions of defectors like Oswald. As Angleton explained in a staff directive, the SIG "maintains and uses sensitive counterintelligence holdings including certain Comint [communications intelligence] and defector materials to match these against operational and personality data and thus to derive operational leads."[72]

This was the arcane language of secret intelligence work: *sensitive counterintelligence holdings . . . match defector materials . . . derive operational leads.* Dense, complex, and allusive, the words have to be unpacked to be understood. In plain speech, you could say the men and women of the SIG used information about defectors obtained via wiretaps or other illicit means to support covert operations against the Soviet Union.

In short, Angleton's mole hunters were running operations and they were interested in Oswald. So was Angleton himself. Someone, most likely Angleton, gave Oswald's name to a subordinate in the CI/PROJECT. That person created a note card in the LINGUAL file bearing Oswald's name, and the handwritten words "SECRET EYES ONLY." This notation put Oswald in a rather select group.[73] The former Marine Corps radio operator was now one of three hundred Americans whose international mail was opened, copied, and filed for future use.

Why did Angleton do this? He was interested in Oswald. As he told the FBI, the purpose of the LINGUAL program was "to identify persons behind the Iron Curtain who might have some ties in the U.S. and who could be approached in their countries as contacts and sources for CIA."[74] A note scrawled on the card provided the details: "Recent defector to the USSR—Former Marine."

THE PROOF OF ANGLETON'S special interest in Oswald emerged in the Counterintelligence Staff's unusual handling of his defection. Standard CIA procedure for collecting information on a defector required the opening of a "personality" file, known in the lingo of many federal agencies as a "201 file." The CIA's Central File Registry had tens of thousands of 201

files, some fat, some thin. Some were crammed with classified information. Others consisted only of newspaper clippings. Oswald, an ex-marine
with a security clearance who had threatened to share military secrets
with the Soviets, certainly qualified for a 201 file.

Angleton's people knew that. Jane Roman and Betty Egerter didn't have
to read the latest edition of the *Clandestine Services Handbook* to know that
a 201 file should be opened on persons "of active operational interest at any
given point in time." They also knew the informal three-document rule:
As soon as the Agency received three incoming reports on a person, it was
time to open a 201 file.[75]

Oswald qualified on every count. Nonetheless, the Special Investigations
Group chose not to open a file on him. Instead, the Office of Security opened
a file on the itinerant ex-marine on December 9, 1959. This file, labeled
OS-351-164, then became the repository of all the information that the
Agency received about Oswald.[76]

Needless to say, the Office of Security did not create Oswald's file without consulting Angleton's staff. CI/SIG served as "a liaison office between
CI Staff and the Office of Security," Egerter later explained. "We worked
very closely with the Office of Security."[77] In the case of Oswald, the unusual
procedure had to be approved at higher levels. Robert Bannerman, deputy
director of the Office of Security in 1959, told historian John Newman that
"Jim Angleton was in on this."[78]

ANGLETON'S INTEREST IN OSWALD was finely tuned. The effect
of creating an Office of Security file, instead of a 201 file, was to ensure
information about the ex-marine was held more tightly. For Angleton's
counterintelligence purposes, an OS file had clear advantages over a 201
file. A 201 file was accessible to anyone in the Directorate of Plans who had
a clearance to draw from the Central File Registry. By contrast, an OS file
could not be seen by anybody outside of Office of Security and the SIG.

So, if someone inside the Agency—say a KGB mole—wanted to know
more about the ex-marine whose defection *The Washington Post* had reported, the person would have to ask for his file in writing—and provide
his or her name, office, and phone number. By creating a restricted OS

file and not a 201 file for Oswald, Angleton could determine who in the ranks of the CIA was interested in him. The unusual handling of the Oswald file was one technique among many for finding the mole who had betrayed Popov.

In the next year, a series of FBI and State Department memos flowed into Angleton's Oswald file.

IN OCTOBER 1960, THE STATE Department sent a notice to the CIA stating that it wanted up-to-date records on all recent defectors to the Soviet Union. The notice came attached with a list of a dozen known defectors, one of whom was Lee Oswald. That missive, according to the CIA's account, prodded the Counterintelligence Staff to act. In December 1960, thirteen months after Oswald's defection, Betty Egerter completed the paperwork to create a 201 file. In the process, she inexplicably gave Oswald the wrong middle name, labeling the file "Lee Henry Oswald."[79]

More important than the name on the file was its contents. Egerter took all the material that was collected in the OS file and transferred it to the new 201 file. The Oswald file now contained a dozen items: four documents from the State Department, two from the CIA, two from the FBI, one from ONI, and three newspaper clippings.[80]

The mole hunt was the most sensitive of Angleton's operations, which is why he put Egerter in charge of the Oswald file. All new information on Oswald was routed to her. In June 1962, for example, the LINGUAL team opened and read a letter written by Oswald's mother, Marguerite. "This item will be of interest to Mrs. Egerter, CI/SIG, and also to the FBI," said the cover memo on the intercepted letter.[81]

Neither the CIA nor Angleton shared this early interest in Oswald and his family with the Warren Commission, which investigated the assassination of JFK. Not until the mid-1970s did people start to ask questions. In 1978, an attorney for the House Select Committee on Assassinations put the question to Angleton. Given the Agency's standard procedures, he asked, what could explain the yearlong delay in opening Oswald's 201 file?

"I don't know the circumstances," Angleton replied. "I don't know why it would take that long."[82]

In fact, Angleton *did* know the circumstances. He had created the SIG to track defectors. He was alarmed by Popov's arrest in late 1959 and he worried about moles. He had put Oswald's name on the LINGUAL list. He wanted to monitor the ex-marine closely and guard all information about him. And he needed to hide a damning fact: Oswald figured in his mole hunt a thousand days before he became world-famous.

IN MAY 1960, ANGLETON crashed.[83] Stressed by the demands of his impossible job, drinking to excess, and gasping for breath from a recurrence of tuberculosis, he was a shambling wreck. His doctor insisted he take a medical leave at a sanatorium in Virginia, and suddenly he was outside the world of secret intelligence. Angleton recuperated for months. He did not return to the house in Arlington until November 4, 1960. The next Tuesday was Election Day. When the votes were all counted, Senator John F. Kennedy had defeated Vice President Richard Nixon in the closest presidential election since 1876.

Angleton knew Nixon from policy discussions about Cuba. He knew Jack Kennedy personally from dinner parties at the Meyers' and the Bradlees'. Like most people in their social crowd, Jim and Cicely Angleton found Kennedy and his wife, Jacqueline, enormously attractive, but they were not always impressed by Kennedy's politics. Angleton usually voted Republican. He had supported Wendell Willkie in 1940 and Dwight Eisenhower in 1952. Kennedy's ironic charm reminded Cicely of a certain Shakespearean aristocrat. After Kennedy was elected, she quipped, "Prince Hamlet is in the White House."[84]

JFK

JAMES JESUS ANGLETON WAS almost exactly the same age as John Fitzgerald Kennedy. Both men were born in 1917, seven months apart. Both grew up in cosmopolitan families, where they mastered the privileges of elite education and new wealth. Both returned from World War II exuding the hopes and ambitions of a new generation. As they made their way toward positions of power in Washington in the 1950s, they saw each other with their mutual friends Cord and Mary Meyer. But if they were friendly, they were not close. Now Kennedy was the president-elect of the United States of America, and Angleton worked for him.

With the arrival of a new administration came new issues and new assignments for Angleton. One of them concerned Israel.

THANKS TO A LONG-STANDING agreement with Dulles, Angleton served as the Israel desk officer at CIA headquarters. He also controlled the CIA station in Tel Aviv. In 1960, he brought in Peter Jessup, a career officer whom he trusted, to serve as station chief. Angleton continued to visit Israel often, meeting with Jessup as well as with Isser Harel, Amos Manor, Memi de Shalit, and other senior figures in the Israeli government. What he didn't do was report on Israel's efforts to build a nuclear reactor and nuclear weapons.

Others were more attentive. Henry Gromberg, a physicist from the University of Michigan, visited Israel's civilian nuclear facilities in November 1960 and came away with the distinct impression that a research reactor in the Negev desert town of Dimona was part of an effort to develop nuclear weapons.

"I feel sure its design is far beyond any kind of training reactor and that it will be capable of producing weapons grade plutonium," he told the CIA.[85]

The Agency sent up a U-2 spy plane, which returned with high-altitude images of unusual construction at Dimona. A formal CIA intelligence estimate, produced January 31, 1961, concluded, "The secrecy and deception surrounding the undertaking [at Dimona] suggest that it is intended, at least in part, for the production of weapons grade uranium."[86]

The Israelis had managed to keep the secret of Dimona from the CIA for more than two years.[87] At the time, Angleton was briefed by Agency photo analysts about the U-2 imagery. He never evinced much interest, said Dino Brugioni, deputy director of the CIA's National Photographic Interpretation Center.

"He was a real funny guy," Brugioni recalled. "I'd meet with him, brief him; he'd ask a few questions, you'd leave—and never know what he's holding. Sometimes he'd have his office real dark and have a light only on you. He was a real spook."[88]

The U.S. Intelligence Board, which reviewed CIA operations on behalf of the White House, recommended the Agency "expeditiously disseminate all information that it collects on this subject" to the rest of the government.[89]

As the Israel desk officer, Angleton was responsible for following the board's guidance. He ignored it.

CUBA

ANGLETON WAS MORE INTERESTED in Cuba. It was closer to home and more pressing. In his view, Israel was a friendly country, while Cuba had fallen to the enemy. Fidel Castro, the leader of the national uprising that ousted pro-American dictator Fulgencio Batista on January 1, 1959, had been consolidating power ever since. Unlike his liberal friends, Angleton was immune to the idea that Castro was a nationalist and a social reformer with whom the United States could do business. Angleton thought Castro was a Marxist-Leninist who predictably dispensed with bourgeois formalities like due process and jury trials in favor of putting his class enemies before a firing squad en masse.

The CIA had been expelled from Havana, a city where the Agency had once had a free hand. David Phillips, a rising star of the clandestine service, had to flee the island when the Cubans learned he was a CIA man. Havana, once a playground for American tourists and investors, had become inhospitable to the CIA, while the KGB was building an operational platform in the western hemisphere for the first time.

In the last year of the Eisenhower administration, Angleton argued for a more aggressive U.S. policy. He found a sympathetic audience in Vice President Richard Nixon.

"Nixon is taking a very dominating position on Cuba," Angleton told an FBI friend in January 1960. He reported that he had "held lengthy discussions with Nixon and other officials concerning a 'getting tough' policy, which will be centered around possible U.S. Government refusal to purchase Cuban sugar."[90]

The struggle for Cuba was a turning point for the CIA. For perhaps the first time in the Agency's thirteen-year history, the CIA men faced organized public opposition from their fellow citizens. On April 6, 1960, *The New York Times* published a full-page advertisement with the headline WHAT'S REALLY HAPPENING IN CUBA?

The ad criticized U.S. news coverage of the Cuban Revolution as biased. Signatories included French philosophers Jean-Paul Sartre and Simone de Beauvoir, as well as novelists Norman Mailer, James Baldwin, Dan Wakefield, and Truman Capote, the poet Allen Ginsberg, and the scientist Linus Pauling. The letter was also signed by leading African American intellectuals, among them historian John Henrik Clarke and civil rights activist Robert F. Williams.

The advertisement announced the creation of a Fair Play for Cuba Committee, dedicated to the proposition that the Cuban revolution posed no threat to the United States. The FPCC was the brainchild of Robert Taber, a CBS news correspondent who had obtained a rare exclusive interview with Castro in 1957,[91] and Richard Gibson, an African American CBS correspondent who was also sympathetic to Castro.[92]

The FPCC was inundated with more than a thousand letters from people ready to take action. Across the South, black college students fighting Jim Crow–era laws were inspired by Castro's summary abolition of racial segregation laws in Cuba. Within six months, the FPCC had an estimated seven thousand members in twenty-seven chapters and forty campus affiliates.[93] The FPCC was one of the first manifestations of the popular oppositional movements that would become known as the New Left.

The CIA was roused to action. Two days after the ad appeared, Bill Harvey, who had been called back from Berlin to take over the anti-Castro operation, bragged to FBI liaison Sam Papich that "this Agency has derogatory information on all individuals listed in the attached advertisement."[94]

From the start, the CIA targeted the FPCC. Within four years the Agency would succeed in destroying it.

WHEN ANGLETON RETURNED TO his desk in early 1961, he was apprised of the latest development in the Cuba operation. The Agency was training a brigade of fifteen hundred exiles at a ranch in Guatemala. They would sail to Cuba, declare a beachhead, and call on the people to rise up against the Castro government. Under the combination of military attack and diplomatic isolation, the CIA expected the young Cuban leader would fold, as Arbenz had in Guatemala in 1954.

President Kennedy had been briefed on the plan by Allen Dulles and the deputy director of the CIA, Charles Cabell. Preoccupied with confronting the Soviet Union in Europe, Kennedy's only questions were whether the United States would be blamed for overthrowing Castro and whether the invaders would need U.S. air support. The answer on both points, he was told, was no. The rebels were indigenous Cubans and they needed no outside military help to prevail. JFK asked for the opinion of the Joint Chiefs of Staff, who pronounced the plan sound from a military point of view.

In the United States, public support for the Cuban leader seemed to be growing. Suddenly, Cuba was not just an issue, but a cause. The Fair Play for Cuba Committee announced the formation of a San Francisco chapter at a street rally in January 1961. To a crowd of thousands, poet Lawrence Ferlinghetti read an apocalyptic homage to the young Cuban leader, whom he expected would soon be dead at the hands of the CIA. It was entitled "One Thousand Fearful Words for Fidel Castro."[95]

> It's going to be a tragedy
> I see no way out
> among the admen and slumming models
> and the brilliant snooping columnists
> who are qualified to call Castro psychotic
> because they no doubt are doctors
> and have examined him personally
> and know a paranoid hysterical tyrant when they see one

> *because they have it on first hand*
> *from personal observation by the CIA . . .*
> *it looks like Curtains for Fidel.*

This was not Jim Angleton's kind of poetry.

THE MEN OF THE CIA always underestimated Fidel Castro. In their Anglo-Saxon chauvinism, many thought he was a Latin hysteric who could be easily disposed of. This view was not held by Angleton's colleague Dick Helms, however. As top deputy to Richard Bissell, the brainy deputy director of plans, Helms was quietly skeptical about the Agency's plans for a coup in Cuba. Castro was no Arbenz, he said.

"His well-propagandized enthusiasm for land reform, universal education and social change had a significant appeal to Cuban peasants and the urban working class," Helms wrote later. "He was young, energetic, forceful and without question possessed a considerable romantic charisma."[96] Helms thought the CIA plan to overthrow him with a small invasion force was doomed to fail and that the United States would have to intervene with its own armed forces.[97]

Castro had studied the CIA. His comrade in arms, Ernesto "Che" Guevara, an Argentine doctor, had lived in Guatemala during the 1954 coup and seen the CIA's tactics close-up. Castro and Guevara fully expected the United States to mount a Guatemala-style operation against them. So they took every defensive measure that Arbenz had not. They shut down radio stations and newspapers that did not support the government. They organized and armed civilian militias and neighborhood watch groups. They mobilized the population against the American invaders with a nationalist battle cry, *"Patria o Muerte"* ("Fatherland or Death"). They were waiting for the CIA.

CUBAN INTRIGUE BOILING IN MIAMI AS CASTRO FOES STEP UP EFFORTS, ran the headline for an article by Tad Szulc in *The New York Times* in early April 1961.[98]

On April 17, the ships of the CIA-trained brigade landed at a remote coastal area of Cuba known as the Bay of Pigs, or Playa Girón. Castro ordered his army to the area. A Cuban air force plane bombed the ship disgorging the rebels. The invaders lost the element of surprise and were pinned down on the beach by gunfire.

In Washington, the CIA men were frantic and disorganized. Allen Dulles had arranged to be out of the country to enhance the cover story that the Agency was not involved. Deputy Director Cabell appealed to President Kennedy for help. Kennedy, attending a gala ball in the White House, was called away from the festivities for a conference. Cabell told the tuxedo-clad president that only U.S. air support could ensure the rebels' survival. Recalling that President Eisenhower had authorized air support in Guatemala in 1954, Angleton and most other CIA men assumed JFK would do the same.[99]

Kennedy said no. He had been told no U.S. air support would be needed, and he would not authorize it now.

One hundred and seventeen of the CIA-trained Cuban men were killed in the fighting. A handful escaped into the mountains. The rest, more than eleven hundred men, were taken prisoner. The battle was over less than seventy-two hours after it had begun.

The Cuban David had defeated the American Goliath. Castro exulted and Communists crowed. The Cubans paraded the captured rebels before TV cameras. It was the most humiliating defeat in the history of the CIA and arguably the worst blow to U.S. geopolitical credibility since World War II. It was, in the words of one Agency postmortem, a "perfect failure."[100]

Publicly, Angleton would attribute the defeat to the work of Castro's intelligence service in South Florida.

"I think the whole Bay of Pigs failure was because of penetration," he said. "In other words, I think that when you're running an operation as massive as the Bay of Pigs, where journalists like Tad Szulc can learn the secrets and publish them in the *New York Times*, and where everybody and his mother down in Miami knew something was going on . . . obviously, they sent provocateurs and agents into the United States."[101]

It was a counterintelligence failure.

KENNEDY WAS ANGRY WITH the CIA for presenting him with an operational plan that had proved so weak, and at his generals for endorsing it. Mostly, JFK berated himself for trusting the soldiers and the spies. "I've got to do something about those CIA bastards," he moaned. "How could I have been so stupid?"[102] In a moment of venting, he vowed "to splinter the CIA in a thousand pieces."[103]

For the first time since 1947, the men of the CIA had reason to fear the man in the White House. Dick Helms recalled the spring and summer of 1961 as "a busy interregnum marked with flashes of abrupt change, dampened by the anxiety most of us shared about the shape and future of the Agency."[104]

Fortunately for the CIA, Robert Kennedy, the president's brother and now the attorney general, did not regard the defeat as insuperable. He wanted revenge.[105] Upon reflection, President Kennedy rejected proposals for abolishing the clandestine service. Instead, he created a new planning cell for overthrowing Castro and assigned RFK as a member.[106] As Robert Kennedy learned about the workings of the CIA's covert operation directorate for the first time, he became convinced that the Bay of Pigs defeat could be avenged before the 1964 election. Overthrowing Castro, he told a well-attended Pentagon meeting in early 1962 "is the top priority of U.S. government—all else is secondary—no time, money, effort or manpower is to be spared."[107]

"HIT HIM"

AS KENNEDY'S GOVERNMENT REGROUPED, Angleton was drawn deeper into Cuban operations. On May 4, 1961, the National Security Council tasked the Counterintelligence Staff with a new job: to cooperate with the Cuban Revolutionary Council, the coalition of anti-Castro organizations funded by the CIA. The CRC was supposed to unify the opposition to Castro's one-party government and, when Castro was overthrown, establish a pro-American government in Havana.

Angleton's assignment was to "create, train, and support a highly motivated and professionally competent apolitical and career security service which will be dedicated to the preservation of the democratic form of government." He was asked to "assign carefully selected and qualified Agency personnel to work with the service during the current and post-Castro eras."[108]

Angleton wanted to make a difference in Cuba, just as he had in Italy and Israel. Among other things, he wanted to assassinate Castro.

"WOULD YOU HIT HIM?" asked Bill Harvey.[109]

Angleton was sitting with his longtime colleague in the familiar confines of Harvey's Seafood Grill, along with a British friend named Peter Wright, a scientist at MI5, who would go on to write a best-selling memoir. Wright was visiting Washington on official business, and Angleton was his escort. As the three men poked at their food, they discussed the merits of murdering the president of Cuba.

Would you hit him?

The mood was businesslike. While Angleton and Harvey were not exactly friends, they had settled into a wary respect. Their guest, Wright, had been invited to Washington for a meeting at the National Security Agency. When Wright shared the latest innovation in British wiretapping capabilities, Harvey cursed him for not providing the information sooner. Harvey demanded to know why the CIA should trust him. The memory of being fooled by Angleton's phony friend Kim Philby still rankled Harvey. He was a man who nursed his grudges.

Now they were talking about the assassination of an impudent demagogue, and Harvey could not help but wonder if his guest was serious. He put it to him straight.

Would you hit him?

"I paused to fold my napkin," Wright later recounted. "Waiters glided from table to table. I realized now why Harvey needed to know I could be trusted."

"We'd certainly have that capability," Wright told him, "but I doubt we would use it nowadays."

"Why not?" Harvey asked.

"We're not in it anymore, Bill," he replied, referring to the assassination business. "We got out a couple of years ago, after Suez."

"We're developing a new capability in the company to handle these kinds of problems," Harvey explained. "We're in the market for the requisite expertise."

The capability was known in the CIA by the code name ZR-RIFLE, and Dulles had put Harvey in charge. With his contacts in the European crime syndicates, Harvey was thought to be most qualified for the job. In his notes for ZR-RIFLE, discovered years later by Senate investigators, he stressed that the CIA should recruit a gunman from the ranks of organized crime, and an assassin should have no roots or contacts in the place where he did the killing.[110] Harvey, often caricatured as a drunken oaf, was, in fact, a meticulous planner.

Wright, suddenly uncomfortable, tried to deflect their interest.

"I began to feel then I had told them more than enough," Wright wrote. "The sight of Angleton's notebook was beginning to unnerve me. They seemed so determined, so convinced this was the way to handle Castro, and I was slightly put out that I could not help more."

Wright was not a sentimental man. A scientist, he had no patience for liberal pieties. As a Catholic, he had no interest in Marxist-Leninist materialism. He admired the determination of Angleton and Harvey to get rid of Castro. He also had misgivings.

"There was a streak of ruthlessness and lawlessness about the American intelligence community, which disturbed many in the senior echelons of British intelligence," Wright said.[111]

THE STORMY INTERREGNUM AT the CIA ended in November 1961. President Kennedy fired both Dulles and Richard Bissell for their leading role in the Bay of Pigs fiasco. Angleton understood the need for change, but he hated to see Dulles go.

To replace Dulles, President Kennedy brought in an outsider, John McCone, a Republican, a corporate executive, and the former chairman of the Atomic Energy Commission. McCone had a reputation as a no-nonsense administrator. His conservative politics would help insulate the liberal president from Republican criticism while taking final decisions out of the hands of the CIA veterans, whom Kennedy no longer trusted.

The only consolation for Angleton was that his friend Dick Helms would succeed Bissell as deputy director of plans. As they had risen in the ranks since their OSS days, Helms had gained a reputation as a plodder, at least compared to activist officers like Frank Wisner and Bill Harvey. But his doubts about the Bay of Pigs operation had been wholly vindicated. Like many a CIA hand, Angleton thought the prudent, steady Helms would establish the sort of discipline the Agency badly needed.

As Angleton's stature grew, so did his penchant for running agents and operations outside of normal CIA reporting channels. Cuba was no exception. In the spring of 1961, the Israeli government sent a diplomat named Nir Baruch to serve in Havana.[112] He was also an intelligence officer reporting to Amos Manor back in Israel.

Baruch soon became Angleton's man in Havana.

"At a certain stage, in order to shorten the processes, the Americans supplied me with a more sophisticated coding device," Baruch recalled. "A few times I flew to Washington and met with Angleton. On several occasions he asked me to be a courier and meet with CIA agents in Cuba, but I declined. I thought this was too dangerous."

WASHINGTON CIRCA 1961 WAS a unique place in the history of the world. Never had there been a country so dominant, so wealthy, so influential, so attractive, and so feared as the United States of America. Never had the U.S. Army, Navy, Air Force, and Marine Corps, as well as the new multibillion-dollar intelligence agencies, the CIA, the NSA, and the DIA, been so fully funded. Never had the corporations that built the planes, submarines, and aircraft carriers been so large or so profitable. Never had the press been so trusting of the government. Never had the men who led these organizations felt so confident, so powerful.

Yet even the most conventional and dependably conservative man in the country perceived a problem. In his farewell address on January 17, 1961, outgoing president Dwight Eisenhower talked about what he called "the military-industrial complex." Dull as Kansas and pale as a pickle, Eisenhower looked back on the events of his own lifetime and forward to events to come. Like the man, his words were plain:

We now stand ten years past the midpoint of a century that has witnessed four major wars among great nations. Three of these involved our own country. Despite these holocausts, America is today the strongest, the most influential and most productive nation in the world. Understandably proud of this pre-eminence, we yet realize that America's leadership and prestige depend, not merely upon our unmatched material progress, riches and military strength, but on how we use our power in the interests of world peace and human betterment.

In taking his leave, Eisenhower warned Americans of a new threat born in America's Cold War prosperity. He referred to the network of arms manufacturers and military officers that had elevated him to supreme power. All the same, he didn't trust it.

This conjunction of an immense military establishment and a large arms industry is new in the American experience. The total influence—economic, political, even spiritual—is felt in every city, every Statehouse, every office of the Federal government. We recognize the imperative need for this development. Yet we must not fail to comprehend its grave implications. Our toil, resources and livelihood are all involved.

Eisenhower emphasized he was talking about "the very structure of our society."

In the councils of government, we must guard against the acquisition of unwarranted influence, whether sought or un-sought, by the military-industrial complex. The potential for the disastrous rise of misplaced power exists and will persist.[113]

The influence of the military-industrial complex feared by Eisenhower was felt after the Bay of Pigs debacle. The hostility to President Kennedy in his own government was so pervasive and palpable, two enterprising news reporters thought they should write about it.

In September 1962, Fletcher Knebel, a reporter for the biweekly magazine *Look*, and Charles Bailey II, Washington correspondent for *The Minneapolis Tribune*, published *Seven Days in May*, a fictional thriller about an incipient military coup in contemporary Washington. It resonated in the capital and with the public at large.

In the book, the embattled liberal president was named Jordan Lyman, his last name linking the fictional tale to its real-life inspiration, Gen. Lyman Lemnitzer, the chairman of the Joint Chiefs of Staff. The fictional coup leader was "Gentleman Jim" Scott, a popular general and war hero who bore a passing resemblance to the real-life U.S. Air Force general Curtis LeMay, the man who had firebombed Dresden and Tokyo during World War II.

To rescue the nation from Lyman's misguided liberal policies, Scott orchestrates a plan to force the president to cede powers to his generals. With the help of a wily aide, President Lyman thwarts the overbearing general and makes peace with the Soviet Union. It was a liberal fantasy grounded in Washington's conservative realities. It quickly became a bestseller.[114]

Never had the Joint Chiefs and the commander in chief been so alienated. Knebel thought Lemnitzer's private tirades about Kennedy showed disrespect for the office of the presidency and for democratic government. LeMay was even more contemptuous of JFK. A burly man fond of cigars, LeMay commanded the U.S. nuclear missile arsenal and its nuclear-armed aircraft. He thought the world a dangerous place, where the United States sometimes had no choice but to bomb its foes into submission. He had no fear of nuclear war. Indeed, he thought the time might come when it would be necessary. In retirement he would liken JFK and his entourage to "cockroaches."

The top CIA men were not quite so harsh on Kennedy. As a group, they were more educated, more liberal, and more cosmopolitan than the uniformed men in the Pentagon. Many of them knew JFK socially, if not personally. Some thought he embodied the organization man: a bright, self-seeking conformist. Allen Dulles liked JFK until Kennedy fired him for the Bay of Pigs. After that, Dulles thought Kennedy had lost his nerve[115] and began acting more like a god than a president.[116]

EMPIRE

ANGLETON WAS NOW ACCORDED a mixture of deference and awe. He consciously enveloped himself and his staff in an aura of mystery, hinting at knowledge of grave secrets and hidden intrigue too sensitive to share.[117]

Only J. Edgar Hoover controlled as much secret information. Angleton's team at the post office in New York was opening ten thousand letters a year for the LINGUAL/HUNTER program. Angleton received a steady stream of actionable intelligence on leftists in touch with people in the Soviet Union, as well as the correspondence of senators and congressmen who visited Moscow. He was assembling files on thousands of individuals and hundreds of organizations.

His relationship with the FBI was strong. He had purchased Hoover's grudging cooperation with the hard currency of useful secrets. William Sullivan, the assistant director of the FBI's Intelligence Division, had become a friend of Angleton's and a student of his counterintelligence theories. The Bureau and the Agency had collaborated effectively in rolling up a Soviet spy network headed by an intelligence officer named Rudolf Abel.[118]

Through Cord Meyer's International Organizations Division, Angleton waged intellectual Cold War in dozens of countries, supporting the National Student Association (the largest student group in the country), the Congress for Cultural Freedom (a prestigious group of European anti-Communist activists), *Encounter* magazine (a leading intellectual journal), and even the Iowa Writers' Workshop (home to many budding American novelists). Allen Ginsberg would argue that Angleton had even succeeded in turning American literary criticism against the so-called Beat writers like himself and Jack Kerouac.[119]

Angleton's friendship with Jay Lovestone and Louise Page Morris enabled him to keep the actions of the American Federation of Labor (now joined with the Congress of Industrial Organizations in the AFL-CIO) aligned with CIA operations around the world.

He had his own network of agents operating outside the CIA's reporting system, including Morris and Nir Baruch.[120] His friend George White still operated two CIA safe houses, funded under MKULTRA accounts, where White ran LSD experiments on unwitting subjects. And Angleton had scores of others friends, assets, agents, and sources whom he never talked about. "I probably recruited more agents than any person in the CIA who would be known to you," he later told investigators.[121]

Angleton had good relations with the National Security Agency. He personally investigated the case of Sidney Joseph Petersen, an NSA employee and suspected homosexual arrested in 1954 for passing sensitive cryptographic material to the Dutch government. Angleton came away satisfied that the information had not reached the KGB, and he allowed Petersen to plead guilty and avoid a public trial.[122]

Angleton's ties to British intelligence remained robust thanks to friendships with senior officials, including SIS chief Maurice Oldfield; senior officer Nicholas Elliott, whom he knew from his OSS days; and newer acolytes in MI5, such as Arthur Martin and Stephen de Mowbray, who were intrigued by his analysis of KGB deception operations. He kept up with Kim Philby, now working as a journalist in Beirut.

Angleton retained sway over CIA operations in Italy through his connections in the Vatican and the intelligence services. In the mid-1950s, when Rome station chief Gerry Miller and political action officer Bill Colby proposed an "opening to the left"—funding center-left parties to increase American influence with more progressive political forces—Angleton resisted, regarding all leftist parties as the cutting edge of communism. Thanks to his influence, the Agency's funding continued to go to the more compliant centrist Christian Democrats, as well as to the anti-Communist right, including his longtime ally Valerio Borghese, now running the neofascist National Front movement.

Angleton was welcome in Israel, where he visited with friends Amos Manor in Shin Bet, Isser Harel in the Mossad, and even Prime Minister Ben-Gurion.[123]

And his influence on Cuban operations was growing now that Bill Harvey had taken over the Agency's Cuban task force.

Angleton was running his own personal intelligence service.

"His secret travels in Western Europe, not to mention Israel, to meet with senior liaison officials with whom he had developed confidential relationships constituted a form of independent operational activity," wrote George Kalaris, the man who succeeded him as counterintelligence chief, in a secret report. ". . . [T]he local station would effectively be cut out and command channel and communications would run direct to counterintelligence headquarters in Washington."[124]

And he had the permission of his bosses. The new CIA director, John McCone, was an outsider who knew little of how the Agency operated. On all but the biggest policy issues, McCone deferred to Deputy Director Helms, who trusted Angleton completely. A firm believer that "no intelligence service can for very long be any better than its counterintelligence component," Helms let Angleton do as he pleased, few questions asked.[125]

President Kennedy thought he had reined in the CIA by firing Dulles and Bissell after the Bay of Pigs, but his actions did not much affect Angleton's power. The counterintelligence chief was now the third-most-powerful man in the CIA and he was accountable to no one.

GOLITSYN

ON A COLD NIGHT in Finland in December 1961, a heavyset man with hazel eyes presented himself at the home of Frank Friberg, the chief of the CIA station in Helsinki. He explained that he was not "Anatoly Klimov" as Friberg thought.[126] His name was Anatoly Golitsyn, and he was chief of the KGB *rezidentura* in Finland. He said he wanted to defect to the United States—immediately.

Angleton was notified. Never before had such a high-ranking KGB officer offered his services to the CIA. Angleton approved. In the moment, Friberg regarded Golitsyn's defection as the highlight of his career. In time, he would regret it as the fateful first step toward an epic fiasco.[127]

The Agency's first psychological evaluation of Golitsyn arrived on Angleton's desk a few days later.

"The Subject himself is a very alert, perceptive and shrewd individual," the Agency's doctor wrote. "Part of this may stem from his intelligence training and experience but no doubt some of this is a reflection of his make-up."

Golitsyn required more study, the doctor judged.

"There are indications of rather grandiose and omnipotent ideas as well as some paranoid feelings about his own intelligence service," he went on. "These are highly suspect as far as motivation for his defection go [sic], but additional data is needed from a psychiatric standpoint to further substantiate the possibility of emotional illness or imbalance."[128]

Angleton forwarded the report to J. Edgar Hoover.

ANATOLY GOLITSYN WAS BORN to a poor family in Ukraine. He joined the Soviet army in 1944 and was assigned to a military counterintelligence unit. After the war, he was transferred to the KGB's First Chief Directorate, where he ran operations against the United States. He claimed he had personally presented his proposals for reforming the KGB to Josef Stalin in 1952. According to Golitsyn, Stalin had accepted his proposals but died before they could be implemented. The CIA could never corroborate any such meeting, but the story was consistent with Golitsyn's style.

"He wanted to immediately meet with the president and with the Attorney General and with the Director of CIA," said Vasia Gmirkin, a CIA officer who worked with Golitsyn. "He didn't want to deal with anybody below that level. So he came with grandiose demands, saying that he had very valuable information to present, and we bought it."[129] Pyotr Deriabin, another KGB defector working at the CIA, recalled Golitsyn "had a big mouth and tended to invent stories which would make him look important."[130]

In terms of actionable intelligence, Golitsyn offered some real revelations.[131] He detailed the organization of the Helsinki *rezidentura*. "This information was specific, accurate, and useful, though not exactly earth-shaking," said one analyst. Golitsyn said the Soviets had a spy in the British Admiralty, which proved to be true. He provided insights into Soviet efforts to penetrate NATO. Golitsyn had delivered "a wealth of information on KGB personnel, organization, and methods," said one CIA memo. "His counterintelligence and penetration leads, however, were considerably less helpful."[132]

Golitsyn intrigued Angleton. He said he had learned that the KGB had a high-level source inside the CIA, someone they called "Sasha." This mole supposedly had been recruited by the KGB in 1950, or perhaps even earlier, he said. According to information Golitsyn had picked up, Sasha's real name began with the letter *K* and ended in *ski* or *sky,* he said.[133] Sasha, he said, had been stationed in Germany after the war and had technical skills in electronic eavesdropping.[134]

Golitsyn's information about the mole meshed with Angleton's fears about the betrayal of Pyotr Popov. Angleton was impressed when Golitsyn's information led straight to a suspect: a career officer in the Technical Service Division named Peter Karlow. He had served in the OSS, where he lost a leg when his PT boat hit a mine off the Italian coast.[135] Recruited by the CIA in 1950, he served for six years in Germany before returning to headquarters.[136] Karlow fit the profile of Sasha in more than one way. His last name began with a *K* and, it turned out, he was born Peter Klibansky. He possessed technical skills—he had studied a cavity resonating microphone found in the U.S. embassy in Russia—and a check of his file revealed there had been security issues in some of the TSD projects he worked on.

Angleton told Helms that Karlow might be the mole and insisted that he be removed from any position where he would have access to intelligence. In January 1962, Helms put Karlow on administrative leave without offering an explanation. The FBI interviewed him and administered a polygraph test, which he passed. Still, he was not returned to duty.[137]

Angleton was intrigued by another story Golitsyn told, which was supported by the documents he had brought with him. In May 1959, the KGB had held a conference, attended by two thousand officers, where chairman Alexander Shelepin announced an aggressive long-range strategy toward the West.[138]

The United States did not know much about how Premier Nikita Khrushchev and other top officials in the Kremlin made their decisions. Angleton was skeptical that anything had changed since the death of Stalin in 1953, and Golitsyn's account strengthened his conviction. Shelepin called for mobilization of the security and intelligence services to destabilize the Soviet Union's enemies and to weaken the alliances among them. Traditionally, Communist doctrine held that the Soviet Union's "main enemies" were the United States and the NATO countries. Shelepin had broadened this criteria to include West Germany, Japan, and smaller U.S. allies.[139] He called on the KGB Department of Disinformation to coordinate with all ministries and undertake joint political operations with allied Communist countries. The goal, according to Golitsyn, was nothing less than a KGB strategy that would affect the fundamental reasoning power of the Western powers.[140]

Angleton appreciated the potency of deception operations. He had seen how the British used the ULTRA secret to fool the Germans on D-Day. He analyzed how the Polish Communists had created and coopted WiN. He had studied the history of the Trust and Rote Kapelle, two ingenious operations mounted by the Cheka, a predecessor organization of the KGB, which effectively dismantled the tsarist opposition to Soviet rule in the 1920s.

"Golitsyn's defection from the elite of the KGB was a premeditated political act of a high moral order," Angleton later wrote. "An act not lacking in great courage, not to mention a significant lifelong sacrifice. . . . He was moved by a conviction to warn the West of the new uses which the communist countries had devised in stealth for their improved political, intelligence and military potential and of the new menacing dimensions which these developments added to the Soviet threat."[141]

BLACKMAIL

ANGLETON WAS RISING. IN late 1961, the CIA moved from its scattered offices in Foggy Bottom and the Mall to a new headquarters, a shiny seven-story office block nestled in the woods of Langley, Virginia. With his stature and reputation, Angleton claimed prime real estate in the new building.

The Counterintelligence Staff, now comprising nearly two hundred people, occupied the southwest corner of the second floor. Angleton's office was room 2C43.[142] In the outer office, there was a large reception room with a sofa, chairs, magazines, and three secretaries. In the inner office, Angleton pulled the venetian blinds shut and sat behind a large executive-style wooden desk that dominated the room.[143] Angleton overawed most everyone who disagreed with him and proved persuasive to the rest.

Angleton supported Golitsyn when he asked for a meeting with President Kennedy. When told that was unlikely, Golitsyn said he would accept a meeting with the president's brother Robert. Angleton supported that, too. The FBI objected, saying they would lose control of Golitsyn if they allowed him to meet with policy makers. Angleton prevailed. A meeting at the attorney general's office was arranged for July 2, 1962. In attendance, according to RFK's calendar, were Dick Helms and "John W. Stone," the Agency's alias for Golitsyn.[144]

ROBERT KENNEDY THOUGHT OF himself as a tough-minded man, not so liberal or intellectual or detached as his urbane older brother. RFK was more Catholic, more emotional, and more viscerally anti-Communist. Unlike Jack, Bob hadn't had much of a problem with Joe McCarthy, for whom he had worked in the Senate. Bob hadn't worried about the Red Scare or the Lavender Scare. He thought Communists working for the government should be fired, and the homosexuals, too.

Bob Kennedy had fewer reservations about the CIA than did his brother.

Since serving as JFK's eyes and ears on the committee to review the Bay of Pigs fiasco, RFK had become friendly with Allen Dulles. On Cuba, he clashed with the president's liberal advisers who thought Castro would survive.[145]

RFK wanted to hear Golitsyn out. The meeting was tape-recorded for the protection of all concerned, according to George Kisevalter, who later heard the tape. Golitsyn raised the idea of a multimillion-dollar institute dedicated to destroying the Soviet Communist Party. Bob only promised to tell the president about their meeting. In taking his leave, Golitsyn said he had a letter for the president explaining the problem of Soviet penetration; Bob said he would deliver it.[146]

Angleton thought this was a splendid idea.

Kisevalter and his colleagues in the CIA's Soviet Russia Division thought it was a terrible idea. So the CIA men told Golitsyn that Kisevalter would deliver his letter.

"I was authorized to promise to deliver it to the President," Kisevalter recalled, "and, if it was not innocuous, to stop it."[147]

When the two men met, Golitsyn handed over the letter. Kisevalter scanned it, his attention lingering on a key passage: "In view of the fact that the President who has promised me things through his brother, Robert, may not be the President in the future, how can I be sure the United States government will keep its promise to me for money and a pension?"

"You SOB," Kisevalter snarled at the heavyset man with hazel eyes. "You're a first-class blackmailer. This is *shantazh*."

Hearing the Russian word for blackmail, Golitsyn started to reconsider his gambit. Maybe issuing demands to the leader of the free world wasn't such a good idea.

Golitsyn asked for the letter back.

"Oh no," Kisevalter purred. "You want it delivered to the President. I'll *deliver* it."

In retirement, Kisevalter relished the memory of Golitsyn's panic.

"Golitsyn jumped up on top of the desk and then jumped down on my side and we began wrestling for the letter. I let him win."

Golitsyn never asked for a meeting with JFK again.

Yet Angleton's faith in Golitsyn never wavered.

"For reasons most intelligence professionals still do not understand, Angleton accepted at face value virtually every judgment Golitsyn rendered over more than a decade," said two Agency historians.[148]

WHEN ANGLETON FIRST HEARD of the story of Yuri Nosenko in June 1962, he thought it improbable.

Nosenko, a veteran KGB officer in Geneva, had approached the U.S. embassy saying he needed some Swiss francs to replenish official funds blown in a drinking spree with some dubious women. In return, he said, he would supply the U.S. government with information that it would find useful.[149]

Nosenko was turned over to Pete Bagley in the Soviet Russia Division. Bagley initially found his story convincing.[150] Angleton did not.

Angleton referred to Golitsyn, who had said the defectors who came after him "would all be phonies," meaning they would be agents dispatched and controlled by the KGB.[151]

Nosenko's father was the Soviet minister of shipbuilding in the 1950s, no small position. He was friends with senior Politburo members. Was it really probable, Angleton asked, that such a well-connected man would sell out his country for a few hundred dollars?[152]

With his powers of persuasion, Angleton was able to bring Bagley and David Murphy, the chief of the Soviet Russia Division, around to his view that Nosenko was a false defector, dispatched by Moscow Center to distract the CIA.[153]

But for everyone at the CIA who found Golitsyn credible, there were others who balked.

Golitsyn "certainly showed every indication of having a severe paranoid disorder," said CIA doctor John Gittinger. "I had an opportunity to see a great deal of information that he had provided and the various things he had done. . . . Much of it was so absurd that it was impossible to believe that anybody would believe it."[154]

Angleton believed it.

———

ON THE NIGHT OF October 15, 1962, the CIA's National Photographic Interpretation Center in Southwest Washington, D.C., was a busy place. The latest surveillance imagery from U-2 flights over Cuba showed new construction near the village of San Cristóbal. The star-shaped battery of missiles was identical to Soviet nuclear missile bases described in material passed on by Oleg Penkovsky, a Soviet official who was spying for the CIA. "The Penkovsky Papers," as they were dubbed, confirmed what the analysts were seeing in the U-2 photos: The Soviet Union was installing nuclear missiles in Cuba.

On Tuesday morning, October 16, 1962, CIA deputy director Marshall Carter briefed President Kennedy and his brother at the White House on what the photographs showed. All concerned realized the gravity of the revelation. The installation of the Soviet missiles so close to the American homeland was unprecedented. It was another test of the mettle of the man in the Oval Office.

HAMLET

THE CUBAN MISSILE CRISIS of October 1962 was, in the words of historian Arthur Schlesinger, "the most dangerous moment in the history of the world."[155]

The story of how that moment came and went has evolved over the decades. First told in daily news stories, the saga of the "October crisis," as it was called, was then fleshed out in longer magazine articles.[156] Then came the memoirs and the histories with portentous titles such as *Thirteen Days, The Missiles of October,* and *Eyeball to Eyeball.*

Thirty years later came the accounts of most of the officials involved, American, Russian, and Cuban, who spoke at a conference in Havana. Since then a dominant narrative of the crisis has emerged, at least in English-language accounts. It is a tale of heroic liberal statesmanship.

President Kennedy resisted the advice of a majority of his military advisers. The so-called hawks urged air strikes to destroy the Soviet missile sites, followed by a U.S. invasion to remove and replace the Castro government. JFK was a dove and opted for diplomacy. After thirteen days of tense deliberations, Kennedy managed to coerce and persuade Soviet premier Nikita Khrushchev to remove the missiles without going to war.

The accounts of the former officials strengthened the dominant interpretation.[157] It turned out that the U.S. military planners who assured Kennedy that the Soviets would step aside and acquiesce to a U.S. invasion were ill informed. They estimated the Soviet Union had fifteen thousand troops on the island and that the nuclear missiles were not yet operational.

Former Soviet officials told the Havana conference that they actually had forty-two thousand troops on the island and the field commanders in Cuba had authority from Moscow to fire tactical nuclear weapons if attacked.[158] A U.S. invasion, which the Joint Chiefs predicted would end with a quick victory, probably would have resulted in thousands of U.S. soldiers dying in the first use of atomic weapons since 1945.

In the event of such an attack, U.S. military doctrine called for massive nuclear retaliation on scores of Soviet cities. Soviet doctrine also called for massive retaliation if the USSR was attacked by the United States.

So if the United States had invaded, as the Joint Chiefs of Staff unanimously urged, the world might well have experienced a nuclear holocaust. With the benefit of hindsight, many scholars regard the peaceful resolution of the crisis as JFK's finest moment as president of the United States.

WHAT THE LIBERAL ACCOUNT of the October crisis tends to overlook is the impact on President Kennedy's government. JFK's refusal to go to war in October 1962 despite the advice of the Joint Chiefs stoked the *Seven Days in May* mood of rebellion that already pervaded the councils of U.S. national security agencies.

The generals felt the president was abandoning the U.S. policy of containment of the Soviet Union in favor of accommodation. When JFK asked General LeMay how the Soviet military would respond to a U.S invasion, LeMay assured him there would be no reaction. After all, the United States had overwhelming military superiority.

The United States had fifteen hundred long-range B-47 bombers and five hundred B-52s armed with nuclear bombs, as well as two hundred intercontinental ballistic missiles. The Soviet arsenal, by contrast, consisted of a few long-range missiles, whose unreliability was so great that it was uncertain exactly whom they threatened. The Soviet's long-range bomber forces consisted of one hundred Tu-95 Bear bombers and thirty-five Bison bombers, whose range and flight characteristics made them easy targets for U.S. fighter jets and surface-to-air missiles.[159]

Kennedy doubted U.S. military superiority would overawe the Soviets.

"They, no more than we, can let these things go by without doing something," he told LeMay. "They can't, after all their statements, permit us to take out their missiles, kill a lot of Russians, and then do nothing."[160]

LeMay argued that *not* attacking Cuba would invite aggression in the heart of Europe.

"This blockade and political action . . . will lead right into war," he warned.

LeMay feared a strategic misjudgment similar to that of the European powers facing Nazi Germany in the 1930s.

"This is almost as bad as the appeasement at Munich," he said to the president. "In other words, you're in a pretty bad fix at the present time."

"What did you say?" JFK asked.

"You're in a pretty bad fix."

Kennedy wouldn't be bullied.

"You're in there with me," he said coolly.

LeMay went silent, chewing his unlit cigar in disgust.

JFK walked out of the meeting, furious.

"These brass hats have one great advantage in their favor," he snapped to his aide Ken O'Donnell afterward. "If we . . . do what they want us to do, none of us will be alive later to tell them that they were wrong."

JFK had recently read Barbara Tuchman's bestselling book *The Guns of August,* about how the leaders of Europe had stumbled into a world war in August 1914 that few wanted or anticipated. Kennedy talked about the miscalculations of the Germans, Russians, Austrians, French, and British.

"The great danger," he said, "is a miscalculation—a mistake in judgment."

His cautious view differed radically from the confidence of men like Le-May and Angleton. They thought the greatest danger was not war but Castro and the spread of Cuban-style revolutions in the western hemisphere.

The tension between the White House and the national security agencies came to a boil in a meeting at the Pentagon in the middle of the crisis. Bill Harvey announced he had ordered six scouting teams to infiltrate Cuba in advance of the expected invasion.

Bob Kennedy told him to call it off.

Harvey said the mission was urgent. Kennedy told him to recall the teams. Harvey objected. The attorney general insisted. The younger man was staring down the older man when Harvey exploded.

"If you fuckers hadn't fucked up the Bay of Pigs, we wouldn't be in this fucking mess," he sneered.[161]

Bob Kennedy didn't have his brother's coolness. He just walked out of the meeting.

"Of course, I was furious," he said later. "You're dealing with people's lives. The best of the Cubans, the ones who volunteer, and you're going to go off with a half-assed operation such as this?"[162]

Most of the CIA men in the meeting agreed with Harvey, but they held their tongues.[163]

"Harvey has destroyed himself today," said John McCone. "His usefulness has ended."[164]

Not to Angleton it hadn't.

THE FISSURES IN KENNEDY'S government widened as Khrushchev balked at Kennedy's demand that the missiles be withdrawn. The chiefs started to mobilize U.S. armed forces for the invasion they favored. Almost overnight South Florida became an armed camp.

"Military convoys clogged highways, the railroad line to Homestead Air Force Base was jammed with military supplies," recalled Justin Gleichauf, a CIA man who was there. "Barbed wire went up along the beach in Key West and rockets sprouted along the Overseas Highway. As one of my last support activities, I obtained six thousand road maps of Cuba for use in what we felt would be an invasion."[165]

In Cuba, soldiers wheeled out artillery guns onto the Malecón, the waterfront boulevard of Havana. Across the island, Castro's government called up the armed forces, the militias, and the neighborhood block committees to fight the expected Yanqui invasion.[166]

After ten days of impasse, nuclear war was no longer a theoretical proposition; it was a looming reality. JFK sent his wife, Jackie, and their children, Caroline and John-John, to their country house in Virginia. He invited one of his paramours, a nineteen-year-old college student named Mimi Beardsley, to the White House to divert him as he tried to manage his predicament.

Kennedy spent his days wondering if he was going have to start a war that might end with whole cities and millions of people incinerated by atomic bombs. Beardsley, who spent the night of October 27, 1962, in JFK's bed, observed his tense mood. Coming out of one meeting and going into another, he told her something he could never have admitted in public: "I'd rather my children be red than dead."[167]

Throughout the crisis, Jack and Bob relied on a Russian diplomat and friend, Georgi Bolshakov, to pass private messages to the Soviet leadership. When the Kremlin's answers seemed conflicted and confusing, JFK sent Bob to see Ambassador Anatoly Dobrynin with one last message.

Dobrynin could see from Kennedy's eyes that he had not slept for days.

"The President is in a grave situation," RFK told him, "and does not know how to get out of it. We are under very severe stress. In fact, we are under pressure from our military to use force against Cuba. Probably at this very moment the President is sitting down to write a message to Chairman Khrushchev."

Bob Kennedy said he was delivering the last U.S. statement on the subject.

"President Kennedy implores Chairman Khrushchev to accept his offer and to take into consideration the peculiarities of the American system. Even though the President himself is very much against starting a war over Cuba, an irreversible chain of events could occur against his will. That is why the President is appealing directly to Chairman Khrushchev for his help in liquidating this conflict. If the situation continues much longer, the

President is not sure that the military will not overthrow him and seize power. The American army could get out of control."[168]

Another point not emphasized in the liberal narrative of the October crisis: The president feared that 186 years of constitutional government in the United States of America was in jeopardy. A military coup was a real possibility.

The American army could get out of control.

That wasn't paperback fiction. It was the reality of power in John Kennedy's Washington.

WAR NEVER CAME. AT noon on Sunday, October 28, the White House received a communication from Chairman Khrushchev that began "Dear Mr. President." The missiles would be removed, he told Kennedy. The Soviet leader said he had installed the missiles only to help Cuba deter the threat of an American invasion. With the president's assurances that there would be no invasion, Khrushchev said the missiles were unnecessary.[169]

The crisis was over.

"Most of us felt limitless relief," wrote Arthur Schlesinger.[170]

Not the men at the Pentagon. They felt limitless dismay. The chiefs heard about the end of the crisis at the same time as the American people did, via a wire-service report read on the radio. President Kennedy had made a strategic decision about national and hemispheric security without involving his military commanders.[171]

Curtis LeMay wanted to repudiate the deal.

"Why don't we go in and make a strike on Monday anyway?" he asked. He was appalled that Kennedy, who had many hundreds more strategic and tactical nuclear weapons at his disposal than did Khrushchev, had not extracted more gains.

"We could have not only gotten the missiles out of Cuba," LeMay said, "we could have gotten the Communists out of Cuba."[172]

WHAT HAS BEEN ALL but forgotten over time is the conservative critique of Kennedy's diplomacy, which prevailed in the Pentagon, the CIA, the Cuban colony in Miami, and much of the Republican Party. This interpretation would influence a generation of U.S. policymakers. In this view Khrushchev had successfully bullied Kennedy. By inserting the missiles and then ostensibly backing down, the Russian leader extracted a concession from Washington in the form of Kennedy's guarantee that the United States would not invade Cuba. With a much weaker military hand, the wily Communist had come out ahead.

The conservative narrative, retailed in popular books with titles like *Stab in the Back, Illusion and Reality,* and *Thirteen Mistakes,* argued that Kennedy had chosen a popular but illusory "peace."

"By the time the Cuban missile crisis ended, relations between the Kennedy administration and the Joint Chiefs of Staff (Taylor excepted) were at an all-time low," wrote Pentagon historian Steven L. Rearden. "In contrast, Kennedy's public stature and esteem had never been higher. Lauded by his admirers and critics alike for showing exemplary statesmanship, fortitude, and wisdom in steering the country through the most dangerous confrontation in history, the President emerged with his credibility and prestige measurably enhanced."

"But to end the crisis," Rearden went on, "he made compromises and concessions that his military advisors considered in many ways unnecessary and excessive. . . . The consensus on the Joint Staff was the United States had come out on the poorer end of the bargain."

Angleton believed JFK's concessions had not only fumbled an opportunity to liberate Cuba; they also signaled a fatal compromise of U.S. policy with regard to containing communism.

"There was first Kennedy's unmistakable faltering of will at the Bay of Pigs," Angleton said, "and, then, a year and a half later, his reluctance to make good the showdown and exact fair price in the missile crisis by forcing Castro's expulsion from Cuba for having conspired with the Kremlin to bring Soviet nuclear power into the Western Hemisphere."[173]

For Angleton, his wife's analogy of JFK to Hamlet was apt. Like the Danish prince, the American president was intelligent, self-absorbed, and indecisive. He lacked will, and the United States was weaker for it.

Origins

TOP: James Angleton grew up in a modest house in Boise, Idaho. *(Google Maps)*

CENTER: Angleton enrolled at Yale in 1937 and graduated in 1941. *(Manuscripts & Archives, Yale University)*

While attending Harvard Law School, he met his future wife, Cicely D'Autremont, Vassar Class of 1944. *(Vassar Yearbook 1944)*

BOTTOM: His family prospered when his father launched a business in Italy and they moved into a grand building in Milan. *(Giovann Dall'Orto)*

Education

TOP LEFT: He helped launch a literary magazine called *Furioso*. *(Beinecke Rare Book and Manuscript Library, Yale University)*

MIDDLE LEFT: As coeditor of *Furioso*, Angleton befriended the poet Ezra Pound and other famous writers. *(Carl Mydans/The LIFE Picture Collection/Getty Images)*

MIDDLE RIGHT: *(Manuscripts & Archives, Yale University)*

BOTTOM: Angleton (back row, second from right) pursued his interests in poetry on the staff of the *Yale Literary Magazine*. (Board of Editors of the *Yale Literary Magazine: Yale Banner. Manuscripts & Archives, Yale University.*)

Rome

TOP LEFT: Relaxing with an OSS and future CIA colleague, Win Scott. *(Michael Scott)*

TOP RIGHT: Angleton recruited fascist Eugen Dollman as a source. Dollman was a translator, seen here with Germany's Adolf Hitler and Italy's Galeazzo Ciano. *(Photo by Heinrich Hoffmann/ullstein bild via Getty Images)*

BOTTOM LEFT: After joining the Office of Strategic Services, Angleton was sent to Rome where he worked out of an office on the Via Sicilia. *(Google Maps)*

BOTTOM RIGHT: Angleton also saved the life of Prince Valerio Borghese, a leading fascist military commander. *(Mondodori Portfolio / Getty Images)*

Washington

TOP LEFT: In 1949, Jim and Cicely Angleton bought a house in Arlington, Virginia. *(private source with permission)*

CENTER LEFT: *(National Security Archive)*

TOP RIGHT: As a top official in the newly created CIA, Angleton grew close to Kim Philby, the senior British intelligence officer in the capital. *(Keystone Pictures USA/Alamy Stock Photo)*

BOTTOM LEFT: Philby was a KGB spy and so was his housemate, the openly gay Guy Burgess. *(PA Images/Alamy Stock Photo)*

BOTTOM RIGHT: When Carmel Offie, a CIA colleague, was accused of being homosexual, Angleton offered him a job. *(John Phillips/The LIFE Picture Collection/Getty Images)*

CIA

TOP LEFT: In the 1950s, Angleton was personally close to CIA director Allen Dulles and social friends with Senator John F. Kennedy. *(AP Photo/WCC)*

TOP RIGHT: In 1961, the Agency moved into its new headquarters in Langley, Virginia. *(Bettman/Getty)*

MIDDLE LEFT: Among Angleton's closest friends were Cord Meyer, also a top CIA official, and his ex-wife Mary. *(Alfred Eisenstaedt/The LIFE Picture Collection/Getty)*

MIDDLE RIGHT: Mary had an affair with JFK starting in 1961. After she was murdered in 1964, her diary was delivered to Angleton. *(Robert Knudsen, White House/John F. Kennedy Presidential Library and Museum, Boston)*

BOTTOM: In 1967, Angleton helped his friend Richard Helms, CIA director from 1966-1973, win the confidence of President Lyndon Johnson. *(Everett Collection Historical / Alamy Stock Photo)*

END OF MESSAGE

WH CMT: "According to LIENVOY 1 Oct, an American male who spoke broken Russian said his name Lee Oswald (phonetic) stated he at Sov Emb on 28 Sept when spoke with Consul. He discussed sending a telegram to Washington. No local Dissemination had been made.

Oswald

TOP LEFT: In the summer of 1963 ex-Marine Lee Oswald leafleted in support of Cuban president Fidel Castro, then went to Mexico City where he contacted the Cuban and Soviet embassies. Angleton's staff was notified.

LEFT: On October 10, 1963, five of his subordinates, shown below, drafted and approved a cable about Oswald. Six weeks later, Oswald allegedly killed JFK.

THIRD ROW: Jane Roman *(Smith Yearbook 1936)*, Elizabeth Egerter *(Croton-on-Hudson News, Croton Historical Society)*, John Whitten (identified as "Scelso") *(Courtesy of the author)*

BOTTOM LEFT: Tom Karamessines *(Keystone USA via ZUMA)*

BOTTOM RIGHT: William J. Hood *(© Harvey Stein 2013)*

Israel:

TOP LEFT: Angleton forged friendships with top officers in the Israeli Mossad, including Efraim Halevy. *(private source with permission)*

LEFT: Meir Amit, Mossad chief in the 1960s. *(Pictorial parade / Staff / Getty Images)*

TOP RIGHT: Isser Harel, Mossad chief in the 1950s. *(Israeli Intelligence Heritage Center)*

LOWER LEFT: Israel's Dimona nuclear reactor. *(Reuters / Alamy Stock Photo)*

LOWER RIGHT: Tel Aviv station chief John Hadden concluded Israel stole fissile material for its nuclear arsenal from the United States. *(Courtesy of author)*

Fall

TOP LEFT: CIA director William Colby fired Angleton in December 1974. *(Keystone Pictures USA / Alamy Stock Photo)*

TOP RIGHT: With the approval of FBI director J. Edgar Hoover and President Richard Nixon, Angleton sought to expand domestic spying in America. *(SCU Archives/Everett Collection/ALAMY)*

LEFT: Accused mole Yuri Nosenko was later cleared by the CIA. *(private source with permission)*

BOTTOM LEFT: Former KGB officer Anatoly Golitsyn's accusations fueled Angleton's mole hunt. *(unknown source)*

BOTTOM RIGHT: Angleton's career ended on national TV in December 1974. *(Vanderbilt Television News Archive)*

PART III

IMPUNITY

KIM

"AN EVEN-HANDED ASSESSMENT OF Angleton's career would discern two distinct phases to it, although most of his detractors concentrate on the second," wrote CIA historian David Robarge. "From the late 1940s to the early 1960s, he and his staff provided a useful voice of caution in an Agency seized with piercing the Iron Curtain to learn about Soviet intentions and capabilities."

And then he lost his way.

"For roughly the next ten years, distracted by unsubstantiated theories of Soviet 'strategic deception,' Angleton and his staff embarked on counterproductive and sometimes harmful efforts to find moles and prove Moscow's malevolent designs," Robarge said.

In the Agency's institutional perspective, Angleton faltered at a time when U.S. intelligence was vulnerable.

"He was losing his sense of proportion and his ability to live with uncertainty right around the time, 1959–63, when it became startlingly evident—agents compromised, operations blown, spies uncovered—that something was seriously amiss with Western intelligence and more aggressive CI and security were needed."[1]

Angleton's disintegration was hastened by a cable from Beirut station that brought sickening news: Kim Philby had turned up in Moscow.

THE NEWS WAS ALMOST incomprehensible to Angleton. Philby had taught him the profession. They had worked together on Albania, Italy, Germany, and Ukraine. They had analyzed NSA material and studied KGB techniques. They remained friends after Philby's dismissal in June 1951. Angleton had believed Philby when he said he knew nothing of Burgess's and Maclean's spying. For a while, Jim had thought his friend would be cleared and would return to the top of SIS. Later on, he disbelieved Bill Harvey and J. Edgar Hoover, both of whom insisted Philby was a Red.

And when Angleton did have suspicions, Kim had allayed them.

After his expulsion from Washington in 1951, Philby retired from secret intelligence work to become a journalist, while taking on occasional missions for SIS. He moved to Beirut, where he wrote about politics and business for the *Economist* magazine. In 1957, Angleton had asked his colleague Miles Copeland, then working undercover as an oil company executive, to investigate. Copeland arranged for a senior official of the Lebanese security service to subject Philby to occasional spot surveillance. The policeman reported back that Philby habitually shook off anyone who was following him. But Philby wasn't meeting up with his KGB handler. He was sneaking off for a regular rendezvous with the wife of a friend. Angleton and Copeland were satisfied: Kim was a rogue, not a Red.[2]

What Angleton didn't know was that his British friends had reopened their investigation of Philby in 1962. New information received from recent defectors made it increasingly clear to the SIS that the Soviets had placed another spy in Washington between 1949 and 1951, someone other than Burgess and Maclean.

Nicholas Elliott, one of Philby's oldest friends, decided not to tell Angleton. He flew to Beirut to confront Philby.[3] The abashed Philby executed an artful maneuver, offering a partial confession that wove together the indisputable facts—he had tipped off Maclean with additional lies—that he had stopped spying for the Soviets after 1946. He agreed to meet Elliott again to explain further. Another lie.

On January 22, 1963, Philby skipped out on his wife and a dinner party. Four days later, he was at Moscow Center, headquarters of the KGB, where he received a warm reception from the comrades whom he had served for decades yet never met.

ANGLETON WAS CRUSHED. PHILBY was his friend, his mentor, his confidant, his boozy buddy. And through every meeting, conference, debriefing, confidential aside, and cocktail party, his friend had played him for a fool.

The news that Philby had fled to Moscow came as a "terrible shock," said Cicely Angleton.[4] The betrayal affected her husband "terribly, deeply," she said. "It was a bitter blow he never forgot."[5]

"I tried to repair the damage by telephoning Jim Angleton," said Nicholas Elliott, "but it was too late."[6]

Angleton had already heard. Philby's final flight was desolating. Angleton's faith in the goodness of his fellow man had never been strong. He had at least clung to the British notion that the inner ring of good men could always be trusted. No more.

"Poor old Jim Angleton," Elliott told John le Carré, the former SIS man turned novelist. "He'd made such a fuss of Philby when he was the head of the Service's station in Washington, and when Angleton found out—when I told him that is—he sort of went the other way."[7]

That was British understatement: *went the other way.*

"He had trusted him and confided in him far beyond any routine relationship between the colleagues of two friendly countries," Elliott said. "The knowledge that he, Jim, the top expert in the world on Soviet espionage, had been totally deceived had a cataclysmic effect on his personality. Jim henceforward found it difficult to trust anybody, to make two and two add up to four. Over-suspicion can sometimes have more tragic results than over-credulity. His tragedy was that he was so often deceived by his own ingenuity, and the consequences were often disastrous."[8]

"The uncovering of Philby as a mole was, without a doubt, one of the most important events in Jim's professional life," said Walter Elder, a senior CIA officer. "The affair had a deep and profound effect on Jim."[9]

Angleton suffered "severe psychic damage," said Cleveland Cram, a senior operations officer, who later wrote a top secret study of Angleton. "If Philby achieved nothing else in the Soviet service," said Cram, "he would have earned his keep by the peculiar thralldom he obtained over Angleton's thinking."[10]

BEREFT AND BETRAYED, ANGLETON sought certainty. He gravitated to the theories of Anatoly Golitsyn. The former KGB man lent credence to the suspicions Angleton had entertained since Popov's arrest and execution. Golitsyn's insider account of KGB deception operations was intellectually appealing, suggesting a historic continuity in Soviet intelligence since the 1920s. If one of his long-buried fears—about Philby—had been confirmed, Angleton concluded, not quite logically, that another long-buried fear—about the mole—must be true, as well.

Compounding Angleton's unease, Golitsyn had left the United States. After a second meeting with Robert Kennedy in December 1962, the former KGB man gave up on the U.S. government. The FBI didn't trust him. The CIA's Soviet Russia Division, led by George Kisevalter, was uninterested in his theories and unwilling to share their files.

In contrast, MI5, the British FBI, embraced him. In February 1963, Golitsyn and his wife and daughter moved to England, where he was greeted by Arthur Martin, chief of counterintelligence for MI5.[11] Golitsyn told his new hosts a disturbing story. Just before he left the Soviet Union in 1961, he had had contact with the KGB's Department Thirteen, responsible for assassinations, where he heard the KGB was planning to kill a high-level figure in Europe in order to get a Soviet asset into a top position.[12] The sudden death of Hugh Gaitskill, leader of the British Labour Party, in January 1963 was suspicious, he said. After a short illness, Gaitskill had died of a rare blood condition. Gaitskill, Golitsyn said, was poisoned by the KGB.[13]

Golitsyn pointed out that Gaitskill was pro-American, while his most likely successor as Labour Party leader, Harold Wilson, took a more independent and leftist position toward Washington. The assassination of Gaitskill, he said, delivered Wilson, Moscow's agent of influence, into a position of power. The British, spooked by Philby's defection, believed him. Angleton would later deny that he believed Gaitskill was assassinated, but he would come to express certainty that Wilson was a Soviet agent of influence, which he most certainly was not.

As Angleton lost perspective, he retained authority. As he repudiated uncertainty, he was entrusted with complexity. As his judgment failed, he won more responsibility. His convoluted certitudes, soaked in alcohol, would eventually bring him to the brink of being a fool. Christopher Andrew, a leading historian of Anglo-American intelligence, concluded Angleton's belief that the hostility between the Soviet Union and China was a KGB deception operation demonstrated that he did not have "the judgment required even of a junior intelligence officer."[14]

Yet men of power called on Angleton for assistance. In May 1963, for example, Angleton advised the Joint Chiefs of Staff on U.S. policy toward Cuba, which had been foundering since the October crisis. Declared U.S. policy still called for the immediate overthrow of Castro and his government. Angleton was asked to assess Cuba's defenses.

PROVOCATION

"THE CASTRO-COMMUNIST REGIME WILL remain in power for the indefinite future with its security and control apparatus relatively intact."[15]

That was Bill Harvey writing in a comprehensive memo on the state of the CIA's operations in Cuba one month after the October crisis. Harvey had gained prestige in the Agency for his tunnel into Communist East Berlin and other feats of derring-do. Dulles brought him into the Cuba operation when talk turned to assassinating Castro. Dick Helms put him in charge of the Cuba Task Force that the Kennedy brothers shut down. Now Harvey was on the way out for cursing Bob Kennedy, and he was blunt about the CIA's poor prospects.

Castro, he wrote, had "the capability not only of crushing unsupported resistance activity but of making operational conditions in Cuba increasingly difficult."

Harvey's memo, all seventeen single-spaced pages of it, arrived on Helms's desk on November 27, 1962. Helms forwarded it to Director McCone, who agreed with its principles.

Kennedy's government was fractured. The liberals in the White House assumed Harvey had been relieved of all Cuban responsibilities after his profane outburst at RFK during the missile crisis. Arthur Schlesinger said,

"The CIA, taking care of its own, made Harvey station chief in Rome, where he was soon sodden with drink."[16]

Not that soon. In his memo, Harvey soberly explained to Helms and McCone how Kennedy's handling of the missile crisis undermined the CIA's ability to operate on the island.

"The assurance of no invasion and no support of an invasion will, in effect, constitute giving to Castro and his regime a certain degree of sanctuary," he wrote.[17]

Angleton agreed. He thought Harvey had been mistreated by Bob Kennedy. He thought U.S. policy toward Cuba was adrift, if not feckless. And he thought the Rome station was a worthy reward for Harvey's service.

"I got him the job," Angleton boasted.[18]

IN MID-1963, ANGLETON MADE his most ambitious contribution to U.S. policy toward Cuba, a secret working paper entitled "Cuban Control and Action Capabilities."

For the CIA men and other advocates of overthrowing Castro, the spring of 1963 was disheartening. In late March, Attorney General Robert Kennedy ordered the FBI to crack down on Cuban exiles who were using South Florida to stage armed attacks on ships doing business with the Communist regime. Two dozen militants were ordered not to leave metropolitan Miami without permission. The Cuban colony exploded in outrage. The Cuban Revolutionary Council, the umbrella organization of exile groups that planned to establish a new pro-American government in Havana, dissolved in acrimonious denunciation of President Kennedy. The national security agencies in Washington were concerned. Castro was getting stronger. The Communists were solidifying their foothold in the western hemisphere, while Kennedy was pursuing a nuclear test ban treaty with the Soviets that the Joint Chiefs of Staff thought was ill advised.

The situation was urgent. In a meeting on May 1, 1963, the Joint Chiefs resurrected a secret plan known by the deceptively bucolic code name of NORTHWOODS. The NORTHWOODS plan, first developed after the Bay of Pigs, sought to create a justification, a pretext, for a U.S. invasion of Cuba. Since Castro could no longer be overthrown from within (thanks to Kennedy's weakness), the only solution was to remove him from without. The idea was to orchestrate a crime that placed the U.S. government "in the apparent position of suffering defensible grievances from a rash and irresponsible government in Havana." Then the president could declare war and send in the Eighty-second Airborne Division.

One NORTHWOODS scenario envisioned the use of violence on the streets of America.

"We could develop a Communist Cuban terror campaign in the Miami area, in other Florida cities, and even in Washington. . . . The terror campaign could be pointed at Cuban refugees seeking haven in the United States. We could sink a boatload of Cubans en route to Florida (real or simulated)."[19]

That merciless parenthetical makes it clear that the Pentagon's planners were willing to kill innocent persons who opposed Castro and to blame their deaths on the Cuban leader in order to justify a U.S. invasion.

Kennedy wasn't interested in so-called pretext operations. When Lyman Lemnitzer had first presented the NORTHWOODS concept at a White House meeting in March 1962, JFK had brusquely rejected it.[20]

With Castro emboldened in the spring of 1963, the Joint Chiefs revived the NORTHWOODS option. They recommended an "engineered provocation," which would provide advantages in "control, timing, simplicity, and security." The chiefs passed their recommendation to Secretary of Defense Robert McNamara, who ignored it. The Kennedy White House preferred the idea of "autonomous operations" against Castro. The result was that, after May 1, 1963, the U.S. government effectively had two divergent Cuba policies.

The White House policy, led by Robert Kennedy, sought to foment a rebellion against the Cuban government, possibly in conjunction with the assassination of Castro. The Defense Department, the armed forces, and the CIA had a different approach: They sought to create or find a pretext for a fullblown U.S. invasion, possibly in conjunction with the assassination of Castro.

With U.S. policy in flux, Angleton offered clarity. Under the counterintelligence responsibilities entrusted to him, he contributed his assessment of the Cuban target: What were Cuba's capabilities? What would the U.S. military have to overcome in order to retake Cuba from the Communists?

Could Castro be overthrown from within, as the Kennedy brothers assumed?

Angleton studied the files and wrote up his findings in a twenty-seven-page paper. On May 23, 1963, he distributed the document to the Joint Chiefs of Staff and heads of fifteen other U.S. agencies. The paper, he stated in his cover letter, was not "merely a provisional statement on the Cuban situation" but an all-source assessment of the Communist control system. Angleton intended his paper to serve as nothing less than the foundation of a new national policy.

The distribution of his "Cuban Control and Action Capabilities" paper illuminated more than Angleton's high standing in the U.S. intelligence community. It also revealed the alienation of the Kennedy White House and U.S. national security agencies in mid-1963. Angleton sent his analysis to the Pentagon, the CIA, and NSA, as well as to the intelligence chiefs of the State Department, army, navy, and air force. He also copied domestic security agencies such as the Customs Service, the Immigration and Naturalization Service, and the Justice Department's Interdepartmental Committee on Internal Security.

Angleton chose not to send his assessment to the White House, the National Security Council, or the attorney general, who styled himself the leader of his brother's Cuba policy.

The "Cuban Capabilities" memo is one of the most important documents bearing Angleton's name to ever surface. It confirms his leading role in U.S.-Cuba policy in 1963 while also demonstrating his intellectual power. Angleton's analysis of the strengths of Castro's government was lucid, historical, and comprehensive.

"Before the events of late October 1962," he began, "the Cuban government had been engaged for a little over two years on measures to insure a complete control over the Cuban population under a centralized authority resting largely in the hands of the prime minister, Fidel Castro, and his immediate coterie."[21]

Angleton's analysis echoed Bill Harvey's: President Kennedy's no-invasion pledge had demoralized Castro's foes.

"After the promise of outside interference was dispelled," Angleton wrote, "greater caution in expression of sentiments appeared. The disappointment in cancellation of action also caused the withdrawal of many persons from any show of support for anti-government ideas or actions and produced an attitude of reserve and mistrust."[22]

Castro had emerged from the October crisis with up to 400,000 men and women now serving in the army and navy. Another bulwark of support for the Communist regime, Angleton noted, were foreign friendship societies like the Fair Play for Cuba Committee, which sent sympathizers to the island who came back indoctrinated with pro-Communist messages. Angleton had reviewed multiple reports of travelers who wished to conceal their visits to Cuba.[23]

"An American citizen, for example," he explained "can enter Mexico with a tourist card, not even a passport, and *obtain a separate visa to Cuba from the Cuban consulate in Mexico City* [emphasis added]. He can go to Cuba and return supplied with a new tourist card obtained in Cuba without any indication that he has ever been there."[24]

Angleton was prescient. That is exactly what the defector Lee Oswald would attempt to do four months later. Thus Angleton's Cuban Capabilities memo is also an important document related to the assassination of President Kennedy. The paper reveals Angleton's personal interest in the Cuban consulate in Mexico City in mid-1963. It illuminates a fact that Angleton would hide for the rest of his life. When the defector Lee Oswald showed up at the Cuban consulate in September 1963, Angleton was not surprised or uninformed. He was prepared.

"GO EASY"

ON A JUNE NIGHT in 1963, four FBI agents sat in a car outside the lone terminal of National Airport in Washington, D.C. They were watching for the arrival of an old friend, Johnny Rosselli, incoming from Los Angeles. Rosselli was a mobster who cultivated attention. He wore silk suits and dated pop singers and Hollywood actresses. Skimming the take from casinos in Las Vegas was one of his specialties. Killing competitors was another. He was suspected of involvement in thirteen murders. The FBI men wanted to take him down.

Rosselli knew he was being tailed by the FBI and pretended not to care. If the feds crowded him too much, he could say, truthfully, that he had friends in high places. When the FBI men saw him get into a waiting car, driven by Bill Harvey of the CIA, they were irked. Why was a senior government official meeting socially with an organized crime figure? One of them called their liaison to the Agency, Sam Papich, who just so happened to be having dinner with Jim Angleton at his house in Arlington.

Papich took the call and then told Angleton.

"Look, let's go very easy on this," Angleton said.[25]

With practiced dexterity, Angleton called Harvey's house and spoke to his wife, Clara Grace Harvey, known as "C.G." She said Bill was at Duke Zeibert's, the plush restaurant on L Street that had succeeded Harvey's Seafood Grill as the restaurant for people who wanted to be seen. Angleton dialed up the restaurant and was put through to the table where Harvey sat with Rosselli. There were murmured exchanges. Papich called off the FBI surveillance team.

The FBI felt obliged to report Harvey's contact with a known crime figure to their bosses; Angleton did not.[26] He was under no illusions about what the two men were discussing. As recently as March 1963, Harvey was still in charge of the Agency's ZR-RIFLE assassination program.[27] "I knew he was not a frivolous man," Angleton said.[28] He did not have to guess that assassination was on the menu at Duke Zeibert's that night.

ANGLETON WAS THINKING ABOUT assassination himself. In July 1963, he asked the wizards of the Agency's Technical Services Division if they could hypnotize an assassin to kill a certain Cuban leader.

"Castro was naturally our discussion point," said a CIA officer who worked on the MKULTRA program under Angleton's direction. The challenge was, "Could you get somebody gung-ho enough that they would go in and get him?"[29]

Angleton's people set up an experiment in Mexico City. They tried to hypnotize a Mexican agent, and failed utterly.

Angleton saw no harm in experimenting. Hypnotizing an assassin to kill Castro wasn't irrational or immoral or even crazy to his way of thinking. It was the applied science of counterintelligence in service of defeating communism. It was necessary.

AT FORTY-FIVE YEARS OF age, Angleton was impressive and ominous. Most nights, he worked late at his office. He sat behind the raised desk stacked with files. As always, he kept the room dim, with just one desk lamp spotlighting his work. "The only lights came from the tip of Angleton's inevitable cigarette," wrote biographer Tom Mangold, "glowing like a tiny star in the dark firmament of his private planet, and the dirty brown sun of his desk lamp, permanently wreathed by nicotine clouds."[30]

One awestruck FBI man saw him as a wraith: "His hair was slicked back from a pale forehead, a bony blade of nose, sunken cheeks, and an elegantly pointed chin—a chiseled, cadaverous face. His deep set eyes were emphasized by arched brows, framed by horn-rimmed bifocals and lit with controlled fire. He was stooped and slightly twisted."[31]

He was "very British in cut and manner," said Joseph Persico, a historian of espionage, who saw his face close-up in an interview.

"A collection of angles. . . . Clearly impatient with stupidity. Tall and cadaverous . . . the most sinister man I have ever seen."[32]

MOLE HUNTS

ANGLETON WAS NOW ACTING out his intellectual passion on a grand scale. Even if his hand remained hidden, his decisions made headlines. One appeared atop the front page of London's *Daily Telegraph* in July 1963:

SOVIET DEFECTOR
GETS BRITISH ASYLUM
Major Defection,
Say Americans[33]

Anatoly Golitsyn, living in a cozy MI5 safe house in the British country-side, read the headline with dread. He was comfortable, to say the least, receiving a stipend of ten thousand pounds a month from the British officials intrigued by his theory that Hugh Gaitskill had been assassinated by the KGB.[34] Now someone had leaked his presence.

The *Telegraph,* citing "unimpeachable U.S. sources," reported that the British intelligence service had given asylum to "a major Soviet defector." *The New York Times* reported the leak might have come from "Benjamin Bradlee, chief of *Newsweek* magazine's Washington bureau and a friend of the president."[35] Ultimately, the leak would be traced back to Langley.

"Angleton wanted Golitsyn back," says Robarge, the CIA historian, "and may have contrived (through a leak to a British tabloid) to force him out of England."[36]

Golitsyn felt he had little choice but to return to the United States.

Questions about Golitsyn's reliability returned with him. A CIA evaluation in September 1963 reported Golitsyn was "dangling before the Agency very enticing and intriguing statements in exchange for acceptance, entrée, support and control. On the face of these statements [about Hugh] Gaitskill and [Harold] Wilson they are far removed from reality but are accusations which, if true, would be a great significance."

Golitsyn's statements, the doctor concluded, were evidence of "his feeling of omnipotence and omniscience, which is viewed as abnormal psychologically."[37]

Angleton dismissed the diagnosis. He thought Golitsyn the sanest man in the world. The notion that he might be considered mentally ill "would set off the greatest peals of glee in the KGB," he said.[38]

ANGLETON WANTED—NO, NEEDED—to believe. He was undaunted by the paucity of evidence to support Golitsyn's theories. In the spring of 1963, the FBI investigation of Peter Karlow had found nothing to confirm that he was Golitsyn's Sasha, the putative mole. Karlow, after waiting on administrative leave for more than a year, was still hoping to become chief of the Technical Services Division.[39] In September 1963, he was forced to resign, the first victim of Angleton's mole hunts, but not the last.[40]

Golitsyn had settled in upstate New York, where Angleton brought him raw source reports and classified CIA files, which was illegal and operationally reckless. Angleton didn't care.[41]

"Golitsyn was so enormous to the Western world," Angleton gushed after his return in the summer of 1963. "We immediately moved on those cases which were perishable," he said: "the French, the British, and ourselves."[42]

SO BEGAN THE DISASTROUS "mole hunt" that would paralyze and divide the CIA for the next seven years. Angleton's mole hunt is often described in singular terms, as a unified search for the spy (or spies) lurking in the ranks of the Agency. Operationally, however, Angleton's mole hunt was multifaceted, consisting of dozens of different mole hunts—some targeting individuals, others focused on components within the CIA—and always employing a variety of investigative techniques.

Angleton's first mole hunt focused on the British intelligence services. Golitsyn said his study of British files indicated Graham Mitchell, deputy to MI5 chief Roger Hollis, was a KGB spy. Angleton's British acolytes endorsed the charge. In September 1963, Hollis himself flew to Washington with the embarrassing mission of reporting to the Americans that his own aide was under investigation. Mitchell, it was later determined, was never a Soviet spy.[43]

The second mole hunt targeted the French intelligence service, SDECE, which Angleton believed, with more reason, had been penetrated by the KGB.[44] Indignant French officials demanded a meeting to respond to Angleton's charges, which were supported by Philippe Thyraud de Vosjoli, a disaffected French counterintelligence officer.[45] Angleton agreed to see Col. Georges de Lannurien, chief of French counterintelligence, in late November.

Angleton's third mole hunt in 1963 targeted the CIA's station in Mexico City, and it involved the defector Lee Oswald. It, too, ended badly.

OSWALD AGAIN

ANGLETON'S PEOPLE HAD NOT forgotten about or lost track of Lee Oswald since his defection in October 1959. In the offices of the Special Investigations Group, located around the corner from Angleton's suite, Betty Egerter still controlled access to Oswald's 201 file.

All U.S. government reporting on Oswald went into the SIG file—a 1961 State Department cable on Oswald's marriage to a Russian woman, a 1962 navy memo about his return to the United States, an FBI interview with a surly and uncooperative Oswald outside his home in Fort Worth, Texas, in August 1962.[46] If Oswald was a "lone nut," as cliché would later have it, he was the rare isolated sociopath of interest to the CIA's Counterintelligence Staff.

The attention was justified. If there was anything more important to the CIA than a defector to the Soviet Union, it was a returning defector like Oswald, who had presumptively been contacted by the KGB and Soviet domestic security agency, the MVD, during his two years of residence. Oswald's redefection should have been "the highest priority for the intelligence community," Angleton later told investigators.[47]

It was. Angleton paid attention when J. Edgar Hoover sent him three more reports on Oswald in the fall of 1963.

The first, an FBI memo from Dallas, arrived on September 24; Jane Roman signed the routing slip to accept delivery. FBI agent James Hosty had been assigned to keep tabs on Oswald's wife, Marina. Hosty reported that Oswald "drank to excess and beat his wife" and had once passed out leaflets for the Fair Play for Cuba Committee. He helpfully attached material on the un-American ways of the FPCC.[48]

Two weeks later, Roman signed for another FBI report. Oswald had been arrested in August while passing out FPCC leaflets on a New Orleans street corner. The ex-marine had gotten into a heated argument with three members of an anti-Castro organization called the Cuban Student Directorate; he was arrested for disturbing the peace.[49]

Angleton was certainly interested in the Fair Play for Cuba Committee, which Oswald now purported to represent. It was one of those friendship societies that sustained the Havana regime. It was also a target for Agency action, as Angleton probably knew. As liaison to the FBI, Angleton was privy to all CIA communications with the Bureau. On September 16, John Tilton, an officer in the CIA's Cuba operation, told Sam Papich that the Agency was "giving some consideration to countering the activities" of the FPCC in a foreign country.[50] Given Angleton's reputation and stature, it would have been unusual, if not unthinkable, for Tilton's branch to mount an operation against the FPCC without Angleton's knowledge.

Naturally, Jane Roman paid attention when another report on Oswald came clattering in by Teletype on Tuesday afternoon, October 8. From Mexico City, station chief Win Scott reported that a man calling himself Oswald had contacted a consular officer at the Soviet embassy.[51] In another cable, Scott reported that Oswald had also visited the Cuban embassy in Mexico City, where the consulate was located.[52]

Oswald's visit was Angleton's responsibility. Scott's cable was slugged LCIMPROVE, the Agency's code name for "counter-espionage involving Soviet intelligence services worldwide," Angleton's undisputed domain.[53]

Angleton responded with discretion. Jane Roman drafted and sent a cable to the FBI, the navy, and the State Department, reporting that Oswald, wrongly described as a six-foot-tall, heavyset man, had been seen in Mexico City. Then she and Betty Egerter drafted a separate and different cable to Win Scott, which they then gave to Bill Hood, chief of operations in the western hemisphere, for approval.

The second cable, sent on October 10, provided the Mexico City station with biographical information about Oswald, as well as a more accurate physical description. The cable, also approved by Tom Karamessines, said nothing about Oswald's recent arrest in New Orleans and his pro-Castro activities on behalf of the FPCC.

With the three FBI reports in hand, Angleton's people could have described Oswald to Scott as a law-breaking Communist and sometimes violent supporter of Castro. Instead, the October 10 cable was oddly reassuring.

Citing a May 1962 State Department cable, headquarters said "twenty months of life in Soviet Union have had a maturing effect on Oswald."

The Agency had not received any new information on Oswald since, according to the second cable drafted by Angleton's aides.

> LATEST HDQS INFO WAS ODACID [State Department] REPORT DATED MAY 1962 SAYING OSWALD IS STILL US CITIZEN AND BOTH HE AND HIS SOVIET WIFE HAVE EXIT PERMITS AND DEPT STATE HAD GIVEN APPROVAL FOR THEIR TRAVEL WITH THEIR INFANT CHILD TO USA.[54]

If the October 10 cable was to be believed—and Win Scott believed it—the CIA had gathered no information about the "maturing" Oswald since his return from the Soviet Union seventeen months before. In fact, the CIA knew all about his latest doings.

The cable was intentionally deceptive, as Jane Roman would later admit. When shown a copy of the cable many years later, she said, "Yeah, I mean, I'm signing off on something I know isn't true."[55]

In retirement, Bill Hood had no explanation for why the CIA didn't share the most recent FBI reporting on Oswald with Mexico City, save that he didn't think it was "smelly."

"I don't see any master hand in it," he said.[56]

If there was a master hand, it was Angleton's. The CIA's "latest headquarters information" on Oswald was not seventeen months old. It was less than two weeks old. Angleton's staff had received virtually all of the FBI's reporting on Oswald and shared none of it. In the parlance of CIA operations, Angleton's omission was justifiable: If Oswald's activities were part of an authorized covert operation, Win Scott had no "need to know" that Angleton was using Oswald for an intelligence purpose.

The time stamp on the cable dates Angleton's deception with precision: 10 Oct. 1963, 5:29 P.M. Washington time.[57]

At that moment, President John F. Kennedy was finishing up a busy day in the Oval Office. He had spent the morning meeting with his national security advisers about the deteriorating situation in Vietnam. He ended the day conferring with two leaders of newly independent African nations.[58]

He had forty-two days to live.

WITHIN A WEEK OF Oswald's visit to Mexico City, Angleton launched the mole hunt in Mexico. This mole hunt underscores a reality overlooked by Angleton's admirers and critics alike: Angleton's mole hunting extended beyond the Agency's Soviet Russia Division.

In the fall of 1963, the CIA's Mexico City station was mounting multiple operations to recruit spies in the Cuban consulate and to disrupt the embassy's political activities.[59] These efforts were led by David Phillips, a protégé of Dick Helms. They were reported to Bill Harvey, who was still involved in Cuban operations from the Rome station. Win Scott boasted of the thoroughness of his coverage of the Cuban compound, which housed the embassy and the consulate.

"We intercept their mail, photograph all people who go in and out of the Embassy, cover their telephones completely, and within a few hours of the conversations have resumes of all the telephone calls," he said in early 1963.[60]

Angleton worried that these operations might be compromised by an FBI informant who was actually a Soviet double agent. He wanted to determine if the KGB had any spies in the Mexico City station. The mole hunt in Mexico began on October 8, 1963, when a team of technicians from the Office of Security flew to the Mexican capital, their luggage bulging with tape recorders and polygraph equipment. They were acting on orders from Bill Hood, chief of western hemisphere operations and Angleton's longtime friend.[61]

Between October 8 and 18, the Office of Security team grilled twenty-one CIA employees in Mexico about their loyalties. The mission was to discover if anyone "has been or is now reporting to or employed by another intelligence organization (including local police)."[62] The employees were hooked up to the polygraph machine used to detect physical stress. In CIA lingo, they were "fluttered."

The first employees questioned were the three men who watched the

Soviet and Cuban diplomatic offices in Mexico City—the very offices that the defector Oswald had visited ten days before. Whether they were asked about Oswald is unknown.[63] By early November, the interrogation team had written up reports on them and eighteen other CIA employees in Mexico City and Monterrey.

The mole hunt in Mexico found some financial irregularities and some loose talk among family members, but no security breaches.[64] As far as the Office of Security and the Counterintelligence Staff were concerned, there was no mole in the Mexico City station.

ALL THE WHILE, LEE Oswald remained a figure of continuing interest. Angleton received no further reports on Oswald's contacts with Soviet or Cuban intelligence officers, at least none that we know of. He received no indication that Oswald had obtained the visa that he sought to travel to Cuba and the Soviet Union. But he remained concerned about Oswald's visit to the Cuban consulate.

In his May 1963 memo to the Joint Chiefs, Angleton identified the consulate as a locus of Cuban intelligence activity in the western hemisphere. From the latest FBI reports, he knew of Oswald's involvement with the Fair Play for Cuba Committee. If Sam Papich knew the CIA operatives had targeted the FPCC for COINTELPRO-style dirty tricks, Angleton surely knew it. For all of these reasons and more, Angleton had to be concerned about Oswald's Cuban contacts in Mexico City. But he did not care to share his concern. He would conceal what he knew about that sensitive subject for the rest of his life.

On November 15, Jane Roman signed for the latest FBI report on Oswald. From New Orleans, senior agent Warren de Breuys had filed a more detailed memo on Oswald's pro-Castro activities. If Angleton scanned the first page, he learned that Oswald had gone back to Texas after contacting the Cubans and the Soviets in Mexico City. Angleton knew Oswald was in Dallas.

Angleton always sought to give the impression that he knew very little about Oswald before November 22, 1963. For the chief of the Agency's counterintelligence staff, that was a frail defense. His staff had monitored

Oswald's movements for four years. As the former marine moved from Moscow to Minsk to Fort Worth to New Orleans to Mexico City to Dallas, the Special Investigations Group received reports on him everywhere he went.

An epic counterintelligence failure culminated on Angleton's watch. It was bigger than the Philby affair and bloodier.

DALLAS

"YOU COULD HEAR THE parade coming down Main Street," recalled Bill Newman. "You could hear the cheering of the people and I could remember seeing the president's car turn right onto Houston Street and go that short block and turn left on Elm. His car was out the width of one lane from the curb. He was not right against the curb. . . . We were, of course, looking at the car coming towards us and it was a hundred feet, or more maybe, from us, and the first two shots rang out. Kind of like a boom . . . boom, like that. At the time I thought somebody threw a couple of firecrackers beside the car, and I thought, you know, That's a pretty poor trick to be pulling on the president."[65]

Bill Newman was twenty-two years old, a plumber's apprentice. He had come to Dealey Plaza with his wife, Gayle, and their two children. They were excited to see the president and the First Lady coming down Elm Street: JFK and Jackie sitting side by side, waving.

"But as the car got closer to us," Newman went on, "you could see the blood on Governor Connally; you could see the president. He had a . . . he was sort of turning his head in toward the crowd, and you could tell something was most definitely wrong. Just as the car got straight in front of us, in the backseat of the car where he was sitting, ten or twelve feet from us . . . the third shot rang out."

Newman spoke with a steady, well-modulated voice forty-plus years later. His account had not changed since the day it happened, when he told the story to a TV reporter. Now retired from the plumbing business, he and Gayle had nine grandchildren. Newman could still see the nightmare unfolding.

"Of course, I knew most definitely that was a gunshot," he said, "and the side of his head blew off. You could see the white matter and the red and he fell across the seat over into Mrs. Kennedy's lap, and she hollered out, 'Oh my God no, they've shot Jack,' and I turned to Gayle. I said, 'No, that's it,' and I hit the ground, because at that moment, what was going through my mind was that shot was coming right over the top of our heads."

That shot was coming right over the top of our heads.

As Bill and Gayle Newman and their kids lay on the grass, the crowd around them roiled in panic at the sound of gunfire.

Dallas police chief Jesse Curry was riding in the lead car of the motorcade. When he heard the shots, he shouted into his radio, "Get a man on top of that triple underpass," the area above and behind the Newmans, "and see what happened up there."[66] What Curry meant to say, he later told the Warren Commission, was "Get someone up in the railroad yard and check."[67] He was talking about the place that would come to be known as the "grassy knoll."

As the motorcade careened away toward the Stemmons Freeway, the shocked crowd looked to the upper floors of the Texas Schoolbook Depository, from which some of the shots had sounded.

The fifth car behind President Kennedy's limousine was the press car. It carried four men: Malcolm Kilduff, Kennedy's acting press secretary; Merriman Smith, the White House correspondent for United Press International; and two other wire-service reporters. The hard-drinking Smith had shaken his daily hangover, straightened his tie, and was paying close attention. No sooner had he heard the report of multiple gunshots than he glimpsed the crowd's freeze-frame reactions: a man sitting on the curb . . . a couple and their kids sprawled on the grass . . . some colored kids running away . . . a lady wearing a babushka . . . a man with an umbrella . . . a motorcycle cop abandoning his Harley-Davidson and running up a grassy embankment.

Nine minutes later at a pay phone in Parkland Hospital, Smith dictated to his editor the details of what he had seen. Shots had been fired at President Kennedy.

"Some of the Secret Service agents thought the gunfire was from an automatic weapon fired to the right rear of the president's car, probably from a grassy knoll to which police rushed,"[68] Smith said.

He had coined a phrase that would never be forgotten: . . . *a grassy knoll to which police rushed.*

Scores of eyewitnesses were later interviewed by the FBI, the Dallas police, and reporters. By the most conservative reading, about 40 percent of them, some fifty people, including twenty-one law-enforcement officers, had the same experience as Bill Newman and Merriman Smith.[69] They believed a gunshot had come from in front of the motorcade, from the grassy knoll.

Bystanders converged on the spot and the parking lot by the railroad yard. Behind a stockade fence, they found a sea of cars, some cigarette butts, and footprints. If there had been a gunman hidden there, he was gone.

ROBERT KENNEDY WAS EATING a chicken-salad sandwich and talking Justice Department business with an aide at Hickory Hill when he received a phone call from J. Edgar Hoover, and then another call, confirming the president was dead.

Kennedy's world vanished. He called John McCone at CIA headquarters and told him to come over. The two men had become close over the last two years. Like Bob Kennedy, McCone was a practicing Catholic. They shared politics and personal tragedy. Bob and Ethel helped McCone when his wife succumbed to cancer. "There was almost nothing we could say to another," recalled McCone of that day.[70]

The two men went outside and strolled on the vast lawn of Hickory Hill. They talked about the president's enemies in the CIA and in Miami. Robert Kennedy would later tell Arthur Schlesinger about the conversation. "You know at the time I asked McCone . . . if they [meaning CIA-backed enemies] had killed my brother and I asked him in a way that he couldn't lie to me, and they hadn't."

When Kennedy and McCone returned to the house, the TV news reported that a suspect had been arrested in the shooting of the president, a defector named Oswald, a supporter of Castro, a leftist, a Communist.

———

AFTER LUNCH ON NOVEMBER 22, Angleton had just started his long-awaited confrontation with French intelligence officials over Golitsyn's allegations of penetration.[71] He was making his case to Colonel de Lannurien, the chief of SDECE, when someone came into the room to report that President Kennedy had been shot dead. The meeting was canceled.

Angleton hastened back to Langley. When the transistor radios around the CIA offices reported that a suspect named Oswald had been arrested, a senior analyst in the Counterintelligence Staff named Paul Hartman spoke up.

"You know, there's a 201 file on this [expletive]," he said, "and SIG has it."[72]

Indeed, the Special Investigations Group did have a file on Kennedy's accused killer. It was a pregnant moment for Angleton. He was responsible for tracking defectors. He had put Oswald's name on the LINGUAL mail-opening list in 1959. Jane Roman had signed for three FBI reports on Oswald in the last two months. His friend Bill Hood had signed off on the mole hunt in Mexico. He had called attention to the intelligence function of the Cuban Consulate in his Cuban Capabilities memo. Angleton would never speak publicly of such things.

Later that day, Angleton was called into a meeting in Dick Helms's office. The deputy director was worried that CIA personnel might be involved in the killing of JFK. "Make sure we had no one in Dallas," Helms told an aide when he heard the news that day.[73]

Helms wanted all of his top lieutenants in the same room. His deputy Tom Karamessines was there. So were Desmond FitzGerald, the chief of the anti-Castro operation, and John Whitten, chief of the Mexico desk. Helms gave orders: Angleton would handle liaison with the FBI. FitzGerald would review Oswald's Cuban contacts. Whitten would write up all incoming information in a summary report.

Whitten was well qualified for the assignment. A career officer who spoke excellent German, he had distinguished himself in several counter-espionage investigations in Europe.[74] Whitten spent the rest of the day collating reports. Late that night, he wrote up the Agency's first report on Kennedy's assassination, which Helms passed to John McCone. The director shared it with the new president, Lyndon Johnson, on the morning of November 23.

"As far as we could see," Whitten explained, "Oswald was the assassin and there was no indication that we had that there were other participants in the assassination, and there was no indication, visible indication, that he was a Soviet or Cuban agent, even though the possibility could not be excluded."[75]

MILLIONS OF PEOPLE IN the United States and around the world winced and wept. On a Hollywood back lot, costumed cowboys sat down on the job, heads bowed. In New York City, construction workers put hard hats to their hearts. In Harvard Square, a crowd rushed a newsstand for the latest news.[76] In Columbus, Mississippi, high school students cheered the death of the liberal president and a teacher ordered her class to sing "Dixie" in gratitude.[77]

People everywhere gathered around their televisions and radios, which amplified and spread the news from Dallas. The suspected assassin was a Communist. He had even defended Fidel Castro on a New Orleans radio station. NBC News played a tape recording of Oswald. The president hadn't been dead two hours, and tens of millions of Americans heard the voice of the suspected assassin defending "the principles of the Fair Play for Cuba Committee."[78]

Unbeknownst to the American people, the effort to link the accused assassin to the notorious FPCC emanated from CIA propaganda assets. The tape of Oswald's radio appearance had been made by a man named Edward Butler. He ran a right-wing organization called the Information Council of the Americas, which promoted an anti-Communist political agenda in Cuba and the Caribbean. Butler mixed with the FBI and CIA men working in New Orleans. When Oswald appeared as an FPCC spokesman, Butler taped his radio appearance as evidence of Communist perfidy. After JFK was dead, he was glad to share the tape with NBC News.

The linkage of Oswald to the FPCC was corroborated by the Agency's assets in Miami and New Orleans. Within hours of the announcement of JFK's death, the leaders of the Miami-based Cuban Student Directorate were calling reporters with details of their encounter with Oswald and his pro-Castro ways. The reporters they spoke to did not know the leaders of the directorate were paid by a CIA program with the code name of AMSPELL. The Cuban agents were run by George Joannides, chief of the Psychological Warfare branch of the WAVE station in Miami. He gave the directorate $51,000 a month. Within forty-eight hours, the CIA's favorite young Cubans published a news sheet declaring Oswald and Castro were "the Presumed Assassins." It was the first JFK conspiracy theory to reach public print. It was funded by Joannides, who was Dick Helms's man in Miami.

LATE ON THE NIGHT of November 22, Angleton received a call from the Secret Service. They had learned from the FBI that Oswald had visited Mexico City in October. What did the CIA know?

A lot, said Angleton. He shared several cables he had received from Win Scott. One concerned surveillance photographs of six unidentified visitors to the Cuban embassy in Mexico City. Another concerned a passenger manifest identifying three recent air travelers from Mexico City, one of whom might have been Oswald. Angleton passed this material to the Secret Service, on the condition that it not be shared with anyone.

The next day, Angleton shared more intelligence with the FBI. He handed Sam Papich six items about Oswald. They were letters intercepted by the LINGUAL mail-surveillance program. Three came from Oswald's mother. Angleton thought they were significant.

Two of the letters, he told Hoover in a memo, indicated Oswald was known to his wife's friends in the Soviet Union as "Alik." He noted that the FBI had already discovered that "a rifle of the same type used in the assassination" had been ordered in the name of "Alek Hidell" and delivered to a post office box registered in Oswald's name. Under the circumstances, Angleton told Hoover, "the fact Oswald was known to his Russian friends as 'Alik' may be significant."[79]

In Dallas, Oswald was in police custody and denying everything. He denied he had gone to Mexico City. He denied he had ordered the rifle found in the Texas School Book Depository. When brought before reporters, he denied shooting the president.

"I'm just a patsy," he shouted before he was led back to his cell.[80]

ANGLETON TOOK A CALL from Anatoly Golitsyn, who said that the Soviet government would have monitored any defector who, like Oswald, had served in the U.S. Army, Navy, or Marine Corps.

"The modus operandi with any defector from anybody's arm[ed forces] to the Soviet Union required that he go through processing by the Thirteenth Department of the KGB, their assassination department," Golitsyn said.[81]

Angleton had to suspect Moscow or Havana might be behind the crime in Dallas. Like the CIA-funded Cuban students, he was not averse to linking Oswald to Castro. On the panicky night of November 23, Helms's deputy Tom Karamessines sent Win Scott a message warning him not to take any actions that "could prejudice [U.S.] freedom of action on the entire question of [Cuban] responsibility."

Questioned about the event many years later, Angleton allowed that he had a "vague recollection" of Karamessines's order. "If Tom intervened it was for good reason . . . because he had superior information," Angleton said. He, too, wanted to preserve the U.S. "freedom of action" in the wake of JFK's death.

The CIA's gambit wasn't hard to figure. It was the NORTHWOODS concept: If the crime in Dallas could be blamed on Castro, the United States would have a justification for the overdue elimination of the Communist regime in Havana.

In the Cuban capital, Fidel Castro intuited the CIA's machinations. The Cuban leader was brooding aloud into a microphone. When he first heard the news from Dallas, Castro was worried. *"Malo noticias,"* he told a visitor. "Bad news."[82] Now he was speaking publicly about the killing of the American president. As a revolutionary, Castro said, he hated systems, not men. Yes, Kennedy had once sought to destroy his revolution. Since the October crisis, he had also shown moderation.

"¿Qué es tras el asesinato de Kennedy? ¿Cuáles fueron los motivos reales?" "What is behind the assassination of Kennedy? What were the real motives?" Castro asked.

"What forces, factors, circumstances were at work behind this sudden and unexpected event that occurred yesterday? . . . Even up to this moment, the events that led to the murder of the President of the United States continue to be confused, obscure and unclear."

He warned that Cuba would be blamed.

"We foresaw that from these incidents there could be a new trap, an ambush, a Machiavellian plot against our country," he declared. "That on the very blood of their assassinated president there might be unscrupulous people who would begin to work out immediately an aggressive policy against Cuba, if the aggressive policy had not been linked beforehand to the assassination . . . because it might or might not have been. But there is no doubt that this policy is being built on the still warm blood and unburied body of their tragically assassinated President."[83]

"DEAR MR. ATTORNEY GENERAL," wrote Dick Helms on his personal stationery on November 23. "There is nothing for me to say that has not been said better by many others.

"When you sent me to see the president on Tuesday afternoon, he never looked better, seemed more confident or appeared more in control of the crushing forces around him. Friday struck me personally."[84]

When Bob Kennedy read the letter, he put it aside, temporarily incapable of response. Helms was referring to a meeting just a few days before, in which Helms and RFK had urged the president to get tougher on Castro. Helms had brought a machine gun, supposedly captured from the Cubans, into the Oval Office to support his point. Jack had made a joke about the gun. Three days later, a pro-Castro gunman blew his head off in broad daylight—or so the CIA's propaganda assets wanted him to believe.

Grief overwhelmed Bob Kennedy's emotions as suspicion dominated his thoughts. A week later, he and Jackie sent a private message to Premier Khrushchev via their friend William Walton, a painter who was traveling to Moscow. The president's brother and widow wanted the Soviet leadership to know they did not believe press reports suggesting the Soviet Union was involved with Oswald. RFK and Jackie told the Soviets they believed that the president was killed by domestic opponents.[85]

Robert Kennedy knew Fidel Castro had not killed his brother. He knew the KGB wasn't involved. He could not be so sure about the CIA men or their allies in Miami and in the Mafia. And that was the punishing hell of it for Bob Kennedy: his naïveté. He had trusted the CIA. He had believed in their mission. And now that Jack was gone, he had their condolences.[86]

NOAH'S CLOAK

ANGLETON WOULD LATER SAY his instinct was to suspect a Communist conspiracy. The facts, which he knew before almost everybody, justified such an inference. Oswald was a former defector, a Marine Corps radio operator who had a security clearance. He was an open leftist. He affiliated himself with the FPCC, designated by executive order as a subversive organization, and targeted by the CIA and FBI for years. Oswald had visited the Cuban consulate in Mexico City, which Angleton had identified as a contact point for U.S.-based sympathizers. At the Soviet embassy, Oswald had met with a consular official named Vladimir Kostikov, who was known to Angleton. Just six months before, Hoover had asked Angleton if Kostikov was with the KGB's Department Thirteen, responsible for assassinations.[87] Angleton said no.

"Putting it baldly," said Pete Bagley, deputy chief of the Soviet Russia Division, "was Oswald, wittingly or unwittingly, part of a plot to murder President Kennedy in Dallas?"[88]

Angleton didn't contact Win Scott himself. He delegated the task, ordering that the surveillance records be checked. Who was Kostikov? Whom had he met with?

Within the day, the Mexico City station sent a list of all persons known to have been in touch with Kostikov in recent months. The Counterintelligence Staff then shared the list with Desmond FitzGerald, chief of the

Cuba operation. FitzGerald saw that Kostikov had been visited by a Cuban government official named Rolando Cubela, and he had a huge problem.

FitzGerald knew Cubela. He knew that Cubela was a moody doctor turned revolutionary *commandante* who thought Castro was ruining Cuba. The CIA had dubbed him AMLASH and recruited him as an assassin in 1961 and 1962. Just three weeks before, FitzGerald had traveled to Paris to meet with him personally. At the suggestion of Dick Helms, FitzGerald had presented himself as a representative of Bob Kennedy, even though he had not spoken with RFK about the matter. FitzGerald and Cubela had discussed their options in murder weapons.[89]

FitzGerald faced trouble, if not disgrace. If Cubela/AMLASH had met with Kostikov, maybe he had told him and the KGB about FitzGerald's recruitment pitch. Maybe Cubela had played him and the CIA for fools, enabling Castro to strike first in Dallas, using Oswald as his pawn.

Under the circumstances, FitzGerald didn't want to have anything to do with Angleton. He regarded Angleton as mentally unstable, drunken, and conspiratorial. He handed the list back without saying anything.[90]

"Des was usually very imperturbable, but he was very disturbed about his involvement" in the assassination business, recalled Walter Elder, aide to John McCone.

FitzGerald had fought in wars, led men toward the sound of gunfire, and he was scared about the forces behind the murder of the president. He stayed home that weekend, monitoring the constant TV news coverage from Dallas. On Sunday morning, he sat on the family couch with his wife and son. On the screen of the black-and-white television, Dallas policemen in their wide-brimmed hats escorted Oswald, the suspected assassin, to a waiting police wagon. A man stepped out of the crowd and stuck a pistol in Oswald's stomach. The screen spun into chaos. The accused assassin was dead.

FitzGerald's fears erupted into tears. It was the first and last time his wife and children saw him cry.

"Now we'll never know," he wept. "We'll never know."[91]

———

ANGLETON WAS NOT SO discomposed. He thought JFK's death a pity, not a tragedy. A couple of days later, he was at home when the phone rang. It was Allen Dulles calling. He said that President Johnson had asked him to serve on a blue-ribbon commission that would investigate the assassination. Dulles wanted to talk about the history of such commissions, and whether he should accept.

Angleton wasn't fooled.

"I could tell very easily that he wanted to be on it," Angleton recalled. "He was looking for approbation from me and not criticism. . . . He said he wanted tips on anything relevant to the Agency."[92]

Dulles wanted to steer the commission's investigation away from the CIA, and Angleton was obliging. A conspiracy theorist would say Angleton masterminded the JFK cover-up. A prosecutor would say he obstructed justice. A bureaucrat would say he covered his ass. In every practical sense, his actions were invisible. In the tragedy of Dallas, Angleton played a ghost.

"AMERICA IS IN DANGER of upheavals," said French president Charles de Gaulle after the death of JFK. De Gaulle had survived a rightist assassination attempt on the back roads of France the year before. He knew his way around an ambush—and American officialdom.

"But you'll see," he told an aide. "All of them together will observe the law of silence. They will close ranks. They'll do everything to stifle any scandal. They will throw Noah's cloak over these shameful deeds. In order to not lose face in front of the whole world. In order to not risk unleashing riots in the United States. In order to preserve the union and to avoid a new civil war. In order to not ask themselves questions. They don't want to know. They don't want to find out. They won't allow themselves to find out."[93]

One CIA man tried to find out, and he paid a price.

JOHN WHITTEN WAS A career civil servant, a GS-16 with supergrade status. His mistake was understandable. He assumed Angleton was interested in a serious counterintelligence investigation of President Kennedy's accused killer. He assumed wrong.

After November 22, Whitten worked eighteen-hour days, assisted by thirty officers from the Western Hemisphere Division, and another thirty clerical workers.[94] They compiled every report about Oswald from anywhere in the world. Much of it was rubbish, but it all had to be processed. Whitten then wrote up his findings and solicited comments from all the CIA offices involved. He incorporated their input. The secretaries retyped his drafts, and the process was repeated.

Angleton didn't share anything of what his office had learned about Oswald over the past four years. He didn't offer any evidence of KGB involvement. He didn't argue that Castro was behind Oswald. Instead, he tried to thwart Whitten.

"In the early stage Mr. Angleton was not able to influence the course of the investigation," Whitten testified in secret session years later. "He was extremely embittered that I was entrusted with the investigation and he wasn't."

Whitten persevered. Based on all the information received, he concluded that Oswald was an erratic man of leftist sympathies who was disturbed enough to shoot the president. Whitten knew that Oswald had been a person of interest to the Counterintelligence Staff before November 22. That did not trouble him. The Agency monitored thousands of people. That was the nature of its work.

Then Whitten found out there was a whole lot he had not been told about Oswald.

PUBLICLY, PRESIDENT JOHNSON CALLED on the nation to rally around the memory of its fallen leader. Privately, LBJ and J. Edgar Hoover made clear to their underlings that they wanted an investigation that showed that Oswald had acted alone and that no other parties were involved, foreign or domestic. The investigation had not yet begun, but the now-dead Oswald had already been judged the sole author of JFK's murder.

The Bureau's agents did their best to oblige their bosses. They compiled a report on the assassination, running to five volumes, and scheduled it for release on December 9, 1963. Whitten went to FBI headquarters to read an advance copy, accompanied by Birch O'Neal, chief of the Special Investigations Group, which had controlled Oswald's file since 1959.

The FBI report confirmed the story of a lone gunman who acted for no apparent reason. Oswald, the Bureau said, had grown up as "a peculiar boy" and become "a disaffected man." He had come to the attention of the Bureau due to his obnoxious left-wing political views, but he seemed to pose no threat.

All of which seemed plausible to Whitten, but some details begged for investigation. Oswald, for example, had written his political views in a "historical diary," according to the FBI. He had carried a card identifying himself as member of the pro-Castro Fair Play for Cuba Committee. He had been known as "Alik" in the Soviet Union, and he had ordered the murder weapons under the alias "Alek Hidell."

Whitten realized he had been deceived.

"Angleton might have received all this information," he testified. "But I did not."

Whitten complained to Helms. The deputy director called both men into his office on Christmas Eve, 1963. Whitten explained to Helms what he had learned from the FBI.

"My report is irrelevant in view of all the added information," he said. "This now takes [us] in an entirely different dimension."[95]

Whitten was both surprised and not surprised by the response of the counterintelligence chief.

"Angleton started to criticize my report terribly without pointing out any inaccuracies," he recalled. "It was so full of wrong things, we could not possibly send it to the Bureau, and I just sat there and I did not say a word. This was a typical Angleton performance. I had invited him to comment on the report, and he had withheld all of his comments until he got to the meeting."

Helms deferred to Angleton. The ambitious deputy director didn't want to make waves at the White House or the Bureau. His predecessors had lost their jobs over the Bay of Pigs. Helms did not intend to lose his job over Dallas.

"Helms wanted someone to conduct the investigation who was in bed with the FBI," Whitten maintained. "I was not, and Angleton was."[96]

Angleton's power had reached a peculiar apex. The ambush in Dallas on November 22 marked the worst failure of U.S. intelligence since December 7, 1941, when the Japanese attacked Pearl Harbor. It had happened on Angleton's watch. Yet such was his bureaucratic genius that he managed to wind up in charge of the Agency's investigation of the accused assassin. During Kennedy's presidency, his staff knew more about the obscure and unimportant Lee Oswald than just about anyone in the U.S. government. After the president was dead, he orchestrated the cover-up of what the CIA knew. Angleton intuited the devastated mood of the men and women who ran the U.S. government in late 1963. *They don't want to know. They don't want to find out. They won't allow themselves to find out.*

LOATHING

"**I AM AFRAID TO** sleep for fear of what I might learn when I wake up," wrote journalist Hunter S. Thompson to a friend on the night of November 22, 1963. Thompson was living in a remote mountain town in Colorado. The shock and rage induced by the murder of President Kennedy inspired Thompson to coin the term that would become his signature: "fear and loathing."

"I was not prepared at this time for the death of hope, but here it is," he wrote. "Ignore it at your peril. This is the end of reason, the dirtiest hour in our time."[97]

Whatever Angleton's reaction to the murder of the thirty-fifth president, allegedly by a pro-Castro defector, he did not commit his thoughts to paper. Remarkably, the chief of CIA counterintelligence generated no known reports, memoranda, or analyses on Oswald, on his defection, his life in the Soviet Union, his Russian friends, his hunting trips, his marriage to a Russian woman, or his contacts with Cuban and Soviet personnel in Mexico City.

Angleton did not author any studies of the possible role of the KGB, Castro, the Miami Cubans, or anyone else in Kennedy's assassination. He never even made a formal finding about the six Oswald letters intercepted by the LINGUAL program. On the key counterintelligence questions raised by JFK's murder, he did very little.

Angleton acted more concerned about exposure of his long-standing interest in Oswald and his more recent attention to the activities of the Cuban consulate in Mexico City. He and Helms constructed an artful cover story depicting the Agency as inattentive to Oswald.

"After the assassination of President Kennedy and the arrest of Lee Oswald an intensive review of all available sources was undertaken in Mexico City to determine purpose of OSWALD's visit," Helms told Warren Commission counsel Lee Rankin in a January 31, 1964, memo. "[I]t *was learned that Oswald had also visited the Cuban Consulate* [emphasis added]."[98]

In other words, the CIA claimed it did not know the purpose of Oswald's visit to Mexico and did not know that Oswald had contacted the Cubans in late September until after JFK was dead. That was a lie. Win Scott knew about Oswald's visit to the Cuban consulate at the time it happened. He wrote as much in his memoirs and reported it in cables read by Angleton's successor George Kalaris.[99] But the cover story seemed plausible to the Warren Commission, which published it in its final report. It just wasn't true.

Within weeks, Angleton had gained effective control of the JFK investigation. In February 1964 the commission's staff attorneys learned that Angleton had shared three CIA cables with the Secret Service on the night of the assassination. Lee Rankin asked the Agency to produce the cables.

Angleton resorted to deflection. He was loath to share anything about Oswald's Cuban contacts, probably because they related to sensitive operations such as LCIMPROVE (counterespionage), LIENVOY (sensitive signals intelligence), and AMSPELL (anti-Castro psychological warfare). But he wanted to make sure he had Helms's support.

"Jim does not desire to respond directly," Ray Rocca, his deputy, told Helms in a memo. "Unless you feel otherwise Jim would prefer to wait out the Commission," rather than turn over the CIA's records in their original form.

Jim would prefer to wait out the Commission.

Why would a senior CIA official want to "wait out" the investigators of a presidential assassination? Rocca later claimed that none of the cables were "of substantive new interest." Oswald was not among the people photographed at the Cuban consulate, nor was he among the passengers on the manifest, he said.

But in intelligence work, the source of information matters as much as its content. The very existence of the Cuban embassy photographs and the Cubana Airlines passenger manifest were substantive. They illuminated the fact that the CIA had the ability and the desire to photograph and identify every visitor to the Cuban consulate in Mexico City, and to identify every potential American traveler to Cuba. Lee Harvey Oswald was no exception. Angleton preferred to wait out the Warren Commission rather than explain the CIA's knowledge of and interest in Oswald's visit to the Cuban consulate.

"If they come back on the point," Rocca told Helms, "he [Angleton] feels that you or someone from here should be prepared to go over to show the Commission the materials rather than pass them to them in copy."[100]

Howard Willens, attorney for the commission, did come back on the point. He asked to see the three cables. A graduate of the University of Michigan and Yale Law School, Willens had been serving in the Criminal Division of the Justice Department when JFK was killed. He joined the Warren Commission as an assistant counsel. He had admired the president, just as he admired the CIA.

He assumed, wrongly, the CIA men shared his interest in finding out the truth.

"I consider the CIA representatives to be among the more competent people in government who I have ever dealt with," Willens wrote in his diary after meeting with Ray Rocca on March 12, 1964. "They articulate, they are specialists and they seem to have a broad view of government. This may be, of course, because they do not have special axes to grind in the Commission's investigation."[101]

Willens never imagined the CIA was deceiving him on fundamental facts about the events leading to the death of the president. In the fullness of time, he realized he had been duped.

"My journal comments about the CIA were naïve, to say the least," Willens wrote in 2015. "The CIA did have axes to grind."[102]

In particular, Willens said, the Agency's failure to disclose the plots to kill Castro compromised the integrity of the Warren Commission's investigation.

ANGLETON PARTICIPATED IN THAT cover-up, too.

On May 8, 1964, Angleton received a memo from Harold Swenson, chief of counterintelligence for the Agency's anti-Castro operations. Swenson had started working for the FBI before Pearl Harbor. He had a quarter century of experience. Swenson had learned from a reliable source that Oswalt had been in contact with a suspected intelligence officer during his visit to the Cuban Consulate. A year later, Swenson reported to senior CIA officials that Fidel Castro had probably known of the CIA's recruitment of Rolando Cubela as an assassin in late 1963.[103]

"The AMLASH operation," Swenson wrote in a 1963 memo read by Angleton, "might have been an insecure operation prior to the assassination of President Kennedy."

The counterintelligence implications were obvious. If Castro knew about the AMLASH plot, then he had a motive for killing Kennedy—self-defense—possibly corroborated by Oswalt's Cuban contact.[104]

Angleton chose not to investigate, tantamount to obstruction of justice.[105] He knew about the AMLASH plot and its possible compromise. He said nothing.

Angleton's willingness to risk violating the law is not hard to understand. A serious counterespionage investigation of Lee Oswald would have uncovered Angleton's abiding interest in him. It would have uncovered the various operations to kill Castro and Angleton's knowledge of them.

No matter who fired the fatal shots in Dallas, Angleton had failed disastrously as counterintelligence chief. He could have—and should have—lost his job after November 22. Had the public, the Congress, and the Warren Commission known of his preassassination interest in Oswald or his postassassination cover-up, he surely would have.

Instead, his malfeasance, abetted by Dick Helms, went undetected. Angleton would remain in a position of supreme power for another decade.

DEFECTOR

ANGLETON WAS, IN THE words of George Kisevalter, "a combination of Machiavelli, Svengali, and Iago."[106]

By the mid-1960s, Angleton reigned as the Machiavelli of the new American national security state, a thinker and strategist of ruthless clarity. Like the Florentine philosopher Niccolò Machiavelli, who wrote in the fifteenth and sixteenth centuries, Angleton did not think ethical claims of virtue could or should restrain a man of power. His way of thinking had enabled him to build the Counterintelligence Staff into an invisible bastion of power, with influence in all the major Western intelligence services; with allies in London, Rome, and Tel Aviv; with interlocutors in organized crime, organized labor, the Vatican, the Ivy League, the Pentagon, and the Washington press corps. He was an unseen broker of American power.

Like Machiavelli, Angleton believed conspiracies were a key to understanding power. "Many more princes are seen to have lost their lives and states through these [plots] than by open war," Machiavelli wrote. "For being able to make open war on a prince is granted to few; to be able to conspire against them is granted to everyone."[107]

Angleton acted as a Svengali to a generation of Anglo-American intelligence officers and intellectuals. Svengali, the fictional hero of a nineteenth-century French novel, was a show business impresario who hypnotized a young girl into becoming an international singing sensation and then led her to doom. Angleton was a seductive maestro of ideas and action. His theories persuaded experts, editors, spies, journalists, novelists, and diplomats to follow him faithfully, sometimes to their own regret.

Angleton played Iago to four U.S. presidents. He was perhaps not so evil as the villainous adviser in Shakespeare's *Othello*. But, like Iago, Angleton was a sympathetic counselor with his own agenda, which sometimes verged on the sinister. Angleton served the men in the Oval Office with seeming loyalty and sometimes devious intent.

Angleton suspected conspiracies everywhere. That was a requirement of his job. Sometimes he was right. Often he was wrong. And never was he more wrong than in the case of Yuri Nosenko.

NOSENKO, THE DISSOLUTE KGB officer who had sold a few secrets to the CIA in 1962, showed up again in Geneva in January 1964, saying he wanted to defect. Angleton was more skeptical than ever. George Kisevalter and Pete Bagley were sent to debrief Nosenko, who told them a sensational story. He said he had supervised the case of Lee Harvey Oswald when the ex-marine arrived in Moscow in October 1959.[108] He said Oswald had been watched by a KGB unit in Minsk between 1959 and 1962 but was not recruited or utilized in any way. Oswald was regarded as unstable and his Russian wife, Marina, was described as "stupid, uneducated and anti-Soviet."

"The KGB was glad to see them go when they left for the United States," he said.[109]

Kisevalter and Bagley were curious about how Nosenko could give such confident assurances about the KGB's lack of interest in Oswald. He replied that when his bosses heard a man named Oswald had been arrested for killing Kennedy, they ordered Oswald's file flown from Minsk to KGB headquarters in Moscow. He told Kisevalter and Bagley that he was there when his fellow officers paged through the entire file. He said they were relieved to find nothing incriminating.[110]

Nosenko told his American interrogators he wanted to leave the Soviet Union for good.

"He said, 'I've been ordered home,'" Kisevalter recalled, a claim that Nosenko later admitted was untrue.[111] Despite reservations about his veracity, the CIA accepted him. On January 30, 1964, Dick Helms approved a $50,000 payment to Nosenko, with an annual contract of $25,000 a year for an indefinite period, along with provisions for retirement and benefits.[112]

The CIA men were keen to hear his story. Angleton made the case that Nosenko was a false defector, sent by the KGB to mislead the Agency. Bagley agreed. So did David Murphy, the chief of the Soviet Russia Division.

DAVE MURPHY WAS ONE of those strivers who worked their way into the upper ranks of the CIA without the advantages of an Ivy League degree or family money. Born in upstate New York, Murphy had graduated from high school at age sixteen, and college by age twenty. He joined the army and married a Russian woman who had fled communism. After the war, Murphy enrolled in the army's language school, where he learned Russian to complement the German and French he had already mastered. His language skills won him a promotion from Washington to the Berlin base, where he worked for Bill Harvey. In 1961, he was promoted to chief of the Soviet Russia Division. He had responsibility for handling and resettling Nosenko.

Nosenko was flown to the United States, where he was admitted as a temporary resident under a secret arrangement that gave the CIA the authority to admit up to one hundred persons a year. He was interrogated by Pete Bagley, and it did not go well. Bagley found Nosenko's responses to be evasive, inconsistent, and inaccurate.[113]

Angleton connected Nosenko's defection to Soviet propaganda about Kennedy's assassination.[114]

"Nosenko's defection," he later told investigators, "came after the Soviets had been asked [by the Warren Commission] to provide all information about Oswald's visit [to Mexico City] and around the time Khrushchev pulled aside a journalist in Egypt and said that Kennedy's death was the work of an American conspiracy."[115]

Angleton reasoned that if the Kremlin had gone so far as to murder the American president, it almost certainly would attempt to conceal its involvement by talking up a right-wing conspiracy. He hypothesized that Nosenko was sent with the improbable message that the Soviets had taken no interest in Oswald in order to shield the KGB's real role.

At Angleton's behest, the CIA reneged on its promises to Nosenko. On orders from Dave Murphy, he was taken to a CIA safe house in southern

Maryland and "involuntarily detained" in the attic.[116] The room featured a metal bed attached to the floor. He was fed weak tea, watery soup, and porridge. There was no air-conditioning or ventilation.[117] Nosenko had landed in what a future generation would call "a black site," an extrajudicial CIA prison. He would remain in detention for more than four years.

ANGLETON WOULD LATER CLAIM he had opposed the incarceration and hostile interrogation of Yuri Nosenko. Pete Bagley knew better.

"Angleton never opposed the incarceration," he said.[118]

Not only did Angleton support incarceration; he agreed that Nosenko needed to be "broken."

Time was running out. On June 27, 1964, Angleton, Rocca, and Murphy questioned Anatoly Golitsyn about Nosenko with a tape recorder running.

"He is a provocateur, who is on a mission for the KGB," Golitsyn insisted. "He was introduced to your Agency as a double agent in Geneva in 1962. During all the time until now he has been fulfilling a KGB mission against your country."[119]

When Murphy raised "the problem of breaking Nosenko," Angleton did not object or propose any alternatives.[120] He only expressed the opinion that it was going to be difficult.

"We have a limited body of information," he told Murphy, "And you've already thrown up to him a very great number of questions that are complex and he managed to get through the histrionics and not break. In fact, [he] has been a long way from breaking. He is nowhere near breaking now."[121]

On July 24, Helms accompanied Murphy and Bagley to a closed-door session with the Warren Commission's seven members. They wanted to know if Nosenko's claim that the KGB didn't have anything to do with Oswald was credible.

"Nosenko is a KGB plant," Bagley declared, "and may be exposed as such sometime after the commission's report."[122]

That was all Chief Justice Earl Warren needed to hear. Much to Angleton's satisfaction, the commission decided to exclude Nosenko's information from its report.

———

ANGLETON ESCAPED ACCOUNTABILITY. ON September 29, 1964, the Warren Commission presented its findings to President Lyndon Johnson. The commissioners endorsed the December 1963 FBI report: Oswald alone and unaided had killed the president for reasons known only to himself. The findings were stated categorically, as if there was no dispute about any of the facts.

There was no hint of intelligence failure in the report. Just the tragedy of inattention. The FBI had received no information that Oswald might pose a threat to the president, the commission said. The CIA had simply missed him when he contacted the Cubans in Mexico City. As for the Agency's extensive covert intelligence activities regarding Oswald, Angleton and Helms effectively erased the story from the historical record.

When the Italian press weighed in on the Warren Commission report, Bill Harvey, now settled in Rome, sent a cable to Angleton. He noted approvingly that the Christian Democratic paper *Il Popolo* gave the report "excellent straight coverage stating that Oswald was the killer of Kennedy and the crime was committed without the assistance of foreign or domestic conspirators." By contrast, the "cryptocommunist" afternoon daily *Paese Sera* said the report contained "many contradictions, and omission and concealment of testimony." The Warren Commission "had arrived at arbitrary facts and conclusions."[123]

Harvey's alcoholism soon consumed him, and Dick Helms removed him from the Rome station and active duty. Harvey was the proverbial burnout. His hatred of the Kennedys was as legendary as his big gut and fondness for guns. More than one associate in Rome told of Harvey ending arguments by pointing a loaded pistol at the head of the person daring to disagree with him. His admiring but appalled biographer called him a "flawed patriot."[124] His longtime colleague John Whitten described him as "a thug."[125] When Sam Giancana, a mobster who had worked with the Agency, was shot dead in his Chicago apartment in 1975, Whitten thought Harvey might have been the killer. Some JFK authors wondered if he had a role in JFK's death. One CIA associate told a journalist that he saw Harvey on a commercial flight to Dallas in November 1963, an odd destination for a Rome station chief. Thanks to Angleton and Helms, the Warren Commission never interviewed Harvey.

The Warren report was supposed to put to rest "rumors" and "speculation" about the causes of Kennedy's murder. It did not quell Angleton's curiosity. He wanted to see the evidence for himself.

On October 9, 1964, Jane Roman asked Sam Papich for the FBI's copy of the home movie of JFK's assassination made by Abraham Zapruder, a Dallas businessman. The film, obtained by *Life* magazine, had never been shown publicly. It would only be used for "training purposes," Roman said. Angleton's friend, deputy FBI director Bill Sullivan, approved the request. And so it is likely that Angleton saw Zapruder's film eleven years before the American people did.

It would not have been easy to watch the murder of a man he knew from many a dinner party. It would not have been reassuring, either. The Warren Commission's report, written with the help of Allen Dulles, quoted Secret Service agent Clint Hill saying he saw JFK "lurch forward and to the left" when hit.[126]

Watching Zapruder's twenty-six seconds of color film, Angleton would have seen how mistaken Hill and the Warren Commission were. The footage showed Kennedy grimacing and raising his arms as he was jolted by the first gunshot, which hit him in the back. And then, a few seconds later, he was blasted *backward* and to the left by the fatal shot.[127]

Angleton lived in a violent world. Three days after Jane Roman requested a copy of Zapruder's film, Angleton experienced another murder. His friend Mary Meyer was killed in broad daylight.

MARY

MARY MEYER WAS WALKING west on the towpath next to the old Chesapeake and Ohio Canal in Georgetown at lunchtime on October 12, 1964. She was forty-four years old, the mother of two teenage boys. She was now divorced from husband Cord, whose youthful idealism had hardened into mature self-righteousness. Liberating herself from the narrow role of CIA wife, Mary had moved to Georgetown and become a painter, while remaining friends with Jim and Cicely Angleton. She walked the towpath almost daily, loving its shady trees and lovely vistas of the Potomac River. She was accosted by a light-skinned African American man. They struggled. He produced a pistol and shot her twice. She tumbled onto the grass by the canal and died. An auto mechanic fixing a car on nearby Canal Road saw the man walk away from her body and head down toward the Potomac River. He called the police.

That afternoon, Cicely Angleton was at home in Arlington when she heard a bulletin on the radio reporting a woman had been killed in Georgetown on the C&O Canal towpath. She knew Mary often walked there and feared the worst. When Angleton came home, he dismissed his wife's anxiety. They would see Mary that evening, he said. She was going with them to hear Reed Whittemore speak on Capitol Hill. His former Yale roommate was giving a droll talk on "Ways of Understanding Poetry and Being Dismal."[128]

Cicely was panicky as Jim drove the Mercedes to the front of Mary's town house on N Street in Georgetown. Mary had a painting studio in the back, where a canvas, still damp from her velvety strokes, was drying under a whirring fan.[129] Mary's car was in the driveway, yet the lights were out inside. A sign hanging on the door said FREE KITTENS—RING BELL OR CALL.

Angleton pushed the doorbell. No answer. He tried the door, which was unlocked. He went into the house. It was empty. In the car, Cicely was close to tears. She had told Mary not to walk along the canal. It used to be safe; it wasn't anymore. Mary had paid her no mind. To reassure his wife, Angleton called Mary's answering service.

The voice on the phone informed him that Mrs. Meyer had been murdered earlier that day.

CICELY WEPT AND JIM blinked. They went straight to the home of Ben and Tony Bradlee, who lived a few blocks away. Their gathering friends, were shocked as they were. Ben Bradlee had been pulled out of a meeting at *Newsweek* to go down to the police station. He returned, still stunned by the sight of Mary's lifeless body in her angora sweater.

More friends gathered. The phones rang; doorbells buzzed. Someone remembered the cats that Mary was trying to give away. Angleton walked back to Mary's house and rescued the three kittens.[130] Food and drink materialized, ordered by Cicely, Tony, and the other women. The radio said a suspect had been arrested.

Cicely never cared to talk about that awful day, but she did remember Anne Truitt's phone call. The Truitts had recently moved to Japan, where Anne's husband worked as a *Newsweek* correspondent. Anne called from Tokyo, asking to speak to Angleton.

Angleton took the call in a quiet room. Anne Truitt told him that Mary had kept a diary in her sketchbook, a journal about her life and her thoughts, along with her drawings. She said that Mary had told her that if anything ever happened to her, she wanted Angleton to have the sketchbook for safekeeping. Truitt said that Mary usually left it in the bookcase in the bedroom.[131]

Bradlee, then in line to become the next editor of *The Washington Post*, recognized how Angleton's aura of intrigue attracted his friends. They trusted him with their most intimate confidences, he observed, "as if the secret would be somehow safer in his keeping than in theirs."[132]

Together, these friends combed Mary Meyer's house for the diary. They tapped walls and looked in the fireplace. They turned over bricks in the garden but found nothing. Given the dismal circumstances surrounding Mary's death, drinking came easily as night fell. Angleton washed the dishes, and the whiskey flowed. Someone wandered out into the garden and shouted to the sky, "Mary, where's your damned diary?" Cord Meyer lit a fire to ward off the chill.[133]

Everyone agreed that Angleton should have Mary's diary—everyone save Ben Bradlee.

IN HIS MEMOIR, the *Washington Post* editor told a different story.

"We didn't start looking until the next morning, when Tony and I walked around the corner a few blocks to Mary's house," Bradlee wrote. "It was locked, as we had expected, but when we got inside, we found Jim Angleton, and to our complete surprise he told us he, too, was looking for Mary's diary."

Bradlee's surprise suggested that he did not know what Anne Truitt had said—that Mary wanted Angleton to have the diary

"We asked him how he had gotten into the house, and he shuffled his feet," Bradlee wrote. ". . . We felt his presence was odd, to say the least, but we took him at his word, and with him we searched Mary's house thoroughly. Without success. We found no diary."

The next day, Bradlee said he returned to look for the diary in Mary's padlocked studio. He had brought along some tools to pick the lock. He recounted that he was surprised to run into Angleton again. He was already picking the lock, according to Bradlee.

"He would have been red-faced, if his face could have gotten red, and he left almost without a word," Bradlee wrote. He said Tony Bradlee found the diary an hour later, and they turned it over to Angleton.[134]

The story had a ring of truth when published in 1995. Angleton was a legendary covert operator and an accomplished lock picker. Bradlee was an honored editor with a Pulitzer Prize. But in this storytelling contest, at least, the spy was perhaps more credible than the scribe.

"Much has been written about this diary—most of it wrong," Bradlee wrote.[135] Since Bradlee took thirty years to publish his account of the search for Mary Meyer's diary, more aggressive journalists had beaten him to the story, tainting ever so slightly his reputation as the fearless, crusading leader of *The Washington Post*'s Watergate coverage. Those reporters inevitably made some minor factual errors when they broke the story, but Bradlee knew that the story they reported was true in all of its essentials: His sister-in-law Mary Meyer did have an affair with his friend, the president. She did keep a diary that made reference to their relationship. And Bradlee did acquiesce in giving it to a top CIA man rather than write anything about it.

In his social circle, Angleton was a reassuring figure, a man with a record and reputation that seemed beyond reproach. Perhaps Angleton was furtive in his searching of Mary's home and studio. If so, he was merely engaged in the same task as Bradlee: preventing the diary from falling into the wrong hands.

Bradlee's story was self-serving. In 1964, he didn't think twice about turning Mary's journal over to the CIA. A decade later, he didn't care to admit it. So he wrote an account of the incident that made himself look good (or less bad) by portraying Angleton as a would-be thief. Cicely Angleton had reason to complain to *The New York Times*.[136]

MARY MEYER'S DIARY MATTERED because she mattered to the man who had been president. During her affair with JFK in 1961–1963, Meyer sought to bring her lover the kind of unique experiences he would never encounter in his work or in the embrace of his conventional friends and family. Meyer had become friends with Timothy Leary, a professor at Harvard Medical School with an interest in the uses of LSD. She asked Leary how to take LSD so that she could introduce the drug to her circle in Washington.

"I have this friend who's a very important man," she told Leary without mentioning names. "He's impressed by what I've told him [about LSD]."[137] Meyer later told Leary that she had smoked marijuana and taken LSD with her important friend. The day after the assassination, Meyer called Leary. "He was changing too fast," she said. "They couldn't control him anymore." Mary's use of "they" implied that she thought JFK had been struck down by powerful enemies.[138]

"I remember her inability to fathom violence," recalled Kary Fischer, a male friend who had a crush on her. "It was more than a personal loss for her. I remember saying, here was a punk [Oswald], rejected by all, looking for a golden boy, the one upon whom all riches and power and beauty had been bestowed, as his victim. And she seemed to agree with that."[139]

At least for a while. Mary saved newspaper clippings about the assassination. And she wondered. The Warren Commission's report came out and supposedly laid all the rumors to rest. The loner Oswald had killed the president for reasons known only to himself. Like many Americans, Mary Meyer wanted to believe it. Like many others, she just couldn't.

They couldn't control him anymore.

AT MARY MEYER'S FUNERAL service in the Bethlehem Chapel of the National Cathedral, Angleton served as an honorary pallbearer.[140] Afterward, he read the diary of his deceased friend. He learned that Mary had taken LSD with Kennedy, after which they had made love. Or so

Angleton would claim.[141] He showed the sketchbook to Mary's son Quentin. Angleton did not destroy it, despite having told Anne Truitt that he would.

Rather, he sifted its counterintelligence implications.

"Did the death of a woman in whom the late president might have confided have anything to do with the Soviet penetration that Golitsyn had warned about?" Angleton asked journalist Joseph Trento. "Had someone in Kennedy's inner circle been compromised? Was Hoover's FBI, which kept track of such personal matters with astonishing competence, the Soviets' source? Had the Soviets penetrated the FBI as well as the CIA?"[142]

As was often the case, Angleton's conspiracy theories lacked substance. There was—and is—nothing to indicate Meyer's death had anything to do with Golitsyn. There was no compromise of Kennedy's inner circle. Hoover did not tell the Soviet Union about JFK's love affair with Mary Meyer, and, no, the Soviets had not penetrated the FBI or the CIA, at least not in any way that pertained to Meyer.

ANGLETON PRESSED ON WITH the mole hunt, playing Svengali to CIA director John McCone. He convinced McCone that Golitsyn's suspicions of a mole had to be investigated. McCone met no fewer than eleven times with the former KGB man. Golitsyn told him that at least five Agency employees, and possibly as many as thirty, were KGB agents.[143] McCone discussed the allegations with J. Edgar Hoover, who in November 1964 finally agreed to a joint FBI-CIA investigation.[144]

Angleton was grimly pleased. Instead of one-off investigations of individual suspects, such as Peter Karlow, a team of Bureau and Agency operatives would collaborate in studying the penetration problem comprehensively. To honor its leading spirits, Angleton dubbed the investigation HONETOL, a combination of letters from the FBI director's last name and Golitsyn's first name. HONETOL was run by a six-man committee, including Angleton and Bill Sullivan and Sam Papich, both of the FBI. The Special Investigations Group, run by Birch O'Neal, reviewed CIA files.[141] The HONETOL committee developed a list of forty suspected moles, thirteen of whom would be investigated in depth.

CICELY

ANGLETON DID NOT HAVE the time or the interest to attend the trial of Ray Crump, Jr., a twenty-five-year-old African American man who was arrested and charged with killing Mary Meyer. In the summer of 1965, Cicely did have the time.

Much had changed in the months since Mary's murder.[146] President Johnson had ordered a massive escalation of the war in Vietnam. The newspapers carried a story about a group of people arrested for planning to destroy the Washington Monument, the Statue of Liberty, and the Liberty Bell. The Beatles were dominating the music charts. *Time* magazine had a cover story on LSD. The chemical once controlled by the men of the MKULTRA program was now known as "acid" and was sold on college campuses as a drug of liberation, not mind control. The secrets of the CIA were seeping into American consciousness with unexpected results.

In the Washington courtroom, Cicely listened as the prosecutors presented the testimony of a witness, Henry Wiggins, the mechanic who had seen the light-skinned black man walk away after Mary cried for help. Crump's lawyer, a righteous lady named Dovey Roundtree, noted that not a hair of Mary's blue angora sweater had been found on Crump's hands or clothing. The police claimed Crump had thrown the gun in the river or the canal. The Marine Corps divers found nothing.

Cicely tried to make sense of it all—for herself, for the kids, for Jim.

"It was a struggle, a terribly long struggle to keep your family together, and yourself together, and your husband together in the Cold War, in the CIA," she later told an interviewer. "That was one of the great traumas that I had. . . . It was something you had to wrestle with all the time."[147]

When Cicely looked around the courtroom, she wanted to think things were working. Judge Corcoran was objective. The prosecuting attorney, Mr. Hantman, was competent. So was Mrs. Roundtree. The jurors, colored and white alike, seemed attentive. She missed Mary's warmth, her concern, her joy.[148]

On July 30, 1965, the jury found Ray Crump not guilty of murdering Mary Meyer.

"They apparently decided there was just not enough evidence to remove all reasonable doubt," she told Cord Meyer when she got home.

Meyer typed out the news in a terse letter to his mother-in-law, Ruth Pinchot. He added the passing suggestion that she talk to Cicely about the verdict. He was not going to. Cord Meyer did not want to talk or think about his ex-wife's death.[149]

Angleton made his own inquiries. Later that summer, Peter Jessup, the former Tel Aviv station chief, wrote a note to Angleton saying that he'd had a long conversation with the wife of Judge Corcoran, the man who had presided over Crump's trial. Mrs. Corcoran advised Angleton not to press her husband on the details, "as he was too upset by the case."[150]

Cicely was left alone in her sorrow. She knew all too well how to stifle her grief. The deaths of her own brothers, Charles and Hugh, in 1944 and her family's stoic reaction never left her. She would write a poem about the desolating effects of sorrow called "Erosions," in which she said, *"Our family wrapped their grief in heavy parcels."* The poem ended:

> *On sad occasions*
> *a ball of string was always rolling*
> *and fish hooks seal our eyes.*[151]

Cicely had lost her brothers; she had lost Jim, who was often absent from her life; and now she had lost Mary, who had been like a sister to her. All she had were her children and the blinding pain of a CIA wife.

> *. . . and fish hooks seal our eyes.*

BOMB

ANGLETON WAS A MAN unbound. His empire now stretched from Mexico City to London to Rome to Jerusalem. He was in Israel when he heard the news: The Soviet Russia Division had decided to subject Yuri Nosenko to hostile interrogation.[152] Although Angleton had talked with Dave Murphy and Ray Rocca about how to "break" Nosenko, he would say he felt that he hadn't been consulted on the final decision.

The news did not disrupt his trip. Even as the mole hunt consumed more and more work hours at Langley—reading personnel files, analyzing travel records, and collating interrogation reports—Angleton did not miss his regular trips to Israel.

"He used to come from time to time, to meet the head of Mossad, to get briefings," recalls Efraim Halevy, who served as the Mossad's liaison officer to the CIA station in Tel Aviv in the early 1960s. Halevy escorted Angleton on his rounds and recorded his meetings with Israeli officials.

"He used to meet with David Ben-Gurion, who[m] he knew for many years," Halevy recalled. "Ben-Gurion ultimately left office [in 1963] and Angleton went down to Sde Boker [Ben-Gurion's home in the Negev] to meet him. I didn't attend those meetings. Those were just the two of them. He had business to transact."[153]

Angleton's appreciation for the men who built the Jewish state had only grown over the years. He admired Isser Harel and the Mossad for capturing Adolf Eichmann in 1960 and did not fail to notice that operational prowess translated into respect at Langley.[154] But it was Harel's dynamic conception of secret intelligence, as much as any individual act of derring-do, which most impressed Angleton.

Angleton shared his impetus for action.

"Harel was a key player and strategist in implementing the concept of Ben-Gurion to reach out to the 'periphery' beyond the Arab world,"

Halevy explained. "He set up relations with the Shah of Iran and the Turkish Intelligence service, the MIT. He created the threesome of Israel, Turkey, and Iran under the name Trident."[155] The three services met annually in Tel Aviv, Ankara, and Tehran to plot strategy against their common Arab enemies.

For Angleton, the Mossad's operations showed that Israel wasn't just a partner or a client of the United States. It was a strategic ally around the world. The Israelis noted that the African policies of Egypt's Nasser blended into the overall interests of the Soviet Union. The Moscow-Cairo axis sought to win over the emerging independent states of Africa as allies. So Harel and the Mossad countered by establishing links with national leaders across Africa, with friendly offers of security training, timely intelligence, and commercial contracts, or more subtle approaches involving bribery and blackmail.

"At that time, the East-West conflict—USA versus the Soviet Union—raged throughout the continent," Halevy noted. "The struggle for control over the mineral and other natural assets, many of key strategic importance, was a major feature of the Cold War. Angleton immediately understood the significance and value of the Israeli role and applauded it and encouraged it."

In March 1963, Harel had a falling-out with Ben-Gurion in part because of the latter's handling of Israel's secret nuclear project.[156] Harel resigned, and Ben-Gurion replaced him with Meir Amit, the methodical military man who had led the Israeli forces in the Suez War.

"Angleton also had a good relationship with Amit," Halevy said, which strengthened the CIA-Mossad relationship.

"We did not discuss Middle East affairs with the Agency until the 1960s, when Amit came in," Halevy said. "Amit demanded Israel and Mossad be able to talk to the CIA about the Middle East and the Soviet Union, and they agreed."

One result was KKMOUNTAIN—KK being the CIA's designation for messages and documents dealing with Israel. Millions in annual cash payments flowed to Mossad. In return, the Israelis authorized their agents to act as American surrogates throughout North Africa and in such countries as Kenya, Tanzania, and the Congo.[157]

Angleton was at ease in Israel. "Jim had a weakness for Jews," said his friend Peter Sichel. "He just liked us."[158] When doing business in Jerusalem, Angleton still stayed at the King David. He found a spot down the hill from the hotel where he could get a closer look at the ancient walls of the Old City. There he contemplated and harmonized his struggles.

One CIA man started to wonder if Angleton wasn't too close to his Israeli friends.

"I REMEMBERED A LONG drive out into the desert in his Ford Falcon," wrote John Hadden, Jr., in a memoir about growing up in a CIA family. Hadden was twelve years old when his father, John Hadden, Sr., served as CIA station chief in Israel in the mid-1960s.

"We stopped in the middle of nowhere," the son wrote. "Pop got us all out of the car and passed out peanut butter sandwiches wrapped by my mother in wax paper. He dove into the trunk and withdrew a small pruning shears. I'd never seen him handle a garden tool. He darted about quickly, clipping bits of shrubbery, keeping a lookout on the horizon. There was a fantastic dome a mile or two in the distance beyond some barbed wire. It was the nuclear reactor at Dimona."[159]

Angleton had selected Hadden for the job as station chief, and the two men got along personally, but they had very different conceptions of their mission.

"I thought we ought to learn things about the Israelis, like whether or not they had a bomb," said Hadden. "He didn't think so."[160]

John Hadden's espionage picnic produced one critical clue: the isotopic signature of the radioactive deposits on the plants he collected near the Dimona site. The plant samples indicated a radiation source of 97.7 percent enriched uranium.[161] For CIA scientists, that was notable. Almost all the nuclear reactors in the world used 93 percent enriched uranium. The more highly enriched uranium, which generates nuclear power more efficiently, was reserved for special purposes, such as powering U.S. nuclear submarines.

Subsequent samples from around Dimona confirmed Hadden's finding.[162] The Israelis had obtained their nuclear fuel from an unusual source. But where?

THE STATE OF ISRAEL'S pursuit of the ultimate destructive deterrent originated in the mind of David Ben-Gurion. Even as Israel secured its independence and its borders in 1948, Ben-Gurion felt its vulnerabilities keenly. He decided early on that the Jewish state needed nuclear weapons to defend itself, an audacious idea at a time when only four nations possessed atomic arsenals.

Ben-Gurion vowed to use science and technology to ensure the Jewish people would never be as helpless as they were in Nazi Germany. Mastering atomic energy was Jewish self-defense, he said. "What Einstein, Oppenheimer, and Teller—the three of them are Jews—made for the United States, could also be done by scientists in Israel for their own people."[163]

To advance this ambition, Ben-Gurion surrounded himself with a group of like-minded men who could keep a secret. Angleton knew at least six of them.

In Washington, he and Cicely had spent many evenings with Memi de Shalit, a Lithuanian-born military intelligence officer stationed in the Israeli embassy. Angleton "adored" de Shalit and his wife, Ada, said Efraim Halevy.[164] The de Shalits moved back to Israel in the 1950s, but the friendship continued, and it brought Angleton into the circle of other knowledgeable Israelis.

Amos de Shalit, Memi's brother, was a professor of nuclear physics at the Weizmann Institute of Science in Tel Aviv. He would be a major contributor to the Israeli nuclear program. Angleton's close ties with the de Shalit family and others in Israel "made it inevitable that he would learn about the construction [of the Dimona reactor] in the Negev," wrote reporter Seymour Hersh.[165]

Angleton had first encountered Asher Ben-Natan, chief of nuclear procurement for the Israelis, as an OSS informant during the war. Ben-Natan was an Austrian Jew who had been born with the name Arthur Pier. After the war, he reported to OSS on the Jewish Agency's efforts to help war refugees emigrate to Palestine. His code name was CONDUCTOR, and he was probably a source for Angleton's reporting on "Jewish escape routes" after the war.[166]

In 1956, Ben-Natan helped arrange for the initial transfer of French nuclear technology to the Dimona site.[167] When the reactor became active in 1965, his job was to arrange diversion of technology and material from European sources to fuel the reactor and amass a supply of weapons-grade uranium.

Another protégé of Ben-Gurion was Shimon Peres, a Russian-born, kibbutz-raised newcomer in the Defense Ministry, a man whose ego was exceeded only by his ability. With Ben-Gurion's cabinet divided about the enormous expense of pursuing nuclear weapons, the old man put Peres in charge of a private fund-raising campaign for Dimona.

"The bottom line, for me," Peres wrote in a memoir, "was that I would have to raise money 'on the side' to help pay for the reactor. We set up a discreet fund-raising operation, which raised contributions totaling more than $40 million—half the cost of the reactor and a very considerable sum in those days. Most of this money came from direct personal appeals by Ben-Gurion and myself to friends of Israel around the world."[168]

"The idea was to raise money independently and outside the national budget," explained Avner Cohen, historian of the Israeli nuclear program. "Money that would go by very few people. Ben Gurion gave the authority, and Shimon Peres did the actual fund-raising, with wealthy Jews all over the world, and in particular, in the United States. He would say, 'Please give us money for a most secret project to ensure the future survival of the Jewish people.'"[169]

"In the eyes of the Israelis," Cohen explained, "there was no undertaking that was more important, more secretive, more costly, more existential— more sacred—than the nuclear project. Everything is kosher, everything is okay, in order to make it happen. *Everything.* It was almost like a religious commitment to make it happen: The bomb is a way to ensure survival after the Holocaust. So they didn't have to give many details. People understood what they were talking about."

One of those who understood best was David Lowenthal, a business-man from Pittsburgh, Pennsylvania. Lowenthal grew up in the United

States and went to Europe after the war to join the Haganah, the Jewish self-defense force. He helped purchase a ship, the *Pan York,* which enabled some eight thousand Jews to emigrate to Palestine. During the 1948 war, he served in the armed forces under the command of Meir Amit, the future Mossad chief, who was witting of Israel's secret nuclear program. "I remember you as a big Zionist," Amit told Lowenthal late in life.[170]

Lowenthal returned to the United States in 1955 to go into business in Pennsylvania. With two other investors, he bought a shuttered steel-manufacturing plant in Apollo, a small city forty miles northeast of Pittsburgh. While planning to restart the company's steel production, Lowenthal used company stock to buy two other bankrupt firms in order to create a new holding company called Apollo Industries.[171] The merger provided Apollo with usable assets, financing, and a rationale for the creation of another subsidiary, the Nuclear Materials and Equipment Corporation, or NUMEC.[172] Lowenthal and his investors planned to develop a new product: nuclear fuel for use in commercial reactors.

To run NUMEC, Lowenthal turned to Zalman Shapiro, a metallurgist then working for the Atomic Energy Commission. Shapiro was undeniably brilliant. The son of an Orthodox rabbi from Lithuania, he earned undergraduate and graduate degrees in engineering from Johns Hopkins University.[173] Before age forty, Shapiro had four patents concerning the production of pure metals. He was considered one of the leading metallurgists in the U.S. nuclear industry, if not the world.[174] Within months of NUMEC's founding, Shapiro had applied for and received a nuclear materials license from the AEC.[175]

At the CIA, John Hadden would note the coincidence: The AEC issued its first license to handle highly enriched uranium to a private company financed by a group of active Zionists at a time when Israel was accelerating its efforts to acquire nuclear weapons.

NUMEC started processing highly enriched uranium at Apollo in 1959.[176] At that time, the U.S. government owned all supplies of the nuclear fuel, which private companies like NUMEC were allowed to use but had to return. Within a few years, worrisome signs appeared that the Apollo plant's security and accounting were deficient—even by the lenient standards of the day. Enriched uranium was disappearing from the NUMEC operation with unusual frequency. Unexplained handling losses occurred at other commercial plants, but Apollo's were proportionately larger. In October 1965, the AEC estimated that 178 kilograms of highly enriched uranium had gone missing from the Apollo plant. By March 1968, the figure was 267 kilograms.[177]

And that, John Hadden would conclude many years later, was the answer to his question: Where did Israel get its nuclear material? The Israelis had stolen highly enriched uranium for the Dimona reactor from NUMEC. The unexplained losses at the Apollo plant were the result of a heist.

IN THE SPRING OF 1965, a technician working the night shift at the NUMEC plant went out on a loading dock for a breath of fresh air. It was around nine in the evening. The technician saw an unusual sight. Zalman Shapiro, owner of the company, paced on the dock while a foreman and truck driver loaded cylindrical storage containers, known as "stovepipes," onto a flatbed truck. The stovepipes, the technician explained, were used to "store canisters of high enriched materials in the vaults located at the Apollo nuclear facility." These were "highly polished aluminum tubes with standard printed square yellow labels, approximately three inches in diameter by six inches tall. They were used to store high enriched uranium products . . . defined as 95 percent uranium." He was sure the men were handling canisters of highly enriched uranium "due to the size and shape of the container and the labeling." He saw the shipping order, which said the material was bound for Israel.

"It was highly unusual to see Dr. Shapiro in the manufacturing section of the Apollo nuclear facility," the employee went on. "It was unusual to see Dr. Shapiro there at night; and very unusual to see Dr. Shapiro so nervous."

The next day, NUMEC's personnel manager visited the technician and threatened to fire him "if he did not keep his mouth shut" concerning what he had seen on the loading dock. It would be fifteen years before the employee told the story to the FBI.[178]

WHAT DID ANGLETON KNOW about NUMEC?

He knew that the AEC and FBI were investigating the loss of uranium at the Apollo plant as early as 1965. As Israel desk officer, Angleton had to talk about the NUMEC case with Sam Papich, who was following it for the FBI.[179] He also talked about it with John Hadden, who returned from Tel Aviv to serve Angleton in Washington.

On the crime-scene particulars, Hadden defended his former boss.

"Any suggestion that Angleton had helped the Israelis with the NUMEC operation was totally without foundation," he told journalists Andrew and Leslie Cockburn.[180] But Hadden didn't deny that Angleton helped the Israeli nuclear program.

"Why would someone whose whole life was dedicated to fighting communism have any interest in preventing a very anti-Communist nation getting the means to defend itself?" he asked.

"The fact they stole it from us didn't worry him in the least," he said. "I suspect that in his inmost heart he would've given it to them if they asked for it."[181]

Hadden knew better than to investigate further.

"I never sent anything to Angleton on this [the nuclear program] because I knew he wasn't interested," he told his son. "And I knew he'd try to stop it if I did."[182]

With the Israelis facing Arab enemies allied with the Soviet Union, Angleton had other priorities.

WAR

IN MAY 1967, ANGLETON met with Dick Helms in the director's office suite on the seventh floor of CIA headquarters. Less than a year before, Helms had assumed the job as director of Central Intelligence. He wanted Angleton to read a memo that he was about to deliver to President Johnson concerning the growing military confrontation between Egypt and Israel.

Helms and Angleton had known each other for twenty-two years. They collaborated, one way or another, in hundreds of secret operations. Some

CIA hands would wonder why Helms was so tolerant of Angleton's eccentricities. One reason was Angleton's performance during the Six-Day War.

"BY LATE 1966 EVERYBODY was anticipating there would be an Israeli-Egyptian war one of these days. And we had reports about who was going to strike first," said Tom Hughes, then the director of the State Department's Intelligence and Research Bureau.[183]

Egypt's Gamal Nasser was probing for advantage. Ever since surviving the British-French-Israeli attack at Suez in 1956, Nasser had positioned himself as the champion of the Arab world, the person who would reverse the humiliation of Israel's existence. In response to Nasser's aggressive rhetoric, the Israelis engaged in a wide-ranging effort to upgrade their tanks and fighter jets.[184] A CIA estimate in April 1967 concluded that "both sides appear to appreciate that large-scale military action involves considerable risk and no assurance of leading to a solution."[185]

That equilibrium began to change in May, when Nasser requested the withdrawal of UN peacekeeping forces, which had provided a buffer between Egyptian and Israeli forces since the Suez War. To the dismay of U.S. officials, UN secretary-general U Thant agreed. On May 22, Nasser announced the closure of the Gulf of Aqaba to Israeli ships.

Not only did Israel regard access to the Gulf as a vital interest but also the United States asserted that the Gulf was an international waterway. President Johnson called on all parties to exercise restraint.[186]

Helms wanted Angleton's take on the Agency's latest assessment. The memo, written by the Intelligence Directorate, asserted the Israelis were likely to strike first. They would prevail quickly over Egypt and other Arab armies because of their superior weapons, training, and discipline. Helms, the ever-cautious bureaucrat, hesitated due to the memo's categorical tone.

"We're really throwing everything on this one," he said.

Angleton counseled certainty.

"It only takes a 'maybe,'" he told Helms, "and you don't get the direct attention of the recipient. They begin to have a hundred thoughts rather than one thought."

Helms sent the memo to President Johnson without qualifications.[187]

———

"THE ATMOSPHERE IN ISRAEL was very grim," recalls Efraim Halevy. "We called it the 'three weeks of suspense.' The atmosphere was very gloomy. Isser Harel said, 'There's going to be a war.' He wanted to consecrate a number of places for mass graves, like the garden in the center of Tel Aviv. Meir Amit was very outspoken in the way he described the situation."[188]

When Amit asked John Hadden to come to his house, the CIA man counseled patience.

"I said, "You've got to wait three weeks," Hadden recalled. "You've got to give Johnson three weeks to try to broker peace . . . that you know and I know won't work, but we got to let him try, so that he can stand before the world and say, 'I tried.' To save face. You go to war now he'll be in position of not having kept you under control and not having tried to keep the peace. Let him go three weeks, and he'll give you the green light and you can do whatever you want."

Amit lost his temper, Hadden recalled.

"You're condemning six thousand, twelve thousand, Israelis, by making me wait three weeks," he shouted. "They're all going to get killed."[189]

The Israelis wanted to go to war on their own terms but feared they might be abandoned by the United States as they had been at Suez. President Johnson sympathized but was consumed by the enormity of managing the war in Vietnam. In the Sinai, IDF field commanders virtually demanded orders to attack. When Prime Minister Levi Eshkol hesitated, seeking more time for diplomacy, his cabinet rebelled and forced him to appoint Moshe Dayan as defense minister.

The Israeli war hawks wanted another answer from Washington. Could they count on U.S. support, or at least neutrality, if they attacked? The advocates of a preemptive strike sent Amit to Washington; John Hadden flew with him. When they landed, Amit went straight to Langley to see Angleton.

In his memoir, Amit described Angleton as "a long-legged intellectual" and "a very talented person, but controversial" for his "far-reaching theories regarding the Soviet Union. . . . At the CIA, he was regarded with a certain mockery, but to us, this did not matter. His total identification with Israel was an extraordinary asset for us."[190] He was, in Amit's words, "the biggest Zionist of the lot."[191]

Efraim Halevy says Angleton then escorted Amit to see Defense Secretary Robert McNamara.

When Amit arrived, McNamara called the president by phone and spoke to him. "After the call Amit deduced that we had the green light, or at least a 'flexible' light," Halevy said.[192]

EARLY ON THE MORNING of June 5, Dick Helms was roused from his bed by the news that fighting had begun in the Middle East.[193] The Israelis had launched a sneak attack. They sent a squadron of low-flying jets to decimate the planes of the Egyptian air force as they sat on the runways of a desert air base. And when Jordan and Syria entered the war, Israel destroyed their air forces, too. Within hours, Israeli troops were beginning to sweep over the Sinai Peninsula and surging into the Old City of Jerusalem and across the west bank of the Jordan River.[194]

For President Johnson, the CIA had delivered. The Agency's memoranda not only predicted that Israel would attack its Arab neighbors but was accurate almost down to the day and time.[195] The U.S. intelligence performance was not flawless. While reporting of events prior to the outbreak of the war was excellent, the coverage once the fighting began left much to be desired. At times, the U.S. government was blinded by technological issues.

Making matters much worse, the National Security Agency's signal intelligence coverage of the war zone was violently degraded on the fourth day of fighting—by Washington's putative ally Israel.

ON THE MORNING OF June 8, 1967, the USS *Liberty* was the eyes and ears of the U.S. government in the Middle East war zone. A lightly armed frigate, loaded with sophisticated radar, radio, and telemetry equipment, the *Liberty* loitered in placid international waters twenty-five miles north of the Egyptian coast. The NSA analysts working below deck were recording and analyzing the radio communications of the various armies fighting in the Sinai and in Syria.

The fog of war enveloped the State Department.

"The explanations for the *Liberty*'s presence in the area are so totally bizarre that you have to think Angleton was behind it," said Tom Hughes, the State Department's intelligence chief. "Here's an NSA ship, a covert listening ship, that is taken off the African coast, prepositioned just before the Israelis attack, off the Egyptian coast, in international waters, and is sitting there. Who ordered it to go there and why? NSA didn't seem to know. CIA didn't seem to know. [The] State Department certainly never knew. The Pentagon couldn't figure it out."

Hughes speculated that Angleton wanted to preposition the *Liberty* off Egypt as a hedge against Israeli battlefield reverses.[196] For whatever reason, the Israelis treated the *Liberty* as a threat to be eliminated.

TWO UNIDENTIFIED AIRCRAFT CIRCLED the *Liberty* three times starting at ten thirty in the morning, causing little concern.[197] The ship was flying a five-by-eight-foot American flag; her name was painted on the stern in English. The ship's configuration, as shown in naval identification books, was, in the words of the subsequent navy inquiry, "clearly sufficient for the aircraft to identify her properly as a non-combatant ship."[198]

The *Liberty*'s commander, William L. McGonagle, testified that at two in the afternoon he saw "an aircraft of similar characteristics, if not identical" to the jets seen earlier, which began firing on the ship.[193] Eight men were killed or died as a result of injuries suffered during the initial bombardment.

Then three high-speed boats approached in flank formation, with the middle boat flying an Israeli flag.[200] An explosion blasted a hole thirty-nine feet wide on the starboard side of the ship, killing another twenty-five NSA personnel. The *Liberty* came to a dead stop and started to list.[201] When sailors began to lower lifeboats into the water, the Israelis fired on them, too.

Eventually, the attacks ceased. A total of 34 men had been killed and 171 injured. The attack was deliberate, according to McGonagle. Secretary of State Dean Rusk passed a stern note to the Israeli ambassador, calling the incident "an act of military recklessness reflecting wanton disregard for human life."[202] Clark Clifford, a veteran presidential adviser and chairman of the President's Foreign Intelligence Advisory Board, declared it was "inconceivable" that the shelling was an accident.

The Israelis quickly apologized, asserting their forces had mistaken the *Liberty* for *El Quesir,* an Egyptian steamer reported in the vicinity. They called the attack a "tragic error."[203]

President Johnson ordered an investigation. The next day, the CIA produced its first analysis, which exonerated the Israelis. The paper concluded, erroneously, that there was "little doubt that the Israelis failed to identify the *Liberty* as a U.S. ship before or during the attack."[204] The *Liberty* "could easily have been mistaken" for *El Quesir,* the memo asserted, a claim that the U.S. Navy would soon repudiate.[205] The report was "compiled from all available sources," probably by Angleton, the Israel desk officer.

"Israel knew perfectly well that the ship was American," said Adm. Thomas Moorer, chief of naval operations at the time. Moorer, who later became chairman of the Joint Chiefs of Staff, concluded the attack was intended to maximize Israel's territorial gains.

"I am confident that Israel knew the *Liberty* could intercept radio messages from all parties and potential parties to the ongoing war, then in its fourth day, and that Israel was preparing to seize the Golan Heights from Syria despite President Johnson's known opposition to such a move," Moorer said. "I think they realized that if we learned in advance of their plan, there would be a tremendous amount of negotiating between Tel Aviv and Washington."

"What is so chilling and cold-blooded, of course," he said, "is that they [the Israelis] could kill as many Americans as they did in confidence that Washington would cooperate in quelling any public outcry."[206]

Angleton cooperated.

WHEN A CEASE-FIRE TOOK effect on June 11, Israel had defeated all three of its Arab enemies, a resounding victory that expanded the land of Israel from the Sinai to the West Bank to the Golan Heights.

The CIA had won a victory, too. Thanks to Angleton's Israeli contacts, the Agency had correctly predicted when the war would start, who would win it, and why the Soviet Union could not, or would not, intervene.[207]

President Johnson was impressed. After the Six-Day War, Johnson started inviting Dick Helms to his weekly Tuesday lunches with Secretary of State Dean Rusk and Defense Secretary Bob McNamara. Angleton burnished the CIA's reputation and delivered Helms into the good graces of the president. Helms had every reason to be eternally grateful to him.

CHAOS

LATER THAT SUMMER, ANGLETON was back in Dick Helms's office for another meeting about a war—the war that had come to the streets of America. Tom Karamessines, whom Helms had promoted to deputy director of operations, was there, too. The weather outside was balmy, the mood inside grim.

Angleton felt besieged by the growing criticism of the Agency. In 1965, he had learned from his sources at *The New York Times* that the paper was querying its reporters worldwide about CIA activities. The very questions, he told *Times* editor Harrison Salisbury, "betrayed the hand of Soviet operatives."[208]

Then, in February 1967, *Ramparts* magazine, a left-wing monthly, laid bare the international operations of Cord Meyer, Angleton's friend and fishing companion. In a series of articles, the magazine exposed the CIA's funding of the National Student Association and of the AFL-CIO's Jay Lovestone, his longtime friend and a frequent houseguest. One corner of Angleton's intelligence empire was exposed and subjected to scrutiny, questions, and denunciation for the first time.

Opposition to the war in Vietnam was growing and spreading. The sort of patriotic unity seen during World War II and the Korean War was gone. In April 1967, antiwar rallies in New York City and San Francisco attracted hundreds of thousands of people, including Nobel Prize winner Dr. Martin Luther King, Jr., who had never before involved himself in foreign policy issues. Philosopher Bertrand Russell made headlines by convening a war-crimes tribunal in Sweden to judge U.S. actions in Vietnam. Antiwar groups from around the world gathered in Stockholm to plan their next actions.

At the same time, racial disorder turned many of America's urban neighborhoods into battle zones. The country suffered more than 160 civic disturbances in 1967 alone, eight of which were classified as major riots.[209] In Newark, New Jersey, a protest march against police brutality was followed by stone throwing, looting, and gunfire. The National Guard was called in to restore order. In the course of a week, twenty-three people were killed.

Ten days later, Detroit, the country's fourth-largest city, erupted in violence when police shut down a string of private social clubs patronized by blacks. The National Guard could not control the streets, so President Johnson sent in U.S. Army paratroopers. In a week of rioting, thirty-four people were killed and hundreds injured.

"Detroit was the new benchmark, its rubble a monument to the most devastating race riot in U.S. history—and a symbol of domestic crisis grown graver than any since the Civil War," said the editors of *Newsweek* magazine.[210]

President Johnson suspected a conspiracy behind the antiwar movement and the black nationalist insurgency. In his now-regular meetings with Helms, Johnson nagged the CIA director for help.[211]

On August 15, Helms called in Angleton and Karamessines. He ordered them to set up a new intelligence-collection program to keep tabs on antiwar leaders and black militants traveling abroad. The mission of spying on U.S. citizens, even if they were overseas, had "definite domestic counterintelligence aspects," as Karamessines delicately put it.[212] It was a job for Angleton.

Helms wanted suggestions for a senior officer who could run such a program. Angleton offered Richard Ober. Like Angleton, Ober had a bookish pedigree. His father had run a literary agency and he had attended Harvard before joining the CIA.[213] Ober was already investigating possible foreign intelligence connections to the *Ramparts* stories, so he was prepared to expand the scope of CIA interest, per the president's wishes.[214] Karamessines asked Angleton to assign a cryptonym to the project, "so that cable traffic can be suitably handled on a limited basis."[215]

Operation CHAOS was born. Before it was terminated six years later, CHAOS would spy on and infiltrate the entire antiwar movement, not just people or organizations that engaged in violence or contacted foreign governments. Angleton's program indexed the names of 300,000 Americans in the Agency's Hydra computer system. CHAOS opened files on 7,200 individuals and more than 100 organizations.[216] More than 5,000 reports were sent to the FBI.[217]

CHAOS expanded Angleton's empire of surveillance.

AND STILL ANGLETON WORRIED. There were so many dangers to deter, so many secrets to keep, so few who could be trusted. His family was drifting away. His colleagues were daring to question his theories. The multiple martinis at lunch blurred his judgment and compounded his paranoia. And his annual fishing trips with work pals on the Brule River in Wisconsin or the Matapedia River in Canada provided only temporary respite from the perils he battled.

Angleton still sought to convince British and American colleagues that Labour Party leader Harold Wilson was a Soviet agent of influence. He still argued the supposed diplomatic spat and shooting war between the Soviet Union and China was an elaborate exercise in disinformation to deceive the West.

In March 1966, Angleton and Golitsyn flew to London unannounced to make their case to Sir Maurice Oldfield, a longtime friend who was a senior SIS officer. They spun a theory of a monstrous KGB plot to disarm the West without firing a shot. The whole performance, one British official noted drily, "was somewhat extraordinary, but then Jim and Anatoly are quite extraordinary chaps."[218]

The continuing detention of Nosenko provoked growing criticism inside the Agency. Nosenko had been removed from his spartan attic in Clinton, Maryland, in August 1965 and shipped to an even harsher black site at Camp Peary, the CIA base in southern Virginia. Angleton would deny that he ever visited the Camp Peary site, but a memo later surfaced that showed he had been informed about the details of its construction and was provided with photographs of its completion.[219]

Under the persistent questioning from Pete Bagley, Nosenko was caught in many misstatements but never changed his story. He was a defector who wanted to help the U.S. government. For his temerity on insisting he was telling the truth, Nosenko says he was dosed with LSD.[220]

"I was simply floating," he later recalled. "I was almost half-conscious and suddenly I couldn't breathe. I couldn't take air in. I couldn't take [sic] air out. I almost died. They [the prison guards] noticed on the TV camera. They immediately came, and took me out of the cell. Next door was my shower stall. They put me under shower: Cold water, hot. Cold, hot. Cold, hot. . . . I couldn't even describe it. I never had such an experience in my life. I'm sure it was LSD."[221]

MKULTRA still haunted the CIA, the dream that drugs could serve the ends of espionage. Angleton was responsible.

"They had tried everything, lie detector tests, so on and so forth," said CIA psychologist John Gittinger. "They decided to try some kind of drugs on him."[222]

Word of Nosenko's plight reached George Kisevalter and other officers who thought he was a bona fide defector. One of them, Leonard McCoy, a reports officer, implored division chief David Murphy to share the results of Nosenko's interrogation with others.[223] Murphy finally did, and the CIA war over Nosenko escalated.

In December 1965, McCoy wrote up a forty-one-page memo, making the case that Nosenko was a bona fide defector, not a KGB asset. Helms then asked the Soviet Russia Division and Angleton's staff to come to a consensus on the man's authenticity. Angleton and Murphy rejected McCoy's analysis. They insisted that Nosenko was a false defector. McCoy countered that Angleton's belief that all Soviet defectors since Golitsyn were fakes had "generated a widespread feeling of frustration, futility and impotence."[224]

In February 1967, Pete Bagley replied to McCoy with a report running to eight hundred pages, arguing that Nosenko was under KGB control.[225] He listed hundreds of unexplained gaps and discrepancies in Nosenko's story. But the sheer volume of Bagley's argument was greater than its persuasive power. In the words of one Agency historian, Angleton and his acolytes had "developed substantial circumstantial evidence but no hard proof in the form of a confession from Nosenko."[226]

Angleton was still flailing after the elusive mole known as Sasha. He suspected a man named Orlov, who had worked for the Agency in the 1950s. Orlov ran a picture-frame shop in Alexandria, Virginia. The FBI put his store under constant surveillance. No suspicious activities or contacts were observed.[227]

Golitsyn offered a new theory to Angleton: Maybe Dave Murphy, chief of the Soviet Russia Division, was the mole. Golitsyn found it suspicious that Murphy had agreed so readily to the hostile interrogation of Nosenko. Maybe he was protecting the mole by confining Nosenko so he couldn't be followed, Golitsyn said.

Golitsyn had no real evidence for this theory, but Angleton was persuaded, at least enough to ask Helms to transfer Murphy to a less sensitive position. Murphy was assigned to be station chief in Paris.[228] He was suspected of being the mole he had been attempting to find.

IN OCTOBER 1967, HELMS overruled Angleton for the first time. Vexed by the impasse over Nosenko's bona fides, Helms transferred responsibility for the case to the Office of Security. Nosenko was moved to a safe house in Washington.[229] He was scheduled for controlled release to civilian life in January 1969.

Angleton had lost control of his prize prisoner. He feared the KGB was prevailing. He believed he knew who was responsible: Kim Philby.

TWO BOXERS

UNTOUCHABLE AND ISOLATED IN his work and family, Angleton grew more angular, a stork among men. His suits grew baggier, his eyes more hollowed. Most days he arrived at headquarters midmorning and read through stacks of files. He favored long liquid lunches, often with Ray Rocca, other colleagues, or foreign friends. He returned to the office late in the afternoon and worked at his desk until the late hours of the night.

Angleton traveled often. He went to London to see top MI6 men. He stopped in Rome to see old friends. He spent time in Pretoria, then under apartheid. He attended conferences in New Zealand and Australia. And he always returned to Tel Aviv and Jerusalem. He took his vacations at the family homes in Tucson and Wisconsin, or on remote rivers in Idaho or the Adirondacks. At the house on 33rd Road in Arlington, he liked to spend time in his steamy greenhouse conceiving intricate plans to bring forth perfect beauty. As his orchids bloomed, his mood blackened.

Intoxicated with alcohol and Anatoly Golitsyn's theories about KGB moles, Angleton saw suspects everywhere. He thought Americans at the highest levels of power were succumbing to the "monster plot" of Soviet strategic deception. The forces of despotic communism, led by a masterful KGB, were advancing, and the free world was in retreat. The Russians, he feared, had even penetrated CIA's headquarters.

In violation of the law and all security procedures, Angleton shared sensitive CIA personnel files with Golitsyn, who used them to finger more suspected spies. Their methods were sloppy, speculative, and not subject to review. The mole hunt had become a witch hunt.

Angleton concluded Vasia Gmirkin, a Russian-born officer, might actually be a KGB sleeper agent. He wasn't, but Angleton blocked his promotion for years. Angleton became convinced, on the slightest of evidence, that Leslie James Bennett, a senior counterintelligence official for the Royal Canadian Mounted Police, was a Communist spy. Angleton hounded him into retirement. Bennett was innocent. Angleton insisted that Yuri Loginov, a KGB officer who defected in South Africa, was just another dispatched agent and returned him to his former colleagues. Loginov was a genuine defector; rumor had it the KGB sent him to a firing squad.[230]

Angleton was a lethal man who had real reason to worry about the lingering suspicions surrounding the assassination of President Kennedy. A series of popular books in 1965 and 1966 challenged the findings of the Warren Commission. The editors of two of the country's most popular magazines, *Life* and *Look,* called for a new investigation of the Dallas tragedy. In March 1967, syndicated columnist Drew Pearson reported that the CIA had enlisted Mafia figures, including Harvey's pal Johnny Rosselli, in a plot to kill Fidel Castro. The column offered the opinion that Castro had learned of the plot and struck first. It was a sensational story and, as Angleton knew full well, accurate, at least with respect to Harvey and Rosselli.

Worst of all, New Orleans district attorney Jim Garrison had arrested a local businessman, Clay Shaw, and charged him with conspiring to assassinate President Kennedy, with the help of Lee Harvey Oswald and others. Garrison didn't know much about how the clandestine service actually operated, but he was correct that Shaw was a CIA operative. As a traveling businessman, Shaw had been periodically debriefed by the Agency's Domestic Contact Service between 1949 and 1956.

Agency officials would later tell reporters that Shaw was an unpaid informant, but that was a cover story. Kenneth McDonald, a CIA historian who reviewed Shaw's file in the 1990s, described him as "a highly-paid contract source."[231]

The growing skepticism about the Warren Commission had even infected Win Scott in Mexico City. Angleton's friend from OSS days had served as chief of station in the Mexican capital since 1956. Under State Department cover, Scott had built one of the most effective CIA outposts anywhere. In a country where nationalist resentment of Yanqui power was the norm, Scott charmed three Mexican presidents onto the CIA payroll and made friends everywhere he went. He had reported on Lee Harvey Oswald in a timely way both before and after JFK was killed. He had cooperated with the Warren Commission without compromising any Agency operations. Needless to say, he was well-informed and nobody's fool. Elena Garro de Paz, a poet and friend of his wife, told Scott she had seen Oswald at a party in Mexico City and that Oswald had had a brief affair with Sylvia Duran, a receptionist in the Cuban consulate. Scott initially dismissed the story, but Charles Thomas, a State Department officer in Mexico, had also heard the story and did some investigating on his own. He found reason to believe the story of an Oswald-Duran fling, and Scott came to believe it, too.[232] "That Sylvia Duran had sexual intercourse with Oswald . . . is probably new but adds little to the Oswald case," he advised headquarters.[233]

Angleton was not happy when Scott shared his view of the JFK case with a longtime British friend Ferguson Dempster, the chief of the SIS station in Mexico. When Dempster wrote a letter to his bosses in London summarizing Scott's JFK thoughts, someone at the CIA—probably Angleton—managed to obtain two pages of the letter.[234]

Dick Helms was not happy, either. He ordered Bill Broe, chief of the Western Hemisphere Division, to reprimand Scott. Broe sent Scott a blind memo under his cryptonym, "Thomas Lund."

> We have received from a very sensitive source two pages only of a letter almost certainly by LIOSAGE [the CIA's code name for Dempster] to his home office reporting on comments he claims made by you. We recognize that any such remarks by you could well be taken out of context no matter how carefully made. . . . Nevertheless, you should be aware the letter was written and be guided accordingly."[235]

Scott did not fail to appreciate the sharp edge sheathed in his bosses' politesse: "be guided accordingly. . . . It would be most unfortunate if there should ever be any leak."

Scott had clashed with Angleton before. In 1961, the counterintelligence chief sought to set up offices in Mexico City that would report to Angleton directly. Scott objected vehemently, and their friendship cooled.[236]

"They were like two boxers in the ring, eyeing each other, who's going to strike," said one station officer who knew them both. "They were two tigers who are looking at each other, who was going to pounce first. Win didn't say much about Angleton. He wasn't someone to make statements about other people that were derogatory. He was a very fair guy, but I don't think he trusted Angleton."[237]

Angleton's message to Scott was clear: Shut up about JFK or else.

IN SEPTEMBER 1967, DICK Helms convened a committee of CIA men that came to be known as the Garrison Group for its close attention to the New Orleans district attorney, who was trying to prove a JFK conspiracy. The Garrison Group was controlled by Angleton. The executive director was his friend Wistar Janney. His deputy Ray Rocca was the most active member.

The Garrison Group did not investigate the conspiracy theories that Angleton would espouse later in life. Mostly, it sought to gauge what Garrison had learned about CIA operations in New Orleans in the summer of 1963, a point of vulnerability for both Helms and Angleton.

Ray Rocca feared the worst. At the group's first meeting in the fall of 1967, Rocca opined that "Garrison would indeed obtain a conviction of Shaw for conspiring to assassinate President Kennedy," a prediction that was noteworthy less for its inaccuracy (Shaw would be acquitted) than for the fact that it was made at all.[238] At a time when many in the Washington press corps, relying on government sources, publicly dismissed Garrison's case as flimsy, one of Angleton's top deputies said privately that Garrison might be able to persuade a jury that a CIA man had connived with Oswald.

HEIST

AS THE CIA'S ISRAEL desk officer, Angleton was responsible for reporting on the Jewish state's continuing efforts to secure a nuclear arsenal. He didn't do a very good job. The last chapter of the great Israeli uranium heist took place on his watch, and he was apparently none the wiser.

It happened on September 10, 1968, when four men arrived at the two-story brick building in Apollo, Pennsylvania, that housed the offices of the Nuclear Materials and Equipment Corporation. Across the street was the long, low-slung building where NUMEC packaged and stored enriched uranium.

The four men were authorized by the U.S. government to visit NUMEC. The company's president, Zalman Shapiro, had written to the Security Office of the Atomic Energy Commission seeking permission to host a group of Israeli scientists. The men were visiting the facility "to discuss thermo-electric devices (unclassified)," he wrote.

Shapiro lied to the AEC, albeit plausibly. The four men who got out of their cars could have passed for scientists. One of them, Avraham Hermoni, actually was a scientist. He served as scientific counselor at the Israeli embassy in Washington. He came to that position from serving as technical director of Israel's national center for weapons development, known as RAFAEL.

Hermoni was accompanied by Dr. Ephraim Biegun. According to Shapiro's paperwork, he supposedly worked for the "Department of Electronics at the Ministry of Defense" in Israel. Actually, Biegun ran the technical department of Shin Bet, the Israeli domestic security force. He was a master of things "we had only read about in books," said his colleague Avraham Bendor.

Bendor was the third man in the crew. He also worked in the Electronics Department, according to Shapiro. In fact, he was on special assignment to LAKAM, the Science Liaison Bureau, a secret Israeli operation, which had responsibility for stealing nuclear technologies and materials.

The fourth man visiting NUMEC that day was Rafael Eitan. He was not a "chemist" as Shapiro claimed. He was the mastermind of the whole operation.

Eitan was a small man with an outsized reputation for trickery. Of Russian ancestry, he grew up in Palestine and joined the Haganah as a boy of twelve. In the 1948 war, he fought under the command of Yitzhak Rabin. He joined the Mossad and distinguished himself on dangerous operations, such as the kidnapping of Adolf Eichmann. He came to Apollo, Pennsylvania, in September 1968 to advance another operation in defense of the Jewish people.

Zalman Shapiro didn't talk about such things. After meeting with the four Israelis, Shapiro informed the AEC via letter that his "[d]iscussion with Israeli nationals concerned the possibility of developing plutonium fueled thermoelectric generator systems."[239]

The presence of Rafi Eitan was the tip-off to U.S. officials in the know.

Anthony Cordesman, a former Defense Department official, said the meeting in Apollo constituted "extremely hard evidence" that Eitan was operating with Israeli intelligence in the United States. "There is no conceivable reason for Eitan to have gone [to the Apollo plant] but for the nuclear material."[240]

John Hadden, now working for Angleton in Washington, concluded Eitan was the mastermind of the great uranium heist. Absconding with a couple hundred pounds of contraband from an unguarded facility, Hadden noted, was an easier task than absconding with a war criminal.[241]

When Zalman Shapiro died in 2016, much of his obituary was devoted to denials that he had diverted nuclear material to Israel.[242] The hundreds of pounds of highly enriched uranium had simply gotten lost in the Apollo plant, said Mark Lowenthal, son of NUMEC financier David Lowenthal, in an email. His father, who had died in 2006, "never mentioned anything about the supposedly missing materials. . . . David was an ultra-American patriot and would never break any American laws, so while the myth surrounding NUMEC makes for a great conspiracy theory, when all the dust (or half-life of the dust) settles, I'm sure it will show that there wasn't any theft."[243]

But neither Shapiro nor Lowenthal could explain why Rafi Eitan and company had visited the NUMEC plant in 1968 disguised as nuclear scientists.

"It was obviously some intelligence operation, a special operation," says historian Avner Cohen. "Rafi Eitan, he is not a scientist. He is not directly related to the nuclear project. He is an operational person, a secrecy person, if you do something that you need a great deal of secrecy. . . . This is a signal that the Mossad is involved in something, which is probably extraordinary."[244]

KIM AGAIN

AS HIS FIFTIETH BIRTHDAY approached, in December 1967 Angleton took refuge in Israel, where his troubles seemed farther away and his friends closer. For companionship, he brought along his intellectual soul mate Anatoly Golitsyn. Upon arrival, Angleton was greeted by John Denley Walker, a career officer who had succeeded John Hadden as chief of the Tel Aviv station.

Angleton asked Walker to arrange to have a case of whiskey delivered to his hotel room. When it arrived, Angleton told Walker he suspected the liquor might have been poisoned by the KGB. Walker explained he had bought the whiskey at the embassy commissary and delivered it himself. Angleton would not be dissuaded. When Walker said Angleton was on the verge of a nervous breakdown and insisted he go home, Angleton shouted he would make sure Walker never got a decent assignment again. Walker relented.[245]

Angleton and Golitsyn went to Eilat, a resort town in southern Israel, on the Gulf of Aqaba. Angleton's Israeli friends had invited him to celebrate his fiftieth birthday.

"We had a big party for him," recalled Efraim Halevy.[246]

ANGLETON RETRIEVED *THE WASHINGTON POST* from his door-step on Wednesday morning, March 15, 1968. He read the front-page head-lines and flipped through the inner pages, scanning the wire-service stories and department store advertisements. He turned to page A12 and found himself reading an article from hell.

PHILBY TELLS OF HIS SPY ROLE
HERE IN BOOK RELEASED TODAY

Angleton was not entirely surprised by the news that his former friend had written a book. A few months before, *The Sunday Times* of London had published an interview with Philby from Moscow in which the now-famous spy said he was writing a memoir.[247]

Angleton was unprepared for the tenor of the *Post* story, which he read with incredulity mounting toward rage.

"'My Silent War'" will be 'must' reading in both the CIA and the Federal Bureau of Investigation," the *Post* reported, "not only for its description of clandestine operations but also for its intimate personal descriptions of the men Philby dealt with in both agencies."

The article reported that James Angleton of the CIA was one of Philby's chief contacts. Furious, Angleton called Ben Bradlee and demanded an explanation. The *Post* had blown his cover, he said. Bradlee insisted Philby's book was news.[248] By the time the conversation ended, their decade-old friendship was over.

Angleton read *My Silent War* not only as a friend betrayed but also as a counterintelligence professional exposed. The book was a witty, malicious account of Philby's sixteen years in the lion's den of the capitalist ruling class. While playing the part of an affable civil servant, Philby relished acting as silent avenger in the class struggle. He enjoyed playing his bourgeois colleagues for fools and took pleasure in sending the CIA's foot soldiers off to certain death. His descriptions of Bill Harvey and Allen Dulles were sketched in acid. His allusions to Angleton were affectionate, condescending, and devastating. Of their last meeting in June 1951, Philby recalled Angleton wanted to convey certain concerns to colleagues in London. "I did not even take the trouble to memorize them,"[249] Philby said. It was a cruel kiss-off for a former friend.

Angleton tried not to take the book personally. He concluded that Philby was targeting him in public in order to protect ongoing KGB operations. Just as he had protected Burgess and Maclean back in 1951, so Philby was seeking to protect other moles now. *My Silent War,* Angleton decided, was the latest gambit in the Soviet strategic deception policy.

In fact, Philby's master conspiracy occurred only in Angleton's wounded imagination. In Moscow, the KGB had made Philby a general but relegated him to training sessions and other nonsensitive assignments, much to Philby's frustration. There's no evidence Philby targeted Angleton. Philby was mostly thinking about Philby.

"The key to Philby, if there is a single one," wrote James McCargar in *The New York Times Book Review,* "is less likely to be found in the surface manifestations of his 'love' or the faults of the [British] Establishment, than it is in a compulsion to betray and deceive which underlay all his relationships."[250]

Angleton knew better than anyone.

DURING ANGLETON'S FREQUENT ABSENCES from home, Cicely and his daughters had talked about the war in Vietnam among themselves. They hated it and opposed it. Truffy and Lucy had come back from college converted. They joined in the antiwar marches that their father disdained. The counterculture had come to another CIA family.

Angleton was not fazed by the so-called Tet Offensive of January 1968. The surprise uprising of Communist forces on Tet, the country's New Year celebration, had brought the war to Saigon, the capital of South Vietnam. A daring squad of Vietcong guerrillas breached the walls of the U.S. embassy before a larger corps of U.S. Marines annihilated them. Angleton argued, with numerical accuracy, that the North Vietnamese had suffered heavy losses in the offensive. He disputed that the Communists had scored a major psychological victory. Even his own family didn't believe him.

ANGLETON WAS NOT A political partisan. He conceived of his job as that of serving the Agency and the president. But he knew how power was wielded or squandered. In spring 1968 he knew he would have a new boss come November, and it mattered who it was. With President Lyndon Johnson forswearing a second term, the innocuous vice president, Hubert Humphrey, announced his intention to become the Democratic presidential nominee. So did Bobby Kennedy, brother of the slain president, who was now a senator from New York while still living at Hickory Hill, in McLean. On the Republican side, former vice president Richard Nixon was running and so was California governor Ronald Reagan.

On April 4, 1968, TV broadcasters announced the news that Martin Luther King, Jr., had been shot to death as he stood on the balcony of a Memphis motel. The Angletons lived in tranquil, tree-lined north Arlington, but they saw on their television what was happening not five miles away in Washington, D.C. Crowds of black people were avenging King's death by smashing windows and looting stores up and down the Fourteenth Street commercial corridor. Hunter S. Thompson's fear and loathing had come to the nation's capital.

Like everyone else, Angleton struggled to comprehend the latest news. On June 5, Robert Kennedy, walking off from a victory speech after winning California's Democratic presidential primary, was shot in the crowded kitchen of the Ambassador Hotel in Los Angeles, apparently by a Palestinian waiter named Sirhan Sirhan. RFK died the next morning. Angleton suspected organized crime figures were behind the assassination.[251]

The secrets and suspicions and cigarette smoke saturated and overwhelmed Angleton. One evening when visiting a friend, he began coughing up blood.[252] He was taken to the George Washington University Hospital, where he was diagnosed with a bleeding ulcer.

"ANGLETON WAS AT THE zenith of his power, although the strain was beginning to tell on him," Peter Wright wrote of his American friend. ". . . [H]e was making enemies throughout the CIA in the Soviet Division . . . and among those officers whose promotion prospects he had adversely affected," Wright said. "He was safe while Helms was director, but the war in Vietnam was rapidly altering the face of the Agency."[253]

Angleton's suspicions had effectively stunted or ended the careers of colleagues who were guilty of nothing. Peter Karlow had been forced into retirement. Paul Garbler had been dispatched to a backwater station in the Caribbean. Richard Kovich had been relegated to a Camp Peary teaching job. David Murphy had been shunted to the Paris station. J. Edgar Hoover had withdrawn the FBI from the HONETOL committee, but Angleton's mole hunt continued.[254]

One evening, Angleton and Peter Wright traded conspiracy theories until four in the morning at a Chinese restaurant in Arlington. As Cicely Angleton said of her husband and his colleagues, "Their nerves were shot."[255]

"We were both on the rack," Wright wrote. "So much depended on making the right assumptions about the defectors—for him the assassination of the President; for me the next move in the mole hunt."[256]

The two men walked back to Angleton's Mercedes. It was parked near the Iwo Jima Memorial, adjacent to Arlington National Cemetery. Angleton was staunch in his reverence for the American flag and patriotic symbols like the statue of U.S. soldiers planting the flag of victory over Japan. He paused to look at the marble men bathed in the glow of spotlights. His own silent war against the KGB was never-ending.

"This is Kim's work," Angleton muttered. His betrayed love had curdled into mad obsession.[257]

PART IV

LEGEND

NIXON

WHEN ALLEN DULLES DIED at age seventy-five in January 1969, Angleton responded with practiced tradecraft. He led an Office of Security team, which passed through Dulles's home in Georgetown. Angleton secured classified papers in the office, while technicians installed secure phone lines to handle the expected flood of condolence calls.

A few days later, Angleton carried the ashes of his friend in a wooden box as he walked out of Georgetown Presbyterian Church and into the rainy Washington morning of February 1, 1969. Allen Welsh Dulles, the friend, mentor, and father figure he had met in that Rome hotel room so many years ago, was gone. In the ritual of memorial, Angleton was given an honored role: to hold the box of dust to which the great man had returned. Angleton emerged from the white church with a full head of gray hair, a distinguished brow, large black-rimmed glasses enlarging his eyes, and a tightly knotted tie. He was not one to let his sadness show.

The CIA men gathered on the cobblestone street outside and in the church's cool wooden interior, spare in the way of Presbyterians. There was the suave Dick Helms, the unpretentious Tom Karamessines, the stoic Cord Meyer, and the dashing David Phillips, who had dubbed Dulles "the Great White Case Officer," an epithet that captured the Anglo-Saxon chauvinism that suffused his career.

Dulles's widow, Clover, sat in the front pew with daughter Joan and son Allen Macy. The Angletons, the Truitts, and the Bradlees mixed with the CIA families and several hundred mourners from the many walks of Dulles's life. In every pew sat columnists and editors, ambassadors and bankers, senators and congressmen, painters and novelists. There was Robert McNamara, the former defense secretary, looking haunted, and William Rogers, the new secretary of state. The corpulent and corrupt vice president of the United States, Spiro Agnew, attended as the representative of newly elected President Richard Nixon.

The eulogy, written by retired diplomat Charles Murphy, with contributions from Angleton, was read by Dick Helms.

"Perhaps we can now find it in ourselves to say that we shall always be with him," Helms declaimed. "To say that for us, as for him, patriotism sets no bounds on the wider pursuit of truth in the defense of freedom and liberty."

That was the consoling message for the mourners, a fitting benediction in the church of spies, a celebration of a patriotism that "sets no bounds on the wider pursuit of truth." Like Dulles, Angleton set no bounds on his patriotism, and, like Dulles, he was glad Richard Nixon was in the White House.[1]

"I KNOW HOW VITALLY important the work of this organization is," President Nixon said to the crowded auditorium on the first floor of CIA headquarters in Langley. It was March 7, 1969, a spring day with a hopeful warmth, outside and in. In the first months of his administration, the thirty-seventh president made the rounds of the largest federal agencies. Nixon wanted to introduce himself to the men and women of the CIA, and in the case of Angleton, to reintroduce himself.

"I also know that this organization has a mission that, by necessity, runs counter to some of the very deeply held traditions in this country and feelings, high idealistic feelings, about what a free society ought to be," Nixon said to the sea of faces before him.

The audience included Helms and Angleton and their top deputies, as well as various division chiefs and their assistants. These were the men and women who spied on America's friends and enemies, stole secrets, opened mail, intercepted radio signals, dispensed with unfriendly governments, organized armies, controlled newspapers, burglarized embassies, and assassinated terrorists.

The Ivy League panache of the CIA men made Nixon sweat. But on this day, he commanded them by embracing their truth: *a mission that, by necessity, runs counter to some of the very deeply held traditions in this country.* Nixon was calling their attention to the obvious, if unspoken, business at hand: The CIA was a law-breaking agency responsible for defending a law-abiding democracy.

"This is a dilemma," Nixon admitted, his jaw jutting. He was a hard man, a plain man, a salesman. "It is one that I wish did not exist."

A humble man, Nixon knew how to flatter.

"I look upon this organization as not one that is necessary for the conduct of conflict or war," he said, ". . . but, in the final analysis [it] is one of the great instruments of our Government for the preservation of peace, for the avoidance of war. . . . I think the American people need to understand—that this [Agency]"—he looked around the auditorium of the clandestine service—"is a necessary adjunct to the conduct of the Presidency."[2]

Nixon's words echoed Angleton's conception of the CIA. *One of the great instruments of our Government . . . a necessary adjunct to the conduct of the Presidency.* Angleton thought Nixon measured up to past presidents. He did not have the gravitas of a Dwight Eisenhower—nor the complacency. Nixon had none of the charisma of Jack Kennedy—and none of the weakness, either. He had little of Lyndon Johnson's crude forcefulness—and rather more subtlety. After eight years of JFK and LBJ in the White House, Angleton regarded Nixon as a welcome improvement. No president, he believed, better understood the threat of communism in all of its dimensions than Richard Milhous Nixon.

Nixon and Angleton had more than a working acquaintance, dating back to their discussions about getting tough on Cuba. They shared an instinct of impatience, an abhorrence of liberal illusion, an intolerance for disorder, a dedication to action, a love of America, and a thirst for information about their enemies. They shared a mission higher than law, and they would share a common fate.

A DEVASTATING EXPLOSION AT 18 West Eleventh Street in New York City on the night of March 6, 1970, gutted the four-story brick town house in a thunderous few seconds. The sound was heard miles away. In Washington, the explosion on the genteel Greenwich Village street would set off something close to panic among the U.S. government's top law-enforcement and intelligence professionals.

The building was the home of Cathy Wilkerson, a college student and member of a revolutionary group that called itself the Weathermen or the

Weather Underground.[3] As federal agents sifted through the smoldering rubble and interviewed Wilkerson's parents, they obtained a more frightening understanding of the group's intentions. The brownstone had been a haven for men and women who styled themselves after Che Guevara and Ho Chi Minh. The FBI counted twenty-one members of the Weather Underground at large who spoke of "bringing the war home." They were violent, elusive, and sure to strike again.

A couple of them had been working in the basement of the town house, preparing a homemade explosive device equipped with several pounds of dynamite.[4] They planned to plant it on the U.S. Army base in Fort Dix, New Jersey. One of the bomb makers made a mistake: A crossed circuit? A stray spark? A drug-induced stumble? The explosives detonated and the bomb maker was obliterated. Three people in the house were killed instantly. Two women climbed out of the ruins and ran away before police or ambulances arrived on the scene.

The top men at the FBI and CIA were disturbed. The antiwar movement had been growing for years and becoming more violent. The civil rights movement had generated the black nationalist insurgency that dismissed the polite agenda of the late Martin Luther King, Jr., in favor of nothing less than reclaiming city streets from white cops. In early 1969, J. Edgar Hoover had reported more than one hundred attacks by "black extremists" on police, double the rate of the previous six months.[5] The Bureau, in league with local police officers, had responded with COINTELPRO measures to harass, disrupt, discredit, and, in Hoover's ominous word, "neutralize" black leaders. None of it seemed to be doing much good to stem the tide of violence in America.

The nation's college campuses were more tumultuous than ever. Eight leaders of the protests at the 1968 Democratic National Convention in Chicago had been indicted on conspiracy charges, although what they had conspired to do was hazy. In Santa Barbara, California, an antiwar crowd torched a Bank of America branch office. In New York, the offices of IBM, Socony Oil, and General Telephone & Electric were bombed. In May, four students were shot dead by National Guardsmen at Ohio's Kent State University. The nation's campuses overflowed with talk of revolution, and the radio airwaves resounded with a dirge of protest: "Four dead in O-hi-o."

Neither the CIA nor the FBI had any sources in the Weather Underground. The group seemed to have logistical support across the United States and internationally. They proclaimed their intention to inflict violence on American targets, and the U.S. government had no solid information about their plans, capabilities, or weaponry—except for what Angleton maintained in his LINGUAL files.[6]

As President Nixon demanded action to combat the tide of what he called "revolutionary terrorism," Angleton was ready to help, along with his friend Bill Sullivan, assistant director of the FBI. With Tom Huston, an aide to Nixon, they developed a proposal for unifying the government's domestic counterintelligence apparatus to deal with the growing crisis.

Their proposal became known as "the Huston Plan," and it generated headlines when exposed by Senate investigators three years later. But Huston was not its intellectual author. A young attorney, Huston was an Indiana political activist who had worked in the White House for little more than a year. He was not the source for the detailed counterintelligence information that filled his memoranda. Huston was schooled by the two men whose policy positions he shared and articulated. If the proposal had been named for its intellectual authors, the Huston Plan would have been called "the Sullivan-Angleton Plan."

THE GERMINATION OF THE Huston Plan went back to Nixon's vision for the CIA. He saw the Agency as an adjunct to the presidency, an instrument of White House power. He expected the Agency to serve. As chief executive, Nixon preferred to insulate himself from cabinet officers and officials by sending his orders through his chief of staff, H. R. Haldeman, and White House counsel John Ehrlichman.[7] They, in turn, used their assistants to deliver Nixon's commands to the offices of the government.

In the summer of 1969, Huston, who worked for Ehrlichman, called on Sullivan at FBI headquarters. He told him that the president was dissatisfied with the work of the Bureau, particularly in regard to antiwar militants. Who was watching them? Who was reporting on their foreign contacts?

Sullivan had no good answers and blamed the problem on his boss. In a fit of pique, J. Edgar Hoover ended the FBI's contacts with the CIA. "I want direct liaison here with CIA to be terminated and any contact with CIA in the future to be by letter only," Hoover wrote in a furious memo.[8] The consequences of Hoover's stubbornness were nothing short of catastrophic, Sullivan told Huston. "The barriers that Hoover had erected between the FBI and other intelligence agencies had led to a condition of total isolation of each organization," he said.[9]

Angleton and Sullivan plied Huston with the best data in the LINGUAL/HUNTER and CHAOS files. The letters of Kathy Boudin, a member of the Weather Underground, who was still at large; reports on the travels of Eldridge Cleaver, minister of information for the Black Panthers; and the finances of the Institute for Policy Studies, a leftist think tank in Washington. Huston fashioned this intelligence into several memos for the White House staff, which evolved into the plan that would bear his name.

After the explosion on Eleventh Street and the disorder on college campuses, Nixon's conservative soul was tormented by America's upheavals: the vicious bombings, the unruly longhairs, the Negroes out of control, and a permissive liberal elite excusing it all.

On June 4, 1970, Nixon summoned the four highest-ranking intelligence directors in the U.S. government: Hoover of the FBI, Helms of the CIA, Lt. Gen. Donald Bennett of the Defense Intelligence Agency, and Vice Adm. Noel Gayler, director of the National Security Agency. These men commanded budgets in the billions and had thousands of subordinates.

Nixon lectured them like schoolchildren.

"We are now confronted by a new and grave crisis in our country—one which we know too little about," he said. "Certainly hundreds, perhaps thousands, of Americans are determined to destroy our society. . . . They are reaching out for the support—ideological or otherwise—of foreign powers and they are developing their own brand of indigenous revolutionary activism, which is as dangerous as anything they could import from Cuba, China, or the Soviet Union."

"I do not intend to sit idly by," Nixon growled, "while self-appointed revolutionaries commit acts of terrorism throughout the land."

He demanded "an intensified domestic intelligence collection effort," beginning with the Huston Plan. He ordered Helms to appoint a sub-committee with an urgent task: "I want to have a full range of options for dramatically expanding our domestic intelligence collection efforts."[10]

Angleton, wreathed in the usual haze of cigarette smoke, seized the moment to identify himself with Huston.

"There was no question in my mind nor in the minds of others that he [Huston] represented the Commander in Chief in terms of bringing together this plan," Angleton said.[11] He said he was ready to "practically drop everything" in order to resolve the "conflicts that had grown specifically between the CIA and FBI."

The Huston Plan offered Nixon a full range of options, but there was one delicate issue. Angleton and Helms had never told President Nixon about the Agency's long-standing mail-opening program, LINGUAL, or about HUNTER, which fed selected correspondence to the FBI. So Angleton wrote a clever lie into the Huston Plan. He told Huston that the CIA had once had a mail-opening program but had shut it down in the face of controversy. The recent emergence of the Weather Underground and other violent groups required "re-activization" of the program, he said.

The plan went to Nixon, who approved of the particulars. The president agreed to lifting existing legal restrictions on domestic intelligence collection. He approved the expansion of NSA operations involving warrantless surveillance of Americans' phone calls and telegrams. He approved of more FBI "black bag" jobs. He agreed to expand the existing CHAOS coverage of the antiwar movement. And he reinstated the CIA's authority to open the mail of Americans.

Sullivan and Angleton had prevailed. The plan bolstered Sullivan's position at the FBI and enhanced Angleton's influence over domestic CIA spying operations. They would be the senior representatives on a new Intelligence Evaluation Committee in the White House, which sought to stem the tide of violence and subversion.

On July 9, 1970, the U.S. intelligence chiefs endorsed the president's directive. The Huston Plan became U.S. policy. Angleton, not Hoover, now controlled domestic counterintelligence.

The Huston plan started fast and faltered faster. Angleton and Sullivan, it turned out, had laid their plans well in all ways but one. No one had thought to inform John Mitchell, the attorney general. The chief law-enforcement officer in the United States knew nothing about the decision to abandon previous legal restrictions on spying on Americans, and nothing about the creation of the Intelligence Evaluation Committee.[12]

Mitchell was appalled. He was no civil libertarian. He was a grumpy, pipe-smoking Wall Street lawyer who specialized in bond issues. He had little tolerance for political adventurism and less for legal improvisation. As Nixon's campaign manager, he worried about the repercussions if such a plan were exposed before the 1972 election.

Mitchell asked to meet with Hoover. Without the blessing of the attorney general, the FBI director suddenly felt vulnerable, too. Hoover told Mitchell he would deploy his men on the expanded domestic counterintelligence mission only with written authorization from the president. Mitchell told Nixon not to sign any such authorization. Hoover replied that the FBI would no longer participate. Nixon did not want a fight with his FBI director or his campaign manager, so he folded. On July 27, 1970, he issued a memo killing the whole arrangement. The Huston Plan, so skillfully advanced by Angleton and Sullivan, was dead.

Angleton was undaunted. In his memo, President Nixon had rescinded the "re-activization" of the mail-opening program, which meant that LINGUAL no longer had presidential approval. As an officer of the CIA, Angleton was obliged to follow the orders of the commander in chief. He chose not to.

The program yielded eight thousand letters a year, a bounty that Angleton could read at his leisure, a guide to the inner thoughts and plans of radicals, senators, and Communist sympathizers around the world.[13] The counterintelligence chief would not surrender such a bounty, not even under written orders from the president. He assumed no one would ever learn of his decision.

As George Kisevalter said, Angleton had a bit of Iago in him. Like the

Shakespearean counselor, he lived by his own creed. What Iago said, Angleton lived.

> But I will wear my heart upon my sleeve
> For daws to peck at: I am not what I am.[14]

GOLEM

IN THE SUMMER OF 1969, Angleton took a new friend out to lunch for the first time. His guest was Yitzhak Rabin, former general staff chief of the Israeli Defense Forces and now Israel's new ambassador to Washington. They met at Rive Gauche restaurant in Georgetown, Angleton's latest favorite dining venue. Angleton was proud to be seen with him. He knew the homely Rabin, far more than the telegenic Moshe Dayan, was the real architect of Israel's victory in the Six-Day War.[15]

With Nixon in the White House, Angleton basked in the mood of improved relations between the governments of the United States and Israel. In September 1969, Prime Minister Golda Meir came to Washington to meet President Nixon, and a new strategic relationship was consecrated. Israel was not just another Middle East country. It was a U.S. ally, like England or France.

"Jim saw this as a wonderful development that should have happened a long, long time ago," said Efraim Halevy, now chief of the Mossad station in Washington, who accompanied Rabin on what became a monthly lunch appointment.

Rabin's English was not fluent, so he relied on Halevy for interpreting and keeping notes. When Rabin returned to the diplomatic party circuit, Angleton cultivated the younger man as a source and a friend.

Angleton's family had found new lives. In 1970, Cicely, Truffy, and Lucy became disciples of Yogi Bhajan, the Indian spiritual leader who introduced kundalini yoga and Sikhism to America. "I was 11 when I saw Yogi Bhajan give a lecture in Tucson," Lucy Angleton later told a journalist. "I had no attention span, but for the first time in my life I paid attention." In their new Sikh faith, Angleton's daughters abandoned the names that Jim and Cicely had given them. Lucy changed her name to Siri Hari Angleton-Khalsa. Truffy became Guru Sangat Kaur Khalsa.[16]

Angleton was more alone than ever. He needed comfort and company, and Halevy was glad to oblige.

"There were weeks in which I met him four or five times a week," Halevy recalls. "There were times he came to my house regularly at ten o'clock at night, and left me around five [in the morning] after polishing off a bottle of Jack Daniel's Black Label. There were times when I used to have lunch with him beginning at twelve thirty, and we were still at the restaurant at six thirty. And sometimes, that very evening, he came again."

For Halevy, Angleton was a mentor.

"Jim was a man who understood, in my view, more than anybody else, the true nature of this ongoing battle of espionage and counterespionage," he said. "He had no illusions."

When Rabin became prime minister, Angleton ran into him at an embassy function in Washington. The event was attended by hundreds of people, but Rabin dropped all protocol. He dismissed his bodyguards and pulled up a chair to talk confidentially with Angleton. The crowd kept a respectful distance as the two men of power chatted. The bystanders, Angleton later joked, could only wonder "who was the goy and who was the golem."[17]

Angleton, of course, was the goy, the non-Jew, so perhaps Rabin was the golem. Or was it the other way around? In Jewish folklore, the golem is a body without a soul, an inanimate being who is summoned to life by magic. In some tales, the golem protects the Jews from their tormentors. In others, he runs wild and terrifies the innocent.

Angleton was both goy and golem.

GHOUL

AT HIS PERSONAL BEST, Angleton was a kindly and avuncular man, an original thinker and a thoughtful friend. He was godfather to Quentin Meyer, Cord Meyer's oldest son, who suffered mental health issues after his mother's murder and his tour of duty in Vietnam. Angleton contributed one of his trademark black homburgs to the hat collection of Ted Jessup, the teenage son of Tel Aviv station chief Peter Jessup. Another college-age friend recalled Angleton giving him the I Ching, the collection of classical Chinese divinatory writings, which enjoyed a revival in the sixties counterculture.[18]

Yet he was also damaged. In his work, he was driven by an all-consuming sense of duty, lubricated by martinis, and suffused with suppressed rage at Philby's betrayal. He was obsessed with his theories and enthralled by his means of surveillance. He read the letters of the Weathermen to their Moscow contacts. He knew about the latest trip of the Black Panthers to North Korea, where they could expect training in sabotage and intelligence collection. He could get access to CHAOS informant reports. He had a special file of the correspondence of Senators Church and Kennedy. All of these secrets crowded the in-box on his desk. With America's enemies emboldened everywhere, he felt he had to guard against them all.

And the damned questions about the assassination of JFK would not go away. Angleton's problem was not the theories multiplying on U.S. college campuses as bootleg copies of Abraham Zapruder's film began to circulate. He worried about official efforts to reopen the JFK investigation.

When he read a news report in January 1969 that Jim Garrison had created a new national committee to investigate the assassination, Angleton ordered his deputy, Jim Hunt, to pass a memo to Sam Papich, asking the FBI to investigate its members. (Under orders from Hoover, Papich was forbidden from meeting Angleton in person.)

Angleton informed the FBI that attorney Bernard Fensterwald had said the committee's purpose was "to embarrass or force the government to make investigations they have been putting off since November 22, 1963." Angleton wanted to make sure that didn't happen. Any reinvestigation of JFK's murder was sure to revisit the question of what the CIA knew about Oswald before the assassination, not something he cared to discuss.[19]

Most ominously, one suggestion that the government investigate further originated within the government itself. In September 1969, Angleton received a detailed report from the State Department, written by Charles Thomas, the earnest Foreign Service officer who had previously reported conversations with several Mexicans who recalled meeting Oswald in September 1963. Thomas had collected credible evidence that Oswald had some kind of relationship with Sylvia Duran, the receptionist in the Cuban consulate in Mexico City, who was known to the CIA for her good looks and Communist sympathies.

Thomas felt obliged to report again what he knew, assuming the FBI or the CIA would want to know more about Oswald's Cuban contacts. The FBI wasn't interested. So the State Department referred Thomas's reporting to Angleton.

Angleton had more than enough reason to act. Thomas was a capable Foreign Service officer. If Oswald had had some kind of relationship with Duran, then, presumptively, he'd had some connection to Cuban intelligence. The accumulating evidence again begged an obvious question: Had Castro, knowing the CIA was out to kill him, deployed Oswald to assassinate Kennedy first?

If Angleton was serious about investigating the possible involvement of a hostile foreign power in JFK's murder, he now had credible evidence and ample opportunity. He wasn't interested. He sent the State Department a note acknowledging receipt of Thomas's information and said he saw "no need for further action."[20]

GOY OR GOLEM? ANGLETON was a ghoul, a specter who showed up around the time of death.

On April 12, 1971, Charles Thomas committed suicide at his home in suburban Washington. In a second-floor bathroom, he shot himself with a gun he had bought in Cuba years before. Thomas was despondent because he felt that his Foreign Service career had been cut short. He blamed himself for pursuing the Oswald story too aggressively.[21]

Angleton was making plans to go to Mexico City to see Win Scott, who had retired as station chief. Angleton had been disturbed to learn that Scott, emulating Philby, was planning to publish a memoir about his life as a spy. He obtained a copy of the manuscript Scott was planning to publish. In 220 typed pages Scott recalled his career at the Agency, and he was not discreet. He alluded to Philby, whom he had known well in

London, but Philby was not the problem. For Angleton, the problem was Scott's appalling chapter on JFK's assassination. Scott's account of Lee Harvey Oswald's visit to Mexico City flatly contradicted the Warren Commission's report—and the CIA—on a key issue: Oswald's Cuban contacts.

Angleton had to handle Scott with care. Scott was one of the original OSS men who built the CIA. In Mexico City, he had earned a reputation as possibly the best station chief in the world. Two years before, Helms had bestowed on Scott the Agency's highest honor, the Distinguished Intelligence Medal. Persuading him not to publish his book was not going to be easy.

Then Win Scott dropped dead.

WIDOW

ON THE AFTERNOON OF April 28, 1971, Angleton knocked on the door of the modern split-level house at 16 Rio Escondido in Mexico City. He was accompanied by another CIA man. The door opened, framing the figure of a brown-haired woman with grim eyes and pursed lips. Janet Scott had been a widow for barely forty-eight hours. She recognized Angleton. Like many CIA wives, she loathed him.

"Why did it take so long?" she said, all sarcasm and turning heels. The vultures had arrived.[22]

Angleton expressed to Janet Scott the condolences of Dick Helms and the entire Agency. He mentioned, briefly and generally, the benefits to which she was entitled, adding that "our current information is tentative." He wanted to make sure she consulted with the legal counsel's office, so that she would obtain "every advantage for herself and her children."[23]

Janet Scott had worked for the Agency. She understood the language of Langley: Do what we say, or else we'll cut off your pension.

"Did Win have a will?" Angleton asked.

"I don't know," she said. "I don't even know who Scottie's lawyer or executor is."

"Could you find out"—he nodded at the man trailing him—"and let John know?"

The man with him, John Horton, was the current station chief in Mexico City.

God, how I hate him, Janet Scott thought, according to her son. It would have killed her husband to see Jim Angleton in his house, in his living room, calling with condolences while seeking to confiscate his memoir. Her husband had died at the breakfast table two days before, the victim of a heart attack. Earlier in the week, Scottie had shown up one morning, his face covered with bruises and scratches. He said he had fallen off a wall in the garden, but no one had seen him fall. The bruises were so unsightly, she closed the casket at his wake.

Some of Win Scott's associates suspected foul play in his death. One of Scott's most trusted agents, George Munro, told his son, "They finally got Win," without betraying whom he thought "they" might be.[24] Tom Mann, the former ambassador in Mexico City, wondered if Scott had been murdered. Janet Scott expressed no such thoughts. She had to worry about her five children and her house and her suddenly uncertain future.

Angleton took her into a side room.[25]

"I have an unpleasant task," he began. "There are some papers. If these are published this violates Win's oath [of secrecy]. We want to recover all of them."

The widow feared this ghoul. Angleton looked like a man whose ectoplasm had run out.[26]

"I knew something was wrong when he told me he was going to see Helms," Janet said. "Why do you think he wrote it?"

That was not a question Angleton was going to answer.

Janet Scott would later tell one of her sons that Angleton was a "drunken idiot." She underestimated him. He knew what he was doing. He was excising Scott's informed opinion about JFK's assassination from the historical record. He was obstructing justice in the case of the murdered president—again.

———

JOHN HORTON RETURNED TO 16 Rio Escondido the next day. He spent several hours behind the locked door of Win Scott's study.

"I was amazed at what I found," Horton wrote in a memo.[27] Scott's office was a mine of precious intelligence: stacks of secret files, as well as tapes and photos of Oswald, and several copies of the unpublished memoir. When no one was looking, Horton lugged three large cartons and four suitcases to an unmarked truck parked at the curb. The packages were shipped by plane back to Angleton's office.

"We have retrieved all papers or will soon have done so," Horton wrote to Langley. He referred to Angleton by his cryptonym, "Hugh Ashmead," and to Janet Scott by Win Scott's cryptonym, "Willard Curtis."

"[I] think worst has been avoided, through Ashmead's persuasiveness and Mrs. Curtis' good spirit," Horton said.[28]

WIN SCOTT HAD WRITTEN his memoir in self-defense. He had read the JFK conspiracy theories and the wild claims of people who knew a lot less about the subject than he did. He wanted to establish some facts. He especially objected to the Warren report's assertion, on page 777, that Oswald's visit to the Cuban consulate was not known until after the assassination.

The passage implied his station had missed something basic and important about the enemy: an American visitor to the Cuban consulate. Scott knew better. He wrote:

> Every piece of information concerning Lee Harvey Oswald was reported immediately after it was received to: U.S. Ambassador Thomas C. Mann, by memorandum; the FBI Chief in Mexico, by memorandum; and to my headquarters by cable; and included in each and every one of these reports was the entire conversation Oswald had, from Cuban Consulate, with the Soviet [embassy].[29]

And Scott had the tapes of Oswald's phone calls to prove his point. Scott wrote to distance himself from the CIA's misrepresentations to the

Warren Commission. Helms and Angleton might have some explaining to do about Oswald. He did not.

Scott did not live to testify about CIA operations and the accused assassin. His chapter on Oswald would not be declassified for thirty years. Angleton had buried his former friend.

HELMS

ON THE MORNING OF June 19, 1972, Dick Helms held the usual Monday staff meeting at CIA headquarters. His demeanor was calm, his tone offhand. Over the weekend, *The Washington Post* had reported that two former Agency employees, James McCord and Eugenio Martinez, had been among five men arrested for breaking into the headquarters of the Democratic National Committee in the Watergate office complex in Foggy Bottom.

Most everybody in the meeting knew the names, Angleton included.

McCord had retired from a twenty-year career in the Office of Security. He had been cleaning up the Agency's dirty work since the fall of Frank Olson in 1953.

Martinez had served in the Bay of Pigs operation and still reported to the WAVE station in Miami.

Making matters worse, veteran officer Howard Hunt had also been implicated in the burglary. Hunt had made a name for himself in Guatemala in 1954 and the Bay of Pigs in 1961.

"We are going to catch a lot of hell because these are formers," Helms said, referring to former CIA employees, "and we knew they were working for the White House."[30]

That was a frank admission, noted by Bill Colby, former chief of the Far East Division and soon to become the CIA's executive director. Colby had distinguished himself in the OSS. After serving in Italy in the 1950s, he moved on to South Vietnam. He now held the new position of executive director, ranking just below the director and deputy director.

Angleton expressed a fear that the press might blame the CIA for the botched burglary. Photographs of Howard Hunt were passed around. Angleton claimed not to recognize him. "I'd never seen him before in my life," he said.[31]

That may not have been true. Hunt said he knew Angleton. When Hunt was serving as station chief in Uruguay in the 1950s, the two men once had an angry confrontation over control of an FBI informant, he said.[32] Angleton and Hunt also once met in room 16 of the Old Executive Office Building, next to the White House, according to a Watergate grand jury witness. Under oath, Angleton said he did not know Hunt and had never been in room 16.[33]

Angleton certainly knew who Jim McCord was. The arrest of the veteran Office of Security man was a hell of a problem for Helms. And Angleton knew that if the DCI had a problem, he had a problem, too.

ANGLETON'S CAREER CANNOT BE understood without reference to Richard McGarrah Helms, his friend and enabler. They had first met in London during the war. Inspired by the can-do example of the British and intrigued by the profession of secret intelligence, they had found their mission in life. They had worked together for a generation, seen their children born, grow up, and go away. Yet Dick Helms and Jim Angleton were not the best of friends.

In the 1950s, Helms and his wife, Julia, invited Jim and Cicely to play charades at their annual New Year's Eve party, but they didn't often visit each other in their homes.[34] Their social styles were different: Angleton was an intellectual, a man of ideas; Helms, a mandarin, a man of power. They admired each other and went their own ways.

Helms's problem in the summer of 1972 was that he had never won the confidence of Richard Nixon, the way he won the confidence of Lyndon Johnson. It wasn't for lack of trying; Helms sent many a flattering letter to Nixon.[35] In the few meetings where Helms was actually in the same room as the president, the CIA director invariably found cause to praise Nixon for his exemplary statesmanship.

The Watergate burglary tested their wary relationship. As far as Nixon was concerned, the men arrested were CIA employees. They had come recommended by Helms. He expected Helms to call off the FBI's investigation. That was the sort of thing a CIA director was supposed to do for his commander in chief.

Helms balked. As far as he was concerned, the Agency had no connection to the burglary, only past relationships with its perpetrators, which he insisted were irrelevant to the FBI investigation. Nixon didn't want to hear it. On June 23, Nixon instructed his chief of staff, H. R. Haldeman, to call in Helms and give him the order. Nixon's temper was boiling.

"We protected Helms from one hell of a lot of things," he growled. "You open the scab there's a hell of a lot of things and that we just feel that it would be very detrimental to have this thing go any further."

Nixon wanted Haldeman to convey a very specific message.

"When you get these people in," he instructed, meaning Helms, "say, 'Look the problem is that this will open up the whole Bay of Pigs thing, and the President just feels that' uh, without going into the detail—don't, don't lie to them to the extent to say there is no involvement—but just say this is sort of a comedy of errors, bizarre, without getting into it. 'The President believes that it is going to open the whole Bay of Pigs thing up again.'"[36]

When Haldeman sat the CIA chief down in his office later that day and delivered the president's veiled threat about "the whole Bay of Pigs thing," the usually composed Helms rose out of his chair.

"The Bay of Pigs hasn't got a damned thing to do with this!"[37] he shouted.

Helms felt threatened. According to Haldeman, "the whole Bay of Pigs thing" was Nixon's way of referring to the CIA's unspeakable secret—the assassination of JFK. Whatever the specifics of Nixon's veiled language, his purpose was evident. Nixon conveyed "a desire to touch a sore spot," said two CIA historians, "to apply pressure."[38]

ANGLETON WAS DILIGENT IN his service to Helms. He retained considerable powers, thanks to the director.

Operation CHAOS remained robust under Dick Ober's leadership. His Special Operations Group now had 40 employees and utilized another 130 agent sources.[39] By 1972 CHAOS accounted for more than 20 percent of the

Counterintelligence Staff. The Agency's analysts had repeatedly concluded that the antiwar movement was not funded or controlled, or even much influenced, by any foreign power. That did not affect the program's growth.

Angleton still guarded the LINGUAL program. Unbeknownst to Nixon, the mail-opening program continued in full force. Per Angleton's standing orders, the Counterintelligence Staff shared with the FBI the personal information culled from the international mail of Americans suspected of no crime. The Bureau's COINTELPRO operatives continued to use Angleton's information to harass, disrupt, deceive, and discredit people and organizations opposed to the policies of the U.S. government. The targets were black nationalist groups, including the Student Nonviolent Coordinating Committee and the Black Panthers, and pacifist organizations such as the Women's Strike for Peace and the American Friends Service Committee.

Angleton had lost sway in the Soviet Russia Division with the release of Yuri Nosenko in early 1969. His warnings about a KGB mole were ignored. His dream of an expanded domestic counterintelligence program had been thwarted by the collapse of the Huston Plan. And his friend Dick Helms was about to get fired.

ON NOVEMBER 7, 1972, Richard Nixon was reelected as president, winning forty-nine of the fifty states, with the largest popular vote in American history. For a man who had been scorned by many during his rise to power, he was not magnanimous in victory. Nixon wanted to remake his second administration with a free hand. He asked for the resignation of his entire cabinet, prompting a round of critical headlines, suggesting he was acting undemocratically.

Nixon informed Helms that he wanted to appoint a new CIA director. What ensued was a delicate negotiation, pregnant with unstated meanings. Senator Howard Baker had observed the tension between the two men. "Nixon and Helms have so much on each other," he said, "neither of them can breathe."[40]

Helms did not want to leave public service under the taint of Watergate. He said he wanted to stay on through his sixtieth birthday, a few months hence. Nixon suggested an ambassadorship. The president mentioned Iran, and Helms said he would consider it.

Within the week, Nixon had reneged on the deal. He surprised Helms by announcing the appointment of James Schlesinger, the chief of the Office of Management and Budget, as the next director of Central Intelligence. Helms quickly cleaned out his office, shredding all files related to MKULTRA and destroying tapes of his phone conversations.

The CIA's farewell ceremony for Helms in February 1973 was an emotional event.

"When Helms left the building, all the troops jammed the headquarters entrance for his departure," said his assistant Sam Halpern. "There wasn't a dry eye in the house. Everyone knew we were in for a bad time after that."[41]

Especially Angleton.

COLBY

THE MUTUAL DISLIKE OF Jim Angleton and Bill Colby was no secret or surprise to colleagues who knew them both. Their differences had flared throughout the course of their intertwined careers.

In Italy in the 1950s, they clashed over the wisdom of the CIA's funding an "opening to the left."[42] In Vietnam, they differed on the need for special counterintelligence units. At home, they disagreed about the value of Operations CHAOS and LINGUAL. Colby distrusted Angleton's methods and mentality. Angleton did not care for Colby's actions, tone, or style.

In one sense, theirs was a professional struggle. Each man was doing what he thought his job required. Colby was a paratrooper, a paramilitary man, a covert operator. He wanted the CIA to focus on running spies and stealing secrets. Angleton was a literary critic, an analyst, a counterintelligence officer. He was looking for double agents, disinformation, and penetration operations.[43] But the antagonism between them flowed from deeper sources, ones that were both personal and political.

Angleton came of age in Italy in the 1930s, when fascism was popular and attractive. In the eyes of his friend Ezra Pound, Benito Mussolini was not a strutting dictator; he was positively Jeffersonian. As a young man at least, Angleton had admired the fascist ideal of a strong cooperative state with some communal ownership of property and a leading role for the church. After the war, he treated fascist allies with care. On Election Day, he tended to vote Republican. Intellectually, he was secular, anti-Communist, and Zionist.

Colby was the son of an army officer. He spent his boyhood on military bases, absorbing the democratic esprit of the mess hall and the barracks. It was a point of family pride that Colby's grandfather, also an army officer, had gotten into trouble for writing an article denouncing the unjust acquittal of a white military officer who murdered a black soldier.[44] Colby came of age supporting the Republicans of Spain, not Wall Street. Politically, he was progressive. Intellectually, he was a liberal Catholic.[45]

If Angleton was a poet-spy, Colby was a soldier-priest. Angleton thought Colby was a naïf; Colby thought Angleton a reactionary. Ultimately, Angleton was a creative theorist, Colby a disciplined moralist, and that made the difference in who would lose his job first.

People had a tendency to underrate Colby. He was slight of build, modest in his manner. Angleton's Israeli friends thought him an unworthy adversary. "They saw Angleton as a man of imagination, of history," said Ted Jessup, son of former Tel Aviv station chief Peter Jessup, who heard his father's conversations with top Mossad officers. "They thought Colby was some clerk."[46]

Colby's advantage was that he had common sense. He understood that the postwar world in which the CIA was born had passed. The Agency had to absorb the new realities in America. The antiwar movement—which many CIA wives and children supported—was not the product of a Communist conspiracy, even if the movement heartened the Soviet Union and its allies. The animosity between China and the Soviet Union was real, not the sham that Angleton still argued it was. Even Nixon, impeccably anti-Communist, had gone to Moscow and Beijing to inaugurate a new spirit of superpower relations called "détente."

Colby tested Angleton's theories against known realities. He said he sat through several long sessions with Angleton, "doing my best to follow his tortuous theories about the long arm of a powerful and wily KGB at work over decades."

"I confess that I couldn't absorb it," Colby said, "possibly because I didn't have the requisite grasp of this labyrinthine subject, possibly because Angleton's explanations were impossible to follow, or possibly because the evidence just didn't add up to his conclusions. At the same time, I looked in vain for some tangible results in the counterintelligence files and found little or none."[47]

PRESIDENT NIXON'S GOVERNMENT WAS falling apart. After being sworn in for his second term in January 1973, Nixon had never seemed more potent. His opening of diplomatic relations with China and his policy of détente toward the Soviet Union surprised and disarmed liberal critics who had long denounced him as a shrill and dogmatic anti-Communist. The antiwar movement that had once plagued him was dying out, thanks to his abolition of the draft. In January 1973, he directed Secretary of State Henry Kissinger to sign the Paris Peace Accords, which promised the war-weary country a plausible plan to finally extricate U.S. troops from Vietnam.

At the same time, Nixon was undermined by the almost daily revelations generated by the investigations of the Watergate burglary, which revealed the burglars worked for the White House. Political reporters, most of them liberals, were appalled by Nixon's lawlessness. With the help of leaks from the FBI and Justice Department, they forged a stream of new stories in the pages of *The Washington Post* and *The New York Times* and in the news broadcasts of the three television networks. They depicted a pattern of perjury and obstruction of justice leading toward the Oval Office. In April 1973, Nixon's chief of staff, Haldeman, and his chief adviser, John Ehrlichman, had no choice but to resign.

The CIA men faced a new challenge. Helms was gone and his artful evasions no longer kept Washington reporters at bay concerning the CIA's support for the burglars. On April 27, 1973, the Department of Justice made an extraordinary disclosure to the judge presiding at the trial of Daniel

Ellsberg. A former national security consultant, Ellsberg had been charged under the Espionage Act for leaking the top secret Pentagon Papers to *The New York Times*. The government revealed that former CIA officer Howard Hunt, on trial for his role in the Watergate burglary, had also burglarized the offices of Ellsberg's psychiatrist, at the behest of the Nixon White House,[48] and he had used equipment and papers supplied by the CIA.

The judge dismissed all charges against Ellsberg, citing egregious governmental misconduct. Ellsberg, who had faced forty years in prison, walked out of the courtroom to claim vindication in front of the TV cameras. America had a new kind of hero, and the CIA had a new kind of notoriety.

The new director James Schlesinger was startled by the revelation. The Agency had furnished Hunt with a camera, disguise materials, and false identification. With another such disclosure, Schlesinger might have feared he would find himself out of a job. In self-defense, he sought to preempt any further revelations. He ordered "all senior operating officials of this Agency to report to me immediately any activities now going on, or that have gone on in the past, which might be construed to be outside the legislative charter of this Agency."[49] He ordered Bill Colby to oversee the preparation of a report of the testimony of those who came forward.

And so Angleton's nemesis inherited the stack of secrets that would become known as "the family jewels." The phrase, Ivy League slang for testicles, evoked the Agency's aristocratic code, its masculine ethos, and the locus of its vulnerability. The family jewels were especially threatening to Angleton because many of the complaints from the ranks of the CIA focused on the propriety of two programs in which he played a leading role—namely, CHAOS and LINGUAL.

And then Bill Colby got the top job in Langley. Nixon suddenly decided he wanted James Schlesinger to ride herd on the Pentagon and named him Secretary of Defense. Almost as an afterthought, Nixon appointed Colby as the eighth director of the CIA.

Angleton was in trouble. Colby had an Ivy League and OSS pedigree similar to Angleton's, but a very different vision of the future. Colby was tested in the summer of 1973 when the story of the Huston Plan was discovered and exposed by the Senate Watergate Committee. The investigators were appalled at the scope of Nixon's domestic surveillance plan and the support it had gained from the CIA and other agencies. The fact that J. Edgar Hoover, of all people, had killed the domestic spying plan only highlighted how out of control the Nixon administration seemed.

Colby thought the CIA had to do a better job of explaining its actions.

At his confirmation hearings in July 1973, Colby said the Agency had to function within "American society and the American constitutional structure. And I can see that there may be a requirement to expose to the American people a great deal more than might be convenient from the narrow intelligence point of view."[50]

Colby harbored "a profound certainty that there must be a 'new' CIA that would be much more forthcoming in its relationship with Congress and the American public."

Such proclamations helped placate a Congress and public disillusioned about the CIA's actions with regard to Vietnam and Watergate. They were ominous for Angleton.

ANGLETON WAS ILL PREPARED to resist Colby's war of attrition. His father had died in March 1973 in a hospital in Boise. James Hugh Angleton was eighty-four years old.[51] Angleton sometimes had let his father down. He had disappointed him by choosing a CIA career over the family business. And he never talked to his father about his working life.

The services were held at the Cathedral of the Rockies in Boise. His mother, now seventy-four, was living in Idaho. So was his brother, Hugh, still running his antique emporium. His sister Dolores Guarneri came from Florence with her Italian husband; Carmen, from Milan with her husband.

Colonel Angleton was a decorated man, the eulogists reminded the assembled mourners. He was a Mason and a member of the Methodist Church. He was president emeritus of the American Chamber of Commerce for Italy, a veteran of the OSS, and recipient of an Italian military star for valor in the field of combat.

Unspoken at the service was that the deceased was also the father of one of the most powerful men in the Central Intelligence Agency. Even among the many friends and family of the late Hugh Angleton, not many knew of that distinction. With his father dead and his family gone, Angleton had never been more alone in his pain. He took to wearing his father's suits.[52]

ANGLETON HAD FEW ALLIES left in Langley. Tom Karamessines had retired with Helms. Cord Meyer was in London. With the exception of David Phillips, chief of the Western Hemisphere Division, all of the Agency's current division chiefs disliked or mistrusted him. Among those who had worked with Angleton, he had a terrible reputation, even for his counterintelligence work.[53]

"Jim virtually destroyed counterintelligence at CIA," said Carter Woodbury, a retired officer. In a letter to a colleague, Woodbury said that when he joined the CIA in 1950, every division and every station had a strong counterintelligence component. Two decades later, "there were almost no such components," he wrote. "They had atrophied over the years as Jim focused more and more on his personal and mythical CIA preoccupations."[54]

Jack Maury, former Athens station chief, who served as the Agency's liaison to Congress, described Angleton's search for moles in the Soviet Russia Division as debilitating "sick think."[55]

Bill Colby heard many such complaints. An audit of Soviet Russia Division officers in 1973–1974 found that a disturbing proportion of them did nothing more than check out Soviet penetrations suspected by Golitsyn and Angleton. Colby concluded Angleton's never-ending mole hunt was "seriously damaging the recruiting of Soviet officers and hurting CIA's intelligence take."

"Because of this we have virtually no positive ops going against our primary targets, the USSR and Soviet officers," Colby wrote in a memo.

Colby suspended LINGUAL, saying the mail-opening operation was legally questionable and operationally trivial, having never produced much "beyond vague generalities."[56] In August 1973, he limited CHAOS activities "to a passive collection of information upon FBI request."[57]

"I hoped Angleton might take the hint and retire in time to secure certain retirement benefits which closed in June 1974," Colby explained. "But he dug in his heels and marshaled every argument he could think of to urge that such an important contact not be handled in the normal bureaucratic machinery."[58]

Angleton worried that Colby was destroying U.S. counterintelligence. Colby worried Angleton was destroying himself.

Angleton was "getting to the point where he had some difficulty separating reality from fiction," said Robert Gambino of the Office of the Security. "I had personal information and personal experience with Angleton during his latter days—he was slipping off the edge. I don't want to suggest he was, you know, that he was having serious mental problems or anything like that. Let me just say, I think it was time for him to go."[59]

ON SATURDAY, OCTOBER 6, 1973, as Israeli Jews observed Yom Kippur, the Day of Atonement, the Egyptian army launched a massive surprise attack across the Sinai Desert, retribution for the surprise Israeli attack of June 1967. The Egyptian invasion penetrated deep into Israeli territory and inflicted unprecedented losses on the unprepared Israeli Defense Forces.

"We were very close to disaster," recalled Efraim Halevy. "After the first week, we lost a third of our air force and close to a third of our tanks. We had over two thousand dead and ten thousand injured. I remember those days vividly because I was there when the U.S. was groping to find out how much damage Israel had suffered."[60]

Over the course of the next three weeks, the United States resupplied Israel while President Nixon managed a geopolitical crisis. As the IDF regained lost territory, the Soviet Union threatened to protect its ally, Egypt, from another humiliation, with nuclear weapons if necessary. Secretary of State Henry Kissinger demanded the Israelis accept a cease-fire, which they reluctantly did.

PRESIDENT NIXON FOUND THE CIA's performance unacceptable. The Agency had not alerted the White House that another war in the

Middle East might be in the offing, much less that it would lead to a nuclear confrontation with the Soviet Union.

It was a classic case of getting too close to a source. Robert Morris, a staffer at the National Security Council, said "the worst common flaw in the reading of the intelligence was an abiding cultural, perhaps racial, contempt in Washington and Jerusalem for the political posturing and fighting skills of the Arabs."[61]

Kissinger diagnosed the CIA's problem with asperity. "The U.S. definition of rationality did not take seriously the notion of [the Arabs] starting an unwinnable war to restore self-respect," he fumed. "There was no defense against our own preconceptions or those of our allies."[62]

As the CIA's most faithful messenger of Israeli thinking, Angleton had contributed to the fiasco. Worse yet, he had made an enemy of Kissinger, the most powerful man in government after Nixon.

Angleton's continuing obsession with Soviet deception operations did not help his credibility. His claim that British prime minister Harold Wilson was a KGB agent of influence was baseless. Yet Len McCoy heard Angleton make the point at length in a speech to senior CIA officers in March 1974.

"What he said was that . . . Wilson was a Soviet agent," McCoy recalled. "That control of Wilson was exercised by a senior KGB officer or officers and that this relationship went back to the time when he was traveling in and out of the Soviet Union on personal assignment."

The CIA never found any evidence to support Angleton's theory.

McCoy thought Angleton's mind-set fit the definition of paranoia: He was incapable of distinguishing what was possible from what was probable. Yet McCoy did not challenge him. "One was a bit cowed in the man's presence," he admitted.[63]

And then an obnoxious newspaper reporter gave Bill Colby the opportunity he had been waiting for.

SMOKING GUN

IN THE SPRING OF 1974, the recurring banner headlines on the front page of *The Washington Post* that Angleton picked up on his doorstep told the tale of a White House besieged.

PRESIDENT HANDS OVER TRANSCRIPTS
NIXON DEBATED PAYING
BLACKMAIL, CLEMENCY[64]

People went about their business in the capital with only three syllables on their lips: *Wa-ter-gate.* The scandalous spectacle of White House aides, charged in a court of law, with diverse counts of conspiracy, perjury, and obstruction of justice preoccupied official Washington. Federal prosecutors and senior editors were pursuing a lawless chief executive who had just won the largest number of votes of any American president.

The discovery of an audiotaping system in the White House created a vast new body of evidence. Nixon said the tapes could not possibly be made public without damaging the presidency. The prosecutors insisted and the court agreed: Nixon had to produce the tapes for the trial of the Watergate defendants.

The results were dispiriting to the Congress and the public. The vigilant editing of the transcripts could not disguise the constant cursing. The censor's euphemism, "expletive deleted," entered the lexicon of a disillusioned nation.

Angleton had other worries. He saw more important stories buried by the Watergate coverage.

WILLY BRANDT RESIGNS
OVER SPY SCANDAL

Willy Brandt, chancellor of West Germany and leftist advocate of Kissinger-style détente, had quit after one of his closest aides, Guenter Guillaume, had been exposed as an East German spy.[65] Guillaume was exactly the sort of long-term penetration agent that Angleton feared was working somewhere in Langley. It was time to expand the use of counterintelligence tools, said Angleton, not discard them.

Angleton still had a vision, even as he was losing his empire. Whatever Nixon's abuses of power, he believed the country still needed more vigorous defense. Kissinger's pursuit of détente had only benefited the Soviet Union, he said. The surge of technological innovation that had lifted the United States and its allies (like Israel) to military ascendancy after World War II had been squandered. Beginning with JFK, he said, U.S. presidents and policy makers had traded the sound policy of containment of the Soviet Union for the illusory benefits of peaceful coexistence, in which the West relaxed its guard while the Communists pursued class warfare ever more vigorously. He thought Harold Wilson's election and Willy Brandt's disgrace showed that détente did not modify Soviet strategy against the West.[66]

As for Vietnam, Angleton thought the United States had peace but hardly with the honor Nixon and Kissinger claimed. The superior resources of the American fighting forces—and, worse still, their spirit—had been wasted in Southeast Asia "for want of a strategy calculated to stand and hold."

"Kissinger diplomacy has not deflected the Kremlin for its basic objectives," Angleton insisted. "Détente is a sham, a tactic; it is Soviet communism's Potemkin Village for waging Cold War."[67]

He was a visionary. He was a crank. He was a victim of his own mentality.

ANGLETON, WHO HAD STUNTED or ended the careers of so many colleagues, suddenly found his own loyalties called into question. Unable to find a KGB spy anywhere in the Agency, one of Angleton's mole hunters finally turned his attention on the counterintelligence chief himself. Clare Edward Petty, a career officer on the Counterintelligence Staff, concluded his boss was either a giant fraud or a KGB agent.[68]

Petty's methodology deserves the adjective *Angletonian*. Assuming the

CIA had been penetrated at a high level, Petty considered the possibility that both Anatoly Golitsyn and Yuri Nosenko had been sent by the KGB under the guidance of the real mole: Angleton himself. Through this analytic lens, Petty saw new meaning in all the anomalies of Angleton's career: his strange indulgence of Philby, his promotion of Golitsyn, his irrational insistence that the Sino-Soviet split was a ruse. Every decision he made seemed to impede U.S. intelligence operations, Petty noted. Perhaps it was intentional.

This was speculation as counterintelligence. Petty took a semiplausible scenario based on a superficial fact pattern and used it to confirm a logical conclusion that flowed from untested assumptions.[69]

As Angleton's mole hunt culminated in absurdity, Nixon's presidency came to an end. It was no coincidence. The spymaster and the president embodied American Cold War policy from its ascendancy after World War II to its failure in Southeast Asia. Angleton and Nixon shared a determination, verging on hatred, to defeat their enemies. They shared a dogged belief in the necessity of domestic counterintelligence—what the liberal headline writers called "spying on Americans." Their willingness to act on that belief, even when it conflicted with the law, ended their long public careers in the span of four months.

NIXON'S LIMITED RELEASE OF the transcripts of the White House tapes did not satisfy the Watergate special prosecutors or the courts. On July 24, 1974, the Supreme Court, by a unanimous vote, upheld the validity of the prosecutor's subpoena seeking additional tapes of fifty-six White House conversations, including the phone calls in the immediate aftermath of the Watergate burglary.

Their release brought another banner headline in the *Post* that had concussive effect on Washington.

PRESIDENT ADMITS WITHHOLDING DATA;
TAPES SHOW HE APPROVED COVER-UP
THE PLAN: USE CIA TO BLOCK PROBE[70]

The *Post* said the tapes proved that Nixon had ordered a cover-up of the Watergate burglary six days after it occurred. The June 23 tape, in which Nixon invoked the "whole Bay of Pigs thing," was a proverbial "smoking gun," incontestable proof of Nixon's guilt.[71]

The end was near. As crowds gathered in vigils outside the White House, the last vestiges of support for Nixon vanished. The eleven Republicans on the Judiciary Committee who had just voted against articles of impeachment announced they would change their votes.[72] Facing all but certain conviction by the Senate, the president had run out of options.

In August, Nixon wrote a letter of resignation to Secretary of State Kissinger. He bade farewell to the White House staff in an emotional ceremony, then flew off to Southern California. Vice President Gerald Ford was sworn in as president before the end of the day.

SEYMOUR HERSH DIDN'T KNOW much about James Angleton besides his name. Hersh was a thirty-seven-year-old reporter for the *New York Times*. He had won the 1970 Pulitzer Prize for his reporting on how U.S. soldiers annihilated several hundred residents of a Vietnamese village in March 1968, raping the women, killing the children, and disemboweling both. His pitiless reporting seared the words *My Lai* into the soft tissue of the American self-regard and won him a job at America's newspaper of record.

Hersh was a genially abrasive man, a kvetcher, and a workaholic.[73] He had no time for politics, only a nose for abuses of power. He exemplified a resurgent, morally confident—some said self-righteous—brand of American journalism that, in a break with the past, dared to publish stories objectionable to senior officials in Washington.

Hersh was hearing from his sources that the CIA had spied on the antiwar movement, something his leftist friends insisted was endemic. People were telling him about Dick Ober's Special Operations Group. They talked about how Tom Huston's plan had stoked CIA action against domestic radicals. They talked about how the mail of certain congressmen had been opened, all of which was true. These stories echoed (or were based on) the family jewels documents that Colby had compiled in May 1973.[74] Many CIA hands objected to CHAOS, saying the Agency was spying on their own wives and children.

When Hersh mentioned Angleton's name in his interviews, he heard expressions of fear and awe. He heard about the man's passion for orchids, his poetry magazine at Yale. He heard that he was an unrelenting Cold Warrior, that he was convinced that the Soviet Union was playing a major role in the antiwar protests, that his reports on the student movement had been forwarded to Nixon and Kissinger.[75]

When Hersh called, Angleton did not hesitate to engage him. Hersh asked if the Counterintelligence Staff had operated in the United States. Angleton denied it. "We know our jurisdiction," he said.

Hersh called Colby, who confirmed the story in its broad outlines, while insisting he had put an end to Angleton's abuses. In December 1974 the reporter then put in a call to Ambassador Dick Helms in Tehran and left a blunt message. The *Times,* he said, "was going to press within six hours with a story very damaging to Mister Angleton."[76]

ANGLETON EXPECTED NOTHING GOOD when Bill Colby asked to see him in his office. Twenty years of rivalry and resentment ended in a terse confrontation.

"I called Angleton to my office to talk the matter out with him," Colby wrote in his memoir, "saying that I had come to the conclusion that a change was necessary in both jobs, the Israeli liaison and counterintelligence but that I wanted to retain his talents for the Agency, and especially his experience. I offered him the prospect of separate status, where he could summarize for us the main ideas he had and conclusions he had reached about counterintelligence and where he would be consulted on, but no longer in charge of, our Israeli liaison."

Angleton scoffed. The imperative of counterintelligence required that he stay on. Did Colby understand what the KGB was doing under the guise of détente?

Colby pressed on without pity. He informed Angleton that *The New York Times* was about to publish an article linking him to domestic spying activities. He had no choice but to resign, Colby said. Otherwise, people might think that he had been fired because of the *Times* story.

"I asked him to think over the matter for a couple of days, to decide if he would like to say on in the way I described," Colby recalled, "or whether he would choose to retire completely."[77]

Checkmate. In one short conversation, Colby had maneuvered Angleton into choosing the method of his professional suicide. It was elegant. It was brutal. It had to be done. Colby took no pleasure in another man's pain, but, as an observant Catholic who attended services at the Little Flower Catholic church in Bethesda, he was glad to have expiated the sins of the Agency.[78]

Angleton shuffled out of the meeting, shocked and uncomprehending. An old friend from the FBI happened to be waiting in the outer office. Behind Angleton's horn-rimmed glasses, the usually sharp brown eyes were blurred with pain. The FBI man took him by the arm.

"Jesus, Jim, it can't be that bad," he said. "What's the matter?"

"It's horrible," Angleton rasped. "It's awful. You'll soon read all about it."[79]

DESOLATE

HUGE C.I.A. OPERATION REPORTED
IN U.S. AGAINST ANTIWAR FORCES,
OTHER DISSIDENTS IN NIXON YEARS
FILES ON CITIZENS

Helms Reportedly Got
Surveillance Data in
Charter Violation

The newspaper article that ended Jim Angleton's career packed a punch for Americans who actually believed they lived in a constitutional republic. Hersh's article described "a massive illegal domestic intelligence operation during the Nixon administration" that maintained files on at least ten thousand Americans associated with the popular movements against the war in Vietnam. These files, the story said, were controlled by a "special unit" reporting to then director Richard Helms. The Agency had also collected evidence of "dozens of other illegal activities" by CIA personnel, including break-ins, wiretapping, and the surreptitious inspection of mail.

Angleton was outraged and anguished. Helms sent a cable to the State Department denying there had been any illegal surveillance in the United States. Ben Bradlee would later say he thought it was a "hell of a story," but at the time *The Washington Post* treated Hersh's scoop with disdain.

The *Post*'s editorial page proclaimed, "While almost any CIA activity can be fitted under the headline of 'spying,' and while CIA activities undertaken on American soil can be called 'domestic spying,' it remains to be determined which of these activities has been conducted in 'violation' of the agency's congressional charter or are 'illegal.' "[80]

Subsequent investigations determined these activities and many more certainly violated the Agency's charter and the law, though politics would preclude prosecution. While Hersh made some errors, his story has withstood the test of time. His sources were well informed about the internal complaints about CHAOS as compiled in the family jewels. Hersh's report was mistaken in attributing the program to President Nixon, when it had actually begun under President Johnson. The story was perhaps unfair to Bill Colby. It might have emphasized more clearly that Colby had restricted some extralegal operations when he became director in 1973.

Citing his unnamed source (Colby), Hersh attributed responsibility to one man.

"The C.I.A. domestic activities during the Nixon Administration were directed, the source said, by James Angleton, who is still in charge of the Counterintelligence Department, the agency's most powerful and mysterious unit."

To be sure, Hersh got the name wrong. Angleton headed the Counterintelligence Staff, not the Counterintelligence Department. But the Agency's "most powerful and mysterious unit" was an apt description of Angleton's empire. Some would dispute that Angleton "directed" the spying on the anti-war movement, as Hersh contended. Dick Ober had directed the day-to-day business of CHAOS from 1967 to 1974.

But Hersh's attribution of ultimate responsibility to Angleton was not misplaced. Angleton had formal responsibility for all of the Agency's counterintelligence operations. Helms had assigned Ober to the Counterintelligence Staff precisely because Angleton's skill in operations requiring extreme compartmentalization. According to Ober's deputy, anyone who wanted to use CHAOS agents had to get operational approval from Angleton or his deputy Ray Rocca.[81] While Angleton did not see all of the reporting that crossed Ober's desk, he made sure that CHAOS was exempted from annual financial audits of Counterintelligence Staff operations.[82]

If Angleton did not run CHAOS, he approved of it in principle and in many of its details. His leading role in domestic counterintelligence was one of the major revelations of the *Times* story, and Hersh got it right.[83]

When Angleton read the story, he called Hersh and angrily told him he had blown his cover. He claimed that his wife had known nothing of his CIA work, and that she had left him because of the story. That was a lie, and not a very subtle one.

Cicely Angleton had known her husband was a "hush hush man" before the CIA was even created. She had not left him over Hersh's story. She had left him three years before because of his absence from their marriage. With a few phone calls to CIA sources, Hersh discovered the truth about Angleton's marriage and was baffled by the fib. Angleton's lie, of course, expressed a terrible personal truth: He felt utterly abandoned.

LATE ON SATURDAY NIGHT, December 21, 1974, the *Times* story was read with mounting fascination by David Martin, a young reporter working the overnight shift at the Associated Press office in Washington. As the junior man on staff, Martin had the chore of reading the first edition of the Sunday *Times* and following up on any especially newsworthy story. With a glance at the triple-decker headline and the photographs of three CIA directors above the fold of the newspaper, Martin knew he had to get to work. He knew something of the CIA world. His father worked as an analyst in the Directorate of Intelligence, but he had never heard Angleton's name before.

Martin found Angleton's home phone number in the Arlington phone book. He dialed the number, while another reporter listened in. They were sure that no one would answer.

"He started talking right away," Martin recalled. "He sounded like a guy straight out of le Carré."[84]

John le Carré, the SIS man turned spy novelist, spun tales of Cold War intrigue into bestselling books. His latest, *Tinker Tailor Soldier Spy*, featured a world-weary British counterintelligence officer, George Smiley, pursuing a Philby-like mole in the upper ranks of the British intelligence service.

"He had a slurred way of speaking," Martin said of Angleton. "He was not hard to understand, but his thoughts were muddled. . . . He gave the impression he'd been drinking too much. We talked to him for an hour, and he complained we had made him burn his spaghetti."

As Angleton suddenly became famous as a powerful spy, he was living the reality of an absentminded bachelor, home alone, talking on the phone to strangers.

THE NEXT DAY, ANGLETON'S home on 33rd Road was besieged by reporters. One of them was Daniel Schorr, a CBS news correspondent famous for his blunt questions. He marched up to the front door and rang the bell. A groggy-looking, stoop-shouldered man in pajamas opened the door and pointed at *The Washington Post* on his doorstep. Schorr was standing on it.

"I certainly didn't expect you, Mr. Schorr, to trample on the press," said Angleton.[85]

Encouraged by his sense of humor, Schorr asked if he could come in. He found himself in a house strewn with books in many languages, mementos of Italy and Israel, and pictures of Cicely and the children. Angleton agreed to talk to Schorr, but only off-camera, saying he would be in mortal danger if recognized.

Each time Schorr asked him about the allegations of improper CIA activities in the United States, Angleton digressed about the Cold War. When

Schorr tried to bring him back to the question he had asked fifteen minutes earlier, Angleton said, "I am not known as a linear thinker, Mr. Schorr. You will have to let me approach your question my way."

When he was done, Angleton donned his black coat and homburg and walked out the front door, down the brick steps, and slowly across the lawn into the wilderness of TV cameras. He stopped as if hypnotized. Schorr grabbed a microphone lying on the ground and the cameraman started filming.

"Why did you resign?" Schorr asked.

"I think the time comes to all men when they no longer serve their countries," Angleton said.

"Did you jump or were you pushed?" someone asked.

"I wasn't pushed out the window," said Angleton.

He got into his Mercedes and drove away.[86]

That night, Christmas Eve 1974, millions of Americans heard the name James Jesus Angleton for the first time. All three TV networks reported on the *Times* story, along with the categorical denials of former CIA director Richard Helms.[87] All three played footage of Angleton emerging unsteadily from his front door.

Angleton's ordeal was surreal and unimaginable, except that it was actually happening: newspaper reporters camped out on his lawn, a career of secrecy expiring in the view of millions, his craft of counterintelligence scorned, his mission mocked, his Agency stripped bare by reporters he thought were righteous and ignorant.

"It was," Dan Schorr intoned, "a personal tragedy."

ON MONDAY MORNING, THE senior CIA staff met as scheduled in a conference room in Langley. Angleton filed in along with two dozen colleagues for the daily rundown of coming activities and events. The meeting opened with a shocking announcement: James Angleton had resigned as chief of the Counterintelligence Staff.

No one said anything, recalled David Phillips, the chief of the Western Hemisphere Division. Angleton lit one of his Virginia Slims filter cigarettes and began to speak one last time to his colleagues.

"It was a gloomy forecast," Phillips said. "We were uncomfortable; while most of us felt the counter-espionage expert to be inordinately inflexible, we also knew he possessed an incubus of deep secrets and a better understanding of the Soviet Union's intelligence operations than many in the West. When the meeting was over we all left hurriedly, almost as if escaping."

That evening, as Phillips was leaving the office, he encountered Angleton in the parking lot.

"I had never seen a man who looked so infinitely tired and sad," he said. "We shook hands. And I got into my car, backed out of the parking space and drove towards the exit. In the rear-view mirror I could see Angleton's tall, gaunt figure growing smaller and smaller. He was still standing beside his car looking up at the building. . . ."[88]

BILL COLBY MOVED TO dismantle the last vestiges of Angleton's empire and eradicate his influence. He replaced Angleton with a longtime colleague, George Kalaris. Originally from Montana, Kalaris had started his Washington career as a civil servant–lawyer in the Labor Department before joining the CIA in 1952.[89] In the course of his tours in Asia, Kalaris became one of Colby's trusted regional specialists. During the Vietnam War, his acquisition of the manuals for the Soviet SA-2 missile was credited with saving literally hundreds of pilots and countless aircraft over Vietnam.[90]

Colleagues described Kalaris as a dependable and fair administrator, someone who grasped complex problems quickly and made shrewd judgments. He had not been part of the Counterintelligence Staff during the Angleton years, nor had he been involved in any of its internal politicking about the mole hunt. With no small amount of trepidation, Kalaris went to Angleton's office in room 43 on the C corridor.[91] He talked to his staff and flipped through the office files. Kalaris called it "a desolate situation."

"Mountains of traffic were coming in to the staff but none of it seemed of much importance," he reported in a memo for the record. "The staff had no relation with the Soviet Division."

The Counterintelligence Staff was supposed to prevent KGB penetration of CIA operations against the Soviet Union. How could it serve its function without communicating with the people running the operations? It made no sense. The office atmosphere, said Kalaris, was "conditioned by double think and mirrors."

Kalaris was disturbed to find Angleton's files on the assassination of President Kennedy and his brother Robert. This was material that had never been incorporated into the CIA's central file registry. It had been concealed from the Warren Commission. Kalaris was stunned to open one file and find autopsy photographs of the naked remains of Robert F. Kennedy. How did the counterintelligence chief obtain the photos? And why? The implications disturbed Kalaris. He thought it was "bizarre" that Angleton had the photos.

He consulted with David Blee, chief of the Near East Division. They agreed that Nosenko's account of the KGB's response to Oswald's defection might explain Angleton's interest in JFK's assassination. They could not think of any reason why it was appropriate for the Counterintelligence Staff files to hold the RFK autopsy photos. Kalaris ordered them destroyed.

As for Angleton's JFK files, they told a story that the CIA, as an institution, preferred not to share. Kalaris ordered some to be shredded and the rest integrated into the Agency's file registry. Thus the many CIA documents held by Angleton's Special Investigations Group from 1959 to 1963 were preserved, complete with routing slips. When the Oswald file was declassified thirty years later, the story of Angleton's preassassination interest in Oswald finally emerged, indicating possible culpability in the wrongful death of President Kennedy.

In another dispiriting moment, Kalaris found Angleton's files on the mole hunt, otherwise known as the HONETOL cases. Here was the evidence, such as it was, that Angleton and Golitsyn had used to blight the careers of those blameless CIA officers: Peter Karlow, Richard Kovich, Igor Orlov, Vasia Gmirkin, and David Murphy, among many others. Kalaris assigned a staff attorney to review the forty files for any evidence of possible Soviet penetration. The task took a year.

"Nothing of merit was found in any of them," Kalaris said.

Angleton's mole hunt was over. At CIA headquarters, it was a moment of reckoning. The *Times* story documented how legitimate foreign counterintelligence operations had evolved into illegal domestic spying. The

Times story only hinted at the existence of the LINGUAL operation. And there were the "skeletons" in Angleton's closet that the *Times* and the Congress and the president knew nothing about: the AMLASH conspiracy to kill Castro; the reckless MKULTRA experiments; the lawless detention of Yuri Nosenko. The multiple congressional investigations into the CIA that followed in 1975 led to what official Washington called "the Year of Intelligence."

Behind Angleton's personal tragedy was a professional travesty. And the travesty invited disturbing questions about everything from unconstitutional spying to extralegal detention to the violent deaths of John and Robert Kennedy.

In this desolate situation, one ambitious young man in Washington knew exactly what to do.

CHENEY

ON THE WEEKEND THAT *The New York Times* broke the story of CIA domestic spying, President Gerald Ford was headed for one of his favorite places in the world, the ski slopes of Vail, Colorado.[92] The athletic president had a passion for sport that could not be denied. The only work on his schedule were meetings about his upcoming State of the Union address. Ford's chief of staff, Donald Rumsfeld, accompanied him on the trip and protected his privacy during the holiday.

As the gatekeeper of the president's time, Rumsfeld brought a gregarious personality and versatile expertise ranging from budgets to engineering. When he read the *Times* sensational headlines on the CIA, he sent a message to the White House Situation Room. The president wanted Bill Colby to address the allegations in writing within forty-eight hours and provide a copy to his deputy, Richard Cheney.

Dick, as he preferred to be called, was thirty-three years old, a native of Wyoming who had come east to Washington to intern for a Republican congressman and never left. An enthusiastic supporter of the U.S. war effort in Vietnam, Cheney used graduate school deferments to avoid getting drafted himself. Rumsfeld was the latest in a series of bosses who were impressed by Cheney's incisive memoranda and prodigious work ethic. Cheney, the junior man in the relationship, did not have Rumsfeld's bluff charm, but he had the more precise mind. Cheney became President Ford's point man on the Angleton story.

The revelations in the *Times* article confounded Ford's advisers. An agitated Henry Kissinger called television journalist Ted Koppel to warn him off the story. Kissinger insisted the CIA had merely assessed "the degree to which foreign countries were infiltrating foreign student movements," which wasn't close to true. "I am so sick of these things," Kissinger said. "They have been in the newspapers thousands of times."[93]

In fact, Hersh's reporting was read with appalled interest on Capitol Hill, in newsrooms, and in living rooms precisely because it documented allegations of surveillance and infiltration that the government had long denied.

In this crucible, Dick Cheney grasped that the issue was neither simply one man nor the spying on Americans. At stake was the power of the president to use the CIA as an instrument of national policy as he saw fit. Cheney did not think small. He pulled his thoughts together in a memo that historian John Prados calls "one of the most significant—and completely ignored—artifacts of the Year of Intelligence."[94]

Cheney's paper disclosed that his acute political instincts were already well developed.[95] He suggested Ford "take the lead in the investigation" and accept "the responsibility for making certain the CIA is adhering to its charter." He proposed public release of all or part of Colby's report. He recommended creating a "special group or commission" to investigate the *Times'* charges. This would demonstrate leadership, Cheney wrote, and convince the nation that government "does indeed have integrity."

A blue-ribbon commission "offers the best prospect for heading off Congressional efforts to further encroach on the executive branch," Cheney added, an argument that would become second nature as he went on to serve as a congressman, secretary of defense, and vice president. Ford accepted Cheney's idea of a commission and named Vice President Nelson Rockefeller to head it. Cheney's strategy was not totally successful.[96] The creation of the Rockefeller Commission did not head off separate investigations by the Senate and the House of Representatives, but Cheney did prove an able advocate of unbridled presidential power.

Jim Angleton's career was ending; Dick Cheney's was just beginning.

ANGLETON'S FRIENDS AND FAMILY rallied to his side. Cicely came back from Tucson. Dick Helms, who had indulged Angleton for years, returned from Iran to deal with the furor. He thought Angleton's dismissal was completely unjust.[97] Tom Karamessines, who had ordered Angleton to set up Operation CHAOS, told Cord Meyer he thought Hersh's piece was "a contemptible shot in the dark with almost no facts to back up his wild allegations."[98]

From Israel, his friend Efraim Halevy wrote a "Dear Jim" letter:

> The wisest of men once said that there is a time for everything. This is not the time for me to write and dwell on all that I feel at this hour or for that matter ever since your move of a few days ago. In so saying, I deliberately refrain from using administrative terms like "retirement" for you never functioned as one of the others. Your sphere of action was never defined by titles and name. What you did for so many years was not at the behest of those fleeting transitory luminaries, the big ones or the more minor ones. And you will not cease to be what you are or do what you believe in because one of them has signed a piece of paper.[99]

"He is not in good shape," his old friend Reed Whittemore said after visiting Angleton. "He is depressed; he doesn't especially want to see people; his friends are not able to help him much and can't seem to persuade him to go to Arizona or Florida for a bit."[100]

AS THE *TIMES*' REVELATIONS about the extent and duration of domestic spying sank in, a sense of anger and betrayal spread in Congress. The now-departed Nixon and his henchmen had violated the law, but they had never compiled files on ten thousand Americans. They had not opened mail or infiltrated peaceful political groups in the United States. The representatives just elected in November 1974 were especially indignant. Ten new senators took their seats in January 1975, along with seventy-five new congressmen and congresswomen. Coming to Washington after the unprecedented debacle of a presidential resignation, "the Watergate babies," as they were known, felt determined to reestablish Congress as an equal branch of government.

The new Congress was hardly satisfied by the creation of the Rockefeller Commission or impressed by the independence of the totems whom Ford had named to investigate the CIA: Ronald Reagan, governor of California, was an instinctive defender of the CIA and the military. Lane Kirkland was chief of the AFL-CIO, which had received secret CIA funding via Jay Lovestone. Lyman Lemnitzer, the retired chairman of the Joint Chiefs of Staff, was still notorious for the militarism that inspired the coup d'état scenario of *Seven Days in May.* And the commission's executive director, David Belin, had also held a position with the increasingly suspect Warren Commission. One poll found that half of all respondents said the Rocke-feller Commission would be too influenced by the White House. Four in ten believed the commission would turn into "another cover-up."[101]

In late January 1975, Senate Majority Leader Mike Mansfield of Montana put together a resolution creating a select committee to investigate the CIA, which passed by a vote of eighty-two to four. The Senate committee would be cochaired by Frank Church, a liberal Democrat from Idaho, and How-ard Baker, of Senate Watergate Committee fame.

Angleton thought the "orgy of self-criticism convulsing the Congress and the press alike was something more primitive than witch burning or the whiplash of Puritan conscience." The indignation was positively evangelical, he said. He took to quoting a German diplomat who said of scandalized America circa 1975, "You don't have a country over there. You have a huge church."[102]

WHAT THE UNITED STATES of America experienced in 1975 and 1976 was a constitutional crisis. The struggle was precipitated by the lawless presidency and unprecedented resignation of Richard Nixon. It was joined by the exposure and firing of James Angleton. The crisis lasted for close to two years, until President Jimmy Carter was elected and the Justice Department decided not to prosecute Angleton.

One witness to this epic conflict was a Capitol Hill veteran named Bill Miller. As Senator Church began to organize the Senate investigation, he called on Miller to serve as the committee's chief of staff. Miller, a former Foreign Service officer, had helped the Nixon administration secure Senate approval of the Strategic Arms Limitation Treaty in 1972. As Miller hired the staff to investigate, he negotiated with his bosses, Church and Baker, in the Senate, and their adversaries, Rumsfeld and Cheney, in the White House, along with Colby and others at the CIA.

Miller found himself navigating between two Washington factions, which he dubbed "the King's Party" and "the Constitutionalists."[103] These were not actual organized entities, and the participants themselves did not use Miller's terminology. But the labels captured the two political tendencies vying for power in the vacuum of legitimacy left by Nixon's resignation.

The King's Party, epitomized by Ford and Cheney, had an expansive view of presidential power. To them, the chief executive embodied the sovereignty of the American people. In their view, any limitation on the powers of the chief executive, and, by extension, the CIA, was, almost by definition, harmful to the American people. The president, they asserted, could and should act in defense of national security as he saw fit.

But the King's Party was on the defensive in the spring of 1975. Its assertive credo had been discredited by the divisive and unsuccessful war in Vietnam and by Nixon's crime spree, as abetted by the CIA. The Constitutionalists, based in the resurgent Congress, demanded a new legal framework to restrain executive power and the CIA. They voiced the widespread belief that no president was above the law. The revelations of domestic spying, they believed, strengthened the case for constitutional principles to protect the liberties of Americans.

Miller noticed one of the most interesting aspects of this struggle: The CIA itself was split. Even in retirement, former director Dick Helms was an influential voice in the King's Party, while the current director, Bill Colby, had effectively joined the Constitutionalists.[104]

Along the way, Miller got to know Angleton. He concluded that his tenure as counterintelligence chief had destroyed him psychologically.

"The Senators looked at Angleton as an example of an extraordinarily intelligent man and interesting phenomenon," Miller said in an oral history of the Church Committee. He embodied the "temptation of falling prey to a fascination with the workings of the dark side."[105]

And the dark side was fast coming to light.

"DEAR CORD," ANGLETON WROTE to his friend Cord Meyer on January 26, 1975. Meyer was now serving as London station chief and anxious about Angleton's condition since his forced retirement.

"Sorry not to have written sooner," Angleton said, "but how can one describe a nightmare?"[106]

With a single word: *assassination.*

WARNING

ANGLETON'S WAKING NIGHTMARE GREW more frightening on February 28, 1975. Daniel Schorr delivered a revelation on the *CBS Evening News* more sensational than anything Seymour Hersh had reported: The CIA faced investigation for the assassination of foreign leaders.

"President Ford reportedly warns associates that if current investigations go too far, several assassinations of foreign officials that had CIA involvement could be uncovered," Schorr said.[107]

The retired orchid grower of 33rd Road knew more than a little about the subject of assassination.[108]

THE SOURCE FOR SCHORR'S story was, in a roundabout way, Dick Helms. In the aftermath of Angleton's firing, Helms returned to Washington. The sleek ambassador was feeling betrayed by his choirboy colleague Bill Colby. To demonstrate that the Agency did not hold itself above the law, Colby had taken it upon himself, without consultation, to share the family jewels documents with the Justice Department to see if there was any criminal behavior. Some of those documents showed that Helms had lied to a congressional committee when he denied that the CIA had sought to overthrow the government of Chile in 1970 by means of an assassination. Some at the Justice Department thought Helms should be indicted for perjury.

Helms had indeed stonewalled the Senate—in service of his legal obligation to protect CIA sources and methods, he said. The story was not pretty. In September 1970, Nixon and Kissinger had ordered Helms to do something, anything, to block the duly elected leftist president Salvatore Allende from taking office in Chile. Helms put his protégé David Phillips in charge. The Agency's allies in Santiago, a clique of ultrarightist officers, took it upon themselves to kidnap the country's top general, René Schneider, who said the military would not interfere with Allende's lawful election.

A gang ambushed Schneider's car in morning traffic, and the general suffered fatal wounds in the shoot-out. Allende assumed office without military intervention. The CIA paid off its thugs and retired from the scene with barely plausible denials of any involvement. Not surprisingly, Helms did not care to explain that homicidal fiasco to the Congress, or to the Justice Department, much less to the television cameras.

In a meeting in early January 1975, Helms had warned Secretary of State Kissinger that he would not take the blame for accusations related to assassination operations.

"If allegations have been made to Justice, a lot of dead cats will come out," Helms said, referring to the nineteenth-century pastime in American politics of hurling feline corpses during appearances of rival candidates.

"I intend to defend myself," he warned Kissinger. "I know enough to say that if the dead cats come out, I will participate."[109] He would sling a few himself.

President Ford wanted to avoid the whole subject. During a meeting with editors of *The New York Times* later that month, Ford expressed concern that the impending congressional investigations might delve into matters the U.S. government simply could not discuss. Like what? a *Times* editor asked. "Like assassination," Ford blurted out before hastily taking his answer "off the record."[110]

The *Times* editors decided they could not take advantage of Ford's blunder and print what he had said. But Dan Schorr heard the story, confirmed it with his own sources, and went on the air.[111]

Schorr's scoop generated another round of damaging headlines in *The Washington Post*.

CIA IS REPORTED TO FEAR LINK
TO THREE ASSASSINATION PLOTS

CIA officials, the story reported, feared exposure of plots to kill Castro in Cuba, strongman Rafael Trujillo in the Dominican Republic, and nationalist Patrice Lumumba in Congo.[112] The resulting disbelief and dismay—America was going around killing the leaders of other countries?—stoked more demands for investigation.

The revelation strengthened Frank Church, Bill Colby, and other Constitutionalists, who favored more accountability for the Agency. It undermined Dick Helms, Dick Cheney, and the stalwarts of the King's Party, who defended the most expansive reading of presidential powers. The Rockefeller Commission, set up to investigate allegations of domestic spying, had no choice but to add CIA assassination plots to its agenda.

Then came another unsettling disclosure: Neither Helms nor Allen Dulles had told the Warren Commission about the plots to kill Castro. The story boosted the credibility of the much-maligned JFK "conspiracy theorists," who had long argued—accurately, it turned out—that the government was hiding relevant information about Kennedy's murder.

On March 6, 1975, Geraldo Rivera, host of ABC's late-night television show *Good Night America,* invited JFK researchers Robert Groden and Dick Gregory on the air to screen Abraham Zapruder's home movie of the assassination, the first time JFK's death had ever been shown on broadcast television.

The footage was grainy—Groden and Gregory had only a third- or fourth-generation copy of the film—but it showed millions of Americans for the first time what had actually happened in Dallas on November 22. The fatal shot had blasted Kennedy's body and head backward and to the left, a grisly reality that the Warren Commission had elided by saying the president "fell to the left."[113]

Defenders of the Warren Commission were hard-pressed to explain how a bullet fired from behind JFK (and traveling a thousand miles an hour) could have driven the victim's head and body *toward* the source of the gunfire. The intrepid reporting of Schorr and Rivera had a combustible effect on public opinion, stirring disbelief and demands for a new JFK investigation. The credibility of the Rockefeller Commission, already stacked with Washington insiders, was in doubt. Executive director David Belin hastened to criticize the CIA's failure to disclose the Castro plots to the Warren Commission. He was joined by David Slawson, a law professor at the University of Southern California, who had also served on the commission's staff.

Slawson rejected criticism of the Warren Commission's findings and disdained the "circus atmosphere" around public discussion of the issue. But when a *New York Times* reporter showed him an FBI document that had just been unearthed in the National Archives, Slawson also felt obliged to speak out. The memo, written by J. Edgar Hoover and sent to the CIA's Office of Security in June 1960, concerned Oswald, who was living in the Soviet Union at the time. The memo asked whether an "imposter" might be using Oswald's birth certificate. The issue had apparently first been raised with FBI agents in Dallas by Oswald's conspiracy-minded mother, Marguerite.

As Slawson read through the fifteen-year-old memo, he decided that there was almost certainly nothing to it. Still, he was angry, because he was certain that he had never seen the memo. So he agreed to go on the record with the *Times*—both to attack the CIA and to join the growing calls for a new investigation of Kennedy's assassination, if only to determine why this document and so much other information had been withheld.

"I don't know where the imposter notion would have led us—perhaps nowhere, like a lot of other leads," Slawson told the *Times*. "But the point is we didn't know about it. And why not?"

There was much more that Slawson didn't know. He didn't know that Angleton's staff had controlled access to Oswald's file from 1959 to 1963 or that his aides had drafted cables on Oswald's visit to Mexico City in October 1963 or that Angleton had participated in planning the assassination of Castro. Slawson didn't know it, but when he criticized the CIA for stonewalling the Warren Commission, he was criticizing Angleton personally.

A few days later, Slawson received an unexpected phone call at his home in Pasadena, California.

"This is James Angleton," the caller said.

The voice was plummy and friendly to Slawson's ears, the name vaguely familiar. Angleton said he wanted to talk about the *Times* article, explaining his background.

"He really piled it on, how important and aristocratic he was," Slawson recalled. Then, Slawson says, the conversation took a menacing turn.

Was it true, Angleton wanted to know, that Slawson was calling for a new investigation of elements of the Kennedy assassination?

Angleton's tone, more than the literal meaning of his words, seemed threatening to Slawson.

Angleton suggested that the CIA needed Slawson's help—his continuing help—as a "partner."

A partner in what? Slawson wondered.

"We want you to know how we appreciated the work you have done with us," Angleton said. Slawson reminded himself that he had never worked for the CIA; he had investigated the CIA, or so he thought.

"We hope you'll remain a friend," Angleton said. "We hope you'll remain a partner with us." He spoke slowly, pausing to allow Slawson to take in what he was saying.

"The message was: We know everything you're doing," Slawson recalled thinking as he put the phone down. "We'll find it out. Just remember that. The CIA is watching you."

Slawson and his wife were both alarmed by the call. It was a warning, Slawson decided: "Keep your mouth shut."[114]

It was the same threat Win Scott had received. Angleton was still obstructing justice in the case of the murdered president. He was still deflecting questions, not answering them. When Seymour Hersh pressed Angleton about who was responsible for the assassination of JFK, he replied cryptically: "A mansion has many rooms. . . . I'm not privy to who struck John."

Whatever did Angleton mean by that?

"I would be absolutely misleading you if I thought I had any f*****g idea," Hersh told author David Talbot. "But my instinct about it is he basically was laying off [blame for the assassination] on somebody else inside the CIA."

The investigative reporter sensed a man with something to hide.

"The whole purpose of the conversation was to convince me to go after somebody else [on JFK] and not him."[115]

THE RITUALS OF WASHINGTON politics were giving way to fear and loathing, and for good reason. The American ascendancy that had elevated Angleton and Helms and the CIA to unlimited power was over. The military-industrial colossus that had defeated Nazi Germany and vanquished the Japanese was spent. The United States was in the final throes of losing the war in distant Vietnam to a disciplined peasant army that barely had an air force.

Henry Kissinger's peace treaty of 1973 was just a scrap of paper as the North Vietnamese launched a wide-ranging offensive in March 1975. In almost every battle, the South Vietnamese army collapsed, leaving the pro-American government in control of Saigon and little more. In early April 1975, Bill Colby ordered the Saigon station to start destroying its files and evacuating its personnel. The CIA men faced a new reality: Things might turn out very badly, not just for the country but for them personally.[116]

The Senate investigation had already drawn blood. The Church Committee gained access to the family jewels documents and found mention of the case of Frank Olson, the U.S. Army scientist who had died after being dosed with LSD. Nobody in Langley wanted to talk about a suspicious death in 1953 that was cleaned up by none other than James McCord, the CIA man now famous as a Watergate burglar.

The idea that Frank Olson had killed himself by hurling his body through a closed window could not withstand much scrutiny, so the Agency quickly offered the Olson family generous financial compensation and a meeting with President Ford, which was coordinated by Dick Cheney. The CIA and the White House adopted the cover story found in the files: that Olson was the unwitting victim of an LSD experiment and had committed suicide.

Nobody was more alarmed about these developments than cool, collected Dick Helms. He had risen through the ranks of the CIA on the strength of his discipline and loyalty. He had prevailed over talented and ambitious men in the competition for the top job. As DCI, he had served two presidents through seven years of war. The revelations of murder plots and mind-control experiments threatened his reputation and his livelihood. He was no longer seen as an apolitical public servant but, in the words of one journalist, as "a gentlemanly planner of assassinations." The prospect of disgrace, if not jail time, was looming.

In April 1975, Helms testified to the Rockefeller Commission in the federal courthouse in Washington's Judiciary Square. As he left the building, he encountered Dan Schorr, who stuck a microphone in his face. A supremely self-satisfied and self-controlled man, Helms exploded in a spluttering, spitting rage.

"You son-of-a-bitch!" he screamed at the newsman. "You killer! You cocksucker! 'Killer Schorr,' that's what they should call you!"[117]

Helms finally managed to compose himself, but his outburst exposed something the sleek former director worked hard to hide: raw fear.

IN THIS SEASON OF upheaval, Angleton was honored by his employer. On April 25, 1975, Gen. Marshall Carter, fishing buddy and former deputy director, presided at an award ceremony in the Langley headquarters. Bill Colby was conspicuous by his absence. Angleton's wife, Cicely, and daughters Siri Hari and Guru Sangat Kaur Khalsa, watched as Angleton received one of the Agency's highest awards, the Distinguished Intelligence Medal. The honor was given for "performance of outstanding services or for achievement of a distinctly exceptional nature in a duty or responsibility, the results of which constitute a major contribution to the mission of the Agency."[118] No one doubted Jim Angleton's contributions to the CIA were major and exceptional.

In a letter to Cord Meyer later that day, Angleton wrote that the ceremony was "especially meaningful" for his family. He made a poignant admission of how little his wife and children knew of his professional life. In his fourteen years working in Langley, he had never once taken them to his office. The occasion of his honor, he said, "was their first and perhaps last visit to the building."[119]

INCONCEIVABLE

ANGLETON ARRIVED AT ROOM 318 of the Russell Senate Office Building on September 24, 1975, anxious for vindication. In June, he had testified behind closed doors to the Rockefeller Commission about what he knew of spying on the antiwar movement (not much, he said, shading the truth) and the mail-opening program (uniquely productive, he insisted). He had followed up his appearance with a thirty-seven-page brief detailing the dire state of counterintelligence under Colby. He warned of the Agency's "mounting inability to cope with the growing menace of hostile clandestine activity."[120]

Angleton peered about curiously through his big glasses, as the hearing room filled up with staffers in skirts, scrappy reporters, well-appointed lobbyists, garrulous lawyers, and interested tourists. Angleton watched the men on the dais in front of him. He saw Senator Church, Senator Baker, Senator Mondale, and the rest. He saw people coming and going, whispering, fussing with papers, adjusting microphones, getting ready, and settling in for the committee's second day of public hearings. The topic was the Huston Plan, President Nixon's abortive scheme to centralize domestic intelligence gathering in the White House, and Angleton was first on the witness list.

Angleton wanted to challenge Senator Church, who was settling into his center-stage seat as the committee's chairman. The two men had a common heritage. Like Angleton, Church had grown up in Boise, Idaho, and had come to maturity in elite institutions (Stanford and Stanford Law School). At the early age of thirty-two, Church was elected to the U.S. Senate, where he served on the Senate Foreign Relations Committee. As President Johnson escalated the war in Vietnam, Church turned into a war critic, and not a quiet one. By 1975, he had served four terms in the Senate. An eloquent (some said long-winded) public speaker, Church lent his voice to the liberal cause of checking the imperial presidency with congressional power.

Church opened the proceedings by referring to one of biggest revelations of the Rockefeller Commission's report: the LINGUAL mail-opening operation, which the commission called "illegal" and "beyond the law." He added new details that his investigators had found in the LINGUAL files: a letter that Senator Hubert Humphrey had written from Moscow; a letter that Richard Nixon had received from his speechwriter Ray Price, who had been visiting in Moscow. The Agency had even swiped a letter that Church had written to his mother-in-law from Europe. With that preemptive strike, Church asked Angleton to stand and swear that he would "tell the truth, the whole truth and nothing but the truth."[121]

Angleton obliged. In a brief opening statement, he sought to identify himself with the mood of public opinion. "It is the ultimate function of the intelligence community as part of our Government, to maintain and enhance the opportunity for peaceful change," he said.[122]

There was something anticlimactic about Angleton's much-anticipated appearance. The vaunted spymaster resembled an old man asking for his porridge, said one reporter.

The senators wanted to know more about the Huston Plan. Nixon's scheme had been abetted by Helms at the CIA and (initially) by Hoover at the FBI. The committee had found Angleton's June 1970 memo in which he sought to gain Nixon's approval for expanding the mail-opening operation. They had found his little lie about the "re-activization" of the LINGUAL program.

The committee's chief counsel, Frederick Schwarz, Jr., asked Angleton to read his memo stating that LINGUAL had been discontinued. Angleton obliged.

"Now the sentence that says 'covert coverage has been discontinued' is a lie," Schwarz went on. ". . . Is that correct?"

Angleton mumbled something.

Senator Church took back the microphone and moved in for the kill.

Wasn't it important, Church asked, given the turbulence of the times, that the president be fully informed about the actions "of the very agencies we entrust to uphold and enforce the law?"

Angleton agreed.

"You have said that there was an affirmative duty on the CIA to inform the President?" Church said.

"I don't dispute that," Angleton replied.

"And he was not informed, so that was a failure of duty to the Commander in Chief; is that correct?"

"Mr. Chairman," Angleton protested, "I don't think anyone would have hesitated to inform the President if he had at any moment asked for a review of intelligence operations."

"That is what he did do," said Church, exasperated. ". . . The President wanted to be informed. He wanted recommendations. He wanted to decide what should be done, and he was misinformed. Not only was he misinformed, but when he reconsidered authorizing the opening of the mail five days later and revoked it, the CIA did not pay the slightest bit of attention to him."

Church had caught Angleton in his little lie and turned it into a big one.

"The Commander in Chief, as you say," he said sarcastically. "Is that so?"

"I have no satisfactory answer for that," Angleton said.

Angleton was silenced, Church victorious.

Senator Baker tried to bolster Angleton by asking if he thought some of the activities he supported should be made legal in consultation with Congress. This was the argument of the Constitutionalists, and it was increasingly popular in Washington. Rein in the CIA; don't destroy it.

Angleton couldn't quite bring himself to agree. The problem wasn't the lack of authorizing legislation. The problem was Kissinger's policy of détente, he said.

"My view is that there is complete illusion to believe on the operative, clandestine side—which is in a sense a secret war that has continued since World War II—that the Soviets or the Soviet blocs have changed their objectives."

When Angleton insisted the Huston Plan was a matter of national security, not politics, Church was roused to attack again. He brought up something Angleton had told the committee in executive session two weeks earlier. Angleton had been asked why the CIA had ignored an order in 1970 from President Nixon to destroy a small stockpile of biological weapons. Angleton could have ducked the question, but he wanted to make his point.

"It is inconceivable," he replied, "that a secret intelligence arm of the government has to comply with all the overt orders of government."

Those were the most notorious words Angleton would ever utter. Under Church's withering interrogation, he tried to withdraw them, but he surely believed what he said. There was nothing shocking to him about the CIA doing its job.

"When I look at the map today and the weakness of this country," Angleton said, "that is what shocks me."[123]

ANGLETON'S ORDEAL IN ROOM 318 was the lead story on all three national news broadcasts that evening.

"James Angleton seems almost typecast as counterspy, rumpled, reflective, avid, and a trout fisherman," said ABC correspondent David Schoumacher. "Angleton was barely settled today when the committee revealed his mail intercept program netted a letter from Richard Nixon to his speechwriter, the mail of Senators Kennedy and Martin Luther King, Jay Rockefeller. Even a letter Chairman Church once wrote his mother-in-law."

On *NBC Nightly News*, Angleton was seen saying, "Certain individual rights have to be sacrificed for the national security."[124]

The millions of Americans who had first seen Angleton tottering out of his house on Christmas Eve 1974 now saw an elderly fanatic who wanted to read their mail and insisted the CIA didn't have to follow orders.

It was a debacle, and Angleton knew it.

"Angleton wanted to hear no more about Washington—or the CIA," said journalist Ed Epstein. Angleton left for the Arizona desert, abandoning his prizewinning orchids and letting his greenhouse fall into disrepair. The next year, he went on a long, solitary fishing trip on the Matapedia River in Canada.[125]

LEGACY

IN RETIREMENT, JAMES ANGLETON was a Svengali to working journalists. In early 1976, when the tabloid *National Enquirer* broke the story of Mary Meyer's affair with JFK, Angleton shared his account of searching for her diary with several writers, including Ron Rosenbaum of *New Times,* a muckraking monthly; Dick Russell, a freelancer interested in JFK's assassination; and Scott Armstrong, a reporter from *The Washington Post.*

Angleton knew how to keep his secrets. He invited Armstrong to his empty house in Arlington and plied him with drinks and gossipy stories about Mary Meyer until his head was spinning. While Armstrong stumbled home drunk, Angleton then called his friend Katharine Graham, the publisher of the *Post,* and said one of her employees was asking inappropriate questions about extramarital hijinks in the Kennedy years. Graham, whose philandering husband suffered mental illness and committed suicide, loathed such loose talk. According to Armstrong, Graham then called *Post* editor Len Downie to complain. Downie saved Armstrong's job by calling him off the story. The *Post* never did a story about how Angleton walked off with Mary Meyer's diary.[126]

Angleton expounded his views to any and all who cared to listen. In long liquid lunches at the Army-Navy Club overlooking Farragut Square in downtown Washington, he spoke to reporters, congressional investigators, freelancers, and friends. In private conversation, Angleton excelled. His conversation was compelling, his ideas original, his breadth of experience impressive, at least at first. Articles began to appear about him, and then books depicting a complex, if not contradictory, man. He soon became semifamous as an intelligence savant, a literary spy, a Cold Warrior, the spymaster who had launched the mole hunt and pierced the KGB's legend about Lee Harvey Oswald.

Edward Epstein, a journalist who estimates he met with Angleton more than one hundred times after his retirement in 1975, said what impressed him most about Angleton was "he invented his own world," and not just professionally. "He designed every piece of furniture in his house. When I went to visit him one time at his house in Tucson, he said, 'It's too bad you got here after sunset. You missed the wonderful view of the mountains.' And then he drew a picture of the sunset and the mountains for me."[127]

The legend of Angleton, however, was not the same as his legacy. The legend was the public version of his story, as recounted by Angleton himself and by those who interviewed him. Harder to discern was the legacy of Angleton: the impact of his actions on the U.S. government and the American people in the years to come. The legend would be confused with the legacy, but they were far from the same. If anything, Angletonian mythology emphasized his compelling personality at the expense of capturing the full dimensions of his intelligence empire and enduring influence.

His mole hunt was his most notorious achievement. Veteran case officer George Kisevalter said Angleton's faith in Anatoly Golitsyn's theories was a form of madness.

"Had there been a real Sasha, he could not have done as much damage to the clandestine services group as this phantom Sasha," Kisevalter told his biographer.[128] "The careers of many were damaged, and some were forced to leave the Agency. Some of those maligned at least had the satisfaction of successful lawsuits settled with monetary compensation and the restoration of their good names, albeit many hard years later."

Kisevalter's opinion was not idiosyncratic. In 1997, he received the Agency's Trailblazer Award, recognizing him as one of the fifty top CIA officers in its first fifty years, an honor Angleton did not receive.[129] There was never any doubt in Kisevalter's mind about the bona fides of Yuri Nosenko. Three subsequent reviews by senior CIA officers reached the same conclusion. So did Cleveland Cram, the senior officer who wrote a still-classified multivolume study of Angleton's operations. So did Benjamin Fischer, a career officer who became the Agency's chief historian.

"The Great Mole Hunt or Great Mole Scare of the late 1960s turned the CIA inside out, ruining careers and reputations in search for Soviet penetrations that may or may not have existed," Fischer wrote.[130]

Those who dissented from the institutional consensus about the mole hunt were mostly officers who had served Angleton on the Counterintelligence Staff. "The Angletonians," as they called themselves, were a dogged bunch.[131] Bill Hood and Pete Bagley asserted that the clandestine service was never penetrated during Angleton's watch—which is true. They also claimed that the CIA's operations against the Soviet Union were not unduly harmed by the mole hunt—which is not.[132]

Angleton and his acolytes would speak many words in his defense and write more than a few books. They cited scores of statements by Yuri Nosenko that they said were misleading or not credible, and indeed Nosenko had exaggerated and embellished, as defectors often do. In retirement, Pete Bagley befriended a retired KGB officer, Sergei Kondrashev, and helped him write a book that expressed doubts about Nosenko's credibility, raising the possibility that Nosenko's defection was somehow sanctioned by the KGB. But Angleton's theory of Nosenko's role in the KGB's "monster plot" asserted much more. Angleton insisted that Nosenko was not merely a controlled agent but that he was sent to protect a source working inside the CIA on a daily basis in 1963 and for many years after. Which begs the question: If there was a mole burrowed into the CIA in the 1950s and 1960s, as the Angletonians claimed, who the devil was it? And what damage did he do?

The CIA learned the consequences of Soviet penetration in the 1980s when the KGB recruited FBI agent Robert Hanssen and CIA officer Aldrich Ames as spies. American agents were arrested and executed. But even after the dissolution of the Soviet Union and the opening of significant portions of the KGB archives, the Angletonians could not identify any CIA operations compromised by the putative mole. They could not even offer up the name of a single plausible candidate from the three dozen suspects whom Angleton investigated. After the passage of five decades, the likeliest explanation is that there wasn't a mole.

Such was the most notorious aspect of Angleton's legacy. But while the mole hunt might have been foolish, it did not violate U.S. law or policy. Angleton's most substantive accomplishments did both.

———

ANGLETON'S MOST SIGNIFICANT AND enduring legacy was to legitimize mass surveillance of Americans. While his mole hunt paralyzed CIA Soviet operations for five years at the most, Angleton's LINGUAL/HUNTER program funneled secret reporting on law-abiding citizens to Hoover's COINTELPRO operatives for eighteen years. The FBI used CIA information to harass leftists, liberals, and civil rights leaders from 1956 to 1974. Angleton was the ghost of COINTELPRO.

Angleton was a ghost in the domestic politics of Italy and Great Britain. In December 1970, Valerio Borghese, the fascist commander whom he had saved from partisan justice in 1945, launched an abortive military coup against a leftist government in Rome. When the coup collapsed, Borghese fled to Spain, amid rumors of American involvement. COMPLOTTO NEO-FASCISTI ("Neofascist Plot") screamed one banner newspaper headline.[133] The Italian parliament investigated the Golpe Borghese, as it was known, and found CIA money had purchased influence in Italy's intelligence services and non-Communist political parties for decades. One State Department official says he personally assisted in the distribution of $25 million in cash to parties and individuals in 1970.[134] For many years, Angleton had played a leading role in doling out such funds. He denied any knowledge of the Golpe Borghese, but the more general CIA-funded corruption of Italian politics is part of his legacy.

Then there was "the Wilson Plot" in England. Angleton's belief that British Labour leader Harold Wilson was a Soviet agent of influence never gained much credence in the CIA or the U.S. government. But it became an article of truth to Peter Wright and other British officers who believed most every word that Anatoly Golitsyn said.[135] In the early 1970s Angleton's allies in London leaked secret intelligence reports to the Fleet Street tabloids calling into question Wilson's loyalty. Wilson eventually resigned.

David Leigh, the first journalist to tell the tale, concluded Angleton "more than any other individual was responsible for the climate of deceitfulness, paranoia, and mutual denunciation of which Harold Wilson became a victim."[136]

ON JANUARY 14, 1977, Angleton got some good news. He would not be indicted for his role in the mail-opening operation.

Without fanfare, the Justice Department issued a fifty-seven-page report on legal questions arising from the Church Committee's findings about the CIA's mail-opening program. The report stated the department would not bring charges against "potential defendants" who created and ran the LINGUAL operation. Angleton's name was never mentioned, but he was the chief beneficiary.

The prosecution of the responsible CIA officials would involve "elements of unfairness and an almost certain lack of success in obtaining convictions," the Justice Department lawyers stated. While offering the "firm view" that the mail-opening operation would be unlawful in 1975, the attorneys asserted that "prosecution of the potential defendants would be unlikely to succeed because of the unavailability of important evidence and because of the state of the law that prevailed during the course of the mail opening program."[137]

The Justice Department had to think about the politics of bringing a case into a Washington courtroom. Indicting Angleton would assure lengthy and difficult disputes about the admission of classified material. Angleton was sure to argue that he had presidential authorization via Dulles, McCone, and Helms. Powerful men in the capital already resented the indictment of Helms. "Retroactive morality," the *Los Angeles Times* called it. The country was in a cynical mood after Nixon's disgrace and the defeat in Vietnam. Washington was eager to welcome President-elect Jimmy Carter and to put Watergate in the past. Discretion seemed the better part of prosecutorial valor, and Angleton walked.

The Justice Department's decision not to indict Angleton set a precedent and sent a message: that the secret intelligence arm of the government could reserve the right to review, without warrant or stated cause, the private communications of Americans—in the name of "national security."

Angleton was the leading champion of this belief in the first twenty-five years of the CIA. He implemented it as U.S. government policy on the barest of authority, confident that any director and president would endorse his actions after the fact. With the fall of Nixon and the exposure of the full dimensions of LINGUAL and CHAOS, Angleton's position became controversial and unpopular.

Yet in the fullness of time, Angleton's thinking would prevail. The Constitutionalists of Washington emerged as the winners after the crisis of 1975–1976. The CIA had to submit to a new regime of legal and legislative oversight. After the terror attacks of September 11, 2001, the King's Party regained the upper hand. With Dick Cheney now serving as a powerful vice president and legislative author, Congress passed the Patriot Act. The government stepped up mass surveillance of Americans' private communications, now focusing on phone calls and e-mail. Thanks to the January 1977 decision not to indict Angleton, there was no legal precedent against it.

Angleton was a founding father of U.S. mass-surveillance policies. To oversimplify only slightly, Dick Cheney picked up where Jim Angleton had left off.

ANGLETON'S LOYALTY TO ISRAEL betrayed U.S. policy on an epic scale, and his former colleague John Hadden knew it. In 1978, Hadden, the retired Tel Aviv station chief, made the long trip from his home in Brunswick, Maine, to Washington, D.C. He had a story he needed to tell the right people: how Israel stole nuclear material from the United States government on Angleton's watch.

The story of the great uranium heist at the NUMEC plant in Pennsylvania continued to attract official interest. Over the years, the story of the loss of hundreds of pounds of fissionable material from the Apollo facility had been examined by several government agencies. The question was whether the Israelis had used NUMEC to divert enriched uranium to Dimona and then used it to build their nuclear arsenal.

The CIA's scientists reviewed the evidence. Without judging the legal questions, they all agreed that enriched uranium from NUMEC had been obtained by the Israelis. "I believe that all of my senior analysts who worked on the problem agreed with me fully," said Carl Duckett, deputy director of the CIA responsible for technical and nuclear intelligence. "[T]he clear consensus in the CIA was that indeed NUMEC material had been diverted and had been used by the Israelis in fabricating weapons."[138]

The Department of Energy and the Nuclear Regulatory Commission looked into the matter and found their efforts stymied by a lack of cooperation from the CIA and from NUMEC president Zalman Shapiro, as well as by a studious lack of interest from Capitol Hill. The investigators found no proof of diversion, but they did not have access to all the classified information available to the CIA scientists. When former NRC staffer Roger Mattson managed to get access to the CIA records, he concluded that NUMEC was the only possible source of Israel's fissionable material.[139]

John Hadden said the same thing. "A crime was committed 10 or 20 years ago," he wrote in a memo for the record, "a crime considered so serious that for its commission the death penalty is mandatory and no statute of limitations applies."

A good CIA man, Hadden never spilled classified information, never reported out of channels. He spoke only with the senior staff of the AEC or the House Interior Committee.[140] He prepared twenty-nine talking points to support his memo's conclusion: that NUMEC was a front company deployed in an Israeli-American criminal conspiracy to evade U.S. nonproliferation laws and supply the Israeli nuclear arsenal.

"If the crime had been committed intentionally and was not the result of carelessness," Hadden went on, "then the circumstances warranted a finding of high treason with a mandatory death penalty."

The only other explanation, he wrote, was "gross incompetence on the part of those responsible for security in certain areas."

It was either treason or incompetence, Hadden said. If one of those terms applied to his former boss, Jim Angleton, so be it.[141]

Angleton had regular professional and personal contact with at least six men aware of Israel's secret plan to build a bomb. From Asher Ben-Natan to Amos de Shalit to Isser Harel to Meir Amit to Moshe Dayan to Yval Ne'eman, his friends were involved in the building of Israel's nuclear arsenal. If he learned anything of the secret program at Dimona, he reported very little of it. If he didn't ask questions about Israel's actions, he wasn't doing his job. Instead of supporting U.S. nuclear security policy, he ignored it.

Angleton thought collaboration with the Israeli intelligence services was more important. And the results proved his point, he believed. When Angleton started as chief of the Counterintelligence Staff in 1954, the state of Israel and its leaders were regarded warily in Washington, especially at the State Department. When Angleton left government service twenty years later, Israel held twice as much territory as it had in 1948, the CIA and the Mossad collaborated on a daily basis, and the governments of the United States and Israel were strategic allies, knit together by expansive intelligence sharing, multibillion-dollar arms contracts, and coordinated diplomacy.

The failure of the U.S. nonproliferation policy to prevent the introduction of nuclear weapons to the Middle East in the 1960s is part of Angleton's legacy, and its effects will be felt for decades, if not centuries. He was a leading architect of America's strategic relationship with Israel that endures and dominates the region to this day. He was, as his friend Meir Amit said, "the biggest Zionist of the lot."

THE JFK STORY IS a blight on Angleton's legacy. His handling of the Oswald file before the assassination of President Kennedy has never been explained by the CIA. His conspiracy theories about KGB involvement have never been substantiated. His animus toward those seeking to investigate JFK's assassination was constant and arguably criminal. If the evidence of his actions had been known to law enforcement, he could have, and should have, been prosecuted for obstruction of justice and perjury.

When it came to the assassination of President Kennedy, Angleton acted as if he had something to hide. The question is, What? Angleton spoke for the record about JFK's murder on four occasions. All four times, he insinuated the assassination of the liberal president might have been influenced by the KGB.

"I don't think that the Oswald case is dead," Angleton told the Church Committee. "There are too many leads that were never followed. There's too much information that has developed later."[142]

It was a curious admission. Angleton was chief of the Counterintelligence Staff for eleven years after JFK's assassination. If there was any new information or any new leads into Oswald's possible contacts with the KGB, Angleton himself was personally responsible for investigating them. He apparently never did so.[143] The documentary foundation of Angleton's KGB conspiracy theories was—and is—vanishingly thin.

Yet whenever the JFK investigation turned to the CIA's preassassination interest in Oswald, Angleton stonewalled. The question was first raised during his appearance before the Church Committee. Senator Charles Mathias, a Republican Brahmin from Maryland posed the question.

"To your knowledge," he asked, "was Oswald ever interrogated when he returned from Russia?"

Angleton fumbled for words.

"I don't, probably would know but I don't know whether the military— normally that would fall with the jurisdiction of the military, since he was a military man who defected," Angleton babbled. "So I don't know the answer to that."[144]

In fact, Angleton did know the answer. The FBI had interviewed Oswald in August 1962 and Hoover had sent the report to Angleton's office, where Betty Egerter signed for it, and Angleton surely read it.

Angleton also lied about his role in the CIA's schemes to assassinate Fidel Castro. When an attorney for the House Select Committee on Assassinations asked about his knowledge of the plots, Angleton hedged.

"The question I want to ask you again is," the attorney said, "do you recall approximately when you learned this information [about the Castro assassination plots] . . . before or after the Warren Commission?"[145]

"I am certain," Angleton said, "it was well after the Warren Commission had completed its work."

Angleton was lying. He had spoken with Bill Harvey and Peter Wright in late 1961 about using nerve gas as an assassination weapon. In June 1963, he knew the substance of Bill Harvey's discussions with Johnny Rosselli, who had been enlisted to kill Castro. In July 1963, the counterintelligence staff had experimented with hypnotizing a potential assassin. Angleton denied knowledge of the AMLASH operation. But he knew of at least four different efforts to kill Castro six months *before* the Warren Commission completed its work.[146]

Angleton was lying to conceal his knowledge of the Castro assassination plots. He had to dissemble because he had used Oswald (or his file) in the mole hunt. He also probably felt duty bound to conceal his knowledge of the CIA's operation against the Fair Play for Cuba Committee in the fall of 1963.

All of which begs the harder question: Was Angleton running Oswald as an agent as part of a plot to assassinate President Kennedy? He certainly had the knowledge and ability to do so.

Angleton and his staff had a granular knowledge of Oswald long before Kennedy was killed. Angleton had a penchant for running operations outside of reporting channels. He articulated a vigilant anti-communism that depicted the results of JFK's liberal policies in apocalyptic terms. He participated in discussions of political assassination. And he worked in a penumbra of cunning that excluded few possibilities. "Angleton possessed a unique grasp of secret operations," Dick Helms wrote in his memoirs. ". . . Jim had the ability to raise an operation discussion, not only to higher level but to another dimension."[147]

Angleton made sure he could plausibly deny his monitoring of Oswald from 1959 to 1963. His admirers today can still plausibly deny he was involved in JFK's assassination.

What cannot be plausibly denied is that Angleton's actions were illegal. He obstructed justice to hide interest in Oswald. He lied to veil his use of the ex-defector in late 1963 for intelligence purposes related to the Cuban consulate in Mexico City. Whether Angleton manipulated Oswald as part of an assassination plot is unknown. He certainly abetted those who did. Whoever killed JFK, Angleton protected them. He masterminded the JFK conspiracy cover-up.

ONE ACHIEVEMENT CANNOT BE denied Angleton: There was no high-level KGB penetration of the CIA on his watch. The Soviets ran hundreds of agents in the United States from 1947 to 1974, but after Kim Philby's departure, they never had an agent with access to the top of the Agency.

Of course, Angleton denied any such achievement. He insisted to the end of his days that the Agency had been penetrated by one or more KGB moles. He had made sure it didn't happen, yet he insisted it had. He deserved credit, but he couldn't take it. About his greatest accomplishment, he was dead wrong. Such was the contradictory legacy of James Angleton.

He was an ingenious, vicious, mendacious, obsessive, and brilliant man who acted with impunity as he sought to expand the Anglo-American-Israeli sphere of influence after the end of World War II. Like his friend Ezra Pound, his mastery was sometimes indistinguishable from his madness. He was indeed a combination of Machiavelli, Svengali, and Iago. He was an intellectual, charming, and sinister. In retirement, at last, he was harmless.

LEGEND

IN JULY 1976, PHOTOGRAPHER Richard Avedon went to Arlington to take a photograph of Angleton. He went at the suggestion of a mutual friend, Renata Adler, a writer and novelist who had known Angleton since the early 1960s.[148] Adler had met him in Washington through Jim's sister Carmen. When Avedon told Adler that he was shooting portraits of the American ruling class for *Rolling Stone* magazine, she insisted he include Angleton.

Angleton's portrait appeared in *Rolling Stone* in October 1976, along with those of Frank Church, Henry Kissinger, Donald Rumsfeld, George H. W. Bush, Jimmy Carter, Barbara Jordan, Ronald Reagan, *New York Times* editor A. M. Rosenthal, and *Washington Post* publisher Katharine Graham. In Avedon's black-and-white minimalist gallery, Angleton had achieved something he had never sought. He was glamorous.

Angleton rarely tired of sharing his ideas with journalist Ed Epstein, who was intrigued by his analysis of the JFK assassination. In 1978, Epstein published *Legend: The Secret World of Lee Harvey Oswald,* which laid out Angleton's "KGB done it" conspiracy theory for the first time, albeit in unattributed form. The book sold well and was important in spreading Angleton's spurious theory of a super KGB manipulating American society and politics.

Angleton took to running reporters like he had once run agents in the field, and for the same purpose: to advance his geopolitical vision. He lunched often with Loch Johnson, a professor of intelligence history at the University of Georgia, who was working for the Church Committee. Johnson came away with his mind reeling. "To paraphrase Mark Twain, listening to Angleton for a half-hour could make you dizzy," he wrote. "Listening to him for a whole hour could make you drunk."[149]

Angleton invited Joe Trento, a reporter on military affairs, to lunch and found they shared a taste for conspiracy theories. From Angleton, Trento came away with the appreciation that "presidents come and go, but the intelligence bureaucracy remains in place as the real ruling class in our political system."[150]

David Ignatius, then a reporter at *The Wall Street Journal*, called him "a character out of fiction. He was so eccentric in his hobbies and his personal manner, that he was a work of art . . . a self-created work of art. He was too self-knowledgeable not to understand what he conveyed. The homburg. The way he looked out over his glasses. He was a piece of artifice."[151]

That was Angleton's first code name in the OSS: ARTIFICE. In retirement, his life became the stuff of art. He became an iconic figure in the Anglo-American imagination, the paranoid genius as spymaster: fisherman, orchid grower, and spy. He was portrayed in a BBC movie about Yuri Nosenko. He figured prominently in a series on Kim Philby and the Cambridge Five. His career served as inspiration for a TV miniseries, *The Company*, and for William F. Buckley's novel *Spytime*. He was the CIA man at the heart of Robert De Niro's movie *The Good Shepherd*. The most private of men, Angleton wound up as the public face of American intelligence in the Cold War.

For Norman Mailer, Angleton was less a hero than an ambiguous oracle, a sardonic teller of bleak truths. In *Harlot's Ghost*, Mailer's biblical novel of the early days of the CIA, the narrator, a retired CIA man, has had a conversation with Hugh Tremont Montague, the retired counterintelligence chief, who was based on Angleton.

"Bobby knows so little about us," the narrator tells us. The scene he describes took place not long after the gunfire in Dallas. Robert Kennedy, the grieving attorney general, confided in the narrator, who later recounted the story to Montague.

"One night he [RFK] began to talk of muffled suspicions and stifled half-certainties, and said to me, 'I had my doubts about a few fellows in your agency, but I don't anymore. I can trust John McCone and I asked him if they had killed my brother, and I asked him in a way that he couldn't lie to me, and he said he had looked into it and they hadn't.'"

Mailer's story was based in fact. Bobby Kennedy did have such a conversation with McCone, the CIA director, in 1963.[152]

"I told that story to Hugh," the narrator went on. "You know how rarely he laughs aloud. He actually struck his thigh. 'Yes,' he said, 'McCone was just the man to ask.'

"'What,' I asked him, 'would you have answered?'"

The narrator then relates Montague's reply: "'I would have told Bobby that if the job was done properly, I would not be able to give a correct answer.'"

That was an Angletonian aperçu to educate innocent Americans. If the ambush in Dallas had been properly planned by CIA men, he advised, even other CIA men would not have been be able to figure out who had done it.

IN RETIREMENT ANGLETON STAYED in touch with Dick Helms. He raised money for the legal defense of two FBI officials charged with COINTELPRO-related crimes. He still expounded on the betrayal of U.S. counterintelligence and the sham of détente, but fewer reporters came calling.[153] He had visits with his most loyal acolytes, Pete Bagley and Bill Hood.[154] He even heard from the reclusive Anatoly Golitsyn, who had written an opus on Soviet deception operations entitled *New Lies for Old*. In 1984, Angleton helped him get it published and contributed a laudatory introduction.

Golitsyn explained, predictably, that signs of change in the Soviet Union in the 1980s were tactical ruses to advance the KGB plans first laid down in 1958. The Solidarity labor movement in Poland, Golitsyn argued, was created by Moscow "to convert the narrow elitist dictatorship of the party into a Leninist dictatorship." It was an absurd description of an authentic social movement whose success in mobilizing Polish civil society foreshadowed the end of the Soviet Union itself.[155]

If the West succumbed to the blandishments of peaceful coexistence, Golitsyn wrote, a powerful, ideologically confident Soviet Union might soon dominate the world. Seven years later, the Soviet Union did not exist. By then, Angleton's reputation as a geopolitical seer had long since expired.

The CIA, for its part, would decide that Yuri Nosenko was more credible than Anatoly Golitsyn. While Golitsyn lived out his life under an assumed name, avoiding all public contact, Nosenko remained a consultant for the CIA into the twenty-first century. In early 2001, Nosenko was invited to give a talk in the Agency's auditorium about his experience handling the Oswald file for the KGB. The crowd of CIA employees listened with rapt attention and gave him a round of applause when he was done.[156]

IN 1986, ANGLETON WAS diagnosed with lung cancer and finally had to give up cigarettes. When he and Cicely had dinner with Dick Helms and his wife, Helms reported to John Hadden that Angleton "was in good fettle, has foresworn liquor and drinks cokes."[157]

Guilty and grateful, Angleton appreciated Cicely's loyalty. "I could never have gone through this without you," he told his wife. He didn't want his final days to burden her, he said. He wanted to "go into the woods on my own like an Indian and deal with the end of my life like an Apache."[158]

He offered reflections, leavened with feelings of mortality, to a favored few.

"Fundamentally, the founding fathers of U.S. intelligence were liars," he told Joseph Trento. "The better you lied and the more you betrayed, the more likely you were to be promoted. These people attracted and promoted each other. Outside of their duplicity, the only thing they had in common was a desire for absolute power. I did things that, in looking back on my life, I regret. But I was part of it and loved being in it. . . . Allen Dulles, Richard

Helms, Carmel Offie and Frank Wisner were the grand masters. If you were in a room with them, you were in a room full of people that you had to believe would deservedly end up in hell." He paused. "I guess I will see them there soon."

He offered secrets, leavened with hints of wisdom, to his allies. He called up former White House aide Dick Cheney, now a Republican congressman from Wyoming, to set up a dinner. He said he had something he wanted very much to tell him. He never got the chance, and the future vice president was left to ponder what fantastic secrets Angleton might have imparted.[159]

Efraim Halevy came from Israel to say good-bye. They exchanged political gossip and greetings for their wives. They understood they would never see each other again. It was an emotional moment for two old friends, and Angleton met it with fortitude.

"He shook my hands," Halevy recalled. "His eyes filled with tears and he gradually became calm. He said, 'Keep the faith.' "[160]

Angleton grew more stoic as he contemplated what he regarded as his own failures. There was a farewell luncheon with former colleagues at the Officers' Club at Fort Myer in Arlington, where he was given time to speak. When asked if he wanted to "come clean in the Philby case," Angleton declined to voice any feelings of love or betrayal.

"There are some matters I shall have to take to the grave with me," he said, heartbroken to the end, "and Kim is one of them."[161]

JERUSALEM

JAMES ANGLETON DIED ON May 11, 1987. He was survived by his former mentor, friend, and enemy, Kim Philby, who would die in Moscow exactly one year later. The first memorial service for Angleton was held at Rock Spring Congregational Church, not far from the Angleton home. Dick Helms and Jim Schlesinger attended the service.

Reed Whittemore read T. S. Eliot's "East Corker," a poem that evoked the ambiguity of Angleton's profession and his life.

Home is where one starts from. As we grow older
The world becomes stranger, the pattern more complicated
Of dead and living. Not the intense moment
Isolated, with no before and after,
But a lifetime burning in every moment
And not the lifetime of one man only
But of old stones that cannot be deciphered.

The ceremony lasted less than an hour, and the crowd dispersed into another day in Washington.[162] Angleton was buried in the same cemetery in Boise where his father had been interred.

The obituaries in *The New York Times* and *The Washington Post* cast him as a flawed man with vision, a man who was betrayed by Kim Philby and disgraced by spying scandals but never discredited and often admired. Angleton was fortunate that so much of his legacy was unknown or classified at the time of his death.

Angleton ably served the United States of America for the first half of his career, and escaped accountability for the rest. He has been condemned for his mole hunt, but he was only doing his job as he saw fit—and his superiors approved. The mole hunt was theoretically defensible. His flouting of U.S. nuclear security policies on behalf of Israel was not. He was never held accountable for suborning justice in the investigation of John Kennedy's assassination. He lost his job for spying on tens of thousands of Americans, but he never had to defend his deeds in a court of law. He often acted outside the law and the Constitution, and, for the most part, he got away with it. He died in his own bed, a lifetime burning to the end.

SEVEN MONTHS AFTER HIS death, Angleton was honored again, this time in Israel. It was in early December 1987. On the side of a winding road in the hills west of Jerusalem, several dozen people gathered, most of them Israeli. They came to remember their good and loyal friend in Washington. Cicely Angleton was there, escorted by deputy Mossad chief Efraim Halevy, one of the organizers. Cicely was accompanied by her daughter Guru Sangat Kaur Khalsa and her granddaughter, Sadhana Kaur. Both wore the splendid all-white garb of Sikh believers, which contrasted vividly with the informal Israeli attire of the rest.

The crowd gathered around a black stone, set in white marble, built into a rocky outcropping. It was engraved with tributes in Hebrew and English.

IN MEMORY OF

A DEAR FRIEND

JAMES J. ANGLETON

1917–1987

Among the celebrants were four past or future chiefs of Mossad, his friends Meir Amit and Amos Manor, and the upper echelon of Amal, the Israeli military intelligence service.[163] These were the men and women who had built the Zionist enterprise, who had transformed the homeland of the Jewish people from an embattled settler state into a strategic ally of the world's greatest superpower. They all wanted to pay their respects to the man who, more than any other American, had made it possible.

"He was a friend you could trust on a personal basis," said Yitzhak Rabin, now the country's defense minister.[164]

Later that afternoon, the same group of people gathered again, converging on a picturesque spot near the King David Hotel.[165] Angleton called it his "observation point," a park bench with an unobstructed view of the teethed ramparts of the Old City. On this spot, with his widow and daughter looking on, Angleton was again eulogized, first by the U.S. ambassador to Israel, Tom Pickering, and then by Teddy Kollek, the mayor of Jerusalem.

"We commemorate a great friend who saw Israel-U.S. relations though their most difficult period in the forty years of Israel's existence," Kollek declared.[166]

Cicely Angleton unveiled another black stone carved in English, Hebrew, and Arabic.

IN MEMORY OF A DEAR FRIEND

JAMES (JIM) ANGLETON

Angleton was buried in Boise, but his spirit came to rest here, far from the American democracy he had served and failed.

Thirty years later, the Angleton stone is still there, still maintained by his admirers, a modest monument unknown to American visitors and unmentioned in the guidebooks of all nations. Angleton's legacy is hidden in plain sight.

ACKNOWLEDGMENTS

I am indebted to John Newman. I did not know it at the time, but my research for this book began in November 1994, when John and I interviewed Jane Roman at her home in Washington. John's seminal work in *Oswald and the CIA* gave me the tools to trace Angleton's role in the JFK assassination story.

Bill Simpich, civil liberties litigator and laugh-a-minute agitator, has spent many nights poring over declassified CIA records. As a result, we have a much deeper and more granular understanding of U.S. spying operations in Mexico City that involved Lee Oswald. Bill introduced me to the previously unknown story of Angleton's mole hunt in Mexico.

Rex Bradford is the genial proprietor of the online archive of the Mary Ferrell Foundation. Without the thousands of documents I retrieved from the Mary Ferrell Web site, I could not have written this book. All historians of the Cold War and the Kennedy presidency who do online research are in Rex's debt.

The aptly named Malcolm Blunt is a wise and funny friend, and he supplied me with many documents and insights about the inner workings of the CIA that I never would have obtained otherwise. Malcolm's generosity reaffirms the truth of Toqueville's observation that there are some things Americans can only learn from foreigners.

My agent, Ron Goldfarb, merely came up with the idea for this book.

Many people gave generously of their time and thoughts about Angleton. They include Michael Scott, Renata Adler, Joseph Augustyn, John Dean, Ed Epstein, William Gowen, John Hadden, Dennis Helms, Tom Hughes,

Peter Janney, David Ignatius, China Jessup, Ted Jessup, Aaron Latham, Simon Lavee, David Martin, Matitiahu Mayzel, Vince Mor, Steven Murphy, Nachik Navot, Tom Pickering, Nancy Reynolds, and Peter Sichel.

Others who shared relevant expertise include Avner Cohen, Peter Fenn, Cliff Karchmer, Roger Mattson, Tim Naftali, John Prados, and Grant Smith.

I'm always impressed by the alacrity with which my fellow journalists share timely tips, useful phone numbers, neglected documents, tantalizing leads, and unexpurgated gossip. Among the guilty are Ronen Bergman, Nina Burleigh, Andrew and Leslie Cockburn, Yossi Melman, Ron Rosenbaum, Elaine Shannon, and Jeff Stein.

Tim Weiner was a constant source of encouragement—as in giving courage. I saw how Tim dealt with the CIA, and I did the same, though not nearly so well. Tim also secured a place for me in the unique nonfiction writers' residency program at the Carey Institute for Global Good in Rensselaerville, New York, where I wrote the first draft of this book.

Carol Ash, Gareth Crawford, Josh Friedman, and Sue Shufeldt made my two stays at Carey Institute delightful. I was content to gain weight eating the fine meals prepared by John Murray and the staff of the Carriage House.

My fellow writers at the Carey Institute were a subversive bunch who made the daily work of writing the first draft of this book an unmitigated pleasure. They were Camas Davis, Sarah Maslin, Justin Cohen, David Zucchino, Sara Catania, Rania Abouzeid, Dan Ellsberg, Scott Rodd, Catalina Lobo-Guerrero, Susannah Breslin, Finnbar O'Reilly, Matt Young, and T. J. Brennan. They are friends for life as far as I am concerned.

I very much appreciated that authors of previous books about Angleton were generous with their thoughts: Ed Epstein, Aaron Latham, Hank Albarelli, and David Martin all responded to my questions. Michael Holzman shared a rare copy of Angleton's FBI file.

This book was a family affair. My late aunt, Lorna Morley, shared memories of working for the CIA. My mother tutored me on the literary importance of Norman Holmes Pearson and located Perdita Schaffner's memoir of Angleton. Mike Heller provided poetic lowdown on Ezra Pound. My sons, Anthony and Diego, made me clarify. Cousins Charley and Chris warned me not to tarnish the Morley journalism brand.

I was sustained in my mission to write this book by the support of constant friends: Brad Knott, Barry Lynn, Eric London, Mark Steitz, Steve Mufson, Agnes Tabah, Patrice LeMelle, Stephen Greener Davis, Clara Rivera, Ken Silverstein, Tom Blanton, Charles Sweeney, Laura Quinn, Janette Noltenius, Robbyn Swan, and Mark Sugg. Stan and Liz Salett were especially supportive.

Old friends like Jodie Allen, Tom Blanton, Sidney Blumenthal, Nina Burleigh, Malcolm Byrne, Kate Doyle, Paul Hoch, Peter Kornbluh, and Phil Weiss encouraged me from day one. So did new friends like James Rosen, Lisa Pease, Alan Dale, and Fernand Amandi.

Tony Summers was, as always, my most exacting editor. David Bromwich, Bill Connell, Val Schaffner, and Bruce Schulman read and commented sagely on draft chapters. Not only did Jim Campbell put me up at his house during my research at Stanford Library, he also goaded me to think more historically. David Talbot inspired.

Jamie Galbraith supported my visit to the LBJ Library in Austin. Jenny Fishmann retrieved key documents from the Stanford Library. Adem Kendir provided invaluable insights into the Eugen Dollmann file. Matt Orehek of Claremont McKenna College volunteered useful research on John McCone.

The faithful readers of JFK Facts keep me apprised of many items of interest about Angleton. Three of them—Damian Turner, Jim McClure, and Leslie Sharp—transcribed a previously unknown audio recording of Angleton talking to the staff of the House Select Committee on Assassinations.

The hospitality of Bill L'Herault, Nic and Gail Puzak, and Anita Kangas enabled me to finish editing the manuscript in the most comfortable of settings.

Thanks to Simon Lavee for his generosity and patience in showing me around the Angleton memorials at Mevaseret Zion and the King David Hotel; Val Schaffner for sharing memories of his mother, Perdita Macpherson Schaffner, and his godfather, Norman Holmes Pearson; Josh Ober for giving me an incisive sketch of his uncle, Richard Ober; Christopher Andrew for answering obscure questions about British intelligence; Albert

Lulushi for sharing his deep knowledge of CIA operations in Albania; Micha Odenheimer for taking in a wandering goy in Jerusalem; and Liron and Mayaan for hosting me in Tel Aviv.

Laura Hanifin provided creative photo research.

I also want to thank Martha Murphy Wagner, head of the JFK Records Collection at the National Archives; Karen Abramson and Abigail Malangone at the JFK Library; Claudia Anderson at the Lyndon B. Johnson Library at the University of Texas; and Dorissa Martinez at the Richard M. Nixon Library.

I also benefited from the help of Nancy Lyon at the Sterling Library at Yale University; Nina Fattal at the Israeli Intelligence Heritage Center; Dean Rogers at the Vassar College Library; Carol Leadenham at the Hoover Institution Archives; Mary Curry of the National Security Archive at George Washington University; and Scott Taylor at the Booth Family Center for Special Collections at the Georgetown University Library.

BIBLIOGRAPHIC NOTE

I am indebted to five authors who were drawn to the Angeltonian flame before me. Robin Winks's *Cloak and Gown* is crucial to understanding Angleton's roots at Yale. Michael Holzman's *James Jesus Angleton, the CIA, and the Craft of Counterintelligentce*, is the most subtle account of Angleton's intellectual formation. David Martin's classic *Wilderness of Mirrors* was the first book to capture the drama of Angleton's career and his friendship and rivalry with Bill Harvey. Tom Mangold's *Cold Warrior* (written with the help of researcher Jeffrey Goldberg) is the most deeply reported book in the Angleton library, with a wealth of interviews about his personal and professional life. David Wise's *Molehunt* is the best informed account of Angleton's search for KGB spies inside the CIA. Without these fine works, I could not have written *The Ghost*.

NOTES

ABBREVIATIONS USED

ACLU: American Civil Liberties Union
CI: Counterintelligence
CI/SIG Counterintelligence, Special Investigations Group
CIA: Central Intelligence Agency
DDP: Deputy Director of Plans
EP: Ezra Pound
EPP: Ezra Pound Papers
FBI: Federal Bureau of Investigation
FPCC: Fair Play for Cuba Committee
GWP: George White Papers
HSCA: House Select Committee on Assassinations
JA: James Angleton
JCS: Joint Chiefs of Staff
KGB: Komitet Gosudarstvennoy Bezopasnosti (Committee for State Security)
NARA: National Archives and Records Administration
NHPP: Norman Holmes Pearson Papers
NSA-GWU: National Security Archive at George Washington University
MFF: Mary Ferrell Foundation
OPC: Office of Policy Coordination
OS: Office of Security
OSO: Office of Special Operations
OSS: Office of Strategic Services
RIF: Record Information Form
SNIE: Special National Intelligence Estimate

PART I: POETRY

1. Angleton's friend John Pauker showed photographs of the naked Pound to classmates, according to Angleton's biographer Robin Winks. Winks interviewed classmates who had seen the photos. Pauker was friends with Angleton, who had photographed Pound and was the most likely source of the photos. See Robin Winks, *Cloak and Gown; Scholars in the Secret War, 1934–1961* (New York: William Morrow, 1988), 334.

2. The sketch appears in Andrews Wanning, "Poetry in an Ivory Tower," *Harkness Hoot,* April 1933, 33–39. Wanning was a close friend of Angleton's.

3. Winks, *Cloak and Gown,* 329.

4. "Ezra Pound Papers," at http://beinecke.library.yale.edu/collections/highlights/ezra -pound-papers.

5. "2 Idaho Boys Married at Border Camp/H. L. Potter Weds Miss Barbara Clyne of Boise and J. H. Angleton is Joined," *Idaho Daily Statesman,* December 19, 1916. The story, repeated by Angleton biographers Tom Mangold, David Martin, and Michael Holzman, that James Hugh Angleton participated in "the punitive expedition" of Gen. "Black Jack" Pershing against Mexican revolutionary Pancho Villa is erroneous, according to historians Charles H. Harris and Louis R. Sadler, authors of *The Great Call-Up: The Guard, the Border, and the Mexican Revolution* (Norman: University of Oklahoma Press, 2015), 478n.104.

6. Ada County Assessor Land Records, "2016 Property Details for Parcel R5538912210"; available at http://www.adacountyassessor.org/propsys/ViewParcel.do?yearParcel=2016R 5538912210.

7. *Boise City and Ada County Directory, 1927* (Salt Lake City: R. L. Polk, 1926), p. 49.

8. "James Hugh Angleton Jr, U.S Army Cpl.," Personnel Files, 1942–1945, box 18, RG 226, National Archives, Washington, D.C.

9. Winks, *Cloak and Gown,* 330.

10. Bert Macintyre, *Spy Among Friends: Kim Philby and the Great Betrayal* (New York: Crown, 2014), 69.

11. Letter from James Angleton (JA) to Ezra Pound (EP), August 13, 1938, Ezra Pound Papers, YCAL MSS 43, Series I: Correspondence, box 2, folder 63, Beinecke Rare Book and Manuscript Library, Yale University. Hereafter, EPP.

12. Letter from JA to EP, August 23, 1938, EPP.

13. Letter from JA to EP, January 19, 1939, EPP.

14. That's what Pound told his friend Mary Barnard. See Mary Barnard, *Assault on Mount Helicon: A Literary Memoir* (Berkeley: University of California Press, 1984), 161.

15. "The Making of a Master Spy," *Time,* February 24, 1975, 2.

16. Reed Whittemore, *Against the Grain: The Literary Life of a Poet* (Washington, D.C.: Dryad Press, 2007), 38.

17. Michael Holzman, *James Jesus Angleton, the CIA, and the Craft of Counterintelligence* (Amherst: University of Massachusetts Press, 2007), 12–13.

18. Letter from JA to EP, December 28, 1939, EPP. "He is really going places here at Yale," Angleton wrote of Mack. He went on to become the chairman of the Yale English Department and a famous critic.

19. Furioso Papers, YCAL MSS 75, Series I: Contributor Correspondence, 1938–1951, box 1, folder 30, Beinecke Rare Book and Manuscript Library, Yale University.

20. Letter from EP to JA, January 10, 1939, EPP.

21. Letter from JA to EP, January 19, 1939, EPP.

22. Letter from EP to JA, March 1939, EPP.

23. Letter from JA to EP, March 23, 1939, EPP.

24. Letter from JA to EP, May 3, 1939, EPP. Angleton and Whittemore proved to be demanding editors. Pound sent them another verse, which read as follows:

    THE DEATH OF THE PROFESSOR
    Is the death of his curiousity. The Professor died the
    moment he ceases hunting for truth, the moment he thinks

> *he knows something and starts telling it to the student*
> *instead of trying to find out what it is.*

This doggerel evidently didn't meet Angleton and Whittemore's standards, because they did not publish it. Letter from EP to JA, May 1939, EPP.

25. Furioso Papers, YCAL MSS 75 Beinecke Rare Book and Manuscript Library, Yale University.

26. Holzman, *James Jesus Angleton*, 25.

27. Author's interview with William Gowen, September 20, 2015.

28. Draft registration card for James Hugh Angleton, June 5, 1917; available at https://www.ancestry.com/interactive/6482/005240752_03982?pid-24559654.

29. Winks, *Cloak and Gown*, 329.

30. Author's interview with Tom Hughes, August 20, 2015.

31. Letter from JA to E. E. Cummings, August 1939, EPP.

32. E-mail from Nancy Lyon, Yale University archivist, to the author, June 10, 2015.

33. *Furioso* 1, no. 2 (New Year's Issue, 1940). Pound's "Five Poems," appears on page 5.

34. Letter from JA to EP, December 28, 1939, EPP.

35. Letter from JA to EP, February 1, 1940, EPP.

36. Letter from EP to JA, June 7, 1940, EPP.

37. Letter from EP to James Hugh Angleton, June 19, 1940, EPP.

38. Doob, Leonard, ed., Ezra *Pound Speaking: Radio Speeches of WWII, Part II, Miscellaneous Scripts #111*, "Homestead"; available at http://www.vho.org/aaargh/fran/livres10/PoundRadiospeeches.pdf.

39. Their last written communication was a postcard from EP to JA, April 11, 1941, EPP.

40. Tom Mangold, *Cold Warrior: James Jesus Angleton, the CIA's Master Spy Hunter* (New York: Simon and Schuster, 1991), 37.

41. Cicely d'Autremont Angleton, *A Cave of Overwhelming: A Collection of Poems* (Cabin John, MD: Britain Books, 1995), 25.

42. Walter Van Brunt, *Duluth and St. Louis County, Minnesota: Their Story and People*, vol. 2, (Chicago: American Historical Society, 1921), 856.

43. "Helen Clara Congdon d'Autremont," https://www.azwhf.org/inductions/inducted-women/helen-congdon-dautremont-1889-1966/.

44. Birth records, for Cecily Harriet d'Autremont, http://people.mnhs.org/finder/bci/1922-57325. Cicely did not use the spelling of her name that is found on her birth certificate.

45. Mangold, *Cold Warrior*, 32.

46. Letter from JA to E. E. Cummings, August 16, 1941, bMS AM 1892, Houghton Library, Harvard University. "Reed has gotten into the army and I have been rejected as a weakling but with few regrets," he wrote.

47. Holzman, *James Jesus Angleton*, 28.

48. Ibid., 28.

49. Pearson's story was told first and best in Winks, *Cloak and Gown*, 247–321.

50. Norman Holmes Pearson Papers, YCAL MSS 899, Letters, box II, Beinecke Rare Book and Manuscript Library, Yale University.

51. Winks, *Cloak and Gown*, 340.

52. Doob, "Ezra *Pound Speaking*," 6.

53. Holzman, *James Jesus Angleton*, 29.

54. Ibid., 30.

55. Records of the Office of Strategic Services, Personnel Files, 1942–1945, box 18.

56. Winks, *Cloak and Gown*, 340.

57. Mangold, *Cold Warrior*, 37.

58. Ancestry.com. *Michigan, Marriage Records, 1867–1952*. Provo, UT, USA: Ancestry.com Operations, Inc., 2015. Original data: Michigan, Marriage Records, 1867–1952. Michigan Department of Community Health, Division for Vital Records and Health Statistics.

59. White's OSS papers and an unpublished memoir are in the George Hunter White Papers, MS111, Department of Special Collections, Stanford University. Hereafter, GWP.

60. George White and Hugh Angleton had a meal on Monday, July 26, 1943, according to White's pocket diary, GWP, carton 7. The diary entry reads "Dinner with Maj Angleton, X-2 sec." Hugh Angleton was in the X-2 (counterintelligence) section of the OSS, where Jim was soon assigned.

61. In his unpublished memoir, White boasted of watching prostitutes ply their trade, the better to blackmail their customers. GWP, folder 11.

62. Perdita Schaffner, "Glass in My Typewriter," *East Hampton Star*, May 15, 1975.

63. Anthony Cave Brown, *Treason in the Blood: H. St. John Philby, Kim Philby, and the Spy Case of the Century* (Boston: Houghton Mifflin, 1994), 298–99.

64. Schaffner, "Glass in My Typewriter."

65. Bryher, H.D.'s companion, captures the devoted friendship of Pearson and Hilda Doolittle in a wartime memoir. See Bryher, *The Days of Mars: A Memoir 1940–46* (New York: Harcourt Brace Jovanovich, 1972).

66. This definition, modified slightly, is quoted in Richard Helms, *A Look Over My Shoulder* (New York: Random House, 2004), 145. Helms, later CIA director, was another one of Pearson's pupils at Bletchley Park.

67. See Cave Brown, *Treason in the Blood*, 87–142, for biographical details concerning Harry St. John Philby.

68. Joseph Trento, *The Secret History of the CIA* (New York: MJF Books, 2001), 37.

69. Timothy J. Naftali, "ARTIFICE: James Angleton and X-2 Operations in Italy," in *The Secret Wars: The Office of Strategic Services in World War II,* ed. George C. Chalou (Washington, D.C.: National Archives and Records Adminitration, 1992), 222.

70. Schaffner, "Glass in My Typewriter."

71. Records of the Office of Strategic Services, 1941–1945, RM 1623, roll 10, vol. 2, July, August, September 1944, London Headquarters, 123–25.

72. Macpherson's observations are from Schaffner, "Glass in My Typewriter."

73. Jack Greene and Alessandro Massignani, *The Black Prince and the Sea Devils: The Story of Valerio Borghese and the Elite Units of the Decima Mas* (Boston: De Capo, 2004), 1–3, 69, 136–37.

74. Ibid., 174.

75. Ibid., 135.

76. Ibid., 177.

77. Naftali, "ARTIFICE," 218.

78. Macintyre, *Spy Among Friends*, 95.

79. Ezio Costanzo, *The Mafia and the Allies: Sicily 1943 and the Return of the Mafia* (New York: Enigma Books, 2007), 146.

80. Naftali "ARTIFICE," 239n.42.

81. Ibid., 225.

82. Interview with James Angleton, *Epoca,* February 11, 1976, 26–27.

83. "Report on the Mission Carried out in Occupied Italy by Captain Antonio Marceglia," original in Italian, CIA FOIA Electronic Reading Room; available at https://www.cia.gov/library/readingroom/docs/PLAN%20IVY_0078.pdf. Marceglia's role in the Decima Mas: Greene and Massignani, *Black Prince*, 166.

84. Interview with James Angleton, *Epoca*, February 11, 1976, 26–27.

85. Greene and Massignani, *Black Prince*, 182. After the war, Fiume Square was renamed Palazzo della Repubblica.

86. Interview with James Angleton, *Epoca*, February 11, 1976, 26–27.

87. Greene and Massignani, *Black Prince*, 184.

88. Naftali, "ARTIFICE," 240n.55.

89. Ibid. See also letter from JA to Commander Titolo, November 6, 1945, box 260, entry 108A, RG 226, National Archives, Washington, D.C.

90. Greene and Massignani, *Black Prince*, 184.

91. Naftali, "ARTIFICE," 220.

92. Dollmann recounts the story of his arrest in his book *The Interpreter: Memoirs of Doktor Eugen Dollmann* (London: Hutchinson, 1967). William Gowen, who attended the interrogation of Dollmann, provided additional details in an interview with the author, October 2, 2015.

93. Michael Salter, *Nazi War Crimes, US Intelligence and Selective Prosecution at Nuremberg: Controversies Regarding the role of the Office of Strategic Services* (New York: Routledge-Cavendish, 2007), 63.

94. Ibid., 65–66.

95. Ibid., 55.

96. Dollmann, *Interpreter*, 102; author's interview with William Gowen, October 2, 2015.

97. Author's interview with William Gowen, October 2, 2015.

98. Michael Warner, *The Office of Strategic Services: America's First Intelligence Agency* (Washington, D.C.: Public Affairs, Central Intelligence Agency, 2008); available at https://www.cia.gov/library/publications/.

99. Richard Breitman, "Historical Analysis of 20 Name Files from CIA Records," April 2001; available at http://www.archives.gov/iwg/declassified-records/rg-263-cia-records/rg-263-report.html. Dollmann's file was selected as one of twenty determined to be representative of the U.S intelligence relationship with Nazis. The Dollmann name file contains forty documents. Angleton is addressed as "Major O'Brien" in these records.

100. Mangold, *Cold Warrior*, 42.

101. Author's interview with William Gowen, October 2, 2015.

102. Aaron Latham, "Politics and the C.I.A.—Was Angleton Spooked by State?" *New York*, March 10, 1975, 34.

103. Mangold, *Cold Warrior*, 45.

104. Burton Hersh, *The Old Boys: The American Elite and the Origins of the CIA* (New York: Scribner, 1992) 179.

105. Peter Grose, *Gentleman Spy: The Life of Allen Dulles* (Amherst: University of Massachusetts Press, 1994), 256.

106. Mangold, *Cold Warrior*, 43–44.

107. Letter from Cicely Angleton to Marion and E. E. Cummings, March 16, 1946, E. E. Cummings Papers, 1870–1969, Am 1823, folder 34, Houghton Library, Harvard University.

108. Find a Grave Web site. https://www.findagrave.com/cgi-bin/fg.cgi?page=gr&GRid=92185892.

109. Ibid. https://www.findagrave.com/cgi-bin/fg.cgi?page=gr&GRid=92185997.

110. Notice of the divorce filing was published in the *Tucson Daily Citizen*, June 15, 1946.

111. Naftali, "ARTIFICE," 219.

112. "Brod, Mario Emanuel aka Broderick, Michael," undated, NARA JFK RIF 104-10120-10358.

113. "Status of Liaison Relations of SSU/X-2 to the Counterintelligence Branches of Foreign Special Services" [1946], Wooden File, box 1, file: "IV Thoreau OK," Norman Holmes Pearson Papers, YCAL MSS 899 Beinecke Rare Book and Manuscript Library, Yale University.

114. Cave Brown, *Treason in the Blood*, 365. Cave Brown's account is based on an interview with Angleton.

115. Macintyre, *Spy Among Friends*, 103.

116. Breitman, "Historical Analysis of 20 Name Files from CIA Records."

117. National Archives, Record Group 263, Records of the Central Intelligence Agency, Series: Second Release of Name Files Under the Nazi War Crimes and Japanese Imperial Government Disclosure Acts, ca. 1981–ca. 2002, Name File, "Dollmann, Eugen," Memo on "Dollmann and Wenner," July 31, 1947; available at https://catalog.archives.gov/id/26195045. The memo states, "The report of Mr. Dulles, who handled the negotiations with General Wolff, indicates that after the initial contact with Baron Parilli, Dollmann appeared representing General Wolff to initiate surrender talks."

118. Dollmann name file, official dispatch to Chief of Station Heidelberg from Chief, FBP (J. Angleton), subject: "Dollmann and Wenner," July 31, 1947. Angleton suggested the two men could write a laudatory history of Operation Sunrise.

119. Eugen Dollmann, *Call Me Coward* (London: William Kimber, 1936), 85.

120. Author's interview with William Gowen, October 2, 2015.

121. Dollmann name file, memo on "Eugenio Dollmann and Eugene Weber." See also Kerstin von Lingen, *Allen Dulles, the OSS, and Nazi War Criminals: The Dynamics of Selective Prosecution* (New York: Cambridge University Press, 2013), 80.

122. Salter, *Nazi War Crimes*, 110n.

123. Author's interview with William Gowen, October 21, 2015. Rauff was never prosecuted for war crimes. He lived the rest of his life as a free man and unrepentant Nazi.

124. Dollmann, *Interpreter*, 117.

125. Salter, *Nazi War Crimes*, 230.

126. Burton Hersh, *Old Boys*, 293.

127. Richard Helms, manuscript entitled "James Angleton," October 27, 1997, Richard M. Helms Papers, box 1, folder 25, Georgetown University.

128. Mark Aarons and John Loftus, *Unholy Trinity: The Vatican, the Nazis, and the Swiss Banks* (New York: St. Martin's Griffin, 1998), 18–19.

129. Naftali, "ARTIFICE," 237.

130. Aarons and Loftus, *Unholy Trinity*, 21–41.

131. Author's interview with William Gowen, October 2, 2015.

132. David F. Rodgers, *Creating the Secret State: The Origins of the Central Intelligence Agency, 1943–1947* (Lawrence: University Press of Kansas, 2000), 147.

133. Ibid.

134. Ibid., 150.

135. Ibid., 167.

136. Andrew Friedman, *Covert Capital: Landscapes of Denial and the Making of U.S. Empire in the Suburbs of Northern Virginia* (Berkeley: University of California Press, 2013), 30–31.

137. James D. Callanan, "The Evolution of the CIA's Covert Action Mission, 1947–1963," (Ph.D. diss., Durham University, 1999), 51; available at http://etheses.dur.ac.uk/4481/.

138. Winks, *Cloak and Gown*, 384.

139. William Hood, James Nolan, and Sam Halpern, eds., *Myths Surrounding James Angleton:*

Lessons for American Counterintelligence (Washington, D.C.: Consortium for the Study of Intelligence, 1993).

140. William Hood, "Angleton's World," in ibid., 9.

141. The best account of the Angleton-Harvey relationship is David C. Martin, *Wilderness of Mirrors* (New York: Harper and Row, 1980). See 37–38.

142. "Italy Faces Her Worst Crisis," *Look,* March 30 1948, 30.

143. Tim Weiner, *Legacy of Ashes: The History of the CIA* (New York: Anchor, 2008), 30. The decision was made by Allen Dulles and Secretary of Defense James Forrestal.

144. Callanan, "The History of the CIA's Covert Action Mission," 65.

145. David Talbot, *The Devil's Chessboard: Allen Dulles, the CIA, and the Rise of America's Secret Government* (New York: HarperCollins, 2015), 147; Grose, *Gentleman Spy,* 284.

146. James E. Miller, "Taking Off the Gloves: The United States and the Italian Elections," *Diplomatic History* 7 (1983): 35–55.

147. This incident is depicted in Aaron Latham, *Orchids for Mother* (Boston: Little, Brown, 1977), a journalistic novel about a CIA official named Francis Xavier Kimball, a version of Angleton. In a 2015 interview, Latham said that he relied on extensive interviews with Angleton and his colleagues to write the book. In the course of his research, he heard the story about Angleton's desire to use Garbo as a propaganda asset, and based the scene in his book on that reporting. The role of the Hollywood studios is recounted in Miller, "Taking Off the Gloves," 49.

148. Board of Trade: Commercial and Statistical Department and successors: Incoming Passenger Lists, 1949–1950, BT26/1255/25, National Archives, Kew, Surrey, England.

149. In his 1949 pocket diary, Win Scott recorded five meetings with Angleton and others between September 26 and October 2. The diary is in the collection of Winston M. Scott's personal papers in possession of his son Michael.

150. Policy Planning Staff memorandum, May 4, 1948, C. Thomas Thorne, David S. Patterson, and Glen W. LaFantasie, eds., *Foreign Relations of the United States, 1945–1950: Emergence of the Intelligence Establishment,* vol. 1 (Washington, D.C.: U.S. Government Printing Office, 1996), 671.

151. Kennan quoted in Anne Karalekas, *History of the Central Intelligence Agency* (Laguna Hills, CA: Aegean Park Press, 1977), 31.

152. Karalekas, *History of the Central Intelligence Agency,* 38.

153. Cave Brown, *Treason in the Blood,* 409.

154. James McCargar, "The Transatlantic Philby," unpublished manuscript, James McCargar Papers, Howard Gotlieb Archival Research Center, Boston University.

155. Letter from Cicely Angleton to Marion Cummings, November 22, 1949, E. E. Cummings Papers, 1870–1969, MS Am 1823.2, folder 11, Houghton Library, Harvard University.

156. Cave Brown, *Treason in the Blood,* 393.

157. Macintyre, *Spy Among Friends,* 134.

158. Kim Philby, *My Silent War: The Autobiography of a Spy* (New York: Modern Library, 2002), 151.

159. McCargar, "Transatlantic Philby."

160. Philby, *My Silent War,* 151.

161. Mangold, *Cold Warrior,* 49.

162. Macintyre, *Spy Among Friends,* 133.

163. Philby, *My Silent War,* 175.

164. McCargar, "Transatlantic Philby."

165. Phillip Knightley, *The Master Spy: The Story of Kim Philby* (New York: Knopf, 1989), 118–19.

166. Cave Brown, *Treason in the Blood*, 405.

167. Verne W. Newton, *The Cambridge Spies: The Untold Story of Maclean, Philby, and Burgess in America* (Lanham, MD: Madison Books, 1991), 305–11. Newton's is the most evocative and best documented of the many accounts of Philby's hospitality.

168. McCargar, "Transatlantic Philby."

169. David K. Johnson, *Lavender Scare: The Cold War Persecution of Gays and Lesbians in the Federal Government* (Chicago: University of Chicago Press, 2004), 2.

170. Ibid., xxv.

171. Ibid., 10.

172. Ibid., 29.

173. Ibid., 28

174. Ibid., 13.

175. The description of Offie comes from Robert Joyce, a retired State Department official, as told to Ben Welles, a journalist who knew Angleton. Welles was the son of Sumner Welles, undersecretary of state from 1937 to 1943. Welles was writing a book about his father, whose homosexual affairs had ended his career, which is probably why he wanted to talk about Offie. Welles took notes on four conversations that he had about Offie, one with Joyce, dated March 26, 1974, and four with Angleton, dated December 25, 1973, early 1975, April 14, 1976, and November 11, 1977. In 2000, Welles gave the file to James McCargar, who included it, with an explanatory note, in the James McCargar Collection, Howard Gotlieb Archival Research Center, at Boston University. Hereafter, "Welles-Joyce Conversation Notes" or " Welles-Angleton Conversation Notes." Joyce's account of Offie's life is confirmed in Irwin Gellman, *Secret Affairs: Franklin Roosevelt, Cordell Hull, and Sumner Welles* (Baltimore: Johns Hopkins University Press, 1995), 241.

176. "Welles-Angleton Conversation Notes," November 11, 1977.

177. Ted Morgan, *A Covert Life: Jay Lovestone: Communist, Anti-Communist, and Spymaster* (New York: Random House, 2011); Kindle Location 4067.

178. "Welles-Angleton Conversations Notes," April 14, 1976,

179. "Welles-Angleton Conversation Notes," November 11, 1977.

180. The call and Hillenkoetter's answers are in a log of the Director of Central Intelligence's phone calls and meetings from May 1 to August 31, 1950, at the CIA's Freedom of Information Act, Electronic Reading Room; available at https://www.cia.gov/library/readingroom/docs/1950-05-01.pdf. The May 8, 1950, call is found on page 17 of the 234-page document. Hereafter, DCI Diary.

181. DCI Diary, May 12, 1950, 26–27.

182. DCI Diary, June 2, 1950, 60.

183. DCI Diary, June 8, 1950, 72.

184. DCI Diary, May 26, 1950, 52.

185. "Welles-Angleton Conversation Notes," March 26, 1974.

186. The claim is asserted as fact in Larry Kramer, *The American People: Volume 1: Search for My Heart: A Novel* (New York: Farrar, Straus and Giroux, 2015).

187. Andrew Boyle, *The Climate of Treason: Five Who Spied for Russia* (London: Hutchinson, 1979), 133.

188. Andrew Lownie, *Stalin's Englishman: Guy Burgess, the Cold War, and the Cambridge Spy Ring* (New York: St. Martin's Press, 2016), 82.

189. Cave Brown, *Treason in the Blood*, 418.

190. Wilfred Basil Mann, *Was There a Fifth Man? Quintessential Recollections* (New York: Pergamon Press, 1982), 84.

191. Philby, *My Silent War,* 165.

192. Boyle, *Climate of Treason,* 227.

193. John S. Mather, ed., *The Great Spy Scandal* (London: Daily Express Publications, 1955), 34.

194. Talbot, *Devil's Chessboard,* 334.

195. The incident recurs in the literature about Kim Philby. The fullest account is found in Newton, *Cambridge Spies,* 305–10. See also Mark Riebling, *Wedge: The Secret War Between the FBI and CIA* (New York: Knopf, 1994), 103–4; Cave Brown, *Treason in the Blood,* 426–27; Mann, *Was There a Fifth Man?,* 82–83.

196. John Hart, *The CIA's Russians* (Annapolis: Naval Institute Press, 2003), 15.

197. This claim appears in Boyle, *Climate of Treason,* 385–86. Boyle attributes the assertion to "confidential information" from "CIA sources." Boyle interviewed Angleton for the book, according to Cleveland Cram, the CIA officer who studied Angleton's career. See *Of Moles and Molehunters: A Review of Counterintelligence Literature, 1977–92* (Washington, D.C.: Center for the Study of Intelligence, 1993), 15.

198. Kollek, quoted in Ron Rosenbaum, "Philby and Oswald," *Slate,* April 2013; available at http://www.slate.com/articles/news_and_politics/the_spectator/2013/04/new_evidence_links_the_cases_of_kim_philby_and_lee_harvey_oswald_in_fascinating.html.

199. G. J. A. O'Toole, *Honorable Treachery: A History of U.S. Intelligence, Espionage, and Covert Action from the American Revolution to the CIA* (New York: Atlantic Monthly Press, 1991), 442.

200. Grose, *Gentleman Spy,* 309.

201. Martin, *Wilderness of Mirrors,* 52.

202. Richard Aldrich, *The Hidden Hand: Britain, America, and Cold War Secret Intelligence* (London: Overlook Press, 2001), 323.

203. Grose, *Gentleman Spy,* 306.

204. Talbot, *Devil's Chessboard,* 186.

205. Author's interview with Cleveland Cram, August 11, 1994.

206. Martin, *Wilderness of Mirrors,* 53; Knightley, *Master Spy,* 180–81.

207. Trento, *Secret History of the CIA,* 81.

208. Ibid., 82.

209. James McCargar, "The Betrothed," unpublished manuscript, James McCargar Papers, box 5, Howard Gotlieb Archival Research Center, Boston University.

210. Karalekas, *History of the Central Intelligence Agency,* 38.

211. Ibid.

212. Morgan, *Covert Life,* Kindle location 4792.

213. Samuel Katz, *Soldier Spies: Israeli Military Intelligence* (Novato, CA: Presidio Press, 2001), 18.

214. Eshed Haggai, *Reuven Shiloah—The Man Behind the Mossad: Secret Diplomacy in the Creation of Israel* (London: Frank Casse, 1997), 168.

215. Author's interview with Efraim Halevy, December 16, 2015.

216. Dan Raviv and Yossi Melman, *Spies Against Armageddon: Inside Israel's Secret Wars* (Sea Cliff, NY: Levant Books, 2012), 33.

217. Haggai, *Reuven Shiloah,* 168.

218. Mangold, *Cold Warrior,* 49.

219. A passenger manifest shows that Angleton returned from Israel on January 30, 1952. Passenger and Crew Lists of Vessels Arriving at New York, New York, 1897–1957, microfilm publication T715 A., RG 85, microfilm roll 8097, page 45, line 14, Records of the Immigration and Naturalization Service, National Archives, Washington, D.C.

220. Raviv and Melman, *Spies Against Armageddon*, 34.

221. Michael Ledeen, "Amos Meets Jesus," *National Review*, August 6, 2007; available at http://www.nationalreview.com/article/221773/amos-meets-jesus-michael-ledeen.

222. Raviv and Melman, *Spies Against Armageddon*, 33.

223. Morgan, *Covert Life*, Kindle location 2706.

224. Ibid., Kindle location 5116.

225. Ibid., Kindle location 5170–79.

226. H. P. Albarelli, *A Terrible Mistake: The Murder of Frank Olson and the CIA's Secret Cold War Experiments* (Walterville, OR: Trine Day, 2009); Kindle page 17.

227. Ibid., Kindle location 24.

228. Ibid., Kindle location 88.

229. John Marks, *The Search for the "Manchurian Candidate": The CIA and Mind Control* (New York: W. W. Norton, 1979), 23.

230. Memo, "Objectives and Agencies," May 23, 1950, document 48. This document is in the John Marks Papers, a collection of declassified government records related to CIA mind-control programs, held by the nonprofit National Security Archive in Washington, D.C. The papers were obtained by Marks via the Freedom of Information Act for the purposes of writing *The Search for the "Manchurian Candidate."* The documents have not been cataloged by subject or date, but they are numbered.

231. *Project MKULTRA, the CIA's Program of Research in Behavioral Modification: Joint Hearing before the Senate Select Committee on Intelligence and the Subcommittee on Health and Scientific Research*, 95th Cong., 1st sess., 3 August 1977, Appendix A, 67–68.

232. Albarelli, *A Terrible Mistake*, Kindle location 16090.

233. TSD was also known at times at the Technical Services Staff. For simplicity's sake, I use TSD throughout.

234. "State Rests Case Against Billie Holiday," *San Francisco Chronicle*, June 3, 1949. See George White Papers, 1932–1970, M1111, box 1, folder 13, Dept. of Special Collections, Stanford University Libraries. Hereafter, GWP.

235. GWP, box 1, folder 12.

236. GWP, Diaries, 1943–1952, box 7. White's 1948 diary mentions several meetings with Angleton and Rocca, as well as the home address of Angleton's parents. White's entry for July 6, 1948, includes the note "12:30 Rocca—borrow pistol."

237. GWP 1, box 7. Diary entry for March 20, 1950, reads "Allen Dulles Etc to 1:30 a[m]."

238. GWP, box 7, diary entry for June 9, 1952.

239. Albarelli, *Terrible Mistake*, Kindle location 5204. Albarelli cites an interview with Gottlieb as his source.

240. GWP, box 7, diary entry for August 25, 1952.

241. GHP, box 7, diary entry for October 30, 1952.

242. Albarelli, *A Terrible Mistake*, Kindle page 240. White told the story in a letter to his attorney, Irwin Eisenberg, December 12, 1952. Albertine White gave a copy of the letter to Albarelli.

243. James Angleton and Charles J. V. Murphy, *American Cause: Special Reports* (Washington, D.C.: American Cause, 1977), 40.

PART II: POWER

1. Burton Hersh, *Old Boys*, 318.

2. Weiner, *Legacy of Ashes*, 76–77.

3. Morgan, *Covert Life*, Kindle location 4793–95.

4. Riebling, *Wedge*, 138.

5. Winks, *Cloak and Gown*, 325–26.

6. Thomas Powers, *The Man Who Kept the Secrets: Richard Helms and the CIA* (New York: Knopf, 1979), 363.

7. Arthur Redding, "A Wilderness of Mirrors: Writing and Reading the Cold War," *Contemporary Literature* 51, no. 4 (Winter 2010): 867–73.

8. "James Angleton: 7 Types of Ambiguity" http://www.brainsturbator.com/posts/225/james-angleton-7-types-of-ambiguity.

9. NARA JFK FBI RIF 124-10326-10098, Memo from V. P. Keay to A. H. Belmont, "Bureau Source 100" (Angleton), June 10, 1953. FBI HQ 62-99724, Section 1, Serial 1.

10. Memo from V. P. Keay to A. H. Belmont, May 17, 1954. FBI HQ 62-99724, Section 1, Serial 10.

11. Mangold, *Cold Warrior*, 44.

12. NARA JFK SSCIA RIF 157-10014-10007, Angleton Church Committee testimony, September 17, 1975, 9.

13. *Berkshire Eagle*, December 6, 2007.

14. *Washington Post*, September 11, 2007.

15. Author's interview with Bill Hood, April 13, 2011.

16. "Extracts of CI History," undated, 24 pages, NARA JFK CIA RIF 104-10301-10011.

17. Frank J. Rafalko, ed., *Counterintelligence Reader*, vol. 3, *Post–World War II to Closing the 20th Century* (Washington, D.C.: National Counterintelligence Center, 1998), 112.

18. For information on Millett, see http://www.powerbase.info/index.php/Stephen_Millett#cite_note-0.

19. Riebling, *Wedge*, 137.

20. Weiner, *Legacy of Ashes*, 176.

21. "ARRB-CIA Issues: Win Scott," NARA JFK CIA RIF 104-10332-10015.

22. Burton Hersh, *Old Boys*, 318.

23. See https://www.theguardian.com/news/2003/feb/20/guardianobituaries.israel.

24. E-mail from Efraim Halevy to the author, March 12, 2016.

25. Yossi Melman and Dan Raviv, "Spies Like Us," *Tablet*, April 8, 2010.

26. Raviv and Melman, *Spies Against Armageddon*, 34.

27. Ibid., 35.

28. Haggai, *Reuven Shiloah*, 170.

29. Melman and Raviv, "Spies Like Us."

30. Morgan, *Covert Life*, Kindle location 4963.

31. Ibid., Kindle location 4819.

32. Raviv and Melman, *Spies Against Armageddon*, 39.

33. Ibid. In fact, Allen Dulles signed a "book message" to CIA stations worldwide, asking them to look for the speech. See Powers, *Man Who Kept the Secrets*, 100.

34. See http://www.theguardian.com/theguardian/2007/apr/26/greatspeeches1.

35. Raviv and Melman, *Spies Against Armageddon*, 41.

36. Michael Ledeen, "Amos Meets Jesus," *National Review*, August 6, 2007; available at http://www.nationalreview.com/article/221773/amos-meets-jesus-michael-ledeen.

37. Raviv and Melman, *Spies Against Armageddon*, 42.

38. Ibid.

39. Powers, *Man Who Kept the Secrets*, 100.

40. Allen Dulles, *The Craft of Intelligence* (Lanham, MD: Rowman and Littlefield, 2006), 84.

41. Ray S. Cline, *Secrets, Spies, and Scholars: Blueprint of the Essential CIA* (Washington, D.C.:

Acropolis Books, 1976), 163. Cline said the speech was "acquired through non-American intermediaries at a handsome price."

42. Andrew Cockburn and Leslie Cockburn, *Dangerous Liaisons: The Inside Story of the U.S.-Israeli Covert Relationship* (New York: HarperCollins, 1991), 79.

43. See http://manythingsconsidered.com/the-spy-from-boise/.

44. This and subsequent Janney quotes are from the author's interview with Peter Janney, July 15, 2015.

45. Nina Burleigh, *A Very Private Woman: The Life and Unsolved Murder of Presidential Mistress Mary Meyer* (New York: Bantam, 1998), 130.

46. Ibid., 127.

47. Ibid., 110.

48. This and subsequent Marshall quotes are from Mangold, *Cold Warrior,* 246.

49. Church Committee Report, Book 3: Supplementary Detailed Staff Reports on Intelligence Activities and the Rights of Americans (Washington, D.C.: U.S. Government Printing Office, 1976), 567. Hereafter, Church Committee Report, Book 3.

50. Ibid., 570.

51. Morgan, *Covert Life,* Kindle location 4906.

52. Church Committee Report, Book 3, 572.

53. Ibid., 571.

54. Ibid., 626.

55. Ibid., 628.

56. Angleton Church Committee testimony, September 19, 1975, 28.

57. Church Committee Report, Book 4: Supplementary Detailed Staff Reports on Foreign and Military Intelligence (Washington, D.C.: U.S. Government Printing Office, 1976), 223.

58. Church Committee Report, Book 2: Intelligence Activities and the Rights of Americans (Washington, D.C.: U.S. Government Printing Office, 1976), 66, citing the testimony of an FBI official to William Sullivan. Hereafter Church Committee Report, Book 2.

59. In the eighteen years Angleton ran LINGUAL/HUNTER, a total of 215,000 letters to and from the Soviet Union were opened. See Church Committee Report, Book 3, 571.

60. Author's interview with Peter Sichel, December 3, 2015.

61. John Tytell, *Ezra Pound: The Solitary Volcano* (New York: Anchor Press, 1987), 325–26.

62. *New York Times,* October 20, 1959.

63. Clarence Ashley, *CIA Spymaster* (Gretna, LA: Pelican, 2004), 95.

64. Ibid., 7.

65. Ibid., 46–66.

66. Ibid., 84

67. William Hood, *Mole: The True Story of the First Russian Spy to Become an America Counterspy* (McLean, VA: Brassey's U.S., 1993), 243.

68. Ibid., 245.

69. David Robarge, "Moles, Defectors, and Deceptions: James Angleton and CIA Counterintelligence," *The Journal of Intelligence History* 3, no.2 (Winter, 2003), 36.

70. U.S. Bureau of the Census, 1930 Census, New York, Family History Library, microfilm 2341393, roll 1659, page 1A, enumeration district 0098, image 4030.

71. Preliminary HSCA interview of Ann Egerter by Dan Hardway and Betsy Wolf, March 31, 1978, p. 3, NARA JFK HSCA RIF 180-10142-10298. Hereafter, Preliminary HSCA Interview of Ann Egerter.

72. "Extracts of CI History," undated, 24 pages, NARA JFK CIA RIF 104-10301-10011.

73. John Newman, *Oswald and the CIA: The Documented Truth About the Unknown Relationship Between the U.S. Government and the Alleged Killer of JFK* (New York: Skyhorse, 2008), 54.

74. In 1975, the CIA explained to Senate investigators that individuals or organizations of particular interest "were specified in Watch Lists provided to the mail project by the Counterintelligence Staff, by other CIA components, and the FBI."

75. Deposition of Richard Ober, March 28, 1975, 4, box 4108, ACLU Collection, Seeley G. Mudd Library, Princeton University. Ober said, "'The normal procedure within the CIA and the Directorate of Operation of Clandestine Services, as it is sometimes called, is to open files on individuals. These files are called 201 files, as a significant amount of information is accumulated. This is a management technique. Information on individuals is kept in files with the name of that individual on the outside of the file folder. In fact, there was a rather standard practice of opening a file on an individual as soon as three documents had been obtained on that individual. This was a sort of working rule."

76. Newman, *Oswald and the CIA*, 57.

77. Preliminary HSCA Interview of Ann Egerter.

78. Newman, *Oswald and the CIA*, 57.

79. The mistaken middle name—if it was a mistake—would sow suspicion and curiosity many years later. "Lee Henry Oswald" might have been an example of what Angleton called a "marked card," or what his British friends called a "barium meal." These were two names for the same technique used by counterintelligence officers seeking to identify internal security breaches. Or perhaps it was, as Egerter later said under oath, an inadvertent mistake.

    The fact that Angleton played marked cards does not necessarily mean that that the misnamed "Lee Henry Oswald" file was a marked card. Angleton explained to Epstein that a marked card was "a selected bit of information about planned CIA operations" that would attract the mole's attention. This definition begs the question of why would one middle name for Oswald, as opposed to another, attract the interest of a KGB mole in the ranks of the CIA? Changing a name on the file would not seem, on the face of it, to be a way to provoke action from a Soviet agent in place. Without more evidence, it would seem premature to conclude that the creation of a file on "Lee Henry Oswald" was one of Angleton's marked cards.

80. "Documents in the Agency's Possession Regarding Lee Harvey Oswald before the Assassination of President Kennedy," NARA JFK, Russ Holmes Work File, RIF 104-10248-10084. This CIA list does not include the document from ONI, which the House Select Committee on Assassinations said was deposited in the new 201 file. See Final Report of the House Select Committee on Assassinations (Washington, D.C.: U.S. Government Printing Office, 1979), 201.

81. Newman, *Oswald and the CIA*, 284. The CIA later told the Warren Commission the letter contained "no information of real significance."

82. HSCA Interview of James Angleton, October 5, 1978, p. 149, HSCA/Security Classified Testimony, NARA JFK HSCA RIF 180-10110-10006.

83. Morgan, *Covert Life*, Kindle location 6361.

84. Ibid., Kindle location 6392–93.

85. National Security Archive, "The U.S. Discovery of Israel's Secret Nuclear Project," Central Intelligence Agency, Information Report, "Nuclear Engineering/Large Nuclear and Electric Power Plant Near Beersheba," February 9, 1961; available at http://nsarchive.gwu.edu/nukevault/ebb510/docs/doc%206C.pdf.

86. National Security Archive, "Post Mortem on SNIE 100-8-60: Implications of the Acquisition by Israel of a Nuclear Weapons Capability," January 31, 1961; available at http://nsarchive.gwu.edu/nukevault/ebb510/docs/doc%2027A.pdf.

87. Author's interview with Avner Cohen, August 4, 2015. Israel's search for nuclear technology started in 1956–1957, when Prime Minster Ben-Gurion endorsed the ongoing efforts of Shimon Peres to build or acquire a bomb. Israel signed a deal with French companies in 1957, paying hundreds of millions of dollars for the installation of a nuclear reactor. The French started to excavate the site in the Negev in mid-1958. The CIA didn't have an authoritative report on the Dimona reactor until December 1960.

88. Seymour Hersh, *The Samson Option: Israel's Nuclear Arsenal and American Foreign Policy* (New York: Random House, 2013), Kindle location 2483.

89. "Post Mortem on SNIE 100-8-60."

90. Memo to A. H. Belmont from F. A. Frohbose, "Cuban Political Situation Activities," January 20, 1960, located in FBI Cuba 109-12-210, Volume 26, Serials 1111–1159; available at http://www.maryferrell.org/showDoc.html?docId=146640&search=Angleton#relPageId=54&tab=page.

91. The interview became the basis of the CBS Special Report "Rebels of the Sierra Maestra: The Story of Cuba's Jungle Fighters," which sympathetically introduced Castro to North Americans.

92. Fair Play for Cuba Committee, hearings before the Senate Internal Security Subcommittee, 87th Cong., 1st sess., January 10, 1961; available at http://www.archive.org/stream/fairplayforcubac0102unit/fairplayforcubac0102unit_djvu.txt. See also Van Gosse, *Where the Boys Are: Cuba, Cold War America and the Making of the New Left* (New York: Verso, 1993), 138–40.

93. See http://www.maryferrell.org/mffweb/archive/viewer/showDoc.do?docId=121887&relPageId=2.

94. Memorandum for Director of FBI, from CIA April 8, 1960, NARA JFK FBI RIF 124-90140-1099; available at https://www.maryferrell.org/showDoc.html?docId=144448.

95. Gosse, *Where the Boys Are*, 216–17.

96. Helms, *Look Over My Shoulder*, Kindle location 3208–12.

97. Ibid., Kindle location 3208. "My impression that the project was entirely too ambitious to be considered a secret activity," Helms wrote, "was partially offset by my assumption that if the *Brigadistas* appeared about to be overwhelmed, President Eisenhower, the old soldier who had initiated the operation, would think—in for a dime, in for a dollar—and provide sufficient U.S. military muscle to carry the day. After all, Eisenhower had reversed his policy when it appeared that Operation PBSUCCESS would fail, and at the critical moment had provided the military aircraft needed to ensure victory."

98. *New York Times*, April 9, 1961.

99. Helms, *Look Over My Shoulder*, Kindle location 3318.

100. Peter Kornbluh, ed., *Bay of Pigs Declassified: The Secret CIA Report on the Invasion of Cuba* (New York: Free Press, 1998), 21.

101. Angleton Church Committee testimony, February 6, 1976, 63–64 NARA JFK SSCIA RIF 157-10014-10003; available at https://www.maryferrell.org/showDoc.html?docId=1434.

102. Richard Reeves, *President Kennedy: Profile of Power* (New York: Simon and Schuster, 1993), 103.

103. JFK quoted in "CIA: Marker of Policy, or Tool?" *New York Times*, April 25, 1966.

104. Helms, *Look Over My Shoulder*, Kindle location 3537.

105. Evan Thomas, *Robert Kennedy: His Life* (New York: Simon and Schuster, 2000), 125.

106. Weiner, *Legacy of Ashes*, 209.

107. Memorandum from the Chief of Operations in the Deputy Directorate of Plans (Helms) to Director of Central Intelligence (McCone), January 19, 1962, *Foreign Relations of the United States, 1961–1963: Cuba 1961–1962*, vol. 10 (Washington, D.C.: U.S. Government Printing Office, 1997), 721.

108. Holzman, *James Jesus Angleton, the CIA and the Craft of Counterintelligence*, 190.

109. Peter Wright, *Spycatcher*: 194–205. *The Candid Autobiography of a Senior Intelligence Officer* (New York: Viking Penguin, 1987), 202–5.

110. "Project ZRRIFLE," December 9, 1960, NARA CIA JFK RIF 1993.06.30.18:51: 34:280330; available at http://bit.ly/2dSJDlt. See also Final Report of the House Select Committee on Assassinations, 204.

111. Wright, *Spycatcher*, 381.

112. Yossi Melman, "Inside Intel: Our Man in Havana," *Ha'aretz*, March 3, 2011; available at http://www.haaretz.com/print-edition/features/inside-intel-our-man-in-havana-1. 346821.

113. *Public Papers of the Presidents of the United States: Dwight D. Eisenhower, 1960–61* (Washington, D.C.: U.S. Government Printing Office, 1999), 1035–40.

114. Fletcher Knebel and Charles Bailey II, *Seven Days in May* (New York: Bantam, 1963).

115. David Atlee Phillips, *Secret Wars Diary: My Adventures in Combat, Espionage Operations and Covert Action* (Bethesda, MD: Stone Trail Press, 1999), 167.

116. Willie Morris, *New York Days* (Boston: Back Bay Books, 1993), 36.

117. Robert M. Hathaway and Russell Jack Smith, *Richard Helms as Director of Central Intelligence, 1966–1973* (Washington, D.C.: Central Intelligence Agency, 1993), 102.

118. Holzman, *James Jesus Angleton*, 142.

119. Ginsberg talked about Angleton and Cord Meyer in a lecture he delivered on June 9, 1977, at the Naropa Institute, Boulder, Colorado. Available at http://ginsbergblog .blogspot.com/2013/11/investigative-poetics-10-conclusion.html.

120. "Intelligence Reports," undated, Louise Page Morris Papers, box 2, folder 11, Hoover Institution Archives, Stanford University.

121. Angleton House Select Committee on Assassinations testimony, October 5, 1978, 67. NARA JFK HSCA RIF 180-10110-10006.

122. Cees Wiebes, "Operation 'Piet': The Joseph Sidney Petersen Jr. Spy Case, a Dutch 'Mole' Inside the National Security Agency," *Intelligence and National Security* 23, no. 4, (2008): 488–535.

123. Author's interview with Efraim Halevy, December 16, 2015.

124. "Extracts from CI History," undated, 24 pages, NARA JFK CIA RIF 104-10301-10011.

125. Helms, *Look Over My Shoulder*, Kindle location 2888.

126. Memo from James Angleton to Director FBI, "Physical Description of Anatoliy Mikhalovich Golitsyn," December 16, 1961, NARA JFK CIA RIF 104-10168-10118.

127. Jerry Ennis, "Anatoly Golitsyn: Long Term CIA Agent?" *Intelligence and National Security* 21, no. 1 (February 2006): 26.

128. Memo from James Angleton to Director FBI, "Anatoliy Mikhaylovich Klimov," December 20, 1961, NARA JFK CIA RIF 104-10263-10004.

129. *Frontline*, "The Spy Hunter," produced by Jenny Clayton; aired on May 14, 1991.

130. Ennis, "Anatoly Golitsyn," 28.

131. Ibid., 33–34.

132. Hathaway and Smith, *Richard Helms*, 120–21.

133. David Wise, *Molehunt: The Secret Search for Traitors That Shattered the CIA* (New York:

Random House, 1992), 27, 181, 99; David E. Murphy, Sergei Kondrashev, and George Bailey, *Battleground Berlin: CIA Vs. KGB in the Cold War* (New Haven: Yale University Press, 1997), 240, 48, 486; Christopher Andrew and Vasili Mitrokhin, *The Sword and the Shield: The Mitrokhin Archive and the Secret History of the KGB* (New York: Basic Books, 1991), 148, 9, 176–77. According to a 2011 CIA study, "Sasha" was "the only substantive CI lead" that Golitsyn provided to U.S. intelligence.

134. Benjamin B. Fischer, "Leon Theremin—CIA Nemesis," *Studies in Intelligence* 46, no. 2: (2002): 29–39.

135. Waldemar Campbell, "Waldo in OSS," typescript memoir, 28. Hoover Institution Archives, Stanford University. Campbell served in the OSS with Karlow.

136. Ibid., 29

137. Ibid., 30

138. Anatoly Golitsyn, *New Lies for Old* (New York: Dodd, Mead, 1984) 49.

139. Ibid., 49.

140. Cave Brown, *Treason in the Blood*, 553.

141. Document obtained from CIA CREST Database, probably written in late 1983 or early 1984 (MORI DocID: 38369).

142. Wise, *Molehunt*, 96.

143. Mangold, *Cold Warrior*, 55–56.

144. Papers of Robert F. Kennedy, Attorney General Papers, 1961–1965, series 05, Desk Diaries, 1961–1964, box 146 (1962), John F. Kennedy Presidential Library.

145. Thomas, *Robert Kennedy*, 100–110.

146. Mangold, *Cold Warrior*, 88.

147. This and subsequent quotes on the exchange between Kisevalter and Golitsyn are in Wise, *Molehunt*, 21.

148. Hathaway and Smith, *Richard Helms*, 105.

149. David Robarge, "Moles, Defectors, and Deceptions: James Angleton and CIA Counterintelligence," *The Journal of Intelligence History* 3, no. 2 (Winter 2003): 36.

150. Nosenko had "conclusively proven his bona fides," Bagley wrote in a cable to Langley. "He has provided information of importance [and is] completely cooperative." Quoted in Hart, *CIA's Russians*, 72.

151. Mangold, *Cold Warrior*, 87.

152. U.S. Central Intelligence Agency, "Fixation on Moles," 44.

153. Edward Epstein, *Deception* (New York: Simon and Schuster, 1989), 60.

154. Gittinger made these comments on camera in the *Frontline* program "The Spy Hunter," produced by Jenny Clayton, which aired on May 14, 1991.

155. Robert Kennedy, *Thirteen Days: A Memoir of the Cuban Missile Crisis* (New York: W. W. Norton, 1999), 7.

156. Stewart Alsop and Charles Bartlett, "In Time of Crisis," *The Saturday Evening Post*, December 8, 1962, 15–20.

157. Laurence Chang and Peter Kornbluh, eds., *The Cuban Missile Crisis 1962: A National Security Archive Documents Reader*, 2nd ed. (New York: New Press, 1998).

158. Author's interview with Daniel Ellsberg, May 16, 2016. Ellsberg was a Pentagon consultant on Cuban issues during the October crisis.

159. Philip Bobbitt, *Democracy and Deterrence* (New York: St. Martin's Press, 1988), 7 Daniel Ellsberg suggests the numbers are 1,400 U.S. ICBMS and 192 T-95 Bears.

160. This and subsequent quotes of the interchange between General LeMay and JFK are in Robert Dallek, "JFK vs. the Military," *The Atlantic*, November 2013.

161. Bayard Stockton, *Flawed Patriot* (Dulles, VA: Potomac Books, 2006), 141.

162. John Bartlow Martin, "First Oral History Interview with Robert F. Kennedy," February 29 and March 1, 1964, 280, John F. Kennedy Presidential Library.

163. Stockton, *Flawed Patriot*, 141. "Everyone had expected something like this to happen one of those days but we were all professionals," said Sam Halpern, assistant to Dick Helms. "We all knew when to keep our mouths shut. Bill was not embarrassed by his outburst."

164. Evan Thomas, *The Very Best Men: Four Who Dared: The Early Years of the CIA* (New York: Simon and Schuster, 1995), 291.

165. Justin Gleichauf, "Red Presence in Cuba: The Genesis of a Crisis," *Army*, November 1979, 38.

166. Memo from James Angleton to Deputy Director (Plans), "Cuban Control and Action Capabilities," May 23, 1963, JFK JCS RIF 202-10002-10039, JCS Central File, pages 2, 6; available at www.maryferrell.org/showDoc.htm/?/docId=184.

167. Mimi Beardsley, *Once Upon a Secret* (New York: Random House, 2012), 94.

168. Nikita Khrushchev, *Khrushchev Remembers*, with an introduction, commentary, and notes by Edward Crankshaw, trans. and ed. Strobe Talbott (New York: Bantam, 1971), 551–52.

169. "Message from Chairman Khrushchev to President Kennedy," October 28, 1962, in *Foreign Relations of the United States*, vol. 11, *Cuban Missile Crisis and Aftermath* (Washington, D.C.: U.S. Government Printing Office, 1996), document 62.

170. Arthur Schlesinger, Jr., *Robert Kennedy and His Times.* (New York: Ballantine, 1978).

171. Steven L. Rearden, *Council of War: A History of the Joint Chiefs of Staff, 1942–1991* (Washington, D.C.: National Defense University Press, 2012), 232.

172. Rearden, *Council of War*, 232–33.

173. Angleton and Murphy, *American Cause*, 40.

PART III: IMPUNITY

1. David Robarge, "The James Angleton Phenomenon: 'Cunning Passages, Contrived Corridors': Wandering in the Angletonian Wilderness," *Studies in Intelligence* 53, no. 4 (2009).

2. Miles Copeland, *The Game Player: Confessions of the CIA's Original Political Operative* (London: Arum Press, 1989), 212.

3. Macintyre, *Spy Among Friends*, 251.

4. Cave Brown, *Treason in the Blood*, 520.

5. Ibid., 551.

6. Macintyre, *Spy Among Friends*, 274.

7. Ibid., 301.

8. Ibid., 287.

9. Cave Brown, *Treason in the Blood*, 553–54.

10. Ibid., 551.

11. Mangold, *Cold Warrior*, 90.

12. Wright, *Spycatcher*, 456.

13. David Leigh, *The Wilson Plot: How the Spycatchers and Their American Allies Tried to Overthrow the British Government* (New York: Pantheon, 1988), 80–81.

14. Bruce Hoffman and Christian Ostermann, eds., *Moles, Defectors, and Deceptions: James Angleton and His Influence on U.S. Counterintelligence* (Washington, D.C.: Woodrow Wilson International Center, 2012), publication of the proceedings of the joint conference held on March 29, 2012, 46.

15. "Operational Plans for Continuing Operations Against Cuba," draft memorandum to

the DCI from William Harvey, November 27, 1962, NARA, JFK CIA RIF 104-10103-10079, page 2.

16. Schlesinger, *Robert Kennedy and His Times*, 575.

17. "Operational Plans for Continuing Operations Against Cuba," 2–3.

18. Martin, *Wilderness of Mirrors*, 183.

19. The NORTHWOODS schemes are contained in "Northwoods," a 197-page compilation of documents from the Joint Chiefs of Staff, discovered and made public by the Assassination Records Review Board in 1997. See NARA JFK JCS RIF 202-10002-10104.

20. Brig. Gen. Edwin Lansdale, "Memorandum for the Record, Meeting with the President," March 16, 1962, U.S. Department of the Army, Califano Papers, NARA CIA JFK RIF 198-10004-10020.

21. "Cuban Control and Action Capabilities," Memo from James Angleton to Deputy Director (Plans), May 23, 1963, page 1. NARA JFK JCS 202-10002-10039, JCS Central File. The memo has three parts, a sixteen-page section, "Cuban Control and Action Capabilities"; a six-page section, "Training of Subversive, Sabotage, and Espionage Agents in Cuba"; and a three-page section, "Communism in Cuba."

22. Ibid., 6.

23. Ibid., 11.

24. Ibid.

25. MFF, Angleton Church Committee testimony, June 19, 1975, 28–30.

26. The next day, Papich called Harvey to remind him of the Bureau rule requiring him to report any known contacts between former FBI employees and criminal elements. He had no choice but to report his dinner with Rosselli to Hoover, he said.

   Harvey, thinking fast, said he understood but just wanted to ask a favor. Could Papich inform him in advance if it appeared that the FBI director might call John McCone about the matter? Harvey helpfully explained that the CIA director should be "briefed on the matter before getting a call from Hoover."

   Papich agreed. So did Dick Helms. The FBI had a rule that meetings with organized crime figures had to be reported. The CIA had no such rule. Was he obliged to inform McCone that the chief of the Rome station had had dinner with a trusted source in Washington? No, Helms decided. There was no need to brief McCone, unless Hoover got involved.

   Papich informed Hoover that Harvey had been seen with Rosselli. Hoover didn't care and didn't contact McCone. The director remained in the dark. See *CIA Targets Fidel: CIA Inspector General's Report on Plots to Assassinate Fidel Castro* (New York: Ocean Press, 1996), 59.

27. Classified message from W. K. Harvey to Luxembourg, "ZRRIFLE QJWIN: PROJECT CONTRACT," March 4, 1963, NARA CIA JFK RIF 1994.03.11.16:03:49:940005.

28. MFF, Angleton Church Committee testimony, June 19, 1975, 29.

29. Marks, *Search for the "Manchurian Candidate,"* 202–3.

30. Mangold, *Cold Warrior*, 56.

31. Riebling, *Wedge*, 136–37.

32. Joseph E. Persico Papers, box 1, "Angleton, James" folder, Hoover Institution Archives, Stanford University.

33. *Daily Telegraph* (London), July 12, 1963.

34. Wright, *Spycatcher*, 398–99.

35. "Appeal Linked to Profumo Case Likely to Add Details of Scandal," *New York Times*, July 15, 1963.

36. David Robarge, *John McCone as Director of Central Intelligence 1961–1965* (Washington, D.C.: Center for the Study of Intelligence, Central Intelligence Agency, 2005), 313.

37. Memo from Charles A. Bohrer, M.D. to Chief, SR Division, "DCI-AELADELE Tapes of 23 August and 4 September 1963, September 19, NARA CIA JFK RIF 104-10172-10403; available at https://www.maryferrell.org/showDoc.html?docId=35166.

38. MFF, Angleton House Select Committee on Assassinations testimony, October 5, 1978, 50.

39. Fischer, "Leon Theremin—CIA Nemesis," 38.

40. Ibid.

41. Robarge, "Moles, Defectors, and Deceptions," 940.

42. MFF, testimony of James Angleton, June 19, 1975, Senate Select Committee on Government Organizations, 64–65, NARA JFK SSCSGO RIF 157-10014-10005.

43. Christopher Andrew, *Defend the Realm: The Authorized History of MI5* (New York: Knopf, 2009), 509.

44. Andrew and Mitrokhin, *Sword and the Shield*, 446. Four French intelligence officers and one former head of department in the Sûreté Générale were active Soviet agents during the period from 1963 to 1966, according to extensive documentation provided by former KGB official Vasili Mitrokhin.

45. P. L. Thyraud de Vosjoli, *Lamia* (Boston: Little, Brown, 1970), 316–17.

46. The routing slips, initialed by CI staffers, are reproduced in Newman, *Oswald and the CIA*, 496, 497.

47. Paul Wallach, "Memorandum for the Record, re meeting with James Angleton on 10/3/75," which is found in a collection of memoranda entitled "Oswald in New Orleans," January 19, 1976, NARA JFK SSCIA RIF 157-10014-10120.

48. From James R. Hosty to FBI Internal Security, "Report on Oswald Subscribing to 'The Worker' and Drinking and Beating," September 10, 1963, NARA JFK RIF 1993.06.1909:31:25:62000.

49. From James P. Hosty, Jr., to FBI Internal Security, "FBI Report on Oswald's Arrests [sic] for Disturbing the Peace," September 24, 1963, NARA CIA JFK RIF 1991.06.19.09:57:36:530000. The CIA routing slips on the September 10 and 24 FBI reports initialed by Roman are reproduced in Newman, *Oswald and the CIA*, 501–03.

50. Memorandum, from S. J. Papich to D. J. Brennan, "Fair Play for Cuba Committee," September 18, 1963, NARA CIA JFK RIF 104-10310-10151.

51. "American Male Who Spoke Broken Russian . . ." cable dated October 8, 1963, JFK CIA RIF 104-10015-10304.

52. George Kalaris, Angleton's successor as counterintelligence chief, reviewed Angleton's JFK files in January 1975 and reported finding "several" cables from October 1963 "concerned with Oswald's visit to Mexico City, as well as his visits to the Soviet *and Cuban Embassies*" (emphasis added). Those cables have never been made public and may have been destroyed. See Confidential memorandum from George J. Kalaris, chief, CI Staff, to executive assistant to the DDO, re Lee Harvey Oswald, September 14, 1975, NARA CIA JFK RIF 104-20051-10173.

53. The House Select Committee on Assassinations requested a definition of LCIMPROVE in "List of Names re Kennedy Assassination." The CIA's response is found on the next page, February 2, 1978, NARA JFK HSCA RIF 104-10061-10115.

54. From Director, CIA, to Mexico City, "Cable Stating that Lee Oswald Who Called SovEmb 1 Oct Probably Identical to Lee Henry Oswald," October 1, 1963 NARA CIA JFK RIF 104-10015-10048.

55. Author's and John Newman's interview with Jane Roman, November 2, 1994. A tape of this interview is part of the JFK Assassination Records Collection at the National Archives, Washington, D.C.

56. Author's interview with William J. Hood, February 5, 2007.

57. The time stamp reads "22:29Z," the letter Z referring to Greenwich mean time, which is five hours ahead of eastern standard time. So the cable was sent at 17:29 local time.

58. "Kennedy Sees Banda and Adoula," *Washington Post*, October 11, 1963.

59. Mexico desk chief John Whitten said that "the main thrust of the station's effort was to recruit Russians, Cubans and satellite people." See deposition of "John Scelso" (aka John Whitten), May 16, 1978, 64–65, NARA JFK HSCA RIF 180-1013-10330.

60. "Excerpts from History: Western Hemisphere Division 1946–1965," 252, NARA JFK CIA RIF 104-10301-10001.

61. From Chief, WH Division, to COS, Mexico City, "Dispatch: LIFIRE/5-LCFLUTTER Interview," NARA JFK CIA RIF 104-10098-10146; available at https://www.maryferrell.org/showDoc.html?docId=30640.

62. To Director from MEXI, "LIEMBRACE Security (LCFLUTTER Exams)," November 7, 1963, NARA JFK CIA RIF 104-10098-10222.

63. Whether CIA employees were questioned about Oswald is unknown. The Agency's records have been tampered with. Each of the CIA's reports on the twenty-one employees came with an attachment that reported the substance of the interrogation. When the reports were declassified in 2007, eighteen of the twenty-one attachments had been removed. See Bill Simpich, *State Secret: Wiretapping in Mexico City, Double Agents, and the Framing of Lee Oswald*, chapter 5; available at www.maryferrell.org/pages/State_Secret.html.

64. "Dispatch: LIFIRE/5-LCFLUTTER Interview."

65. This and subsequent Newman quotes are from the author's interview with Bill Newman, November 21, 2005.

66. Warren Commission Hearings, vol. 23, 913. Commission exhibit 1974, "FBI Report Dated August 11, 1964, at Dallas, Tex., of Transcripts of Dallas Police Radio Transmissions"; available at http://www.maryferrell.org/showDoc.html?docId=1139#relPageId=945.

67. Testimony of Jesse Edward Curry, Warren Commission Hearings, vol. 4, 161.

68. Gary Mack, "The Man Who Named the Grassy Knoll"; available at http://mcadams.posc.mu.edu/gk_name.htm.

69. "21 Cops Who Heard a Grassy Knoll Shot," JFK Facts, July 4, 2016; available at http://jfkfacts.org/21-jfk-cops-who-heard-a-grassy-knoll-shot/.

70. Schlesinger, *Robert F. Kennedy and His Times*, 616.

71. Angleton House Select Committee on Assassinations testimony, October 5, 1978, 79–80, HSCA/Security Classified Testimony, NARA JFK HSCA RIF 180-10110-10006.

72. MFF, Hartman House Select Committee on Assassinations testimony, 47.

73. CBS News correspondent Richard Schlesinger's interview with Richard Helms, February 1992; available at https://www.youtube.com/watch?v=e3nDUEgh05o.

74. MFF, Whitten House Select Committee on Assassinations testimony, May 16, 1978, 111. In 1954, when Helms was running European operations, Whitten had unlocked the baffling case of Otto John, the head of West German intelligence, who defected to East Germany and then returned a year later. Helms "had known me for years as a polygraph operator and as a man who had successfully investigated a number of very, very big operations and security problems," Whitten testified.

75. Ibid., 114.

76. Brian Galindo, "16 Photos That Capture People's Reactions to the News of JFK's As-

sassination," Buzzfeed, November 21, 2013; https: //www.buzzfeed.com/briangalindo /16-photos-that-capture-peoples-reaction-to-the-news-of-jfks.

77. "Reaction to JFK's Death Varied Across the U.S." See Web site of TV10, Columbus, Mississippi, at http://www.10tv.com/article/reaction-jfks-death-varied-across-us.

78. "Translation of Tape re Lee Harvey Oswald," January 21, 1964, NARA CIA JFK RIF 104-10020-10009.

79. James Angleton to D/FBI J. E. Hoover, "Hunter Report #10815 re Fair Play for Cuba Committee," November 26, 1963, NARA JFK CIA RIF 104-10054-10190.

80. See "Lee Harvey Oswald 'I'm just a patsy'"; available at https://www.youtube.com /watch?v=NUTnzfmCJY4.

81. MFF, Angleton Church Committee testimony, June 19, 1975, 66.

82. Jean Daniel, "When Castro Heard the News," New Republic, December 7, 1963, 79.

83. Castro's speech was published in the December 1, 1963, issue of Política, a Mexican weekly, under the title "Cuba Ante el Asesinato de Kennedy." An English version appears in E. Martin Schotz, History Will Not Absolve Us: Orwellian Control, Public Denial, and the Murder of President Kennedy (Brookline, MA: Kurtz, Ulmer, and DeLucia, 1996), 53–86.

84. Letter from Richard Helms to Robert Kennedy, November 23, 1963, Papers of Robert F. Kennedy, Attorney General Papers, Correspondence, Condolences 1963–1964, box 132, John F. Kennedy Presidential Library.

85. Aleksandr Fursenko and Timothy Naftali, "One Hell of a Gamble": Khrushchev, Castro, and Kennedy, 1958–1964 (New York: W. W. Norton, 1999), 344–45.

86. RFK responded to Helms's note with equal politesse. On a printed thank-you card sent to Helms, he added a handwritten postscript: "Dear Dick, My thanks to you. Bob." See Richard Helms Papers, Part 1, box 2, folder 27, Georgetown University.

87. Angleton told Hoover he saw no evidence that Kostikov was part of Department Thirteen. See Simpich, State Secret, 3.

88. Thomas, Very Best Men, 306.

89. Ibid., 300–6.

90. Ibid., 307.

91. Ibid., 308.

92. MFF, Angleton Church Committee testimony, February 6, 1976, 32.

93. Talbot, Devil's Chessboard, 567.

94. MFF, Whitten House Select Committee on Assassinations testimony, 131.

95. Ibid., 115–16

96. Ibid., 62

97. William McKeen, Outlaw Journalist: The Life and Times of Hunter S. Thompson (New York: W. W. Norton, 2008), 85.

98. Warren Commission report, 777.

99. Confidential memorandum from George J. Kalaris, chief, CI Staff, executive assistant to the DDO, re Lee Harvey Oswald.

100. NARA JFK CIA RIF 1993.06.24.14.59:13:840170 Memo, from "Rock" [Ray Rocca, CIA] CIA to "Dick" [Richard Helms, CIA] Re Response to Rankin W/C, March 5, 1964; available at http://www.maryferrell.org/showDoc.html?docId=98075.

101. Howard Willens, Journal, March 12, 1964; available at HowardWillens.com.

102. E-mail from Howard Willens to author, 2015; available at http://jfkfacts.org/qa-with -howard-willens-warren-commission-defender/.

103. Brian Latell, Castro's Secrets (New York: St. Martin's Press, 2013), 107.

104. Swenson described and quoted from his 1964 and 1965 memos in an affidavit for the

House Select Committee on Assassinations, September 14, 1978. Swenson's original memo was turned over to the House Select Committee on Assassinations. See From Office of Legislative Counsel to CIA Security Officer, HSCA, "Volume II/Support Documents for the Helms Hearing at HSCA," September 9. 1978, NARA JFK CIA, Russ Holmes Work File, RIF 104-10406-10113.

105. Tim Weiner asserts the same in *Legacy of Ashes*, 265.

106. Mangold, *Cold Warrior*, 154.

107. Niccolo Machiavelli, *Discourses on Livy* (Chicago: University of Chicago Press, 2009), 218.

108. Ashley, *CIA Spymaster*, 273.

109. Ibid., 274.

110. Ibid., 275.

111. Wise, *Molehunt*, 136.

112. Memorandum To: File from Deputy Chief Security Research Staff, "Subject: BERTO-TALLY, Bruce, A," February 18 1970, NARA JFK CIA RIF 104-10106-10081. This memo, declassified by the CIA in 1999, reports on the Agency's resettlement of Nosenko and includes some history of Nosenko's case. The memo states that Helms approved the funds for Nosenko on January 30, 1964, five days *before* Nosenko said he wanted to defect. Either that date is incorrect or Helms approved of the idea of paying Nosenko in advance.

113. Ashley, *CIA Spymaster*, 279.

114. Robarge, *John McCone*, 382.

115. Angleton SSCIA testimony, February 6, 1976, NARA JFK SSCIA RIF 157-10014-10003; available at http://www.maryferrell.org/mffweb/archive/viewer/showDoc.do?docId=1434&relPageId=1.

116. "Chronology of Soviet Defector's Handling," February 6, 1975, NARA JFK CIA RIF 104-10312-10275.

117. Wise, *Molehunt*, 144.

118. Ibid., 143.

119. Memorandum to W. C. Sullivan from W. A. Branigan, "SAMMY-ESPIONAGE," July, 16, 1964, NARA FBI HQ RIF 124-10333-10009. Attached to the memo are transcripts of seven tape recordings made on June 29, 1964, each paginated individually. Hereafter, CIA Golitsyn transcripts. "He is a provocateur" quote from Golitsyn transcript no. 2, 2.

120. CIA Golitsyn transcript no. 3, 19.

121. CIA Golitsyn transcript no. 5, 1.

122. Riebling, *Wedge*, 217.

123. From: Chief of Station Rome, To Chief, WE, "Italian Press Coverage—Warren Commission Report on President's Assassination," October 11, 1964, NARA JFK CIA RIF 104-10007-10034.

124. Bayard Stockton, *Flawed Patriot: The Rise and Fall of CIA Legend Bill Harvey* (Washington, D.C: Potomac Books, 2006).

125. See deposition of "John Scelso" (aka John Whitten), May 16, 1978, 147 NARA JFK HSCA RIF 180-1013-10330.

126. Memo, To: Mr. W.C. Sullivan From: Mr. D.J. Brennan Jr, Subject: Kennedy assassination film, October 12, 1964. I have no direct evidence that Angleton watched Zapruder's film in October 1964, only inference. Is it possible that the FBI did not share the film or that Angleton chose not to watch it? Both seem unlikely.

127. Warren Commission report, 50–51.

128. Burleigh, *Very Private Woman*, 244.

129. Philip Nobile and Ron Rosenbaum, "The Mysterious Murder of JFK's Mistress," *New Times*, October 1976, n.p.

130. Ibid.

131. Ibid.

132. Burleigh, *Very Private Woman*, 273.

133. Nobile and Rosenbaum, "Mysterious Murder."

134. Ben Bradlee, *A Good Life: Newspapering and Other Adventures* (New York: Simon and Schuster, 1995), 267–68.

135. Ibid., 268.

136. Cicely d'Autremont Angleton and Anne Truitt, "In Angleton's Custody," letter to the editor, *New York Times Book Review*, November 5, 1995.

137. Timothy Leary, *Flashbacks: An Autobiography* (Los Angeles: J. P. Tarcher, 1983), 128–29.

138. Peter Janney, *Mary's Mosaic: The CIA Conspiracy to Murder John F. Kennedy, Mary Pinchot Meyer, and Their Vision of World Peace* (New York: Skyhorse, 2012), 3.

139. Burleigh, *Very Private Woman*, 220.

140. George Eagle, "Grand Jury to Hear Evidence Today in Mary P. Meyer Death," *Washington Post*, October 15, 1964.

141. Burleigh, *Very Private Woman*, 212.

142. Trento, *Secret History of the CIA*, 281–82.

143. U.S. Central Intelligence Agency, "Fixation on Moles," 45.

144. Robarge, *John McCone*, 382.

145. Ibid., 382–83.

146. Burleigh, *Very Private Woman*, 257.

147. Cicely Angleton made these comments in an appearance at the Library of Congress. See "The Poet and the Poem" Audio podcasts, part 1, available at https://www.loc.gov/poetry/media/poetpoem.html.

148. Letter from Cord Meyer to Ruth Pinchot, August 5, 1964, Cord Meyer Papers, box 1, folder 8, Library of Congress, Washington, D.C. See also Burleigh, *Very Private Woman*, 276.

149. Letter from Cord Meyer to Ruth Pinchot, August 5, 1964.

150. "Memorandum for Mr. Angleton, Subject: Minutiae of Possible Interest," September 7, 1965, Ted Jessup Collection.

151. Cicely d'Autremont Angleton, *Cave of Overwhelming*, 5.

152. Angleton House Select Committee on Assassinations testimony, October 5, 1978, 66, HSCA/Security Classified Testimony, NARA JFK HSCA RIF 180-10110-10006.

153. Unless otherwise noted this and subsequent Halevy quotes are from the author's interview with Efraim Halevy, December 15, 2015.

154. Kevin Conley Ruffner, Draft Working Paper, "Eagle and Swastika: CIA and Nazi War Criminals and Collaborators," chapters 11–21; see in particular chapter 14, 9 NARA CREST: document no. 519697e8993294098d50c295.

155. Efraim Halevy, *A Man in the Shadows: Inside the Middle East Crisis with a Man Who Led the Mossad* (New York: St. Martin's Press, 2006), Kindle location 1221.

156. Daniel Raviv and Yossi Melman, *Every Spy a Prince: The Complete History of Israel's Intelligence Community* (Boston: Houghton Mifflin, 1991), 125.

157. Hersh, *Sampson Option*, Kindle location 81.

158. Author's interview with Peter Sichel, December 2, 2015.

159. John Hadden, *Conversations with a Masked Man* (New York: Arcade, 2015), 20. There are two sources for John Hadden's comments. One is *Conversations with a Masked Man;*

the other is a transcript of comments by John Hadden, Sr., on his life in the CIA, on which the book was based (hereafter, Hadden transcript). The transcript includes material that John Hadden, Sr., did not want included in his son's book. John Hadden, Jr., generously shared the transcript with me. Whenever possible, I cite the book version.

160. Hadden transcript.

161. Hadden, *Conversations with a Masked Man*, 22.

162. Roger J. Mattson, *Stealing the Atom Bomb: How Denial and Deception Armed Israel* (self-published, 2016), 239–43.

163. Ibid., 22.

164. Author's interview with Efraim Halevy.

165. Hersh, *Sampson Option*, Kindle location 2480.

166. Ruffner, "Eagle and Swastika," chapter 11.

167. Ibid.

168. Shimon Peres, *Battling for Peace* (New York: Random House, 1995), 119.

169. Author's interview with Avner Cohen, August 4, 2015.

170. "David Lowenthal: Innovative Industrialist Who Helped Jews Settle in Israel," *Pittsburgh Post-Gazette*, March 10, 2006. Citing Lowenthal's FBI file, Grant Smith says Lowenthal traveled to Israel once a month for Zionist functions in the 1950s. See Grant F. Smith, *Divert! NUMEC, Zalman Shapiro and the Diversion of U.S. Weapons Grade Uranium into the Israeli Nuclear Weapons Program* (Washington, D.C.: Institute for Research, 2012), Kindle location 2096.

171. Ibid., Kindle location 549.

172. Ibid., Kindle location 2173.

173. Ibid., Kindle location 480.

174. Mattson, *Stealing the Atom Bomb*, 83.

175. Smith, *Divert!*, Kindle location 551.

176. Victor Gilinsky and Roger J. Mattson, "Revisiting the NUMEC Affair," *Bulletin of the Atomic Scientists*, March–April 2010, 62.

177. Mattson, *Stealing the Atom Bomb*, 77.

178. National Security Archive at George Washington University; "The NUMEC Affair," From SAC Pittsburgh to Director FBI and Criminal Investigative Division, Terrorism Section, March 25, 1980, http://nsarchive.gwu.edu/dc.html?doc=3149997-41-FBI-Internal-Report-of-Interviews-DIVERT-from.

179. Mattson, *Stealing the Atom Bomb*, 9. According to Mattson, the FBI liaison was on the distribution list for most of the Bureau's correspondence concerning NUMEC. It was Papich's job to coordinate with the CIA, and it was Angleton's job to respond. The fact that the CIA distribution of the FBI's NUMEC reports is still classified in 2016 suggests counterintelligence components were involved.

180. Ibid., 255.

181. Hadden, *Conversations with a Masked Man*, 142.

182. Hadden transcript.

183. Author's interview with Tom Hughes, August 29, 2015.

184. Harriet Dashiell Schwar, ed., *Foreign Relations of the United States 1964–1968*, vol. 18, *Arab-Israeli Dispute, 1964–1967* (Washington, D.C.: Government Printing Office, 2000), "Summary."

185. Ibid., document 404, National Intelligence Estimate, Washington, April 13, 1967; NIE 30–67, "The Arab-Israeli Dispute: Current Phase."

186. Harriet Dashiell Schwar, ed., *Foreign Relations of the United States, 1964–1968*, vol. 19, *Arab-Israeli Crisis and War, 1967* (Washington, D.C.: U.S. Government Printing Office, 2004), "Summary."

187. Hathaway and Smith, *Richard Helms*, 144.

188. Author's interview with Efraim Halevy, December 16, 2015.

189. Hadden, *Conversations with a Masked Man*, 110–11.

190. Meir Amit, *Rosh be-rosh: Mabat ishi al eru'im gedolim u-farashiyot alumot* [Or Yehudah, Israel]: Hed Artsi, 1999, 239–41.

191. Tom Segev, *1967: Israel, the War, and the Year that Transformed the Middle East* (New York: Metropolitan Books, 2007), 332.

192. Author's interview with Efraim Halevy, December 16, 2015.

193. Hathaway and Smith, *Richard Helms*, 141.

194. Schwar, *Foreign Relations of the United States*, vol. 19, "Summary."

195. The oft-told story that the CIA predicted the war would last seven days, not six, is more an office legend than documented fact, according to Agency historian David Robarge. The Agency's reports predicted a quick Israeli victory but never gave a specific time estimate for how long it would take. See Hathaway and Smith, *Richard Helms*, 142.

196. Author's interview with Tom Hughes.

197. Transcript of the examination of Comdr. William L. McGonagle, National Security File, Country File, Middle East, folder labeled "Middle East Crisis," vol. 7, cables, 6/21/67–7/10/67 [3 of 3], document 176, page 32, Lyndon B. Johnson Presidential Library. Hereafter, McGonagle testimony.

198. "Narrative Based the Report of Court of Inquiry on the Armed Attack on the USS LIBERTY," National Security File, Country File, Middle East, folder labeled "Middle East Crisis," vol. 7, cables, 6/21/67–7/10/67 [3 of 3], document 175, page 5, Lyndon B. Johnson Presidential Library. Hereafter, *Liberty* narrative.

199. McGonagle testimony, 35.

200. Ibid., 38.

201. *Liberty* narrative, 11.

202. Schwar, *Foreign Relations of the United States*, vol. 19, "Summary."

203. Ibid.

204. Ibid., document 284, page 470.

205. Ibid.

206. Moorer's statement is found on ussliberty.org, a Web site run by Jerry Ennis, a survivor of the attack. See http://www.ussliberty.org/moorer3.htm.

207. Matthew M. Aid, ed., *U.S. Intelligence on the Middle East, 1945–2009*, citing "CIA, Briefing, Draft Briefing by Director of Central Intelligence Helms for President's Foreign Intelligence Advisory Board," June 14, 1967; available at Brill Online Sources, http://primarysources.brillonline.com/browse/us-intelligence-on-the-middle-east.

208. Harrison Salisbury, *Without Fear or Favor: An Uncompromising Look at the New York Times* (New York: Times Books, 1980), 514–17.

209. Otto Kerner, *The Kerner Report: The 1968 Report of the National Advisory Commission on Civil Disorders* (New York: Pantheon, 1988), 113. A major riot was defined as an incident that lasted for more than two days; generated deaths, injuries, or looting; and required the summoning of the National Guard or federal forces.

210. *Newsweek*, July 29, 1967, 22.

211. MFF, Helms testimony, Rockefeller Commission, April 28, 1975, 243–44.

212. Memorandum to Chief, CI Staff, "Overseas Coverage of Subversive Student and

Related Activities," August 15, 1967, American Civil Liberties Union Records, box 4108, folder labeled "Duplicate Records," Seeley G. Mudd Manuscript Library, Princeton University.

213. E-mail from Josiah Ober, professor at Princeton and nephew of Richard Ober, to the author, December 7, 2015.

214. Church Committee Report, Book 3, 690.

215. ACLU Records, Memorandum for Chief, CIA Staff, August 15, 1967, box 4108.

216. Church Committee Report, Book 2: Intelligence Activities and the Rights of Americans (Washington, D.C.: U.S. Government Printing Office, 1976), report No. 94-755, p. 6. Hereafter, Church Committee Report, Book 2.

217. Church Committee Report, Book 3, 716.

218. Andrew, *Defend the Realm*, 513.

219. Mangold, *Cold Warrior*, 207.

220. Ashley, *CIA Spymaster*, 282. Nosenko told Ashley that he was given hallucinogenic drugs, "probably LSD," on many occasions.

221. *Frontline*, "The Spy Hunter," produced by Jenny Clayton, aired May 14, 1991.

222. Ibid. Gittinger denied that he had dosed Nosenko but did not deny it had happened.

223. Ashley, *CIA Spymaster*, 284–85.

224. Undated memo written by Leonard McCoy, found in the JFK Records Collection by Malcolm Blunt. The copy Blunt gave the author did not include an RIF sheet or the first page of the memo.

225. Richards J. Heuer, Jr., "Nosenko: Five Paths to Judgment," in *Inside CIA's Private World: Declassified Articles from the Agency's Internal Journal, 1955–1992*, ed. H. Bradford Westerfield (New Haven: Yale University Press, 1995), 383.

226. H. Bradford Westerfield, ed. *Inside CIA's Private World: Declassified Articles from the Agency's Internal Journal, 1955–1992*, (New Haven: Yale University Press, 1997), 383.

227. Wise, *Molehunt*, 192–97.

228. Author's interview with Steven Murphy, February 24, 2016.

229. Mangold, *Cold Warrior*, 196–201.

230. Wise, *Mole Hunt*, 176 (Gmirkin); Mangold, *Cold Warrior*, 295 (Bennett), 226 (Loginov).

231. Memorandum to director of Central Intelligence from J. Kenneth McDonald, Chief CIA History Staff, February 10, 1992, NARA JFK CIA, Russ Holmes Work File, RIF 104-10428-10104.

232. Jefferson Morley, *Our Man in Mexico: Winston Scott and the Secret History of the CIA* (Lawrence: University of Kansas Press, 2008), 244.

233. Scott's comments are from a JFK assassination chronology compiled by his assistant Anne Goodpasture in 1968. See "Mexico City Chronology," 116, NARA JFK CIA RIF 104-10014-10046.

234. Peter Wright said that "all important communications with British intelligence went through him [Angleton] personally." See Wright, *Spycatcher*, 386. Angleton also had sympathetic British sources, including Wright, Arthur Martin, and Stephen de Mowbray.

235. Letter from "Thomas W. Lund" to "Willard," June 14, 1967, NARA JFK CIA RIF 104-10247-1049.

236. "Mexico City Station History, Excerpts," 35, 355, JFK Assassination Records Collection, Russ Holmes Work File, NARA JFK CIA RIF 104-10414-10124.

237. Morley, *Our Man in Mexico*, 114.

238. Memo from F. W. M. Janney to the record, "Garrison Group Meeting No. 1," September 20, 1967, NARA JFK CIA RIF 104-10428-10023.

239. NSA/GWU, "The NUMEC Affair," Memorandum from SAC, WFO, to Director, FBI, Subject: [Redacted] Atomic Energy Act, September 11, 1968, http://nsarchive.gwu.edu/dc.html?doc=3149962-10-Memorandum-from-SAC-WFO-to-Director-FBI.

240. "Israel Spy Visited A-Plant Where Uranium Vanished," *Los Angeles Times,* June 16, 1986. When Peter Stockton, a congressional investigator, later asked Eitan if he had ever visited NUMEC, Eitan said no. When Stockton informed him the Atomic Energy Commission had a document related to the visit that he had signed, Eitan said, 'Well, OK, I was there . . . but I was getting batteries for listening devices.'" See "What Lies Beneath," by Scott C. Johnson, *Foreign Policy,* March 2015; available at http://foreignpolicy.com/2015/03/23/what-lies-beneath-numec-apollo-zalman-shapiro/.

241. *Panorama,* BBC, June 26, 1978.

242. "Scientist Developed Nuclear Fuel for USS Nautilus," *Pittsburgh Tribune,* July 18, 2016; available at http://triblive.com/obituaries/newsstories/10809808-74/shapiro-nuclear-fuel.

243. E-mail from Mark Lowenthal to the author, April 22, 2016.

244. Author's interview with Avner Cohen, August 4, 2015.

245. Wise, *Molehunt,* 233.

246. Author's interview with Efraim Halevy, December 16, 2015.

247. Knightley, *Master Spy,* 270.

248. Nobile and Rosenbaum, "Mysterious Murder," n.p. The authors cite an anonymous source for Bradlee's reply. See also Martin, *Wilderness of Mirrors,* 215.

249. Philby, *My Silent War,* 99.

250. Christopher Felix, "A Second Third Man," *New York Times Book Review,* May 26, 1968, 8. McCargar's article appeared under his nom de plume.

251. Angleton expressed this thought to Paul Wallach, an investigator for the Church Committee, who recorded it in a memo dated October 28, 1975. The memo can be found in a collection of documents entitled "Oswald in New Orleans," September 19, 1976, NARA JFK SSCIA RIF 157-10014-10120.

252. Holzman, *James Jesus Angleton,* 262.

253. Wright, *Spycatcher,* 386.

254. Wise, *Mole Hunt,* 129 (Karlow), 203 (Garber), 225 (Murphy), 264 (Kovich).

255. Mangold, *Cold Warrior,* 239.

256. Wright, *Spycatcher,* 388.

257. Ibid., 389.

PART IV: LEGEND

1. Talbot, *Devil's Chessboard,* 616–17.

2. Public Papers of the Presidents of the United States: Richard Nixon, 1969 (Washington, D.C.: U.S. Government Printing Office, 1999).

3. Jim Dwyer, "An Infamous Explosion and the Smoldering Memory of Radicalism," *New York Times,* November 14, 2007; available at http://www.nytimes.com/2007/11/14/nyregion/14about.html.

4. Bryan Burrough, "Meet the Weather Underground's Bomb Guru," *Vanity Fair,* March 29, 2015; available at http://bit.ly/29lCLMi.

5. Memorandum to Ron Ziegler from J. Bruce Whelihan, "Domestic Violence/Conduct of Foreign Policy," February 11, 1974, in J. Bruce Whelihan file, "Domestic Violence Chronology," box 1. See White House Staff Files, Staff Member and Office Files, Richard Nixon Presidential Library.

6. *Hearings Before the Select Committee to Study Governmental Operations with Respect to Intelligence Activities of the United States Senate,* 94th Cong., 1st Sess., vol. 2, *Huston Plan,* September 1975, Angleton testimony, 85. Hereafter, Husten Plan.

7. Holzman, *James Jesus Angleton,* 264.

8. Powers, *Man Who Kept the Secrets,* 318.

9. William C. Sullivan, *The Bureau: My Thirty Years in Hoover's FBI* (New York: W. W. Norton, 1978), 208.

10. "Internal Security and Domestic Intelligence Presidential Talking Paper," Nixon Library, White House Subject Files, Confidential Files, box 41, folder ND6, Intelligence 69–70.

11. *Huston Plan,* Angleton testimony, 57.

12. Powers, *Man Who Kept the Secrets,* 319.

13. John Prados, *The Family Jewels: The CIA, Secrecy, and Presidential Power* (Austin: University of Texas Press, 2014), Kindle location 1108, citing LINGUAL production for 1972.

14. William Shakespeare, *Othello,* (New York: Penguin Books, 1978) act I, scene 1, lines 63–64.

15. Information on the lunch and subsequent comments are from the author's interview with Efraim Halevy, December 16, 2015.

16. Peter Haldeman, "Outside Time and Place: Classic Forms Rise Up in a Once-Arid Corner of Northern Mexico," *Architectural Digest,* April 2007.

17. Angleton wrote this in a private letter to Efraim Halevy.

18. Cord Meyers Papers, box 1, folder "Angleton James"; Ted Jessup interview, August 8, 2015; Confidential interview, March 1, 2017.

19. MFF, Memorandum for Federal Bureau of Investigation, Attention Mr. S. J. Papich, Subject: "Garrison and the Kennedy Assassination," January 14, 1969.

20. Philip Shenon, *A Cruel and Shocking Act: The Secret History of the Kennedy Assassination* (New York: Henry Holt, 2013), 528.

21. Ibid., 529.

22. MFF, Angleton House Select Committee on Assassinations testimony, 129.

23. To Director, "Cable re Death Benefits for Mrs. Curtis," April 29, 1971, NARA JFK CIA RIF 104 10129-10097.

24. Author's interview with Michael Scott, August 8, 2015.

25. MFF, Angleton House Select Committee on Assassinations testimony, 129.

26. David Atlee Phillips, *The Night Watch* (New York: Atheneum, 1977), 239.

27. ARRB collection, National Archives. Horton wrote this in a memo to the CIA in 1992, and it was obtained by the Assassination Records Review Board.

28. "Cable re Death Benefits for Mrs. Curtis."

29. Winston Scott, "It Came to Little," unpublished manuscript, Michael Scott Collection, 187.

30. Weiner, *Legacy of Ashes,* 371.

31. Jim Hougan, *Secret Agenda: Watergate, Deep Throat, and the CIA* (New York: Random House, 1984), 262–63.

32. Hunt spoke about Angleton in a video interview with his son St. John Hunt and Eric Hamburg. Hamburg shared a transcript with the author.

33. "Working Draft—CIA Watergate History," 149–50. This document, written by the CIA general counsel, was obtained by litigation of the conservative watchdog group Judicial Watch in September 2016.

34. Author's interview with Dennis Helms, May 16, 2016.

35. The correspondence is dissected in Lucy Komisar, "The Art of Flattery: Letters from a CIA Director to a President," *Washington Monthly*, April 1996, 22–25.

36. "The Smoking Gun Tape," June 23, 1972, http://watergate.info/1972/06/23/the-smoking -gun-tape.html.

37. Helms, *Look Over My Shoulder*, Kindle Location 316.

38. Hathaway and Smith, *Richard Helms*, 191. Haldeman said he got "the whole Bay of Pigs" idea from Daniel Schorr, who thought Nixon was referring to the CIA's plots to kill Castro and the assassination of Kennedy.

39. Prados, *Family Jewels*, 50–51.

40. Stanley Kutler, *The Wars of Watergate* (New York: W. W. Norton, 1992), 202.

41. Weiner, *Legacy of Ashes*, 375.

42. Harold P. Ford, *William E. Colby as Director of Central Intelligence* (Washington, D.C.: Central Intelligence Agency, 1993), 82.

43. Holzman, *James Jesus Angleton*, 282.

44. Carl Colby, Bill Colby's son, talked about his grandfather's defense of the murdered soldier in Hoffman and Ostermann, *Moles, Defectors, and Deceptions*, 13.

45. William Colby and Peter Forbath, *Honorable Men: My Life in the CIA* (New York: Simon and Schuster, 1978), 29.

46. Author's interview with Ted Jessup, August 8, 2015.

47. Colby and Forbath, *Honorable Men*, 364.

48. Prados, *Family Jewels*, 284–89.

49. Weiner, *Legacy of Ashes*, 378.

50. Ford, *William E. Colby as Director of Central Intelligence, 1973–1976*, 10.

51. Epstein, *Deception*, 100–101.

52. Author's interview with Efraim Halevy, December 16, 2015; manuscript, entitled "James Angleton," October 27, 1997, Richard M. Helms Papers, box 1, folder 25, Georgetown University.

53. Powers, *Man Who Kept the Secrets*, 362.

54. Letter from Carter Woodbury to David Robarge, John Hadden, Jr., Collection.

55. Edward Jay Epstein, "The Spy War," *New York Times Sunday Magazine*, September 28, 1980, 11.

56. Ford, *William E. Colby* 83–87.

57. Ibid., 100.

58. Colby and Forbath, *Honorable Men*, 365.

59. Ford, *William E. Colby*, 91.

60. Author's interview with Efraim Halevy, December 16, 2015.

61. Ford, *William E. Colby*, 25.

62. Ibid., 26.

63. David Leigh, *The Wilson Plot: How the Spycatchers and Their American Allies Tried to Overthrow the British Government* (New York: Pantheon Books, 1988), 215–16.

64. *Washington Post*, May 1, 1974.

65. John M. Goshko, "Willy Brandt Resigns Over Spy Scandal," *Washington Post*, May 7, 1974.

66. Angleton and Murphy, *American Cause*, 3. Murphy and Angleton were close friends and coauthored this collection of essays. Their views on détente were very similar.

67. Ibid., 11.

68. Cram, "Of Moles and Mole Hunters," 8.

69. "Clare Edward Petty, Cold Warrior and Spycatching CIA Officer, Dies at 90," *Washington Post*, April 15, 2011; available at https://www.washingtonpost.com/local/obituaries/clare-edward-petty-cold-warrior-and-spycatching-cia-officer-dies-at-90/2011/04/13/AFGpYziD_story.html. The CIA has never declassified Petty's report, which was reputedly mammoth and detailed.

70. *Washington Post*, August 6, 1974.

71. William Greider, "Amidst Mussed Hair and Trivia, a Smoking Gun," *Washington Post*, August 7, 1974.

72. See http://watergate.info/chronology/1974-chronology.

73. Oliver Burkeman, "Scoop," *Guardian*, October 8, 2004; available at http://www.theguardian.com/books/2004/oct/09/pulitzerprize.awardsandprizes.

74. Ford, *William E. Colby*, 97.

75. Seymour M. Hersh, "Huge CIA Operation Reported in U.S. Against Antiwar Forces, Other Dissidents in Nixon Years," *New York Times*, December 22, 1974.

76. To William Colby from Richard Helms, December 22, 1974, Richard M. Helms Papers, box 17, folder labeled "Seymour Hersh," Georgetown University.

77. Colby and Forbath, *Honorable Men*, 377.

78. Randall B. Woods, *Shadow Warrior: William Egan Colby and the CIA* (New York: Basic Books, 2013), 330.

79. Riebling, *Wedge*, 323.

80. "The CIA's 'Illegal Domestic Spying,'" *Washington Post*, January 5, 1975.

81. Testimony of Deputy Chief of CI Staff, undated, American Civil Liberties Union Records, box 4108, Seeley G. Mudd Manuscript Library, Princeton University.

82. Memorandum for Inspector General, "Audit of Chaos Program," August 22, 1975, American Civil Liberties Union Records, box 4108, Seeley G. Mudd Manuscript Library, Princeton University.

83. If anything, the *Times* story underestimated the extent of the Agency's domestic spy operations. While Hersh mentioned that the CIA had opened the mail of Americans opposed to the Vietnam War, the article portrayed the epistolary surveillance as merely one part of the program to spy on the antiwar movement. Unbeknownst to Hersh, the LINGUAL mail-opening operation was separate from CHAOS, much larger and much older.

84. Author's interview with David Martin, June 23, 2015.

85. Daniel Schorr, *Clearing the Air* (Boston: Houghton Mifflin, 1977), 135.

86. Ibid., 134–37.

87. NBC, CBS, and ABC news broadcasts, December 24, 1974, Vanderbilt Television News Archive.

88. Phillips, *Night Watch*, 265.

89. Mangold, *Cold Warrior*, 323–24.

90. "George T. Kalaris, 73, Official Who Changed CIA's Direction," *New York Times*, September 14, 1995; available at http://nyti.ms/2dkI6q7.

91. Wise, *Molehunt*, 41.

92. Prados, *Family Jewels*, 23.

93. Ibid., 26.

94. Ibid., 28.

95. Cheney's memo is in the Richard B. Cheney Files, box 5, folder labeled "Intelligence—Colby Report," Gerald R. Ford Presidential Library.

96. Prados, *Family Jewels*, 34.

97. Powers, *Man Who Kept the Secrets*, 374.

98. Letter from Tom Karamessines to Cord Meyer, January 6, 1975, Cord Meyer Papers, box 2, folder 5, Library of Congress.

99. Letter from Efraim Halevy to James Angleton, January 5, 1975.

100. Letter from Reed Whittemore to Cord Meyer, January 13, 1975, Cord Meyer Papers, box 2, folder 5, Library of Congress.

101. Kathryn S. Olmsted, *Challenging the Secret Government: The Post-Watergate Investigations on the CIA and FBI* (Chapel Hill: University of North Carolina Press, 1996), 49–50.

102. Angleton and Murphy, *American Cause*, 7.

103. Bill Miller, Oral History, First Interview, May 5, 2014, 12, Senate Historical Office.

104. Ibid., 13.

105. Bill Miller, Oral History, Third Interview, 6–7, Senate Historical Office, unpublished.

106. Letter from James Angleton to Cord Meyer, January 26, 1975, Cord Meyer Papers, box 2, folder 5, Library of Congress.

107. Olmsted, *Challenging the Secret Government*, 59.

108. Angleton had taken notes in October 1961 when Peter Wright explained to Bill Harvey the virtues of using poison gas. When Harvey turned to Johnny Rosselli to carry out the hit in June 1963, Angleton protected both of them from the FBI's surveillance teams. He had explored the possibility of hypnotizing an assassin in July 1963. And in 1965, Angleton buried Harold Swenson's memo, warning that the AMLASH operation to assassinate Castro was known to its target before November 22.

109. Prados, *Family Jewels*, 33.

110. Olmsted, *Challenging the Secret Government*, 61.

111. Author's interview with David Martin, June 23, 2015.

112. *Washington Post*, March 6, 1975.

113. Warren Commission report, 3.

114. Shenon, *Cruel and Shocking Act*, 578–79.

115. David Talbot, *Brothers, The Hidden History of the Kennedy Years* (New York: Free Press, 2007), 275.

116. Powers, *Man Who Kept the Secrets*, 367.

117. Schorr, *Clearing the Air*, 147.

118. Smith W. Thomas, *Encyclopedia of the Central Intelligence Agency* (New York: Infobase Publishing, 2003), 15.

119. Letter from James Angleton to Cord Meyer, April 28, 1975, Cord Meyer Papers, box 2, folder 5, Library of Congress.

120. "Report by James J. Angleton," 30, box 7, folder labeled "Intelligence—Report by James J. Angleton," Richard B. Cheney Files, Gerald R. Ford Presidential Library.

121. *Huston Plan*, 51.

122. Ibid., 52–53.

123. Ibid., 59–75.

124. Quotes from all three September 24, 1975, broadcasts come from footage provided by Vanderbilt Television News Archive.

125. Epstein, *Deception*, 100–101.

126. Burleigh, *Very Private Woman*, 298–99.

127. Author's interview with Edward Epstein, June 12, 2015.

128. Ashley, *CIA Spymaster*, 288.

129. "Trailblazer Awards," James McCargar Papers, box 20, folder 23, Howard Gotlieb Archival Research Center, Boston University.

130. Benjamin B. Fischer, "Double Troubles: The CIA and Double Agents During the Cold War," *International Journal of Intelligence and Counterintelligence* 29, no. 1 (2016): 49.

131. Hood, Nolan, and Halpern, *Myths Surrounding James Angleton.*

132. In 1967, Deputy Director Rufus Taylor warned Dick Helms that the situation in the Soviet Russia Division was unhealthy, that fears of Soviet penetration had disrupted the division's effectiveness. An inspector general's report in 1968 reached the same conclusion, attributing the poor performance to a preoccupation with Nosenko. David Robarge, in-house historian, concluded that anti-Soviet operations were most adversely affected between 1964 and 1969.

133. *Serra,* March 20 1971.

134. Wells Stabler, deputy chief of mission at the U.S. embassy in Rome, saw the system first-hand. The cash was divided by "the Ambassador, myself and the station chief," he said in an oral history. "Some was given to the parties, some to individuals." He didn't name the beneficiaries. See "Italy Country Reader," entry for Wells Stabler, 244, Foreign Affairs Oral History Collection, Association for Diplomatic Studies and Training, Arlington, Virginia; available at http://adst.org/wp-content/uploads/2012/09/Italy.pdf.

135. The story is told in Leigh, *Wilson Plot.* In *Spycatcher,* Peter Wright downplayed his own role in the plot but acknowledged a Tory counterintelligence clique did seek to confront Wilson about his Eastern Bloc friends.

136. Leigh, *Wilson Plot,* 22.

137. "Report of the Department of Justice Concerning Its Investigation and Prosecutorial Decisions with Respect to Central Intelligence Agency Mail-Opening Activities in the United States, 3, ACLU Records, Princeton University.

138. Transcript of "Near Armageddon: The Spread of Nuclear Weapons in the Middle East," 14, *ABC News Closeup,* broadcast April 28, 1981. See also "Only CIA Believed Uranium Diverted," *Washington Post,* February 26, 1978.

139. Author's interview with Roger Mattson, December 10, 2015.

140. One of them was investigator Peter Stockton, who said Hadden had showed him "a binder of stuff" when they met at a CIA safe house. "He would pull out a 25 foot make-shift scroll of paper that contained the case against NUMEC," Stockton told a reporter. "This was before computers, and the thing was long and pasted together and that was his evidence. We'd sit there in the safe house and he'd read me portions." See Scott Johnson, "What Lies Beneath," *Foreign Policy,* March 23, 2015.

141. When the NUMEC investigation petered out in the late 1970s, Hadden let the matter drop. He was intelligence officer, not a crusader. He had done what he could as a CIA officer and a citizen. He filed his findings about NUMEC among his personal papers, where his son found them after his death in 2013.

142. MFF, Angleton Church Committee testimony, June 19, 1975, 51.

143. One of his successors as counterintelligence chief, Hugh Tovar, was asked how paperwork related to the JFK assassination was prepared and stored. He testified that Angleton had not passed on any files or reports on Nosenko, the KGB, and Oswald. "I have seen nothing either original or approved or signed by him." See "Deposition of Bernard Hugh Tovar," House Select Committee on Assassinations Security Classified Testimony, June 29, 1978, 38–39, NARA JFK HSCA RIF 180-10110-10014.

144. MFF, Angleton Church Committee testimony, June 19, 1975, 103.

145. MFF, Angleton House Select Committee on Assassinations testimony, 89.

146. Swenson called attention to his memo when the Congress reopened the JFK investigation in 1978, and he made sure Helms got a copy. See "Affidavit, Joseph Langosch,"

September 14, 1978, Richard M. Helms Papers, box 18, folder 7, Georgetown University. LANGOSCH was Swenson's cryptonym.

147. Helms, *Look Over My Shoulder*, Kindle Location 5137.

148. Author's interview with Renata Adler, July 11, 2015.

149. Loch Johnson, "James Angleton and the Church Committee," *Journal of Cold War Studies* 15, no. 4 (Fall 2013); 128.

150. Trento, *Secret History of the CIA*, xii.

151. Author's interview with David Ignatius, July 11, 2015.

152. This and subsequent quotes from the novel are in Norman Mailer, *Harlot's Ghost* (New York: Ballantine Books, 1991), 1144.

153. Schlesinger, *Robert Kennedy and His Times*, 664.

154. Winks, *Cloak and Gown*, 435.

155. Anatoliy Golitsyn, *New Lies for Old* (New York: Dodd, Meade, 1984), 332.

156. Author's interview with Joseph Augustyn, April 12, 2016. Augustyn headed the CIA's program for resettling defectors in the 1990s.

157. Letter from Richard Helms to John Hadden, July 28, 1986; courtesy of John Hadden, Jr.

158. Mangold, *Cold Warrior*, 353.

159. Trento, *Secret History of the CIA*, 479.

160. James Rosen, *Cheney One on One: A Candid Conversation with America's Most Controversial Statesman* (Washington, D.C.: Regnery, 2015), 162–63.

161. Author's interview with Efraim Halevy, December 20, 2015.

162. Cave Brown, *Treason in the Blood*, 565.

163. Mangold, *Cold Warrior*, 354.

164. Andy Court, "Spy Chiefs Honour a CIA friend," *Jerusalem Post*, December 5, 1987.

165. Ibid.

166. Author's interview with Tom Pickering, September 21, 2015.

INDEX

Abel, Rudolf, 104
Abramson, Harold, 58
Adler, Renata, 266
AEC. *See* Atomic Energy Commission
Allende, Salvatore, 246
American Communist Party, 23, 56, 67, 83–84
Amit, Meir, 172, 272
AMLASH, 150
Amory, Robert, 78
AMSPELL, 146
Andrew, Christopher, 126–127
Angleton, Cicely, 30–31, 81, 164–165, 169–170, 269
    following Yogi Bhajan, 209–210
    in Israel, 271–272
    against Vietnam war, 196–197
    in Virginia, 42–43
    watching husband award, 251–252
Angleton, Hugh, 10, 23, 224–225
Angleton, James Jesus. *See specific topics*
Anglo-Iranian Oil Company, 67
antiwar groups, 185, 203–204, 221
    CIA spying on, 231–232
    in college, 204–205
    Soviet Union protest for, 232
Ardeatine Caves massacre, 33
Armstrong, Scott, 256
Artichoke operation, 60
ARTIFICE, 23, 29
Ashmead, Hugh, 215
Atomic Energy Commission (AEC), 176–177
Avedon, Richard, 266
awards ceremony, 251–252

B-47 bombers, 114–115
Bagley, Pete, 149, 187
Bailey II, Charles, 103
Baker, Howard, 219, 243
Baldwin, James, 94
Balkans, 25, 35
Bannerman, Robert, 89
Baranowska, Lucia, 76
Barmor, Yaakov, 77
Baruch, Nir, 101
Bay of Pigs, 97–98
Beardsley, Mimi, 117
Belin, David, 243
Bendor, Avraham, 193
Ben-Gurion, David, 55
    Angleton relations with, 171
    Harel falling out with, 172
    nuclear weaponry development by, 174–178
Ben-Natan, Asher, 174–175
Biegun, Ephraim, 193
Bison bombers, 115
Bissell, Richard, 100
Black Panthers, 206
Blee, David, 239
Boise, Idaho, 273
Bolshakov, Georgi, 117
Borghese, Junio Valerio, 21–22
    capture of, 26–27
    coup of, 259
    in IVY plan, 25–26
    in Operation Sunrise, 26
Borgo Ticino, 22
Boudin, Kathy, 206
Boyle, Andrew, 50
Bradlee, Ben, 81, 164–166

Bradlee, Tony Meyer, 81
Brandt, Willy, 228–229
British intelligence. *See also* Great Britain
    Angleton working with, 105, 135
    KGB defectors working with, 134
    leaders of, 100, 236
    training at, 15
Brod, Mario, 31, 57
Broe, Bill, 191
Brugioni, Dino, 92–93
Brule River, 81
Buckley, William F., 7, 267
Bullitt, William, 46
Burgess, Guy, 44, 48, 49–50, 52
burial, 273

Cabell, Charles, 95
Cambridge Five, 267
Capote, Truman, 94
Carter, Jimmy, 244
Carter, Marshall, 251
Cassani, Alfredo, 28
Castro, Fidel, 93, 247, 264
    Angleton lies about, 264–265
    assassination plans for, 98–104, 129–130,
        132–133, 189–190
    CIA underestimating, 96–97
    after Cuban missile crisis, 131
    after JFK assassination, 146–147
    "One Thousand Fearful Words for Fidel
        Castro," (Ferlinghetti), 95–96
    Oswald case linked to, 157
Central Intelligence Agency (CIA)
    Angleton in, 154–159, 265–266
    Colby director of, 223–224
    Dulles in, 33, 51–52, 62
    FBI ending contact with, 206
    formation of, 35–36
    Golitsyn in, 106–107
    in Havana, 93–94
    Helms career in, 178, 245–246, 251
    investigation of, 243, 245–247
    in Italy, 105
    mind control program of, 59–63
    in New Orleans, 145–146, 191–192
    in postwar world, 221–222
    SIS relationship with, 40–41
    Special Investigations Group files 1959 to
        1963 in, 239

    split in, 244
    underestimating Castro, 96–97
    in Vietnam, 220, 222, 224
cerebral approach, 36–37
CHAOS
    formation of, 186
    growth of, 218–219
Cheney, Richard, 240–241, 244
    strategy of, 241–242
    as vice president, 261
childhood, 4–5
Childs, Marquis, 47
Christian Democrats, 38–39
Church, Frank, 243, 252–255
Church Committee, 245
    on mail surveillance, 260
    in Olson case, 250–251
CIA. *See* Central Intelligence Agency
CI/PROJECT, 88
Clark, Mark, 23
Clarke, John Henrik, 94
Cleaver, Eldridge, 206
Clifford, Clark, 36
Cline, Ray, 77–78
Cohen, Avner, 175
COINTELPRO, 84, 204
Colby, Bill, 105, 221, 240–241
    Angleton relationship with, 220–222,
        232–233
    as CIA director, 223–224
    confirmation hearings for, 224
    as executive director, 216
    with family jewels, 223
Communists, 7
    American Party of, 23, 56, 67, 83–84
    in Balkans, 25, 35
    class warfare of, 229
    control system of, 130
    "crypto-," 162
    Eastern European, 54–55
    in Havana, 97, 118, 127, 129–131, 147
    in Israel, 75
    in Italy, 29, 37–38, 69
    in North Korea, 51
    organized labor of, 56
    Oswald as, 137, 143–144
    Philby, Kim as, 50–51
    in Poland, 76, 109
    rising power of, 35

in Soviet Union, 40–45, 109, 111
in State Department, 44
sympathy with, 49, 208, 212
Tet uprising of, 197
victory of, 197
The Company, 267
CONDUCTOR, 175
Congress for Cultural Freedom, 104
"the Constitutionalists"
formation of, 244
as winners, 261
Cooper, Gary, 62–63
Corcoran, Judge, 169
Cordesman, Anthony, 193
counterespionage, 27, 39–40
Angleton chief of, 70
challenges of, 69–70
in Israel, 55
in Italy, 20
LCIMPROVE, 155
Cram, Cleveland, 125
Criminal Division of the Justice
Department, 156
Crump, Ray, 169–170
Cuba, 96–97. *See also* Havana, Cuba
Angleton in, 98–99
artillery in, 117
colony in Miami, 118–119
defenses of, 127
exiles from, 128–129
Fair Play for Cuba Committee, 94
Harvey role, 94, 99–100, 127
Nixon position on, 93–94
Oswald connections to, 157, 213–216
revolution in, 94–98, 128
Soviet Union in, 114
Task Force, 127
U-2 spy plane over, 113
Cuban Control and Action Capabilities
Angleton writing of, 128
application of, 130
in JFK assassination, 131, 144
Cuban missile crisis, 118
Castro after, 131
Harvey during, 116
JFK during, 95–97, 113–119, 128–129
Khrushchev during, 109, 114, 116
RFK during, 116
Schlesinger after, 118, 127–128

Cubela, Rolando, 150
Cummings, E. E., 9
Curry, Jesse, 142
Curtis, Willard, 215

Dayan, Moshe, 209
de Beauvoir, Simone, 94
de Breuys, Warren, 140
de Gaulle, Charles, 151
de Mowbray, Stephen, 105
De Niro, Robert, 7, 267
de Shalit, Amos, 174
de Shalit, Memi, 75, 173
Dealey Plaza, 141
Decima Mas, 25–27
Dempster, Ferguson, 191
Department of Energy, 262
Deriabin, Pyotr, 107
Detroit, Michigan, 185
Dimona, 92, 173–174
Dobrynin, Anatoly, 117
Dollmann, Eugen, 28, 31–32
Donne, John, 7
Donovan, William ("Wild Bill"), 15, 56
Doolittle, Hilda ("H. D."), 18
Doolittle, James, 69
Downie, Len, 256
Duckett, Carl, 261
Dulles, Allen, 100, 201–202
Angleton meeting with, 30
CIA positions of, 33, 51–52, 62
in JFK assassination investigation, 151
JFK relations with, 104
at the Mall, 54
Dunn, James, 38
Duran, Sylvia, 190, 212

Eastern European Communists, 54–55
education, early, 5–8
Egerter, Elizabeth Ann, 87–88
Egypt, 178–179
Ehrlichman, John, 205
Eichmann, Adolf, 171
Eisenhower, Dwight D., 62, 101–102
Eitan, Rafael, 193–194
El Greco painting, 13
Elder, Walter, 125
Eliot, T. S., 6
Elliott, Nicholas, 105, 124

Ellsberg, Daniel, 223–224
Empson, William, 7–8
Encounter magazine, 104
English 10, 7
Epstein, Ed
    on Angleton attributes, 256–257
    *Legend: The Secret World of Lee Harvey
        Oswald*, 266
Eshkol, Levi, 180
espionage, 39–40
Espionage Act, 223
Exceptional Civilian Service Award, 61

Fair Play for Cuba Committee (FPCC)
    development of, 94
    Oswald connection to, 136–137,
        145–146
Fascist Party, 22, 259
    American collaboration with, 23, 67
    Angleton admiration of, 13, 221
    Angleton penetration of, 18
    in Austria, 50–51
    leaders of, 4, 21–22
    National Front, 105
FBI. *See* Federal Bureau of Investigation
Federal Bureau of Investigation (FBI)
    CIA ending contact with, 206
    in Oswald interview, 264
    Roman liaison to, 71–72
Federal Bureau of Narcotics, 17
Federal Communications Commission, 15
Fensterwald, Bernard, 211
Ferlinghetti, Lawrence, 95–96
The Fifth Decade of Cantos, (Pound), 4
Fischer, Kary, 167
FitzGerald, Desmond, 144
    after JFK assassination, 150
Ford, Gerald
    on CIA assassination plots, 246–247
    power of, 244
    Rumsfeld relationship with, 240–241
    swearing in, 231
Fort Dix, New Jersey, 204
FPCC. *See* Fair Play for Cuba Committee
Franco, Francisco, 22
Free Trade Union Committee of the
    American Federation of Labor, 48
Freedom and Independence Movement
    (WiN), 68–69

Friberg, Frank, 106
Furioso, 9–10, 29

Gaitskill, Hugh, 126
Gambino, Robert, 226
Garbo, Greta, 38
Garrison, Jim, 190
Garrison Group, 191, 192
George Washington University Hospital, 198
Germany
    arms industry in, 10
    catching spies from, 23
    deciphering communications of, 19
    invasion into Poland, 11
    plan IVY in, 24–25
Gestapo, 23
Giancana, Sam, 162
Ginsberg, Allen, 94, 104
Gittinger, John, 112
Gmirkin, Vasia, 107
golem, 210
Golitsyn, Anatoly, 107–108
    Angleton trust in, 112
    at Angleton 50th birthday, 195
    in CIA, 106–107
    evaluation of, 107
    in Gaitskill assassination, 126, 134
    meeting about MI5, 126
    in MI5 safe house, 126, 134–135
    New Lies for Old, 268–269
    paranoia of, 112
    RFK meetings with, 110–112, 126
    theories of, 125–126
Golpe Borghese, 259
The Good Shepherd, 7, 267
Gowen, William, 28, 34–35
Graham, Katharine, 256
Grajewski, Wiktor, 76–77
Great Britain. *See also* British intelligence
    ghost in, 259
    United States allied with, 21
    "the Wilson Plot," 259
Greene, Joe, 34–35
Gregory, Dick, 247
Groden, Robert, 247
Gromberg, Henry, 92
Guarnieri, Luciano, 79
Guatemala, 67–68, 95
Guevara, Che, 204

Guillaume, Guenter, 229
Gulf of Aqaba, 179
Gulf of Tigullio, 6
The Guns of August, (Tuchman), 115

Hadden, John, 173
  in Israel war, 180
  on NUMEC, 178
  on uranium heist, 262
Haldeman, H. R., 205, 218
Halevy, Efraim, 55, 242
  Angleton relations with, 171, 210
  during Sinai attack, 226
  with Rabin, 209
Harel, Isser, 74, 171–172
Harlot's Ghost, (Mailer), 267–268
Hart, John, 50
Hartman, Paul, 144
Harvard University, 7, 14
Harvey, Bill, 36–37
  alcoholism of, 162
  in Cuba, 94, 99–100, 127
  investigating Philby, 53
  during missile crisis, 116
  party for, 49–50
  RFK relations with, 127–128
  in Rome, 128
  Rosselli meeting with, 132
Harvey, Clara Grace, 132
Hauser, Ernest, 29
Havana, Cuba. *See also* Cuba
  CIA in, 93–94
  Communists in, 97, 118, 127, 129–131, 147
Helms, Dick
  as CIA director, 178, 251
  in CIA investigation, 245–246
  at Dulles funeral, 202
  employment of, 98, 101
  in JFK investigation, 153
  letter from, 148
  loyalty of, 106
  McCone relationship with, 106
  Nixon relationship with, 217–218
  paying Nosenko, 159
  release of Nosenko, 219–220
  in retirement, 268
  testimony of, 251
  after war, 184
Helsinki *rezidentura,* 108

Hermoni, Avraham, 192–193
heroin, 61
Hersh, Burton, 67, 73
Hersh, Seymour, 231
High Noon, 62–63
Hillenkoetter, Roscoe, 46–47
Hitler, Adolf, 11–12, 21
hobbies, 4, 42, 73
Holiday, Billie, 61
homosexuals
  Angleton view of, 48
  entertainment of, 49–50
  firing of, 44
  during Lavender Scare, 45
  openly gay, 44, 48
HONETOL
  files on, 239
  formation of, 168
Hood, Bill, 36
Hoover, J. Edgar
  Angleton relationship with, 71
  appointment of, 15
  ending CIA contacts, 206
  in Huston plan, 208
  mail surveillance ideas of, 83–84
  withdrawal of, 198
Horton, John, 214–215
Hosty, James, 136
House Select Committee on
    Assassinations, 90
Hugh Selwyn Mauberley, (Pound), 4
Hughes, Tom, 179
Humphrey, Hubert, 197
Hunt, Howard, 217, 223
HUNTER
  development of, 83
  execution of, 84
  in Huston plan, 207
  letters intercepted, 104
Huston, Tom, 205–209, 206
hypnosis
  of Mexican agent, 132
  for mind control, 59–60, 132–133

Iago, 158–159
Idaho National Guard, 4
Ignatius, David, 267
Intelligence Evaluation Committee, 208
interrogation techniques, 60

Iowa Writer's Workshop, 104
Iran, 67
Iron Curtain, 123
Israel
    Angleton in, 54–55, 73–74, 106, 171,
        261–263, 271–272
    Angleton, C., in, 271–272
    attack of, 181
    cease-fire in, 183–184
    Communists in, 75
    counterespionage in, 55
    desk officer for, 92–93
    Egypt war with, 178–179
    intelligence in, 55
    invasion by, 78
    nuclear weaponry development in,
        174–178, 262
    predictions about, 78
    uranium in, 177
    war in, 180–184
Italian-American Chamber of Commerce, 3
Italy. See also Rome
    Angleton in, 22–23, 29, 259
    CIA operations in, 105
    civil war in, 37–38
    Committee for the Liberation of, 21
    Communists in, 29, 37–38, 69
    counterespionage in, 20
    Croatian fascists in, 34–35
    plan IVY in, 24–25
    Pound in, 3–4, 6
    press in, 162
IVY plan, 25–26

Janney, Peter, 79–80
Janney, Wistar, 80
Jessup, Peter, 92
Jessup, Ted, 211
Jews
    Angleton resentment of, 11
    mobile machines killing, 32
    Zionist, 75
JFK assassination. See also Kennedy, John F.
    Angleton and, 154–157, 239, 263–264
    Castro after, 146–147
    conspiracy theories on, 246–247
    Cuban Control and Action Capabilities
        in, 131, 144
    FitzGerald after, 150

investigation committee for, 211
investigation of, 90, 131, 150–153,
    190–191, 213–214
RFK and, 143, 148–149
Soviet Union after, 148–149
United States after, 145, 151
Warren Commission in, 90, 154–155
Joannides, George, 146
Johnson, Loch, 266–267
Johnson, Lyndon
    conspiracy theories of, 185
    in Israel war, 180–184
    after JFK assassination, 152–153
    Oswald file of, 145
    in Vietnam war, 169
Jordan, 181

Kalaris, George, 238
    after Angleton resignation, 238–239
    comments of, 106
Karamessines, Tom, 16
    in Oswald case, 137, 144, 147
    role in Operation CHAOS, 184
Karlow, Peter, 108
    investigation of, 108, 134, 168
    retirement of, 198
Kennan, George, 39
Kennedy, John F. (JFK). See also JFK
        assassination
    Angleton compared to, 91–92
    Angleton view of, 119
    after Bay of Pigs, 98
    critiques of, 118–119
    during Cuban crisis, 95–97, 113–119,
        128–129
    in Dallas, 141–149
    Dulles relations with, 104
    election of, 91
    hostility towards, 102–103
    LeMay advise to, 114–115, 118
    Meyer affair with, 166–168
    taking LSD, 167–168
Kennedy, Robert (RFK)
    Angleton files on, 239
    after Bay of Pigs, 98
    Bolshakov meeting with, 117
    as candidate, 197
    death of, 197–198
    Golitsyn meeting with, 110–112, 126

Harvey relations with, 127–128
JFK assassination and, 143, 148–149
McCone relationship with, 143, 268
meeting Kisevalter, 111–112
during missile crisis, 116
ordering Cuban exiles out, 128–129
planning Castro assassination, 129–130
Kent State University, 204–205
KGB. *See also* Soviet Union
   conference, 108–109
   deception operations in, 69–70
   defectors, 106–109, 134, 147, 159–161
   department of disinformation, 109
   Department Thirteen in, 126
   investigations of, 168
   mole hunts of, 168, 229–230
   Nosenko in, 112
   paranoia about, 188–189
   Philby meeting with, 124
   Sasha in, 108
   theories of, 125–126
   watching Oswald, 159
Khrushchev, Nikita
   as bully, 118–119
   during missile crisis, 109, 114, 116
   "On the Cult of the Individual and Its
      Consequences," 76–77
Kilduff, Malcolm, 142
King, Martin Luther Jr.
   death of, 197
   popularity of, 184
King David Hotel, 74, 272
"the Kings Party"
   acts out of, 261
   emergence of, 244
Kirkland, Lane, 243
Kisevalter, George, 85
   in Nosenko case, 187
   in RFK meeting, 111–112
   on Sasha, 257
Kissinger, Henry
   as Angleton enemy, 227
   on CIA assassination plots, 246
   Nixon relationship with, 222–223
   Nixon, resignation of, 231
   peace treaty of, 250
   détente, pursuit of, 229
   resignation of, 231
KKMOUNTAIN, 172–173

Klibansky, Peter, 108
Knebel, Fletcher, 103
Knights of Malta, 10, 38
Kollek, Teddy, 50–51, 272–273
Korean War, 60
kundalini yoga, 209

Ladd, Mickey, 44
LAKAM, 193
Lamphere, Bob, 44
Langelle, Russell, 85
Langley
   Angleton at, 225, 237–238
   Nixon speech at, 202–203
Lashbrook, Robert, 58–59
Lavender Scare, 45, 48
LCIMPROVE, 137
le Carré, John, 125, 236
Leary, Timothy, 167
leftist partisans
   in Balkans, 25
   Italian, 21
   in Mussolini death, 25–26
   war against, 22
*Legend: The Secret World of Lee Harvey
   Oswald,* (Epstein), 266
Leigh, David, 259
LeMay, Curtis, 114–115, 118
Lemnitzer, Lyman, 103, 243
LINGUAL
   development of, 82
   execution of, 83
   in Huston plan, 207–208
   investigation of, 253
   letters about, 104
   Oswald file in, 88–89, 144, 146
   suspension of, 225
LIOSAGE, 191
Lovestone, Jay
   Angleton friendship with, 105
   in labor movement, 56, 75–76
   personal life of, 76
Lowenthal, David, 175–176
   in nuclear warfare, 176–177
   in uranium heist, 194
Lysergic acid diethylamide (LSD)
   Angleton experiments with, 61–62
   discovery of, 60
   in Kennedy affair, 167–168

Lysergic acid diethylamide (LSD) (*continued*)
 in *Time* magazine, 169
 White use of, 59–60, 62

Machiavelli, Niccolò, 158
Maclean, Donald, 52
MacLeish, Archibald, 9
Macpherson, Perdita
 account of, 19–20
 career of, 19
 holiday of, 21
mail surveillance
 Angleton legacy of, 82–83, 207–208
 Church Committee findings on, 260
 Hoover view of, 83–84
 in Huston plan, 208
 during Nixon presidency, 219
 Patriot Act out of, 261
 of Soviet Union mail, 82–83
Mailer, Norman
 during Cuban revolution, 94
 Harlot's Ghost, 267–268
the Mall
 Angleton moving into, 71
 Dulles arrival at, 54
 morale at, 68
 move from, 110
Malvern College, 5
Mangold, Tom, 133
Mann, Wilfred, 44, 49
Manor, Amos, 55–56, 74–75, 272
Mansfield, Mike, 243
Marceglia, Antonio, 25
marriage, 14–16
Marshall, Caroline, 81–82
Marshall, George, 35
MARTHA, 57
Martin, Arthur, 105, 126
Martin, David, 235–236
Martinez, Eugenio, 216
Mattson, Roger, 262
Maury, Jack, 225
McCargar, Jim, 42–43, 53–54
McCarthy, Joseph, 45
McCarthy, Mary, 79
McCone, John
 appointment of, 100
 Helms relations with, 106
 RFK relationship with, 143, 268

McCord, James, 59
 arrest of, 216
McCoy, Leonard, 187
McDonald, Kenneth, 190
McGonagle, William L., 182
McKenzie, Robert, 43–44
McNamara, Robert, 129
McNeil, Hector, 49
Meir, Golda, 209
memorial service, 270–271
memory enhancement, 60
Mexico City, Mexico
 hypnotizing agents in, 132
 mole hunts in, 135, 139–140
 Oswald in, 137–138, 146
Meyer, Cord
 Angleton relationship with, 80
 employment of, 79–80
Meyer, Mary, 80–81, 164, 167–168, 169–170
 affair of, 166–167
 diary of, 165–168, 256
 divorce of, 163
Meyer, Quentin, 210
MI5
 Golitsyn working with, 126, 134–135
 spies in, 135
Miami, Florida
 allies in, 149
 Cubans in, 96–97, 118–119
 enemies in, 143, 146
 exiles in, 128–129
military-industrial complex, 101–102
Miller, Bill
 Angleton relationship with, 245
 calling split, 244
Miller, Gerry, 105
Millett, Stephen, 72
mind control
 CIA program for, 59–63
 experiments in, 59–60
 hypnosis for, 59–60, 132–133
Mindszenty, József, 60
Minh, Ho Chi, 204
Mitchell, John, 208
MKULTRA, 59–60
mole hunts
 in British intelligence, 135
 careers ruined by, 257–258
 condemnation of, 271

continuation of, 198
of counterintelligence staff, 229–230
end of, 239–240
"the Great Mole Hunt," 257
Karlow in, 108, 134, 168
of KGB agents, 168, 229–230
in Mexico City, 135, 139–140
Murphy in, 188
Nosenko in, 186–188
for Sasha, 188
Montini, Giovanni Battista
becoming Pope Paul VI, 39
meetings with, 33–34
Morris, Louise Page
friendship with, 105
in labor operations, 56–57
Mosaddegh, Mohammad, 67
Moscow
Americans moving to, 87
Center, 112
Moscow-Cairo axis, 172
Oswald in, 86–87
Mossad
Angleton relations with, 171
founding of, 54–55
operations of, 56, 172
Murphy, Charles, 202
Murphy, David, 112, 160
as mole, 188
in Nosenko defection, 160–161
in Paris, 198
Mussolini, Benito
death of, 25–26
defending Hitler, 11
leftist partisans and, 25–26
in new Europe, 12
Pound admiration of, 4, 221
retreat of, 22
My Silent War, (Philby), 195–196

Naftali, Timothy, 27
Nasser, Gamel, 78, 172, 179
National Cash Register Company, 4
National Front movement, 105
National Photographic Interpretation
    Center, 92, 113
National Security Act (1947), 35
National Security Agency (NSA), 105, 260
National Student Association, 104, 184

Nazi regime
in Ardeatine Caves massacre, 33
in Austria, 25
members of, 27–28
war trials of, 29
nerve gas, 264
New Europe
like United States, 13
Mussolini in, 12
New Lies for Old, (Golitsyn), 268–269
New Orleans
CIA operations in, 145–146, 191–192
Oswald in, 145–146
New York City, New York, 184, 203
Newark, New Jersey, 185
Newman, Bill, 141
Newman, John, 89
The New Critics, 7–8
The New York Times article
Angleton resignation after, 233, 237
Colby address about, 240–241
contents of, 239–240
publishing of, 232
scandals after, 234–237
Ninotchka, 38
Nixon, Richard, 91, 202–203, 219
on Cuba, 93–94
Helms relationship with, 217–218
in Huston plan, 206–209
intelligence collection effort of, 206–207
Kissinger relationship with, 222–223
lawlessness of, 222–223
mail surveillance under, 219
meeting Meir, 209
tapes of, 230–231
after Watergate break in, 218
North Korea
brainwashing in, 60
invasion by, 51
NORTHWOODS, 128–129
Nosenko, Yuri, 112
as Angleton target, 258
continuing detention of, 186–187
as defector, 159
drug dosing of, 187
Helms payment to, 159
incarceration of, 161
interrogation of, 186–188
movie about, 267

Nosenko, Yuri (*continued*)
  Murphy relationship with, 160–161
  Oswald linked to, 239
  in safe house, 160–161, 189
  Warren Commission interrogation of,
    161–162
NSA. *See* National Security Agency
Nuclear Materials and Equipment
    Corporation (NUMEC), 177–178
  Angleton knowledge of, 178
  cooperation of, 262
  development of, 176
  Hadden involvement with, 178
  uranium heist at, 192–194, 261–262
Nuclear Regulatory Commission, 262
nuclear weapons, 193
  Ben-Gurion projects for, 174–178
  de Shalit involvement with, 174
  funding for, 175
  Israel development of, 174–178, 262
  Lowenthal involvement in, 176–177
NUMEC. *See* Nuclear Materials and
    Equipment Corporation

Oakwood Junior High, 5
Ober, Richard, 185
  Special Operations Group of, 231
obituary, 271
"October crisis," 113
O'Donnell, Ken, 115
Office of Policy Coordination (OPC)
  development of, 39
  first mission of, 40
  OSO merger with, 54
Office of Special Operations (OSO)
  formation of, 36
  OPC merger with, 54
Office of Strategic Services (OSS)
  arrival at, 17–18
  changes in, 28–29
  formation of, 15
  training for, 16–17
Offie, Carmel, 45
  Angleton hiring of, 47
  arrest of, 46–47
  employment of, 46
  gay life of, 46
Oldfield, Maurice, 105, 186
Olson, Frank

cover up of, 59
death of, 57–58
investigation of, 250–251
"On the Cult of the Individual and Its
    Consequences," (Khrushchev), 76–77
"One Thousand Fearful Words for Fidel
    Castro," (Ferlinghetti), 95–96
O'Neal, Birch, 72, 152–153
OPC. *See* Office of Policy Coordination
Operation Balsam, 56
Operation Sunrise
  Borghese in, 26
  negotiations of, 32
  Pagnotta in, 28, 31–32
  plan of, 25–26
organized labor, 56–57
OSO. *See* Office of Special Operations
OSS. *See* Office of Strategic Services
OSS: ARTIFICE, 267
Oswald, Lee Harvey
  Angleton case for, 87–91, 154–157,
    248–249
  arrest of, 146–147
  Castro linked to, 157
  conclusions about, 162
  Cuban contacts of, 157, 212–216
  as defector, 136, 149
  Duran fling with, 190, 212
  FBI interview of, 264
  FPCC connection to, 136–137, 145–146
  imposter theory about, 248
  Johnson, Lyndon, file on, 145
  KGB watching, 159
  *Legend: The Secret World of Lee Harvey
    Oswald,* (Epstein), 266
  LINGUAL file on, 88–89, 144, 146
  in Mexico City, 137–138, 146
  in Moscow, 86–87
  in New Orleans, 145–146
  Nosenko linked to, 239
  Roman involvement with, 36, 137
  Special Investigations reports on,
    140–141
  201 file on, 90
Oswald, Marina, 136

Pagnotta, Leo
  as civilian, 33
  Dollman, arrest of, 28, 31–32

Palazzo Castiglioni, 10
Papich, Sam, 72–73
parents, 4–5
Paris Peace Awards, 222
Patriot Act, 261
Paul VI (pope), 39
Pauling, 94
Pearson, Drew, 189–190
Pearson, Norman Holmes
    characteristics of, 9–10
    as spy master, 14–15
    in ULTRA, 19
    as X-2 trainer, 17
Penkovsky, Oleg, 113
Peres, Shimon, 175
Persico, Joseph, 133
Personae, (Pound), 30
Petacci, Clara, 25
Petty, Clare Edward, 229, 230
Philby, Kim, 18, 43, 53–54, 267, 270
    Angleton relationship with, 41–42, 54,
        124–125, 211
    in Beirut, 105
    Burgess relationship with, 49
    as Communist, 50–51
    Elliott relationship with, 124
    in German spy capture, 23
    literary career of, 124, 195–196
    McCargar investigation of, 42–43,
        53–54
    My Silent War, 195–196
    as spy, 52–53, 123–124
    taking SIS station, 39–41
Philby, St. John, 43
Phillips, David
    as division chief, 237
    in Langley meeting, 238
Pickering, Tom, 272
Pierson College, 11
Pinchot, Ruth, 170
Poland
    Communists in, 76, 109
    Germany invading, 11
Popov, Pyotr
    as contact, 85
    exposure of, 86
Pound, Ezra
    Angleton with, 4
    The Fifth Decade of Cantos, 4

Hugh Selwyn Mauberley by, 4
indictment of, 29–30
in Italy, 3–4, 6
letters with, 8
political views of, 4, 11–13
recordings of, 15–16
recovery of, 84
text book of, 9
psychological warfare, 36, 67–68, 146

Rabin, Yitzhak
    at Angleton celebration, 272
    meeting with, 209
racism, 185
Radio Rome, 13
RAFAEL, 193
Rankin, Lee, 155
Rauff, Walter, 32–33
Reagan, Ronald, 243
Rearden, Steven L., 119
Red Scare, 45
religion, 34
Resio, Carlo, 21, 25–26
retroactive mortality, 260
RFK. See Kennedy, Robert
Richards, I. A., 7
riots (1967), 185
Rive Gauche, 209
Rivera, Geraldo, 247–248
Robarge, David, 86, 123
Robeson, Paul, 49
Rocca, Ray
    Angleton meeting with, 31
    in Garrison Group, 192
    in investigation, 155–156
    as research chief, 72
Rockefeller Commission
    Angleton testimony to, 252–255
    Cheney strategy for, 241–242
    formation of, 242–243
Rolling Stone, 266
Roman, Jane Atherton, 71, 86, 137
Rome, Italy. See also Italy
    Angleton legend in, 22–23
    Harvey stationed in, 128
room 318, 252, 255
roommate, 6
Roosevelt, Franklin, 11, 21
Rosenbaum, Ron, 256

Rosselli, Johnny
    accusations of, 189–190
    arrival of, 131
    Harvey meeting with, 132
Rotary Club, 10
Roundtree, Dovey, 169
Rumsfeld, Donald, 240–241
Rusk, Dean, 182–183
Russell, Bertrand, 184–185
Russell, Dick, 256

Salisbury, Harrison, 184
San Cristóbal, 113
San Francisco, California, 184
San Girolamo seminary, 34
Sartre, Jean-Paul, 94
Sasha (suspected mole), 108
    continuing hunt for, 188
    Kisevalter opinion about, 257
Schlesinger, Arthur
    after missile crisis, 118, 127–128
    RFK relationship with, 143
Schlesinger, James
    appointment of, 220
    as Secretary of Defense, 223
    in testimonies, 223
Schneider, René, 246
Schorr, Daniel
    in CIA investigation, 245–247
    interviewing Angleton, 236–237
    public impact of, 248
Schoumacher, David, 255
Schwarz, Frederick Jr., 253
Scientific Intelligence, 60
Scott, Janet, 213–214
Scott, Winston, 16
    book plans of, 212–214
    death of, 213–214
    in JFK investigation, 190–191, 213–214
    memoir of, 215–216
    secret files of, 215
SDECE, 144
Secret Intelligence Service (SIS)
    CIA relationship with, 40–41
    formation of, 15
segregation, 94
Seven Types of Ambiguity, (Empson), 7–8
Shapiro, Zalman, 177
    permission from, 192–193

Shaw, Clay, 190
Shiloah, Reuven
    replacement of, 74
    in Washington, 55
Sicherheitsdienst, 23
SIG. See Special Investigations Group
Sikhism, 209
Sinai Desert attack, 226
Sirhan, Sirhan, 198
SIS. See Secret Intelligence Service
Six-Day War, 209
Slawson, David
    Angleton conversation with, 249–250
    investigation of, 248
Smith, Merriman, 143
Smith, Walter Bedell, 51, 62
Soviet Russia Division, CIA, 225,
    238–239
Soviet Union. See also KGB
    American alliance with, 35–36
    Angleton later efforts in, 123
    in antiwar protests, 232
    arsenals in, 115
    Communists in, 40–45, 109, 111
    in Cuba, 114
    after JFK assassination, 148–149
    mail surveillance from, 82–83
    main enemies of, 109
    missiles in, 113–114
    troops in, 114
    VENONA program in, 68
Spanish Civil War, 22
Special Investigations Group (SIG)
    Angleton secret files from, 239
    formation of, 72
    Oswald reports by, 140–141
Spytime, (Buckley), 267
Statler Hotel, 57–58
Sullivan, William, 104
Sullivan & Cromwell law firm, 51
"the Sullivan-Angleton Plan," 205
Svengali, 158
Swenson, Hal, 157
Syria, 181
Szulc, Tad, 97

Taylor, Myron, 28
Technical Services Division (TSD), 60
Tenth Light Flotilla, 22

Tet Offensive, 197
Texas Schoolbook Depository, 142, 147
thermoelectric devices, 192
Thomas, Charles
  further reports of, 211–212
  initial reports of, 190
  suicide of, 212
Thompson, Hunter S., 154
Tilton, John, 137
Tinker Tailor Soldier Spy, (le Carré), 236
"Total Counterespionage," 27
Trailblazer Award, 257
Trento, Joseph
  Angleton lunch with, 267
  reporting conspiracy theory, 168
Truitt, Anne, 81
Truman, Harry, 28, 51
"truth drugs," 61
TSD. See Technical Services Division
Tu-95 Bear bombers, 115
Tuchman, Barbara, 115
201 file, 90
Tydings, Millard, 45

ULTRA
  Angleton in, 20
  Pearson in, 19
United Fruit Company, 68
United States
  B-47 bombers in, 114–115
  Cuban Revolution and, 94, 97
  as Great Britain ally, 21
  in Israel war, 180–184
  after JFK assassination, 145, 151
  new Europe like, 13
  in 1961, 101
  nonproliferation policy in, 262–263
  after Sinai attack, 226
uranium
  continued interest in, 261
  heist, 192–194, 261–262
  in Israel, 177
  lost, in Apollo plant, 194
  in NUMEC/AEC, 176–177
  processing of, 177–178
  search for, 173
U.S. Army's School of Military Government, 23

USS Liberty
  attacks on, 181–183
  investigation of, 183

Vatican, 33–34
VENONA program, 68
verbal ambiguity, 7–8
Vietnam
  CIA in, 220, 222, 224
  Johnson, L., escalation in, 169
  opposition to, 184–185, 196–197
  report on, 231

Wakefield, Dan, 94
Walker, John Denley, 194–195
War Department, 29
Warren Commission
  in Castro investigation, 247, 264
  challenges to, 189–190
  defenders of, 248
  interrogating Nosenko, 161–162
  Italian press views of, 162
  in JFK assassination cover up, 90, 154–155
Watergate
  "babies," 243
  burglary, 216–217
  Nixon reaction to, 218
  public scandal of, 228
  Senate Committee, 224
WAVE station, 146
Weather Underground, 203, 204, 205
Weizmann Institute of Science, 174
Wenner, Eugen, 31
White, George Hunter, 17
  experiments of, 105
  expertise of, 61
  in LSD experiments, 59–60
  personal drug experience of, 62
Whittemore, Reed, 6
  Angleton friendship with, 242
Whitten, John, 151–152, 153
Wiggins, Henry, 169
Wilkerson, Cathy, 204
Willens, Howard, 156–157
Williams, Robert F., 94
Williams, William Carlos, 9

Wilson, Harold, 126, 186, 259
    accusations of, 227
"the Wilson Plot," 259
WiN. *See* Freedom and Independence
        Movement
Winks, Robin, 69
Wisner, Frank, 16, 47
Wolff, Kurt, 22
Women's Strike for Peace, 219
Wright, Peter, 99, 198

X-2 indoctrination training, 17–18

Yale college, 7–13
The Yale Literary Magazine, 5
Yeats, William Butler, 7
Yogi Bhajan, 209

Zapruder, Abraham, 163, 211
ZR-RIFLE assassination program,
        132